T0211263

Pro PowerShell Desired State Configuration

An In-Depth Guide to Windows PowerShell DSC

Second Edition

Ravikanth Chaganti

Apress®

Pro PowerShell Desired State Configuration: An In-Depth Guide to Windows PowerShell DSC

Ravikanth Chaganti
Saideep Helicon
Bengaluru, India

ISBN-13 (pbk): 978-1-4842-3482-2   ISBN-13 (electronic): 978-1-4842-3483-9
https://doi.org/10.1007/978-1-4842-3483-9

Library of Congress Control Number: 2018941469

Copyright © 2018 by Ravikanth Chaganti

This work is subject to copyright. All rights are reserved by the Publisher, whether the whole or part of the material is concerned, specifically the rights of translation, reprinting, reuse of illustrations, recitation, broadcasting, reproduction on microfilms or in any other physical way, and transmission or information storage and retrieval, electronic adaptation, computer software, or by similar or dissimilar methodology now known or hereafter developed.

Trademarked names, logos, and images may appear in this book. Rather than use a trademark symbol with every occurrence of a trademarked name, logo, or image we use the names, logos, and images only in an editorial fashion and to the benefit of the trademark owner, with no intention of infringement of the trademark.

The use in this publication of trade names, trademarks, service marks, and similar terms, even if they are not identified as such, is not to be taken as an expression of opinion as to whether or not they are subject to proprietary rights.

While the advice and information in this book are believed to be true and accurate at the date of publication, neither the authors nor the editors nor the publisher can accept any legal responsibility for any errors or omissions that may be made. The publisher makes no warranty, express or implied, with respect to the material contained herein.

Managing Director, Apress Media LLC: Welmoed Spahr
Acquisitions Editor: Gwenan Spearing
Development Editor: Laura Berendson
Coordinating Editor: Mark Powers

Cover designed by eStudioCalamar

Cover image designed by Freepik (www.freepik.com)

Distributed to the book trade worldwide by Springer Science+Business Media New York, 233 Spring Street, 6th Floor, New York, NY 10013. Phone 1-800-SPRINGER, fax (201) 348-4505, e-mail orders-ny@springer-sbm.com, or visit www.springeronline.com. Apress Media, LLC is a California LLC and the sole member (owner) is Springer Science + Business Media Finance Inc (SSBM Finance Inc). SSBM Finance Inc is a **Delaware** corporation.

For information on translations, please e-mail editorial@apress.com; for reprint, paperback, or audio rights, please email bookpermissions@springernature.com.

Apress titles may be purchased in bulk for academic, corporate, or promotional use. eBook versions and licenses are also available for most titles. For more information, reference our Print and eBook Bulk Sales web page at www.apress.com/bulk-sales.

Any source code or other supplementary material referenced by the author in this book is available to readers on GitHub via the book's product page, located at www.apress.com/9781484234822. For more detailed information, please visit www.apress.com/source-code.

Printed on acid-free paper

This work, without a doubt, is dedicated to my lovely family. Especially, my wife, Silpa, and my sons, Kaustubh and Srivathsa. We missed many moments of being together as I worked on this. Words cannot express how much I love you all!

Table of Contents

About the Author

Ravikanth Chaganti is a well-known blogger and a member of the PowerShell community. He has been a Microsoft MVP in Cloud and Data Center Management since 2010 and works at Dell EMC as lead engineer in the Converged Platform and Solutions Division. He is passionate about automation and works in his free time writing scripts and tools to help automate management tasks for Windows OS and applications on Windows OS. Ravikanth has more than 15 years of industry experience and a broad set of skills in the IT infrastructure domain ranging from servers to storage to networking. He started scripting in early 2000 and continued to hone in his skills from that point on. In 2006, he fell in love with an early release of Windows PowerShell and has been evangelizing PowerShell ever since.

About the Technical Reviewer

Ben Gelens is a technician in heart and soul. He likes working with cutting-edge technology and implementing innovative solutions, often before the technology has been commoditized. His strength is that he can automate almost anything. Ben transitioned from a traditional infrastructure consultant/engineer to a DevOps- and Cloud-focused consultant/engineer. Ben is an active IT community participant and speaker and has been awarded the Microsoft MVP award for his contributions.

Acknowledgments

When I wrote the first edition of this book, I was overwhelmed because it was my first published book. PowerShell DSC has evolved quite a bit since then and completing the second edition was equally overwhelming because I had to rewrite almost every chapter and then add a few completely new chapters. I certainly wrote this whole thing all by myself, but it would not have been possible without the direct or indirect help from many folks in the community and at Microsoft.

First and foremost, I am grateful to the Almighty and my parents for what I am today. Thanks to every reader of the first edition for your feedback and encouragement; your support made me think about the second edition. I am thankful to the people at Microsoft who made PowerShell DSC possible. These people have been around for me whenever I had questions. Abhik Chatterjee, Travis Plunk, and Narine Mossikyan were very helpful while authoring the first edition, which was the foundation for this book. Hemant Mahawar and Narayanan Lakshmanan (Nana) were always there whenever I had questions. Steven Murawski (former Microsoft MVP) was one of the first ones to write about PowerShell DSC and evangelize it; I owe a lot of my learning to him.

Finally, huge thanks to my friend, fellow MVP, and PowerShell DSC expert Ben Gelens. He was more than just the technical reviewer of this book. His suggestions certainly made this book better. If I ever decide to write another book, I know who I want to review or co-author it with me.

Introduction

When Windows PowerShell DSC was first released in 2013, it was very exciting. I developed a deep interest in exploring the technology. This curiosity helped me understand the internals. The first edition of this book was published in the year 2014 and is still one of the most in-depth books on DSC out there. So, naturally, I wanted the second edition to be a better book than the first one. Therefore, I took the time and effort to rewrite more than 90% of the first edition; in this book, I narrate an end-to-end story with DSC.

Configuration management that is native to the Windows platform is no longer a dream. With DSC, we have a very powerful configuration management platform. As DSC has evolved, there is now more integration with third-party software and there are different methods to use DSC with public cloud platforms. At this time of writing, there are hundreds of custom DSC resources published by Microsoft teams alone. When we combine that with what the community has delivered, it's not an exaggeration to say that there is a DSC resource module for almost everything that runs on the Windows platform. Several companies use DSC as their primary configuration management solution for Windows-based workloads and platforms. I have personally built deployment automations of large hybrid cloud infrastructures that solely use DSC as the configuration management platform.

With all this experience and love for DSC, my goal for the second edition is to show you the end-to-end story with DSC. This means that I start with the very basics, go all the way to the internals of DSC, explain all of the advanced concepts in using and implementing DSC, show how to build release pipelines for your custom DSC resources, and show how to use DSC with different public cloud infrastructure and containers. This is the essence of this book.

An Overview of This Book

Pro PowerShell Desired State Configuration is divided into four distinct parts. Each part contains related chapters that help you understand thoroughly the concepts that are covered.

Part I: Getting Started with Windows PowerShell DSC

Part I provides an introduction to Infrastructure as Code (IaC) and the role DSC plays within IaC. This part also provides an introduction to the basic DSC concepts.

Chapter 1: Introduction to Infrastructure as Code and PowerShell DSC

This chapter introduces you to the concepts of DevOps, IaC, and Configuration as Code (CaC). Once these concepts are well understood, you explore the role that the release pipeline plays in IaC and the role DSC plays in IaC. The chapter ends with a quick overview of what DSC is and how to enable DSC in your infrastructure.

Chapter 2: Windows PowerShell DSC Architecture and Feature Overview

In this chapter, you look at the DSC component architecture and understand how the components relate to each other. This chapter builds upon the foundation supplied by Chapter 1 and provides an in-depth explanation of various components in DSC. I look at the new and updated features in DSC and review each one of them. The subsequent chapters dive into each of these features.

Chapter 3: Windows PowerShell DSC Local Configuration Manager

DSC Local Configuration Manager (LCM) is the core of PowerShell DSC. Think of this as the agent that sits in the operating system and performs the configuration management tasks. Therefore, it is very important to understand this component in-depth and learn how to configure LCM. You look at a subset of the LCM configuration settings and deal with others in subsequent chapters. You learn how DSC is implemented and explore various classes and properties in its CIM-based implementation.

Chapter 4: Writing Configurations

Once you understand the basics of DSC architecture and how to configure LCM for different configuration management scenarios, you can write your first configuration document. You learn different parts of the declarative syntax used in writing these configuration scripts. In this chapter, you also learn how to explore in-box DSC resources and how to download and install resource modules from the official PowerShell gallery. You look at parameterizing configuration scripts and building dependent resource instances in a configuration script.

Chapter 5: Writing Advanced DSC Configurations

In this chapter, you look at the concept of configuration data and why you need it, how you can use configuration data to create flexible and reusable configurations, how to secure sensitive data such as credentials and secure strings in the configuration authoring and enact process, and many other advanced configuration authoring concepts.

Chapter 6: Writing Composite and Custom DSC Resource Modules

You extend the knowledge from Chapters 4 and 5 to create composite resource modules. The composite resource modules enable us to package the parameterized configuration scripts that we author into resource modules so that they become discoverable and can be distributed in a similar manner as the custom DSC resource modules. You then write your own custom DSC resource modules, both MOF-based and class-based. You end the chapter by publishing modules to a local private PowerShell repository.

Chapter 7: Validating DSC Resources

There is a formal way to approach testing of DSC resources and modules. In this chapter, you learn exactly that. You learn some basic testing, you start writing a DSC resource script, and you evolve it into a complete set of tests that validate different code paths in the resource script. This is done using Pester, which is the framework for unit testing and beyond. At the end of this chapter, you should have the necessary knowledge to implement both unit and integration tests for the MOF-based DSC resources. Pester testing for class-based DSC resources is still evolving and there is no standard or method that works across different resources. Therefore, this chapter does not cover class-based resource testing.

Part II: Advanced DSC Concepts

Part II is more than just basics. With a solid understanding of DSC concepts, you move on to the DSC ecosystem and other features such as a pull service, DSC reporting, partial configurations, cross-node synchronization, debugging DSC resource modules, and security in DSC.

Chapter 8: DSC Configuration Delivery Modes

All earlier chapters looked at pushing DSC configurations to target nodes, which is not a very scable method and requires firewall ports to be open, among other things. This is where the pull mode configuration delivery really helps. In this chapter, I discuss a few more concepts around the push model and move towards the other configuration refresh modes.

Chapter 9: Reporting, Monitoring, and Correcting Configuration

DSC provides interfaces to monitor and report configuration from the target systems and also a method to auto-correct a configuration drift. In this chapter, you take a look at the internals of configuration management using DSC, monitoring, and correcting configuration on target systems, and finally, reporting configurations from target systems using built-in methods.

Chapter 10: Partial Configurations

Partial configurations can help in an IT organization where multiple individuals are responsible for the configuration of the infrastructure. Partial configurations enable delegation of configuration management tasks and separation of the common configuration from node-specific configurations. This chapter goes in-depth into partial configurations and provides a walk-through of how partial configurations can be built and used. You look at preparing the necessary infrastructure to start enacting partial configurations. Finally, you see an updated configuration life cycle that presents a complete view of configuration management including partial configurations.

Chapter 11: Cross-Node Synchronization

With WMF 5.0, Microsoft introduced a new feature called cross-node synchronization in DSC. At the surface, what you see are three DSC resources that help you wait for dependencies to be in a desired state before proceeding to finalizing the configuration. But, behind the scenes, there is something more interesting. This chapter explores the xNode synchronization feature in DSC and describes scenarios where it can be useful.

Chapter 12: Debugging DSC Resources

Testing is a great way to ensure that the functionality that you intended to build is indeed available and not broken. You saw in Chapter 9 how DSC debug and analytics logs can help you retrieve more information around DSC operations. However, bugs may get introduced because of an environmental configuration where the resource module is being used or could just be a test miss. If so, you need to use the available debugging techniques to root-cause the bug and fix it. DSC as a platform offers a way to debug resource modules while the enact is in progress. In this chapter, you look at how to debug DSC resource module issues. It's a quick one but I really suggest that you practice the debugging technique that you learn with not just the simple example in this chapter but with a module of your own, too.

Chapter 13: Security in DSC

Securing configuration documents is not just about encrypting the credentials and other sensitive strings in it. The configuration documents describe a blueprint of the configuration on the system where they are enacted. Therefore, you must consider the entire MOF contents as a document containing sensitive information. In this chapter, you look at how DSC secures the MOF documents at rest in the local configuration store and also how you can ensure that the LCM enacts only trusted configurations and uses only trusted resource modules. You look at creating constrained endpoints and delegating DSC-based configuration management to non-administrator users in the IT organization.

Part III: DSC and the Release Pipeline

In Part II, you looked at creating and validating custom DSC resource modules. In this part, you look at automating these tests through the implementation of a release pipeline.

Chapter 14: DSC and the Release Pipeline

In Chapter 6, you learned about authoring your own DSC resource modules and looked at validating these resource scripts in Chapter 7. You looked at how you can publish the module to a private PowerShell repository hosted on an SMB share as well. It was all manual. But, with the help of a release pipeline implementation, this entire process can be automated from source control to a private repository. In this chapter, you will explore one such implementation using a few community PowerShell modules that enable a build-to-release pipeline implementation.

Chapter 15: DSC with AppVeyor CI

Chapter 14 presents an implementation of a release pipeline for DSC resource modules using all open source tooling and libraries. However, within this method, building a complete automated pipeline involves tinkering with Git hooks. Also, this method provides no reporting around the build success or failure and any historical reporting for the builds. This is where more evolved tools such as AppVeyor, among many others, can help. In this chapter, you implement a release pipeline with AppVeyor.

Part IV: DSC Platform, Cloud, and Containers

The final part this book covers DSC as a management platform and how DSC can be used with different public cloud IaaS instances and containers running on Windows Server 2016 or Windows 10 FCU.

Chapter 16: DSC as a Platform

Windows PowerShell DSC is a platform rather than just a set of tools to perform configuration management. DSC uses the CIM standard data representation for node configurations and uses WS-MAN as a standard transport for sending the configurations to the target nodes. This architecture is what makes DSC a platform. The cmdlets in the PSDesiredStateConfiguration module are a way to use the interfaces provided in the

DSC platform. In this chapter, you explore the platform aspect of Windows PowerShell DSC and learn how to perform the DSC operations without the need for any cmdlets in the PSDesiredStateConfiguration module.

Chapter 17: Microsoft Azure and DSC

Microsoft Azure offers different cloud service models, such as Infrastructure as a Service (IaaS), Platform as a Service (PaaS), and Software as a Service (Saas) among many others. With the release of Microsoft Azure Stack (MAS), many of these services can now be extended into on-premises infrastructure in hybrid cloud deployment model as well. As a part of the IaaS offerings, the virtual machines created in the Azure cloud can be configured using PowerShell DSC in a few different ways. For the IaaS VMs on Azure, you can use the Azure VM DSC extension handler to enact configurations in the VM. Another approach that internally uses the DSC extension handler is provided by an Azure service called the Azure Automation DSC (AA DSC) service. In this chapter, you explore how Azure IaaS virtual machines can be configured using the DSC extension handler and how the AA DSC service can be used to manage both Azure IaaS VMs and the systems on-premises.

Chapter 18: DSC and Google Cloud Platform

Google Cloud Platform (GCP) is yet another but very important player in the IaaS public cloud space. As a part of Google Compute Engine (GCE), GCP offers a wide range of IaaS VM instances and operating systems. Windows Server 2008 R2, Windows Server 2012 R2, Windows Server 2016, and Windows Server 2016 version 1709 are parts of the GCE offerings. In this chapter, you learn how to use DSC to configure the GCE Windows instances.

Chapter 19: Amazon Web Services and DSC

The previous two chapters showed you how to use PowerShell Desired State Configuration with Windows instances running on Azure and Google Cloud services. You looked at how the Azure Automation DSC service can help with both cloud and on-premises instances of Windows systems. In this chapter, you look at how to use DSC with AWS Elastic Compute 2 (EC2) instances.

Chapter 20: DSC with Containers

Containers have been around for a while in the Linux world, and with Windows 10 and Windows Server 2016, containers have entered the Microsoft Windows world, too. Containers accelerate application development, testing, and deployment, and are useful in dynamic data centers and cloud environments where DevOps practices are implemented. You can get an application from the development environment to production in a completely automated way by building the container images in the development stage and then shipping the same image through validation and finally to production. The configuration needed for the application to work can be packaged into the image itself. In this chapter, you explore how to use DSC with Windows containers using Server Core.

PART I

Getting Started with Windows PowerShell DSC

Windows PowerShell DSC isn't a new technology anymore. It has evolved from its infant phase into a mature, powerful platform. The first part of the book provides a good overview of DevOps and Infrastructure as Code (IaC) practices and explains where DSC plays a role in these practices. After a quick overview of DSC, you dive into the DSC component architecture and learn the internals of LCM.

With the knowledge of DSC architecture and the internals of LCM, you start writing your first configuration script and learn the declarative syntax provided by DSC. You extend this knowledge into creating advanced configurations that use configuration data, secure strings, and encrypted credentials, and common DSC resource properties such as the `PsDscRunAsCredential`.

The section ends by looking at writing composite DSC resource modules from reusable configurations and writing your own MOF-based or class-based DSC resource modules. You look at performing unit and integration tests for these custom DSC resource modules towards the end of this part.

By the end of this section, you will be proficient in not just the basics of PowerShell DSC but also in writing your own custom DSC resource modules and validating them using Pester.

## CHAPTER 1

Introduction to Infrastructure as Code and PowerShell DSC

> *You can learn from anyone, it doesn't matter who they are or what their experience is.*

—Neil Patel (Entrepreneur)

In this era of cloud computing, communication and collaboration along with an agile way of delivering both infrastructure and software are critical. With the rise of the cloud infrastructure, starting with the Amazon Web Services announcement in 2006, there has been a constant effort to make the infrastructure dynamic and responsive to changes in business. The traditional methods of building and managing IT infrastructure do not help with web-scale infrastructures that are dynamic and work at a different scale than their traditional counterparts. Being an automation and efficiency fanatic, I always find an opportunity to evangelize DevOps practices. When we implement some of the DevOps practices in the context of infrastructure management, we call it Infrastructure as Code (IaC). In fact, IaC is an integral part of DevOps practices. Automation is certainly one of the most important enablers in DevOps practices and it makes Infrastructure as Code possible.

When I talk about these practices to a room full of infrastructure administrators, at least 50% of them think that it is irrelevant in terms of their day-to-day tasks. To explain the relevance of DevOps practices to IT professionals, I usually start with one of my own experiences to set the context around why DevOps practices are relevant in infrastructure management. That said, this chapter isn't about DevOps practices. You will

3

© Ravikanth Chaganti 2018
R. Chaganti, *Pro PowerShell Desired State Configuration*, https://doi.org/10.1007/978-1-4842-3483-9_1

learn about this in the context of what you, an IT professional, can learn from practices usually followed by brothers and sisters from the other side of the wall (developers) and in the DevOps world.

Gene Kim highlighted the issues that are faced by IT organizations very well in his book *The Phoenix Project*. In his book, he narrates how an IT organization evolved to a great business enabler by developing and implementing DevOps practices. For an IT professional like you, DevOps practices sound completely alien. Even though you may not be interfacing with developers and deploying their code in production, it is helpful to understand some of the DevOps practices and how they can be leveraged in the infrastructure world.

Before I dive into what IaC is, let's first look at the infrastructure deployment and configuration challenges faced by IT organizations. I will expand this knowledge into a DevOps discussion and show how practices like IaC and/or Configuration as Code (CaC) can help achieve continuous delivery and deployment. I will conclude this chapter by looking at an introduction to Windows PowerShell Desired State Configuration (DSC), explain the role DSC plays in IaC, and show you how to enable DSC in your infrastructure.

Lab Requirements

In order to try out examples and exercises in this chapter, you will need at minimum a Windows Server 2008 R2 or above system with WMF 5.1 installed. I recommend a system with Windows Server 2016.

The Operations Challenge

I started my career in IT back in 2000. It was the time when the Microsoft Windows NT 4.0 Server operating system was popular for both good and bad reasons. I was managing a small data center at a customer site that had a mix of different operating systems including Windows NT and Unix. I was also responsible for the network infrastructure that had Cisco switches and routers connecting the data center to the public Internet as well as branch offices. Being the only IT administrator was not an easy thing, especially when the IT manager and developers on the systems team had god-mode access to all IT infrastructure. These developers could push configuration and code changes without any prior change requests and approvals. This severely impacted the services running in production. And, not just that! We had issues recovering servers when something went wrong. There was not even a documented way of recovering server configuration.

This is not just my story but the story of several IT administrators. What I really needed was a way to identify changes that were needed, ensure these changes were reviewed, and the ability to deploy the changes through a system that provided a method to document and track these changes. A few IT organizations that realized the value of these change management processes had implemented systems and tools that help them manage change in the data center environment. A typical configuration change management process has different phases, such as change submission, review, approval, deployment, and monitoring and reporting, which combine to form the configuration management cycle. Parts of this process are manual, and others can be automated. Overall, configuration change management is a process that involves both people and systems. Therefore, collaboration between teams and people is an important aspect.

A typical configuration management life cycle is shown in Figure 1-1. This is a high-level representation of the different phases involved in configuration management and does not represent a granular configuration process.

Figure 1-1. *A typical configuration management cycle*

Each configuration change in the data center may include more than one configuration item and may involve disparate systems. For example, deploying a new web application might require changes to the web servers and database servers. Depending on how the application is architected, there might be a middleware tier, too, that gets changed. The initial deployments are always easy and usually adhere to the standards defined in IT service management. However, the subsequent changes are not. Some of these changes may involve only updates at one of the tiers of the application architecture. This is where the stringent process or phases of the configuration life cycle play a critical part in IT service management. Each of the configuration items going through this life cycle finally get stored in a configuration store usually referred to as a configuration management database (CMDB). In an ideal world, the CMDB must be up-to-date, with all changes performed on an entity either on-premises or in the cloud. We should be able to use the information stored in the CMDB to trace faults in the data center management to their exact cause and location and, thus, help data center administrators avoid configuration drift. However, we are not always in an ideal world, especially when talking about enterprise data centers.

What I faced early in my career is a classic example of configuration drift. Often developers (and even an IT manager) changed the configuration of servers and applications running on those servers without following a standard procedure, thereby creating islands of configurations. It was never easy to restore a failed server to its functional configuration. Configuration drift refers to these unmanaged changes made to an entity in the scope of IT service management. Going back to the example of a web application, the changes performed at any tier of the architecture must be properly documented and implemented. Any failure to do so while performing changes to the application or the infrastructure hosting the applications will result in a configuration drift. Simply put, this drift represents a deviation from the known desired configuration state, and such a drift can have bad consequences for service management and can make fault isolation difficult. It is essential for IT managers to address these challenges in configuration management and to eliminate configuration drift. To this extent, we can modify the **Monitor and Report** phase shown in Figure 1-1 to make it **Monitor, Report, and Remediate**. This is shown in Figure 1-2.

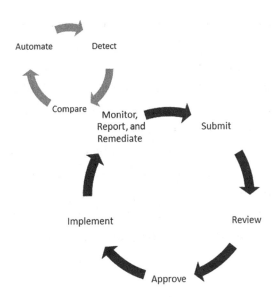

Figure 1-2. *Extended phases of configuration management*

The extended phase (**Remediate**) in the configuration management life cycle, shown in Figure 1-2, is used to enforce the configuration changes. This means we not only have the ability to report but also to take action based on how the remediation policies are created.

Within the extended phases shown within the **Monitor, Report, and Remediate** phase, **Detect** provides a mechanism to detect the state of configuration items. This includes the ability to list what configuration items are being monitored and the means to retrieve the state of each configuration item.

The **Compare** phase should provide the ability to compare the state of the configuration items retrieved in the **Detect** phase to a predefined baseline or a baseline that has been updated through a managed configuration change process. This phase also builds a report of the deviations, if there are any. **Detect** and **Compare** are the most important steps in the **Monitor and Remediate** phase of configuration management. Within the scope of our definition, these two phases provide insights into what has changed or not changed in the system being monitored. Without these insights, there is no meaning in monitoring and remediating a configuration drift.

Through the final phase, **Automate**, we should be able to automate the actions, based on how we configure the remediation policies. You may choose to verify the configuration drift manually and then take action to remediate. This is perfectly fine, and this is what makes automated remediation optional: it is not always mandatory to fix the configuration differences automatically.

The first three phases of the configuration management life cycle are related to IT service processes. There are various tools that help users to submit change requests and appropriate people to approve or reject the same. The next phases in the life cycle can be automated using scripts and existing frameworks. This is generally referred to as Configuration as Code. By saying Configuration as Code, we are not just referring to a bunch of scripts that perform automated deployments or configuration management automation. We need a consistent, reliable, and repeatable method to perform configuration management of the data center infrastructure. This is a major part of an IaC practice, which brings software development best practices to infrastructure deployment and configuration management. Before I dive into what IaC is, let's complete the discussion around the DevOps challenge and then talk about what role IaC plays in it.

The DevOps Challenge

Back in August 2012, Knight Capital lost over $460 million in a span of just 45 minutes due to an issue in its automatic trading system. What and how it happened is a long story and is detailed in the SEC filing (http://azrs.tk/secKCA) by Knight Capital. Here is an excerpt from the SEC filing that briefly indicates what happened:

During the deployment of the new code, however, one of Knight's technicians did not copy the new code to one of the eight SMARS computer servers. Knight did not have a second technician review this deployment and no one at Knight realized that the Power Peg code had not been removed from the eighth server, nor that the new RLP code added. Knight had no written procedures that required such a review.

What happened at Knight Capital is similar to what you as an IT administrator might be facing in your organization. If you remember the operations challenge discussion, this is what I was trying to solve but just within the infrastructure configuration. However, when you are managing infrastructure where code from development teams needs to be deployed, you have a larger problem. For an investment banker such as Knight Capital, the lack of procedures and collaboration between development and operations team was a disaster. This is where DevOps practices play a major role. DevOps shouldn't be a new term and you must have already heard or read about it elsewhere. With the rise of web-scale infrastructures, it is important for IT organizations to be more agile and efficient to support the ever-growing need for flexible infrastructures that a normal IT professional would have ever imagined. Wikipedia reflects upon DevOps:

DevOps (a clipped compound of "development" and "operations") is a culture, movement, or practice that emphasizes the collaboration and communication of both software developers and other information-technology (IT) professionals while automating the process of software delivery and infrastructure changes. It aims at establishing a culture and environment where building, testing, and releasing software, can happen rapidly, frequently, and more reliably.

Let's keep the collaboration and communication part of this definition out of this discussion; they are soft skills that should be nurtured between the development and operations teams. There are even tools that enforce this communication and collaboration. Let's focus on the later part the DevOps definition about automating the process of software delivery and infrastructure changes and building, testing, and releasing software rapidly, frequently, and more reliably. A picture is worth a thousand words. So, Figure 1-3 shows the technical part of the DevOps definition in a picture!

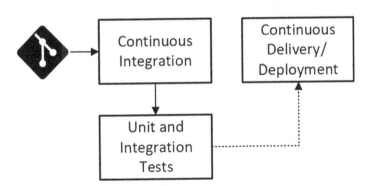

Figure 1-3. *Application development flow from source control to production*

What this picture depicts is the typical application code flow from development to production. The phases such as continuous integration and continuous delivery ensure that the developed application code is tested and is stable for deployment in production. The tests that run at these phases provide an assurance that the code will run as expected in all sorts of environments (development, QA, staging, and production) where the code gets deployed. One thing you must note here is that for the application code to run as expected in any of the environments, you must have the same or similar infrastructure configuration. For example, when you start making changes to the application code, the development infrastructure where you perform unit testing of your code must mimic the production infrastructure. If the application code in development requires infrastructure configuration changes, these configuration changes must move, along with the application code, from development to other environments as the code gets tested and deployed.

While delivering and deploying the application code in a rapid and efficient manner is important, it is equally important to ensure that the infrastructure where this code gets deployed is dealt with the same way we deal with the application code. I already discussed the importance of these processes in the preceding section. For reusable, consistent, and rapid deployments of infrastructure, you need automation. When you have automation, you always want to validate what you are doing because there are no humans sitting and watching the deployment as it happens or clicking buttons to complete the deployment. And, finally, when something goes wrong, you want to quickly see what changed in your infrastructure automation and roll back those changes when needed.

Infrastructure as Code

It is easy to argue that what I described—a need for automated configuration management—is just infrastructure automation, which you and I as IT professionals have been doing for ages. Right? One thing you must notice here is that IaC is not just about code alone. Infrastructure automation does play a role within IaC. After all, how else do we create reusable and repeatable infrastructure without automation? IaC mandates software development practices in managing IT infrastructure.

The three major components of IaC are

- **Source Control**: Enables the method to track and roll back changes to your infrastructure as needed. There are many tools that you can use here. My favorite has been Git.

- **Unit/Integration/Operational Testing**: Enables validation of your infrastructure code within various phases of the infrastructure release pipeline or outside the release pipeline and lets you feel confident about what you are pushing to production. The PowerShell Unit Testing framework, Pester, can be used here. You will learn more about the release pipeline towards the end of this section.

- **Infrastructure Automation**: Enables consistent, reusable, and rapid deployment part of IaC. This is referred to as Configuration as Code and it is the main component within the IaC practice. Within CaC, the configuration management tools or platforms enable a declarative way of handling infrastructure configuration. This automation should always go hand-in-hand with unit/integration/operations testing. When talking about Infrastructure and Configuration as Code, version control and testing become very important. However, to enable a consistent, reusable, and repeatable method of infrastructure deployment and configuration, it is important that we go beyond imperative scripting. You will learn more about the imperative style of scripting in the "Imperative vs. Declarative Syntax" section.

If you want to understand the IaC practices with in-depth examples and real-world scenarios, I recommend *Infrastructure As Code* by Kief Morris (`http://azrs.tk/IacDSC`). It provides an excellent introduction to IaC and explains the concepts with several examples.

The process of getting infrastructure code from source control to production should not be a manual process. The different phases should be completely automated. This is usually referred to as a release or deployment pipeline. Figure 1-4 shows the release pipeline representation of what was shown in Figure 1-3.

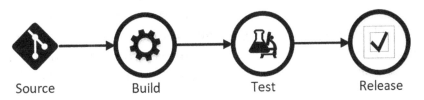

Source   Build   Test   Release

Figure 1-4. *Infrastructure code release pipeline*

What we see in Figure 1-4 can be considered a blueprint for implementing IaC. It represents the essential elements of IaC as implementable artifacts such as build systems, tests, and releases. You will see implementations of this pipeline in Chapters 14 and 15 when you look at using automated release pipelines for publishing custom DSC resource modules from source control all the way to a PowerShell module repository or pull server for resource module distribution. There are several open source and proprietary tools that help us build these release pipelines. Chapter 14 presents one implementation with all open source PowerShell libraries and Chapter 15 discusses more evolved tools such as AppVeyor.

Automated build and release systems are nothing new in the Linux space, and over the last few years we have been seeing these systems or libraries get implemented in the Windows space as well. Historically, Microsoft Windows focused on user experience. Until Windows PowerShell was released, the focus was never on developing a scripting language (VB Scripting existed but had many limitations) or an engine for automating day-to-day administration tasks. There were disparate places where the Windows OS and applications on it stored configurations. For example, OS and application configurations were stored in the Windows registry, in INI and CONFIG files, and many other places. Utilities such as reg.exe were used to manage configuration stored in the Windows registry while INI and CONFIG file changes are done either by underlying OS interfaces or proprietary ways defined within the OS and applications. This resulted in script sprawl.

In the pre-PowerShell era, this meant hundreds of lines of Windows batch scripts or VB Scripts. Even with Windows PowerShell, this still meant a bunch of scripts and often really complex ones. For example, changing the configuration stored within the registry using Windows PowerShell was easy but ensuring that this configuration stayed as-is and any drifts caused by misconfiguration were handled properly wasn't easy. We needed to schedule scripts that checked the configuration of a specific entity within the OS and then set or reset it as needed. The lines of code only increased with the increase in number of configuration items. It wasn't a scalable approach.

With the recent DevOps adoption and growing need for managing CaC, there is a strong desire to build a platform that provides open and consistent configuration management interfaces across Windows and other Operating Systems such as Linux. This is where the Windows PowerShell Desired State Configuration (DSC) feature plays a role.

Understanding Desired State Configuration

Windows PowerShell Desired State Configuration has evolved into a powerful platform since its inception back in 2011. DSC is built on and makes use of a standards-based management platform. DSC uses a common information model (CIM) for representing a device or resource configuration and a WS-Management (WS-Man) remote management protocol for transporting the configuration to target nodes.

To reiterate, DSC should be seen as a configuration management platform rather than a complete configuration management solution. Unlike the other configuration management tools or solutions, DSC does not provide an end-to-end tool set to manage and monitor configuration. Instead, DSC offers an application programming interface (API) and a platform that even other tools and frameworks can leverage. That said, the integrations available with the Azure Automation and Operations Management Suite provide a way to get insights into the configuration being managed by DSC. Other configuration management tools such as Puppet and Chef leverage DSC APIs to perform configuration management of Windows systems. PowerShell DSC supports separation of environmental configuration from structural or resource configuration. You can use the configuration data in your DSC documents to make your infrastructure automation reusable. I will discuss using configuration data in Chapter 5.

Also, understand that PowerShell DSC does not represent the entire IaC practice. It is one of the enablers that is referred to as Configuration as Code. I mentioned CaC as being a major part of IaC. It is where PowerShell DSC comes into play. It enables a declarative way of expressing your infrastructure configuration. Using this declarative syntax, you can create what I referred to as infrastructure automation in the earlier section. Although the declarative syntax might be new to some of you, it is still PowerShell. And it is my favorite part of using DSC. I can use my existing PowerShell skills to write DSC configuration documents and the DSC resource modules. I will discuss writing your own DSC resource modules in Chapter 5.

As mentioned, within CaC, the intent is described in terms of the declarative syntax. The imperative scripts, in this case the DSC resource modules, take care of implementation of the configuration or *make it so*. The following section provides a brief overview of the distinction between the imperative and declarative syntaxes using PowerShell and DSC as examples. You may not understand everything in the DSC syntax but just hang in there. I have an in-depth discussion on that in Chapter 2.

Imperative vs. Declarative Syntax

Windows PowerShell is imperative in nature. What that means is that when we write a script in PowerShell, we tell PowerShell how to perform a specific task, using either the built-in cmdlets or the functions or modules we write. Let's look at an example that describes this in detail. So, the task at hand is to ensure that the Windows Update Service is running and the startup type is set to Automatic. This can be done using just two lines of PowerShell:

```
Set-Service -Name wuauserv -StartupType Automatic
Start-Service -Name wuauserv
```

However, doing this using a production quality script will require some changes. Here is how I put these commands into a script:

```
[CmdletBinding()]
param
(
    [Parameter(Mandatory = $true)]
    [string]
    $Name,

    [Parameter()]
    [string]
    [ValidateSet('Running', 'Stopped')]
    $Status,

    [Parameter()]
    [string]
    [ValidateSet('Automatic', 'Disabled', 'Manual')]
    $StartupType
)

$service = Get-Service -Name $Name -ErrorAction Stop

if ($service.StartType -ne $StartupType)
{
    Write-Verbose -Message "Setting startup type for $Name to $StartupType"
    Set-Service -Name $Name -StartupType $StartupType
}

if ($service.Status -ne $Status)
{
    if ($Status -eq 'Running')
```

```
    {
        Write-Verbose -Message "Starting service $Name"
        Start-Service -Name $Name
    }
    else
    {
        Write-Verbose -Message "Stopping service $Name"
        Stop-Service -Name $Name
    }
}
```

In reality, a production PowerShell script usually contains the following:

- It expresses the intent or the desired state of the service (in this case, the intent is to ensure that Windows Update service is running and its startup type is automatic).

- It contains the logic to get the service to the desired state.

- It has logging, error handling, and reporting.

As you can see, bulk of the code contains how to get the task done and not the intent.

In the declarative style of programming, we describe the end state and not how it needs to be done. In this programming style, we are not concerned about how things are done. We depend on the underlying automation or programming framework to know how to perform a given set of tasks. Of course, there has to be explicit support within the underlying framework to perform these tasks. Essentially, the declarative approach separates the two: the intent and the how to make it so. This enables a developer or an IT pro to understand what the end state or the desired state of the system should look like. PowerShell DSC enables this approach. In this example, the desired state of the system will look like the following:

```
Configuration MyServices
{
    Import-DscResource -ModuleName PSDesiredStateConfiguration

    Node MyServer
    {
        Service WindowsUpdate
```

```
    {
        Name        = 'wuauserv'
        State       = 'Running'
        StartupType = 'Automatic'
    }
  }
}
```

As you can see, the declarative language is a lot easier to understand because it focuses on the intent. Someone who is not familiar with PowerShell can still change the intent of the system since it is more readable and easy to understand.

This is what DSC helps achieve: a declarative way for defining the desired state of the system. The following are the various parts of the declarative syntax:

- **Configuration**: A function that describes that the desired state of the system will be expressed declaratively

- **Import-DscResource**: A keyword indicating which modules to import resources from

- **Node**: A keyword that indicates list of nodes in which this configuration will be applied

- **Service**: A resource whose desired state can be expressed declaratively

- **WindowsUpdate**: A name that identifies this instance of the resource in the PowerShell script

- **Name, State, and StartupType**: Properties of the resource that are configurable

The example showing the declarative syntax in PowerShell is indeed a DSC configuration. Using the DSC configurations, we can specify what configuration items have to be managed and how. You will explore the configurations more and write your first configuration in Chapter 2, but first, how do you get the DSC feature in Windows?

Enabling Desired State Configuration

The Windows PowerShell Desired State Configuration feature was first released with Windows Management Framework (WMF) 4.0. The most recent version of DSC feature is released with WMF 5.1. Windows Server 2016 and Windows 10 operating systems come with WMF 5.1 preinstalled and therefore, there is no WMF 5.1 download for these operating systems.

The WMF 5.1 package is available for down-level operating systems, such as Windows Server 2012 R2, Windows Server 2012, Windows Server 2008 R2 SP1, Windows 8.1, and Windows 7 SP1.

Table 1-1 lists the WMF 5.1 prerequisites and download locations. All examples listed in this book will use only WMF 5.1.

Table 1-1. *WMF 5.1 Prerequisites and Download Locations*

Operating System	Prerequisites	Download Links
Windows Server 2012 R2	NA	https://go.microsoft.com/ fwlink/?linkid=839516
Windows Server 2012	NA	https://go.microsoft.com/ fwlink/?linkid=839513
Windows Server 2008 R2	.NET Framework 4.5.2	https://go.microsoft.com/ fwlink/?linkid=839523
Windows 8.1	NA	x64: https://go.microsoft.com/ fwlink/?linkid=839516
Windows 8.1	NA	x86: https://go.microsoft.com/ fwlink/?linkid=839521
Windows 7 SP1	.NET Framework 4.5.2	x64: https://go.microsoft.com/ fwlink/?linkid=839523
Windows 7 SP1	.NET Framework 4.5.2	x86: https://go.microsoft.com/ fwlink/?linkid=839522

As mentioned, all examples in this book will be based on WMF 5.1 only. Also, I discussed earlier that DSC uses CIM for representing resource configuration and WS-Man for transporting the configurations to the target nodes. Therefore, the target nodes require a WinRM service in running state with listeners configured to accept remote connections. WinRM supports both HTTP (port 5985) and HTTPS (port 5986) listeners. On systems running Windows Server 2012 and above, WinRM service with an HTTP listener is enabled by default. The HTTPS listener can be created and it is the recommended way to perform remote management.

Configuring a WinRM HTTPS Listener

Since we can use WinRM HTTPS listeners with DSC and it is the recommended method, I will quickly look at configuring these listeners. A WinRM HTTPS listener requires deploying certificates on the target node.

For the purpose of this demonstration, you will use self-signed certificates. The HTTPS endpoint requires a Server Authentication certificate with its CN matching the hostname of the target node.

```
$certificate = New-SelfSignedCertificate -DnsName $env:COMPUTERNAME
-CertStoreLocation cert:\LocalMachine\My
```

Once the certificate is created, you can create a listener and associate the certificate.

```
New-Item -Path WSMan:\Localhost\Listener -Transport HTTPS -Address *
-CertificateThumbprint $certificate.Thumbprint


New-NetFirewallRule -DisplayName "Windows Remote Management (HTTPS-In)"
-Name "WinRM HTTPS-In" -Profile Any -LocalPort 5986 -Protocol TCP
```

The connectivity to the HTTPS listener can be tested using the New-CimSession cmdlet. Since you are using a self-signed certificate, you need to ensure that you skip CA checks.

```
$cimSessionOption = New-CimSessionOption -SkipCACheck -UseSsl

$session = New-CimSession -SessionOption $cimSessionOption -ComputerName
S16-01
```

When you run the New-CimSession cmdlet you should not see any errors related to the WinRM connection. This session object can then be used to query remote CIM classes using the CIM cmdlets and as an argument to the -CimSession parameter with the DSC cmdlets as well. And that is what enables you to work with DSC on remote target nodes using the WinRM HTTPS listener.

```
Get-DscConfiguration -CimSession $cimSession
```

Ok, don't worry about that command. I just mentioned it here to show you how to use DSC cmdlets with WinRM endpoints. Chapter 2 provides an in-depth overview of DSC and its components.

Tools for the Job

As with any other technology, it is important that you choose right tools for the job. For working with DSC, you will need PowerShell. Code editors such as Visual Studio Core and script editors such as PowerShell ISE will be very useful in working with DSC. These editors provide IntelliSense, which helps you discover DSC resources and the declarative syntax. For most part of the book, I have used either of these tools.

Summary

This chapter provided an introduction to configuration management and continuous delivery in the context of IaC. You looked at some of the challenges involved in IT service management with regard to configuration management and the role of configuration management as a part of continuous delivery and integration. The need for enforcing automation in IT service management is unquestionable and a necessity. DSC provides the required feature set to enable the automation required for configuration change management and continuous delivery. DSC is designed to be a configuration management platform, and any existing configuration management tools in the enterprise can use the interfaces provided by DSC. The prerequisites for enabling this new feature are a part of the Windows operating system and are configurable using well-known administration interfaces in the Windows OS. For example, you saw how to configure WinRM HTTPS listeners. For IT administrators who are already familiar with Windows PowerShell and with writing PowerShell scripts, the learning curve to adapt PowerShell DSC will be small.

CHAPTER 2

Getting Started with DSC

Chapter 1 discussed the philosophy behind DevOps practices, explained the need for Infrastructure as Code, and looked at different aspects of IaC including Configuration as Code where PowerShell Desired State Configuration plays a role. It ended with a quick introduction to PowerShell DSC and how to install WMF 5.1 on down-level operating systems such as Windows Server 2012 R2. In this chapter, I take this knowledge further down the rabbit hole and show what DSC has to offer—its features and component architecture.

When learning any new technology, it is essential for the learner to understand the different components involved in making that technology functional. PowerShell DSC is no exception. This is how I learned and this book is a reflection of what I followed in an attempt to learn DSC in-depth. So, you'll start your journey into the DSC world by first seeing a list of all the components that make up DSC and then exploring each one. This chapter won't dive into the components fully. You will get an overview of each component and how they glue together to make configuration management possible with PowerShell DSC. Once you have this foundation, the subsequent chapters dive into all of these components and show how they are used in the real world. If you don't understand everything that is explained in this chapter, it is fine. You will get the big picture once you read the subsequent chapters and you will be able to stitch things together easily. On that note, let's get started with DSC!

Lab Requirements

To try out the examples and exercises in this chapter, you will need at a minimum a Windows Server 2008 R2 or above system with WMF 5.1 installed. I recommend a system with Windows Server 2016.

© Ravikanth Chaganti 2018
R. Chaganti, *Pro PowerShell Desired State Configuration*, https://doi.org/10.1007/978-1-4842-3483-9_2

PowerShell DSC: A 10,000-Foot View

A picture is worth a thousand words. So, before we delve into the component details, take a look Figure 2-1. The rest of this chapter uses this component architecture as the basis for this discussion. Figure 2-1 provides a high-level overview of the DSC components and some of its features.

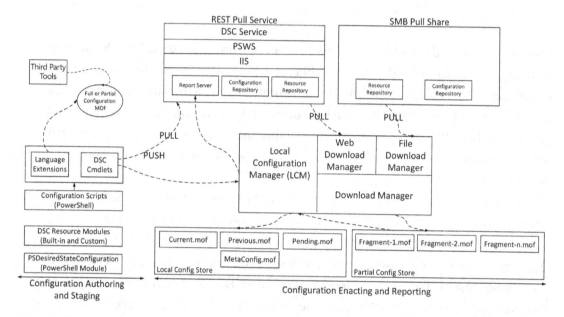

Figure 2-1. *Configuration management phases of DSC and DSC components*

In Figure 2-1, the text at the bottom indicates that there are two distinct phases of configuration management in DSC or rather in any configuration management platform or tool.

1. Configuration Authoring and Staging

2. Configuration Enacting and Reporting

The **Configuration Authoring and Staging** phase is where we write configuration documents that define what and how the resources on target systems must be configured and how this configuration gets staged for enacting. Although **Authoring** and **Staging** refer to two different aspects of configuration management, it is prudent to discuss them together because the **Configuration Authoring** phase leads to **Staging** as a natural next step. I discussed the declarative style of writing configuration documents and reviewed a related example in Chapter 1. You may understand the declarative scripts, but you have not learned how the declarative syntax is made possible. You will do so in this chapter. You will also look at different configuration staging choices available when using DSC.

The **Configuration Enacting and Reporting** phase is when the staged configuration gets enacted on a target system. There are two different modes, push and pull, through which we can deliver the configuration for enacting. While **Configuration Staging** refers to a place where the configuration in managed object format (MOF) gets stored, **Enacting** refers to receiving this configuration MOF on a target system and performing the required configuration changes. In this chapter, I will briefly show the different configuration delivery modes and explain how each of these methods can be used to enact configuration. Finally, the **Reporting** part of this phase becomes very important after the configuration enact is complete. You always want to track the target systems' configuration for any drift and be notified about it. In a larger infrastructure, you may need to get a holistic view of the configuration status on several nodes. I will go through an overview of the tools and infrastructure that DSC provides to support configuration reporting.

Figure 2-1 depicts how different DSC components are used across the two phases of configuration management. As you move forward in your journey towards mastering PowerShell DSC, an understanding of these components and how they fit in the overall DSC configuration management will play a major role in building the foundation to master PowerShell DSC.

Configuration Authoring and Staging

Configuration document authoring is one of the first steps in configuration management. DSC provides a set of PowerShell language extensions that make configuration authoring an easier task by enabling the declarative syntax you looked at in Chapter 1.

Note   The phrases *configuration document* and *configuration script* refer to system(s) configuration definition. There are other definitions that exist as well. For example, Puppet refers to a *configuration document* or *script* as a manifest while Chef refers to the same as a *recipe.* Whatever the name, they all refer to a declarative configuration. In the context of PowerShell DSC, I prefer to call these scripts *configuration documents.*

PowerShell DSC Language Extensions

In PowerShell DSC, a function called `Configuration` and dynamic keywords called `Node` and `Import-DscResource` are used as the starting point for writing configuration documents.

The following is another example to show the declarative syntax enabled by the language extensions in DSC:

```
Configuration FileCopyConfiguration
{
    Import-DscResource -ModuleName PSDesiredStateConfiguration

    Node S16-01
    {
        File FileCopyInstance1
        {
            DestinationPath = 'C:\Scripts\build.tag'
            Type = 'File'
            Contents = 'Version:1.0.0.0'
            Ensure = 'Present'
        }
    }
}
```

In this example, you can see that the `Configuration` function, `Node` and `Import-DscResource` keywords are used. These language extensions are exported by the `PSDesiredStateConfiguration` module. This module lives in `${env:SystemRoot}\System32\WindowsPowerShell\v1.0\Modules`. The functionality provided by this module, in terms of keywords, functions, and cmdlets, is used not just in the authoring but also in the staging, enact, and reporting parts of the DSC-based configuration management.

You can see the `Configuration` function listed as one of the exported commands in Figure 2-2.

```
PS C:\> Get-Module -Name PSDesiredStateConfiguration -ListAvailable | Select -ExpandProperty ExportedCommands | Format-Wide
```

```
Set-DscLocalConfigurationManager                              Start-DscConfiguration
Test-DscConfiguration                                         Publish-DscConfiguration
Update-DscConfiguration                                       Invoke-DscResource
Configuration                                                 Get-DscConfiguration
Get-DscLocalConfigurationManager                              Restore-DscConfiguration
New-DscChecksum                                               Get-DscResource
Get-DscConfigurationStatus                                    Stop-DscConfiguration
Remove-DscConfigurationDocument                               Enable-DscDebug
Disable-DscDebug                                              sacfg
tcfg                                                          gcfg
rtcfg                                                         upcfg
glcm                                                          slcm
pbcfg                                                         cmpcfg
gcfgs
```

Figure 2-2. *Commands exported in the PSDesiredStateConfiguration module*

Note   The `Microsoft.Windows.DSC.CoreConfProviders.dll` located at `C:\Windows\Microsoft.Net\assembly\GAC_MSIL\Microsoft.Windows.DSC.CoreConfProviders` is the root module for the `PSDesiredStateConfiguraton` PowerShell module. This binary module implements the `Start-DscConfiguration` and `Set-DscLocalConfigurationManager` cmdlets. However, this binary module does not export any of these cmdlets. Therefore, the `PSDesiredStateConfiguration` script module is used to export these cmdlets.

The `Configuration` command is like any other PowerShell function but with a special role. `FileCopyConfiguration` is the name given to the configuration example. What follows that name is a script block that defines a set of one or more nodes and resources (inside the *Node* script block) that you need to configure. When this configuration function is loaded into memory, you can access it like any other PowerShell function. You can observe this in Figure 2-3.

Figure 2-3. *FileCopyConfiguration command*

In Figure 2-3, you can observe that the CommandType for FileCopyConfiguration is shown as Configuration and therefore identifies it as a PowerShell DSC configuration. The Get-Help cmdlet output for this configuration shows a few parameters that are automatically added to every command of configuration type. You will learn more about these parameters and why you need them in Chapter 4 when you start writing DSC configurations.

Going back to the discussion of language extensions, in the list of exported commands from the PSDesiredStateConfiguration module, you do not see the Node and Import-DscResource keywords. This is because they are the dynamic keywords and not commands. For example, trying the Get-Command cmdlet for them would not result in anything. This is shown in Figure 2-4.

```
PS C:\> Get-Command -Name Node, Import-DscResource
Get-Command : The term 'Node' is not recognized as the name of a cmdlet, function, script file, or oper
was included, verify that the path is correct and try again.
At line:1 char:1
+ Get-Command -Name Node, Import-DscResource
+ ~~~~~~~~~~~~~~~~~~~~~~~~~~~~~~~~~~~~~~~~~~~~~
    + CategoryInfo          : ObjectNotFound: (Node:String) [Get-Command], CommandNotFoundException
    + FullyQualifiedErrorId : CommandNotFoundException,Microsoft.PowerShell.Commands.GetCommandCommand

Get-Command : The term 'Import-DscResource' is not recognized as the name of a cmdlet, function, script
or if a path was included, verify that the path is correct and try again.
At line:1 char:1
+ Get-Command -Name Node, Import-DscResource
+ ~~~~~~~~~~~~~~~~~~~~~~~~~~~~~~~~~~~~~~~~~~~~~
    + CategoryInfo          : ObjectNotFound: (Import-DscResource:String) [Get-Command], CommandNotFour
    + FullyQualifiedErrorId : CommandNotFoundException,Microsoft.PowerShell.Commands.GetCommandCommand
```

Figure 2-4. *Node and Import-DscResource are not commands*

So, how do you confirm that the PSDesiredStateConfiguration module is where these dynamic keywords coming from? You can verify using the following function:

```
Function Get-CimKeyword
{
    [CmdletBinding()]
    param (
        [Parameter(Mandatory, ValueFromPipeline)]
        [ValidateNotNullOrEmpty()]
        [string] $ImplementingModule
    )
```

```
Begin
{
    [Microsoft.PowerShell.DesiredStateConfiguration.Internal.
    DscClassCache]::ClearCache()
    $functionsToDefine = New-Object -TypeName 'System.Collections.
    Generic.Dictionary[string,ScriptBlock]'([System.StringComparer]::Or
    dinalIgnoreCase)

    $builtInModules = @('PSDesiredStateConfiguration','PSDesiredState
    ConfigurationEngine')
}

Process
{
    #Load the default CIM Keywords
    [Microsoft.PowerShell.DesiredStateConfiguration.Internal.DscClass
    Cache]::LoadDefaultCimKeywords($functionsToDefine)

    if ($builtInModules -notcontains $ImplementingModule)
    {
        #We need to import either CIM or Script or Class keywords
        #Check if the module exists
        $modInfo = Get-Module -Name $ImplementingModule -ListAvailable
        $dscResourceFolder = "$($modInfo.ModuleBase)\DscResources"

        foreach ($resource in (Get-ChildItem -Path $dscResourceFolder
        -Directory -Name))
        {
            $schemaFilePath = $null
            $keywordErrors = New-Object -TypeName 'System.Collections.
            ObjectModel.Collection[System.Exception]'
            $foundCimSchema = [Microsoft.PowerShell.
            DesiredStateConfiguration.Internal.DscClassCache]::Im
            portCimKeywordsFromModule($modInfo, $resource, [ref]
            $SchemaFilePath, $functionsToDefine, $keywordErrors)
```

```
            $foundScriptSchema = [Microsoft.PowerShell.
            DesiredStateConfiguration.Internal.DscClassCache]::Imp
            ortScriptKeywordsFromModule($modInfo, $resource, [ref]
            $SchemaFilePath, $functionsToDefine )
        }
    }

    $keywords = [System.Management.Automation.Language.
    DynamicKeyword]::GetKeyword()
    $keywords.Where({$_.ImplementingModule -eq $ImplementingModule}) |
    Select-Object Keyword, ResourceName
    }
}
```

The Get-CimKeyword function, in the above example, loads all the default CIM keywords from the DscClassCache. The GetKeyword() method of the DynamicKeyword class is then used to get a list of all keywords that are loaded into the DscClassCache. Finally, for the list of keywords, you filter only the keywords that are implemented in the PSDesiredStateConfiguration module.

The output in Figure 2-5 shows all the keywords exported by the PSDesiredStateConfiguration module. In the bottom-most rows, you can see Node and Import-DscResource. Don't worry about other keywords and the associated resource name values in that list; you will explore the rest of the keywords in the coming sections of this chapter or other chapters of this book.

```
PS C:\> Get-CimKeyword -ImplementingModule PSDesiredStateConfiguration

Keyword                                    ResourceName
-------                                    ------------
MSFT_Credential                            MSFT_Credential
MSFT_KeyValuePair                          MSFT_KeyValuePair
OMI_ConfigurationDocument                  OMI_ConfigurationDocument
OMI_MetaConfigurationResource              OMI_MetaConfigurationResource
OMI_ResourceModuleManager                  OMI_ResourceModuleManager
OMI_ConfigurationDownloadManager OMI_ConfigurationDownloadManager
OMI_ReportManager                          OMI_ReportManager
LocalConfigurationManager                  MSFT_DSCMetaConfiguration
File                                       MSFT_FileDirectoryConfiguration
Archive                                    MSFT_ArchiveResource
Environment                                MSFT_EnvironmentResource
Group                                      MSFT_GroupResource
Log                                        MSFT_LogResource
Package                                    MSFT_PackageResource
WindowsProcess                             MSFT_ProcessResource
Registry                                   MSFT_RegistryResource
WindowsFeature                             MSFT_RoleResource
Script                                     MSFT_ScriptResource
Service                                    MSFT_ServiceResource
User                                       MSFT_UserResource
WaitForAll                                 MSFT_WaitForAll
WaitForAny                                 MSFT_WaitForAny
WaitForSome                                MSFT_WaitForSome
WindowsOptionalFeature                     MSFT_WindowsOptionalFeature
Node
Import-DscResource
```

Figure 2-5. *CIM keywords exported by the PSDesiredStateConfiguration module*

Tip   Reading and understanding the contents of
PSDesiredStateConfiguration.psm1 is a great deal of learning.

The Import-DscResouce keyword is used to import the DSC resource modules
that are needed to enact the configuration of the resources in the DSC configuration
document. This dynamic keyword can only be used inside the Configuration script
block. At the time of configuration authoring, including this keyword in the configuration

document helps editors such as PowerShell ISE, and Visual Studio code enables IntelliSense and tab completion for resource names and resource properties.

The Node keyword identifies of the node(s) where the configuration needs to be enacted. As you see in the above sample configuration, you can either put a single node name or a list of comma-separate node names. Following the node name(s) is a script block that contains the resource configuration definitions. As you will see in Chapter 4, adding the Node keyword in a configuration document is not mandatory.

What goes inside the Node script block or the configuration script block directly (in the absence of the Node keyword) is a set of resource instance definitions. In the example above, you are using the File resource which comes in-box with PowerShell DSC. While the DSC configuration documents offer a declarative method to define the resource configurations, the resource modules are the imperative scripts that work behind the scenes to enact the resource instance configuration or make it so. Without the imperative resource scripts, the DSC configuration documentations are just non-functional PowerShell scripts.

PowerShell DSC Resource Modules

PowerShell DSC, by default, comes with a set of in-box resources. Figure 2-6 shows the list of in-box DSC resources on a system with WMF 5.1.

```
PS C:\> Get-DscResource

ImplementedAs    Name                        ModuleName                       Version    Properties
-------------    ----                        ----------                       -------    ----------
Binary           File                                                                    {DestinationPath, Attributes, Checksum, Content...
Binary           SignatureValidation                                                     {SignedItemType, TrustedStorePath}
PowerShell       Archive                     PSDesiredStateConfiguration      1.1        {Destination, Path, Checksum, Credential...}
PowerShell       Environment                 PSDesiredStateConfiguration      1.1        {Name, DependsOn, Ensure, Path...}
PowerShell       Group                       PSDesiredStateConfiguration      1.1        {GroupName, Credential, DependsOn, Description...}
Composite        GroupSet                    PSDesiredStateConfiguration      1.1        {DependsOn, PsDscRunAsCredential, GroupName, En...
Binary           Log                         PSDesiredStateConfiguration      1.1        {Message, DependsOn, PsDscRunAsCredential}
PowerShell       Package                     PSDesiredStateConfiguration      1.1        {Name, Path, ProductId, Arguments...}
Composite        ProcessSet                  PSDesiredStateConfiguration      1.1        {DependsOn, PsDscRunAsCredential, Path, Credent...
PowerShell       Registry                    PSDesiredStateConfiguration      1.1        {Key, ValueName, DependsOn, Ensure...}
PowerShell       Script                      PSDesiredStateConfiguration      1.1        {GetScript, SetScript, TestScript, Credential...}
PowerShell       Service                     PSDesiredStateConfiguration      1.1        {Name, BuiltInAccount, Credential, Dependencies...
Composite        ServiceSet                  PSDesiredStateConfiguration      1.1        {DependsOn, PsDscRunAsCredential, Name, Startup...
PowerShell       User                        PSDesiredStateConfiguration      1.1        {UserName, DependsOn, Description, Disabled...}
PowerShell       WaitForAll                  PSDesiredStateConfiguration      1.1        {NodeName, ResourceName, DependsOn, PsDscRunAsC...
PowerShell       WaitForAny                  PSDesiredStateConfiguration      1.1        {NodeName, ResourceName, DependsOn, PsDscRunAsC...
PowerShell       WaitForSome                 PSDesiredStateConfiguration      1.1        {NodeCount, NodeName, ResourceName, DependsOn...}
PowerShell       WindowsFeature              PSDesiredStateConfiguration      1.1        {Name, Credential, DependsOn, Ensure...}
Composite        WindowsFeatureSet           PSDesiredStateConfiguration      1.1        {DependsOn, PsDscRunAsCredential, Name, Ensure...}
PowerShell       WindowsOptionalFeature      PSDesiredStateConfiguration      1.1        {Name, DependsOn, Ensure, LogLevel...}
Composite        WindowsOptionalFeatureSet   PSDesiredStateConfiguration      1.1        {DependsOn, PsDscRunAsCredential, Name, Ensure...}
PowerShell       WindowsPackageCab           PSDesiredStateConfiguration      1.1        {Ensure, Name, SourcePath, DependsOn...}
PowerShell       WindowsProcess              PSDesiredStateConfiguration      1.1        {Arguments, Path, Credential, DependsOn...}
```

Figure 2-6. *In-box DSC resources in WMF 5.1*

> **Note**   A system with only WMF 4.0 will only have a subset of the in-box resource modules listed here.

Do you find anything common between output in Figure 2-6 and Figure 2-5? Do you see some keywords from the PSDesiredStateConfiguration module appearing in Figure 2-6 as well? Yes, that is because a DSC resource in a resource module is exported as CIM keyword as well. The PSDesiredStateConfiguration module is what houses all in-box DSC resources and therefore you see those resource names appearing as CIM keywords as well in the context of PSDesiredStateConfiguration module.

As you can see in Figure 2-6, the first column in the output shows the type of DSC resources. Table 2-1 provides a brief overview of these different types.

Table 2-1. *Resource Types in DSC*

DSC Resource Type	Description
PowerShell	Resources written as PowerShell script modules using MOF-based schema or written as class modules
Binary	Resources written in C# or written as Management Infrastructure (MI) modules
Composite	Resources that combine predefined DSC configurations into a new DSC resource

And, of course, as you have guessed, the in-box DSC resources are no way sufficient for all the configuration needs in a data center. This is where you can either look for custom DSC resource modules that are community developed or develop your own custom DSC resource modules implemented as one of the above modules types listed in Table 2-1.

The PowerShell product team at Microsoft has a GitHub repository (https://github.com/powershell/dscresources) that has the official DSC resource kit modules. You can download these official resource kit modules and other community-submitted DSC resource modules from the official PowerShell Gallery (www.powershellgallery.com).

Note   You can use the cmdlets from the `PowerShellGet` module to find and install DSC resource modules from the gallery. You will learn about using `PowerShellGet` cmdlets in Chapter 4.

You will learn about the composite resource modules and custom DSC resource module implementations and how to author your own custom DSC resource modules and publish them to the PowerShell gallery in Chapter 6.

So far you have seen how the `PSDesiredStateConfiguration` module helps in DSC configuration document authoring and the need for resource modules. In PowerShell DSC, the configuration document is just a way to author resource configuration definitions in a declarative manner. These configuration documents have to be compiled into an intermediate format (Managed Object Format, MOF) to be able to enact them on the target system. This is necessary because the current implementation of DSC heavily relies on the Common Information Model (CIM) for defining resource configurations in a platform-independent manner.

So, how do you compile a configuration document to a MOF file? Simple; you execute the configuration function in memory. Let's see a quick example:

```
FileCopyConfiguration -OutputPath C:\configurations\ -Verbose
```

This is it, really! If you take a look at Figure 2-3, the `FileCopyConfiguration` function was loaded into memory. You can also see that there are several parameters added to that configuration. You are using only the `-OutputPath` in the above example to ensure that the generated MOF file gets stored at the path specified. This is shown in Figure 2-7.

```
PS C:\> FileCopyConfiguration -OutputPath C:\configurations\ -Verbose


    Directory: C:\configurations


Mode                LastWriteTime         Length Name
----                -------------         ------ ----
-a----        7/4/2017   9:42 AM           2094 S16-01.mof
```

Figure 2-7. *Compiling DSC configuration to MOF*

The MOF format is a standard representation. Here is the MOF file for your configuration:

```
/*
@TargetNode='S16-01'
@GeneratedBy=Administrator
@GenerationDate=07/04/2017 09:42:23
@GenerationHost=S16-JB-01
*/

instance of MSFT_FileDirectoryConfiguration as
$MSFT_FileDirectoryConfiguration1ref
{
    ResourceID = "[File]FileCopyInstance1";
    Type = "File";
    Ensure = "Present";
    Contents = "Version:1.0.0.0";
    DestinationPath = "C:\\Scripts\\build.tag";
    ModuleName = "PSDesiredStateConfiguration";
    SourceInfo = "::7::9::File";
    ModuleVersion = "1.0";
    ConfigurationName = "FileCopyConfiguration";
};

instance of OMI_ConfigurationDocument
{
    Version="2.0.0";
    MinimumCompatibleVersion = "1.0.0";
    CompatibleVersionAdditionalProperties= {"Omi_BaseResource:Configuration
    Name"};
    Author="Administrator";
    GenerationDate="07/04/2017 09:42:23";
    GenerationHost="S16-JB-01";
    Name="FileCopyConfiguration";
};
```

In this MOF that you just compiled, you can see the resource configuration parameters you put in the configuration document along with a lot of other metadata. Generating a MOF from the configuration document completes the **authoring process** of the DSC configuration.

Before you enact a configuration, the associated MOF can be stored either locally or on a pull server, either an SMB share or DSC pull service configuration repository. This is called **configuration staging**. When you stage the compiled configuration locally, you **push** the configuration to a target node. And, when the configuration is staged on a DSC pull server, the target node **pulls** the configuration and enacts it. Therefore, a DSC configuration can be staged either for a push or a pull configuration delivery method. I discuss these methods in-depth in Chapter 8.

Configuration Enacting and Reporting

Once the configuration is staged, the enact phase is when the target node gets into a desired state declared in the configuration document. PowerShell DSC, to be specific the `PSDesiredStateConfiguration` module, provides several cmdlets that are helpful in the configuration staging, enacting, and reporting phases. You saw this list in Figure 2-2 and but Figure 2-8 shows a more refined list.

```
PS C:\> Get-Command -Module PSDesiredStateConfiguration -Noun *DscConfiguration*

CommandType     Name                                Version    Source
-----------     ----                                -------    ------
Function        Get-DscConfiguration                1.1        PSDesiredStateConfiguration
Function        Get-DscConfigurationStatus          1.1        PSDesiredStateConfiguration
Function        Remove-DscConfigurationDocument     1.1        PSDesiredStateConfiguration
Function        Restore-DscConfiguration            1.1        PSDesiredStateConfiguration
Function        Stop-DscConfiguration               1.1        PSDesiredStateConfiguration
Cmdlet          Publish-DscConfiguration            1.1        PSDesiredStateConfiguration
Cmdlet          Start-DscConfiguration              1.1        PSDesiredStateConfiguration
Cmdlet          Test-DscConfiguration               1.1        PSDesiredStateConfiguration
Cmdlet          Update-DscConfiguration             1.1        PSDesiredStateConfiguration
```

Figure 2-8. *Commands that help in configuration staging, enacting, and reporting*

Figure 2-8 provides a subset of cmdlets or functions exported by the `PSDesiredStateConfiguration` module. Table 2-2 provides a brief overview of these cmdlets.

Table 2-2. *An Overview of Cmdlets Used in Staging, Enacting, and Reporting*

Cmdlet or Function Name	Description	Phase of Configuration Management
Get-DscConfiguration	Retrieves the current state of the resource configuration	Configuration Reporting
Get- DscConfigurationStatus	Retrieves the status of completed configuration runs	Configuration Reporting
Test-DscConfiguration	Tests if a target node's configuration is in the desired state or not	Configuration Reporting
Publish-DscConfiguration	Publishes a MOF file to a target node as pending configuration	Configuration Staging
Start-DscConfiguration	Publishes a MOF file to a target node as pending configuration and also enacts it	Configuration Staging and Enacting
Update-DscConfiguration	Publish and enact configuration in one go or enact a staged configuration by using -UseExisting	Configuration Staging and Enacting
Stop-DscConfiguration	Stops a running configuration	Configuration Enacting
Restore-DscConfiguration	Restores target node to a previous configuration	Configuration Enacting
Remove-DscConfigurationDocument	Removes a specified configuration from the target node's configuration store	Configuration Staging and Enacting

You will take a look at each of these commands in-depth in later chapters but for now, take a look at the Start-DscConfiguration command to enact the configuration you generated in an earlier example:

```
Start-DscConfiguration -Path C:\configurations -Wait -Verbose
```

In an earlier example, when you compiled the configuration, you provided
C:\Configurations as the argument to -OutputPath, which copied the generated MOF
to that folder. In this example of a configuration enact, you are using the same path as
an argument to -Path parameter of the Start-DscConfiguration cmdlet. I will go into
the details of what exactly the Start-DscConfiguration cmdlet does later, but for now
just understand that it takes the configuration MOF from the local system and pushes it
to the target node as pending configuration and immediately enacts that configuration.
This is shown in Figure 2-9.

```
PS C:\> Start-DscConfiguration -Path C:\configurations -Wait -Verbose
VERBOSE: Perform operation 'Invoke CimMethod' with following parameters, ''methodName' = SendConfigurationApply,'className' = MSFT_DSCLocalConfigurationManager,'namespaceNam
e' = root/Microsoft/Windows/DesiredStateConfiguration'.
VERBOSE: An LCM method call arrived from computer S16-J8-01 with user sid S-1-5-21-3941074720-3606139424-1940643221-500.
VERBOSE: [S16-01]: LCM:  [ Start  Set      ]
VERBOSE: [S16-01]: LCM:  [ Start  Resource ] [[File]FileCopyInstance1]
VERBOSE: [S16-01]: LCM:  [ Start  Test     ] [[File]FileCopyInstance1]
VERBOSE: [S16-01]:                            [[File]FileCopyInstance1] The system cannot find the file specified.
VERBOSE: [S16-01]:                            [[File]FileCopyInstance1] The related file/directory is: C:\Scripts\build.tag.
VERBOSE: [S16-01]: LCM:  [ End    Test     ] [[File]FileCopyInstance1]  in 0.0940 seconds.
VERBOSE: [S16-01]: LCM:  [ Start  Set      ] [[File]FileCopyInstance1]
VERBOSE: [S16-01]:                            [[File]FileCopyInstance1] The system cannot find the file specified.
VERBOSE: [S16-01]:                            [[File]FileCopyInstance1] The related file/directory is: C:\Scripts\build.tag.
VERBOSE: [S16-01]: LCM:  [ End    Set      ] [[File]FileCopyInstance1]  in 0.0310 seconds.
VERBOSE: [S16-01]: LCM:  [ End    Resource ] [[File]FileCopyInstance1]
VERBOSE: [S16-01]: LCM:  [ End    Set      ]
VERBOSE: [S16-01]: LCM:  [ End    Set      ]  in  0.6720 seconds.
VERBOSE: Operation 'Invoke CimMethod' complete.
VERBOSE: Time taken for configuration job to complete is 2.07 seconds
```

Figure 2-9. *The configuration enacting process using the Start-DscConfiguration cmdlet*

So, how does this cmdlet know which is the target node?

Go back and take a look at the MOF that was generated in an earlier example. It does
not contain the target node name.

For identifying the target node name, the Start-DscConfiguration cmdlet looks
at the name of the MOF file and then derives the target node name. For example, when
you compiled your configuration earlier, the name of the MOF was S16-01.mof with
S16-01 being the name of the node. So, when you enacted this configuration, the Start-
DscConfiguration cmdlet looked at the filename and identified S16-01 as the target
node. If the target folder specified as an argument to -Path contains more than one MOF
file, this cmdlet looks at each file and tries to enact configuration on each target node
that is identified from the filenames. You will take a look at the overall enact process in
Chapter 4 when I discuss writing configurations in-depth.

Once the enacting is complete, you can verify the current state of the configuration
using the Get-DscConfiguration cmdlet. For your node configuration, the current state
of the File resource is shown in Figure 2-10.

```
PS C:\> Get-DscConfiguration -CimSession S16-01 -Verbose
VERBOSE: S16-01: An LCM method call arrived from computer S16-01 with user sid S-1-5-21-3941074720-3606139424-1940643221-500.
VERBOSE: S16-01: [S16-01]: LCM:  [ Start  Get ]
VERBOSE: S16-01: [S16-01]: LCM:  [ Start  Get ]        [[File]FileCopyInstance1]
VERBOSE: S16-01: [S16-01]: LCM:  [ End    Get ]        [[File]FileCopyInstance1]  in 0.0470 seconds.


ConfigurationName    : FileCopyConfiguration
DependsOn            :
ModuleName           : PSDesiredStateConfiguration
ModuleVersion        :
PsDscRunAsCredential :
ResourceId           : [File]FileCopyInstance1
SourceInfo           :
Attributes           : {archive}
Checksum             :
Contents             :
CreatedDate          : 7/4/2017 1:04:19 PM
Credential           :
DestinationPath      : C:\Scripts\build.tag
Ensure               : present
Force                :
MatchSource          :
ModifiedDate         : 7/4/2017 1:04:19 PM
Recurse              :
Size                 : 18
SourcePath           :
SubItems             :
Type                 : file
PSComputerName       : S16-01
```

Figure 2-10. *Current state of the file resource*

Tip   Make it a habit, at least initially, to use the -Verbose switch parameter with all of these DSC-related commands. The verbose output helps a great deal in understanding what is happening behind the scenes.

The Get-DscConfiguration command provides one way of reporting a DSC configuration. However, remember that this is only the current state of the resource, which may not be the desired state. To verify if a resource is in the desired state or not, use the Test-DscConfiguration cmdlet. The output from this is shown in Figure 2-11.

```
PS C:\> Test-DscConfiguration -ComputerName S16-01 -Verbose
VERBOSE: Perform operation 'Invoke CimMethod' with following parameters, ''methodName' = TestConfiguration,'className' = MSFT_DSCLocalConfigurationManager,'namespaceName' =
root/Microsoft/Windows/DesiredStateConfiguration'.
VERBOSE: An LCM method call arrived from computer S16-JB-01 with user sid S-1-5-21-3941074720-3606139424-1940643221-500.
VERBOSE: [S16-01]: LCM:  [ Start  Test    ]
VERBOSE: [S16-01]: LCM:  [ Start  Resource ]  [[File]FileCopyInstance1]
VERBOSE: [S16-01]: LCM:  [ Start  Test    ]  [[File]FileCopyInstance1]
VERBOSE: [S16-01]:                           [[File]FileCopyInstance1] The destination object was found and no action is required.
VERBOSE: [S16-01]: LCM:  [ End    Test    ]  [[File]FileCopyInstance1] True in 0.0310 seconds.
VERBOSE: [S16-01]: LCM:  [ End    Resource ]  [[File]FileCopyInstance1]
VERBOSE: [S16-01]: LCM:  [ End    Test    ]    Completed processing test operation. The operation returned True.
VERBOSE: [S16-01]: LCM:  [ End    Test    ]   in  0.1400 seconds.
VERBOSE: Operation 'Invoke CimMethod' complete.
True
VERBOSE: Time taken for configuration job to complete is 0.642 seconds
```

Figure 2-11. *Output from the Test-DscConfiguration cmdlet*

Within the reporting phase of the DSC-based configuration management, you can use the Get-DscConfiguration, Get-DscConfigurationStatus, and Test-DscConfiguration cmdlets. There are other centralized reporting methods provided through the DSC pull service endpoints. You will learn more about DSC configuration reporting in Chapter 9.

So, are the Start-DscConfiguration and other reporting cmdlets just discussed responsible for configuration enacting and reporting? The answer is yes and no. Yes, because these cmdlets are what you are using to enact and report configuration, like the front end of the web application. Without the application logic and the back-end databases, the beautiful UX that the front end provides is just like a wire-frame with no real use.

Similar to this web application analogy, the real meat of configuration enacting and reporting is not in these cmdlets but rather provided by the DSC Local Configuration Manager (LCM).

Local Configuration Manager

The LCM is at the heart of PowerShell DSC architecture. It is responsible for enacting a pending configuration, and monitoring and managing any drift that happens over a period of time. In summary, the LCM is what takes care of configuration life cycle on a target node. This is implemented as a CIM class named MSFT_DSCLocalConfigurationManager in the root/Microsoft/Windows/DesiredStateConfiguration. This class implements the methods that are necessary for configuration life cycle management.

```
Get-CimClass -Namespace root/Microsoft/Windows/DesiredStateConfiguration
-ClassName MSFT_DSCLocalConfigurationManager | Select -ExpandProperty
CimClassMethods
```

If you run the above command, you will see a list of all methods implemented by the MSFT_DSCLocalConfigurationManager CIM class. This is shown in Figure 2-12.

```
PS C:\> Get-CimClass -Namespace root/Microsoft/Windows/DesiredStateConfiguration -ClassName MSFT_DSCLocalConfigurationManager | Select -ExpandProperty CimClassMethods

Name                                ReturnType Parameters                                                                          Qualifiers
----                                ---------- ----------                                                                          ----------
SendConfiguration                   UInt32 {ConfigurationData, force}                                                             {implemented, static}
SendConfigurationApply              UInt32 {ConfigurationData, force}                                                             {implemented, static}
GetConfiguration                    UInt32 {configurationData, configurations}                                                    {implemented, static}
TestConfiguration                   UInt32 {configurationData, InDesiredState, ResourcesInDesiredState, ResourcesNotInDesiredState} {implemented, static}
ApplyConfiguration                  UInt32 {force}                                                                                {implemented, static}
SendMetaConfigurationApply          UInt32 {ConfigurationData, force}                                                             {implemented, static}
GetMetaConfiguration                UInt32 {MetaConfiguration}                                                                    {implemented, static}
RollBack                            UInt32 {configurationNumber}                                                                  {implemented, static}
PerformRequiredConfigurationChecks  UInt32 {Flags}                                                                                {implemented, static}
StopConfiguration                   UInt32 {force}                                                                                {implemented, static}
GetConfigurationStatus              UInt32 {All, configurationStatus}                                                             {implemented, static}
SendConfigurationApplyAsync         UInt32 {ConfigurationData, force, jobId}                                                       {implemented, static}
GetConfigurationResultOutput        UInt32 {jobId, resumeOutputBookmark, output}                                                   {implemented, static}
RemoveConfiguration                 UInt32 {Force, Stage}                                                                          {implemented, static}
ResourceGet                         UInt32 {ModuleName, resourceProperty, ResourceType, configurations}                           {implemented, static}
ResourceSet                         UInt32 {ModuleName, resourceProperty, ResourceType, RebootRequired}                            {implemented, static}
ResourceTest                        UInt32 {ModuleName, resourceProperty, ResourceType, InDesiredState}                           {implemented, static}
EnableDebugConfiguration            UInt32 {BreakAll}                                                                             {implemented, static}
DisableDebugConfiguration           UInt32 {}                                                                                     {implemented, static}
```

Figure 2-12. *CIM methods in the MSFT_DscLocalConfigurationManager class*

So, how is this all related to what you have learned so far? Go back and take a look at the enact process output in Figure 2-9 and read the first line in the output.

The verbose output clearly tells you that the SendConfigurationApply CIM method from the MSFT_DSCLocalConfigurationManager class is being invoked.

What this implies is that the Start-DscConfiguration cmdlet is just an easy-to-use wrapper around the SendConfigurationApply CIM method. So, for every cmdlet or function shown in Table 2-2, there is method in the CIM class that implements LCM.

Note   You will see a mapping of methods in the MSFT_ DscLocalConfigurationManager CIM class to commands in the PSDesiredStateConfiguration module in Chapter 3.

The LCM itself is a configurable resource in the context of DSC and it can be configured using the declarative syntax that DSC provides.

The PSDesiredStateConfiguration module provides cmdlets that are used to get and set DSC location configuration manager settings.

```
Get-Command -Module PSDesiredStateConfiguration -Noun
*DscLocalConfiguration*
```

```
PS C:\> Get-Command -Module PSDesiredStateConfiguration -Noun *DscLocalConfiguration*

CommandType     Name                                                Version    Source
-----------     ----                                                -------    ------
Function        Get-DscLocalConfigurationManager                    1.1        PSDesiredStateConfiguration
Cmdlet          Set-DscLocalConfigurationManager                    1.1        PSDesiredStateConfiguration
```

Figure 2-13. *Commands that help in LCM configuration*

Figure 2-13 shows the commands exported by the PSDesiredStateConfiguration module to manage the LCM configuration. There are several configurable settings in LCM. The Get-DscLocalConfigurationManager provides the current state of these settings.

```
PS C:\> Get-DscLocalConfigurationManager -CimSession S16-01


ActionAfterReboot                    : ContinueConfiguration
AgentId                              : 74C5780D-2980-11E7-9300-00155D16061F
AllowModuleOverwrite                 : False
CertificateID                        :
ConfigurationDownloadManagers        : {}
ConfigurationID                      :
ConfigurationMode                    : ApplyAndMonitor
ConfigurationModeFrequencyMins       : 15
Credential                           :
DebugMode                            : {NONE}
DownloadManagerCustomData            :
DownloadManagerName                  :
LCMCompatibleVersions                : {1.0, 2.0}
LCMState                             : Idle
LCMStateDetail                       :
LCMVersion                           : 2.0
StatusRetentionTimeInDays            : 10
SignatureValidationPolicy            : NONE
SignatureValidations                 : {}
MaximumDownloadSizeMB                : 500
PartialConfigurations                :
RebootNodeIfNeeded                   : False
RefreshFrequencyMins                 : 30
RefreshMode                          : PUSH
ReportManagers                       : {}
ResourceModuleManagers               : {}
PSComputerName                       : S16-01
```

Figure 2-14. *DSC LCM configuration settings*

Figure 2-14 lists all the settings in their default state. Now these settings can be modified by generating what is called a meta configuration document or a meta MOF once it is compiled. The following code snippet provides a simple example of a LCM configuration:

```
[DscLocalConfigurationManager()]
Configuration metaConfiguration
{
    Node S16-01
    {
        Settings
        {
            ConfigurationModeFrequencyMins = 30
            ConfigurationMode = 'ApplyAndAutoCorrect'

        }
    }
}
```

What is defined in the above example is a meta configuration. This is similar to the FileCopyConfiguration you saw early in this chapter except for the fact that this example configures the LCM itself. There are similarities in the declarative syntax as well. There are minor differences too. Don't worry about that for now. You will take an in-depth look at all this in Chapter 3.

Note   The [DscLocalConfigurationManager()] attribute is available only in WMF 5.0 and above. Chapter 3 discusses the differences in meta configurations between WMF 4.0 and WMF 5.0 and above.

For the sake of clarity, I will refer to configurations such as *FileCopyConfiguration* as node configurations and configurations that change the LCM settings as meta configurations.

```
PS C:\> Get-Command -Name metaConfiguration

CommandType     Name                                    Version  Source
-----------     ----                                    -------  ------
Configuration   metaConfiguration


PS C:\> Get-Help -Name metaConfiguration

NAME
    metaConfiguration

SYNTAX
    metaConfiguration [[-InstanceName] <string>] [[-DependsOn] <string[]>] [[-PsDscRunAsCredential] <pscredential>] [[-OutputPath] <string>] [[-ConfigurationData]
    <hashtable>] [<CommonParameters>]
```

Figure 2-15. *The metaConfiguration command*

In Figure 2-15, you can see that metaConfiguration is also a command of type Configuration and it has similar properties as a node configuration. So, you compile it the same way:

```
metaConfiguration -OutputPath C:\configurations -Verbose
```

```
    PS C:\> metaConfiguration -OutputPath C:\configurations -Verbose


        Directory: C:\configurations


    Mode                LastWriteTime         Length Name
    ----                -------------         ------ ----
    -a----        7/4/2017    2:06 PM           1238 S16-01.meta.mof
```

Figure 2-16. *Compiling a meta configuration to meta MOF*

Do you see anything different from what was generated when we compiled the node configuration (shown in Figure 2-7) and what is generated now with metaConfiguration in Figure 2-16?

There is a difference in the filename. The MOF generated from metaConfiguration has the word *meta* as a part of its filename. This tells you that the contents of this MOF represent LCM meta configuration. So, can you use Start-DscConfiguration to enact this meta configuration?

No! You need to use the Set-DscLocalConfigurationManager cmdlet.

```
Set-DscLocalConfigurationManager -Path C:\configurations -Verbose
```

The syntax used to enact a meta configuration is similar to that of a node configuration. In this example, you point the Set-DscLocalConfigurationManager cmdlet to the same folder as the node configurations. This cmdlet identifies the target node and the configuration to apply by looking at all file names in that folder.

This is shown in Figure 2-17. To show that the Set-DscLocalConfigurationManager picks only the meta MOF, I have listed the contents of the folder as well.

Figure 2-17. *Enacting LCM configuration*

You can see in Figure 2-17 that the Set-DscLocalConfigurationManager cmdlet internally invokes a CIM method called SendMetaConfigurationApply. Now, execute the Get-DscLocalConfigurationManager cmdlet again and see if the settings are applied.

```
PS C:\> Get-DscLocalConfigurationManager -CimSession S16-01


ActionAfterReboot                   : ContinueConfiguration
AgentId                             : 74C5780D-2980-11E7-9300-00155D16061F
AllowModuleOverwrite                : False
CertificateID                       :
ConfigurationDownloadManagers       : {}
ConfigurationID                     :
ConfigurationMode                   : ApplyAndAutoCorrect
ConfigurationModeFrequencyMins      : 30
Credential                          :
DebugMode                           : {NONE}
DownloadManagerCustomData           :
DownloadManagerName                 :
LCMCompatibleVersions               : {1.0, 2.0}
LCMState                            : Idle
LCMStateDetail                      :
LCMVersion                          : 2.0
StatusRetentionTimeInDays           : 10
SignatureValidationPolicy           : NONE
SignatureValidations                : {}
MaximumDownloadSizeMB               : 500
PartialConfigurations               :
RebootNodeIfNeeded                  : False
RefreshFrequencyMins                : 30
RefreshMode                         : PUSH
ReportManagers                      : {}
ResourceModuleManagers              : {}
PSComputerName                      : S16-01
```

Figure 2-18. *Updated LCM configuration*

Compare the output shown in Figure 2-18 to Figure 2-14. You can see that the ConfigurationMode and ConfigurationModeFrequencyMins have been updated.

I will discuss other LCM settings and what they really mean in Chapter 3. But, looking at the available LCM settings leads us into a discussion on PowerShell DSC features.

PowerShell DSC Features

What you have seen so far is about the configuration management phases. You looked at how to author configuration documents and compile them for staging. You also looked at enacting (push delivery) and reporting of DSC configuration on target nodes. LCM plays the central role in most of this except the authoring phase.

The LCM settings offer a peek into other features that PowerShell DSC implements. In this section, let's take a brief look at these features.

DSC Pull Server

I discussed earlier in this chapter that target nodes using DSC can pull configurations and DSC resource modules from a central DSC pull server. The pull mode of configuration delivery resolves the scalability issues and limitations of the push mode while providing a central store for both configurations and DSC resource modules. To implement this, pull mode can be built using a file server (Server Message Block [SMB]) share or an OData web service. A target system can be configured to use the pull mode of configuration delivery, which means the system will periodically poll a central repository or service to get the configuration changes and DSC resource modules required for the change.

In this section, I will show the two pull mode configurations available and explain the pros and cons of these methods. For pull mode, whether over an SMB or OData endpoint, you need this special configuration on the target systems. These settings are defined as the meta-configuration of the LCM.

Pull Mode Over SMB

The pull mode over SMB is the simplest method to implement. All you need to do is create an SMB file share and copy all configurations you generate and the resources required for the configurations. The advantage of this method, of course, is the simplicity in setting it up. The only configuration you need is to assign proper permissions to the SMB file share. You will see this in detail when I discuss configuration delivery methods in Chapter 8.

Pull Mode Over OData or HTTP

This method requires special configuration of an OData endpoint. On Windows Server 2008 R2, 2012 systems with WMF 4.0 or later, or on systems with Windows Server 2012 R2, this OData endpoint can be configured by installing the Windows PowerShell

Desired State Configuration Service (DSC-Service) feature. The target systems can then be configured to pull the configuration and the DSC resource modules from this OData endpoint.

When using the pull mode, either over SMB or REST, you must create a checksum for the configuration MOF files being pulled to the target systems for configuration change. Once again, the PSDesiredStateConfiguration PowerShell module provides the necessary functionality for this. The configuration checksum can be created using the New-DscChecksum function. This function is used only in staging the configuration for delivery in pull mode. It is possible to create a file checksum without using the New-DscChecksum function. This function uses the SHA-256 hashing algorithm and the New-FileHash cmdlet to generate the checksum for each configuration MOF.

You will take a look at configuring DSC LCM as a pull client in Chapter 8 but to give you an overview of what is involved, the following section describes the LCM settings that are used in a pull client configuration.

The ConfigurationDownloadManagers in LCM settings can be used to configure the LCM to download configurations from a central pull server. If you plan on using the SMB share-based pull server for configurations, the ConfigurationRepositoryShare needs to be configured. The ConfigurationRepositoryWeb is what needs to be configured if you have a REST-based pull service to distribute configurations.

Similar to the ConfigurationRepositoryWeb and ConfigurationRepositoryShare, custom resource modules can also be retrieved from a central pull server by configuring the ResourceRepositoryWeb and ResourceRepositoryShare settings in LCM.

As Figure 2-1 depicts, "file download manager" and "web download manager" are used for both configuration and resource module downloads from a pull server implemented as SMB share and REST-based pull service respectively.

The recommended configuration for a pull server is the REST-based DSC pull service endpoint. When you implement the REST-based DSC pull service, the target nodes register with the central DSC pull service endpoint and the state of the configuration on target nodes can be retrieved by querying the report server endpoint.

The ReportManagers configuration (shown in Figure 2-14) in LCM settings is used to configure where the LCM sends configuration status reports to. The report manager endpoint deployed using DSC pull service is an oData endpoint. Querying this with the node details provides access to the configuration status on the target nodes. I will explain more about this topic in Chapter 9.

Partial Configurations

In a typical enterprise IT scenario, there is usually more than one IT administrator deploying and managing the same IT infrastructure. For example, in case of a server hosting Microsoft SQL Server databases, there will be an administrator for taking care of the OS deployment and configuration and there will be another one for managing the SQL database deployment on this server.

In such a scenario where multiple people are responsible for configuration of the infrastructure, it makes sense to have configuration documents authored by these individuals as separate fragments. This enables delegation of configuration management tasks. Each administrator responsible for his/her configuration can author and manage it independently of what the other administrator is authoring by eliminating any human errors involved in updating a single configuration document.

This is why the partial configurations feature was added in WMF 5.0. Figure 2-19 depicts an overview of this feature.

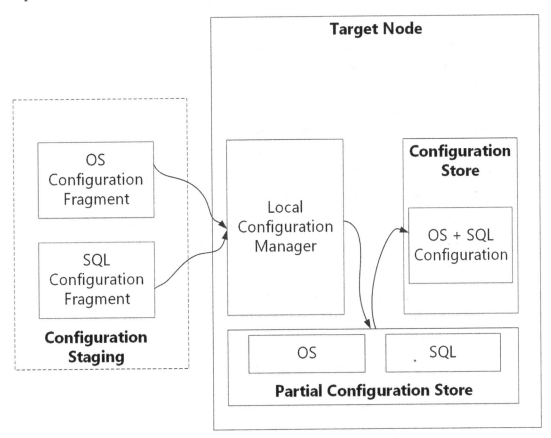

Figure 2-19. *Partial configurations overview*

As you can see in Figure 2-19, two different fragments of the DSC configuration get staged (local system or on a pull server). The LCM then copies these fragments into the partial configuration store and converges these fragments into a pending configuration for enact. The advantage with partial configurations is that these fragments can be updated independently as long as they do not have any conflicts in the resources each fragment is trying to configure.

You will learn more about partial configurations and examine the pros and cons of using partial configurations along with several examples in Chapter 10.

Cross-Machine Synchronization

When you build an application infrastructure, it is apparent that this infrastructure requires multiple instances of the services for high availability and load balancing. Also, the application server instances in the infrastructure will have dependencies on other elements in the infrastructure such as database servers and other application servers. When configuring such an infrastructure, you will need to ensure that these dependencies between instances in the same tier or across tiers are taken care of. In a scenario where an orchestrator is used for infrastructure deployment, the dependencies are handled by the orchestrator's task flow. However, when the application infrastructure is deployed using a configuration management tool, the capability to define inter-node or cross-machine dependencies for configuration is a must.

With PowerShell 5.0, Microsoft added the capability to define inter-node dependencies in the form of in-box DSC resources. These are referred to as the WaitForX resources in general and listed in Figure 2-6.

- **WaitForAll** is used when a node's configuration must wait for all other nodes' configurations of a specific resource or resources to complete.

- **WaitForAny** is used when a node's configuration can start if any one of the nodes completes a specific resource or resources configuration.

- **WaitForSome** is used when a node's configuration needs to wait for at least x number of nodes to complete their configuration of a specific resource.

This new feature can be effectively used to validate if a dependent configuration on remote system exists before configuring the local system for any resource. Chapter 11 provides an in-depth explanation of how these WaitForX resources work with an example of deploying a multi-tier and multi-machine application using PowerShell DSC.

Configuration Encryption at Rest

Figure 2-1 shows a configuration store that contains the current, pending, and previous MOF files. The current.mof is the current configuration on the system, previous.mof is the earlier configuration that can be rolled back to, and pending.mof is the pending configuration that needs to be enacted. I will discuss this in-depth in Chapter 13 but for now understand that these MOF used to be plain-text files in PowerShell 4.0 or the initial release of PowerShell DSC. The DSC configuration MOF files contain sensitive information such as passwords and access keys depending on what resource you are configuring. Passwords are encrypted using certificates. But, if an administrator forces plain-text credentials in a configuration document, these passwords will be seen in plain text even after the configuration enact is complete. And, in general, you can consider the entire MOF itself to be a document containing sensitive information, essentially a blueprint of your node configuration. Therefore, any user who has access to the C:\Windows\System32\Configuration folder can open the MOF files at rest and see the sensitive information in these MOF documents.

To address this, encryption of the configuration MOF files was added in PowerShell 5.0. Using this method, even when the administrator forces plain-text credentials in a configuration document, the configuration MOFs at rest (current, pending, and previous) are always encrypted. The DSC LCM uses Windows Data Protection API (DPAPI) to encrypt the MOFs files.

Since you have a system that you just pushed configuration to, try opening the Current.mof file stored in the C:\Windows\System32\Configuration folder. What do you see? Can you read and comprehend the contents of Current.mof?

Note   The meta configuration MOF is not encrypted at rest. This behavior may change in future.

Configuration and Module Signature Validation

In an earlier section of this chapter, I mentioned downloading and installing community-developed DSC resource modules. While no one wants to reinvent a wheel, downloading from the Internet and using the DSC resource modules in your data center has certain risks associated with it. An attacker with a malicious intent can embed code into the resource modules that can potentially damage your IT infrastructure and cause business loss. The same applies to the configurations that are staged as well. For example, if you have staged all configurations on a pull server and it becomes compromised, an attacker can modify the configuration MOF files with malicious code.

To address this potential security risk in DSC configuration management, Microsoft added a signature validation feature in the LCM for both configurations and modules. When configured, the LCM always looks for the digital signature from trusted authority in both the configuration MOF and resource modules that are used for enact process.

You will look at using signed configurations and modules in Chapter 13.

The PowerShell DSC Platform

So far in this book, I have referred to PowerShell DSC as a configuration management platform and not a tool or a complete solution. This means DSC provides an API that can be used in programming languages other than just PowerShell. Using this API, you can build similar language extensions that PowerShell provides today. This aspect is depicted in Figure 2-1 through the representation of third-party tools. Let's explore this further.

Think about the role of a declarative configuration script written in PowerShell after the MOF is compiled. Do you need it when there are no further changes needed to the configuration? The answer is no.

In the configuration authoring stage, if you have the capability to generate a MOF directly without using an intermediate declarative script, do you still need PowerShell? The answer is no again! Yes, generating a MOF is tricky and complex. You need to understand the resource schema and ensure that there are no errors in the configuration definition. This is where the language extensions helps. Any third party can create those language extensions and in any programming language.

For example, take a look at the Vamp project (`https://github.com/bundyfx/vamp`) by Flynn Bundy. Although this is a PowerShell module, the project aims to use Yet Another Markup Language (YAML) for the declarative definition of resource configurations instead of PowerShell scripts.

So, that clears the air about configuration authoring and generating a MOF. But, what about configuration enacting and reporting? Well, as I discussed in the "Local Configuration Manager" section of this chapter, most or all of the commands used in the enacting and reporting phase of DSC configuration management are just wrappers around the CIM methods implemented in the `root/Microsoft/Windows/DesiredStateConfiguration` WMI namespace. So, if the programming or scripting language that you plan to use has the ability to invoke CIM methods, you have an alternative to using PowerShell.

The DSC Pull Server has an open specification that can be used to develop your own pull service and probably with better features than what Microsoft ships with the Windows Server operating system. Even if you don't, Microsoft's implementation of Pull Server specification provides a report server endpoint that is oData-compliant. Accessing an oData endpoint is relatively straightforward; using most of the modern scripting and programming languages, you can create your own visual dashboards for reporting configuration status of your infrastructure.

In Chapter 16, you will look at the third-party integration opportunities and explore how the CIM methods provided by DSC configuration management platform can be accessed directly in PowerShell.

Summary

This chapter was a whirlwind tour of PowerShell DSC and its components. Understanding the architecture and components involved in making a technology work is the most important thing to master in any technology. This chapter provided an overview of different phases of PowerShell DSC-based configuration management. You looked at the components that are used across these different phases. You also learned about the features that DSC supports in WMF 5.0 and above. As mentioned, this chapter is just an overview of what is coming later in this book. You tackled most of the basics here and you will build on this foundation as you move forward. The next chapter discusses the DSC Local Configuration Manager. You will learn about LCM CIM interfaces, differences in LCM implementation in the first generation of DSC, how LCM is configured using the declarative syntax that DSC implements, and how LCM handles configuration life cycle.

CHAPTER 3

The Local Configuration Manager

The Local Configuration Manager (LCM) is the heart of configuration management in PowerShell DSC. The LCM is like an OS agent that receives the configuration document in the form of a MOF, enacts it, monitors that configuration for any drift, and finally, corrects the drift when configured to do so. As you go forward in this book, a good understanding of the LCM is a must to be able to troubleshoot issues that you may observe during a DSC enact or in overall configuration management. Being this important, the LCM certainly deserves a chapter of its own!

In this chapter, you will dive into LCM fundamentals, look at how the LCM is implemented, what the different LCM settings mean, how the LCM manages the configuration life cycle, and how the LCM does configuration drift monitoring and correction. Chapter 2 provided an overview using the DSC declarative syntax for meta configurations. Therefore, I will not focus on the "how" part of LCM configuration. This chapter will become a reference when you move towards advanced concepts on your journey towards mastering PowerShell DSC.

Lab Requirements

To try the examples and exercises in this chapter, you will need at minimum a Windows Server 2008 R2 or above system with WMF 5.1 installed. I recommend a system with Windows Server 2016.

© Ravikanth Chaganti 2018
R. Chaganti, *Pro PowerShell Desired State Configuration*, https://doi.org/10.1007/978-1-4842-3483-9_3

LCM CIM Classes

As discussed briefly in Chapter 2, the Local Configuration Manager is implemented as a set of CIM classes in the root/Microsoft/Windows/DesiredStateConfiguration namespace. Let's take a look at it again to understand it better:

```
Get-CimInstance -Namespace root/Microsoft/Windows -ClassName __NAMESPACE |
Format-Wide
```

This command will list all CIM providers under the root/Microsoft/Windows namespace. This is shown in Figure 3-1.

Note For the sake of simplicity and to reduce the number of words, I will use DSC CIM namespace wherever I have to refer to the complete path identified by root/Microsoft/Windows/DesiredStateConfiguration.

CIM cmdlets require administrative privileges. Ensure that you try out this and subsequent examples in an elevated session.

```
PS C:\> Get-CimInstance -Namespace root/Microsoft/Windows -ClassName __NAMESPACE | Format-Wide

RemoteAccess                                              Dns
Powershellv3                                              WindowsUpdate
DeviceGuard                                               TaskScheduler
DesiredStateConfigurationProxy                            ManagementTools
SmbWitness                                                Wdac
winrm                                                     ServerManager
AppBackgroundTask                                         SDNDiagnostics
PS_MMAgent                                                Storage
HardwareManagement                                        SMB
EventTracingManagement                                    DesiredStateConfiguration
CI                                                        Defender
```

Figure 3-1. *DSC namespaces in CIM*

As can be seen in Figure 3-1, there are two namespaces that are related to PowerShell DSC: DesiredStateConfigurationProxy and DesiredStateConfiguration. Let's first take a peek at the DSC CIM namespace.

Figure 3-2 shows a list of CIM classes in this namespace.

```
PS C:\> Get-CimClass -Namespace root/Microsoft/Windows/DesiredStateConfiguration -ClassName MSFT_* | Format-Wide


MSFT_WmiError                                    MSFT_ExtendedStatus
MSFT_SignatureValidation                         MSFT_FileResourceManager
MSFT_WebResourceManager                          MSFT_WebDownloadManager
MSFT_FileDownloadManager                         MSFT_PartialConfiguration
MSFT_WebReportManager                            MSFT_DSCConfigurationStatus
MSFT_Credential                                  MSFT_DSCResource
MSFT_ResourceInDesiredState                      MSFT_ResourceNotInDesiredState
MSFT_FileDirectoryConfiguration                  MSFT_ArchiveResource
MSFT_ScriptResource                              MSFT_DSCConfigurationOutput
MSFT_DSCConfigurationOutputResult                MSFT_DSCConfigurationOutputWriteObject
MSFT_DSCConfigurationOutputWriteError            MSFT_DSCConfigurationOutputWriteMessage
MSFT_DSCConfigurationOutputWriteArray            MSFT_DSCConfigurationOutputReboot
MSFT_DSCConfigurationOutputWriteProgress         MSFT_DSCConfigurationOutputWhatIf
MSFT_DSCMethodInvoked                            MSFT_DSCMetaConfiguration
MSFT_DSCLocalConfigurationManager                MSFT_KeyValuePair
MSFT_DscTimer
```

Figure 3-2. *CIM classes in DSC CIM namespace*

While there are many classes in the output shown in Figure 3-2, you are mostly interested, in the context of a basic LCM configuration, in the MSFT_ DSCLocalConfigurationManager and MSFT_DSCMetaConfiguration classes.

The MSFT_DSCMetaConfiguration class implements the LCM properties you saw in Chapter 2 while the MSFT_DSCLocalConfigurationManager CIM class implements methods that support managing node and meta configurations. This can be seen in Figure 3-3.

```
PS C:\> Get-CimClass -ClassName MSFT_DscMetaConfiguration -Namespace root/Microsoft/Windows/DesiredStateConfiguration


    NameSpace: ROOT/Microsoft/Windows/DesiredStateConfiguration

CimClassName                      CimClassMethods     CimClassProperties
------------                      ---------------     ------------------
MSFT_DSCMetaConfiguration         {}                  {ActionAfterReboot, AgentId, AllowModuleOverwrite, CertificateID...}


PS C:\> Get-CimClass -ClassName MSFT_DscLocalConfigurationManager -Namespace root/Microsoft/Windows/DesiredStateConfiguration


    NameSpace: ROOT/Microsoft/Windows/DesiredStateConfiguration

CimClassName                        CimClassMethods     CimClassProperties
------------                        ---------------     ------------------
MSFT_DSCLocalConfigurationManager   {SendConfiguratio... {}
```

Figure 3-3. *DSC meta and local configuration manager CIM class details*

As seen in Figure 3-3, the MSFT_DSCMetaConfiguration class implements the properties that can be used to configure LCM behavior and the MSFT_DSCLocalConfigurationManager class implements the methods that perform node and meta configuration management.

LCM Properties

Let's look at a summary of all LCM properties before I discuss the CIM methods to get and set the LCM configuration. As you learned in the above section, these properties are implemented as an MSFT_DSCMetaConfiguration CIM class. Each of the configurable properties has a certain CIM data type and possible values. The following script will help you investigate these properties in a better way than simply listing them out. It will also serve as a documented reference when you want to quickly check the possible values for a given CIM property in this class.

```
[CmdletBinding()]
param (
    [Parameter(Mandatory)]
    [String] $ClassName,

    [Parameter(Mandatory)]
    [String] $Namespace,

    [Parameter()]
    [String] $PropertyName
)

function extractProperty($cimProperty, $Namespace)
{
    $cimProperty | Select Name, CimType, `
    @{
        l='EmbeddedInstanceOf';e={
            if ($_.Qualifiers.Name -contains 'EmbeddedInstance')
            {
                $embeddedClassName = $_.Qualifiers.Where({$_.Name -eq
                'EmbeddedInstance'}).Value
```

```
            $embeddedClass = Get-CimClass -ClassName $embeddedClass
            Name -Namespace $Namespace
            if ($embeddedClass.CimClassQualifiers['Abstract'].Value)
            {
                $derivedClasses = (Get-CimClass -Namespace $Namespace).
                Where({ $_.CimSuperClassName -eq  $embeddedClassName}).
                CimClassName
                $derivedClasses
            }
            else
            {
                $embeddedClassName
            }
        }
    }
},
@{
    l='IsReadyOnly';e={
        $_.Qualifiers.Name -contains 'read'
    }
},
@{
    l='AllowedValues';e={
        if ($_.Qualifiers.Name -contains 'ValueMap') {
            $_.Qualifiers.Where({$_.Name -eq 'ValueMap'}).Value
        }
    }
},
@{
    l='IsKey';e={
        $_.Qualifiers.Name -contains 'Key'
    }
}
}
```

```
try
{

        $cimClass = Get-CimClass -ClassName $ClassName -Namespace
        $Namespace -ErrorAction Stop

        if ($PropertyName)
        {
            $cimProperty = $cimClass.CimClassProperties.Where({ $_.Name -eq
            $PropertyName })
            if ($cimProperty)
            {
                extractProperty -cimProperty $cimProperty -Namespace
                $Namespace
            }
            else
            {
                throw "${PropertyName} does not exist in the CIM Class"
            }
        }
        else
        {
            foreach ($property in $cimClass.CimClassProperties)
            {
                extractProperty -cimProperty $property -Namespace $Namespace
            }
        }
}
catch
{
    Write-Error $_
}
```

A complete list of properties from the MSFT_DSCMetaConfiguration class along with type and other details is shown in Figure 3-4.

```
PS C:\Scripts> .\GetCimClassPropery.ps1 -ClassName MSFT_DSCMetaConfiguration -Namespace root/Microsoft/Windows/DesiredStateConfiguration  | ft
```

Name	CimType	EmbeddedInstanceOf	IsReadyOnly	AllowedValues	IsKey
----	-------	------------------	-----------	-------------	-----
ActionAfterReboot	String		False	{ContinueConfiguration, StopConfiguration}	False
AgentId	String		True		False
AllowModuleOverwrite	Boolean		False		False
CertificateID	String		False		False
ConfigurationDownloadManagers	InstanceArray	{MSFT_FileDownloadManager, MSFT_WebDownloadManager}	False		False
ConfigurationID	String		False		False
ConfigurationMode	String		False	{ApplyOnly, ApplyAndMonitor, ApplyAndAutoCorrect}	False
ConfigurationModeFrequencyMins	UInt32		False		False
Credential	Instance		False		False
DebugMode	StringArray		False	{None, ForceModuleImport, All, ResourceScriptBreakAll}	False
DownloadManagerCustomData	InstanceArray		False		False
DownloadManagerName	String		False		False
LCMCompatibleVersions	StringArray		True		False
LCMState	String		True	{Idle, Busy, PendingReboot, PendingConfiguration}	False
LCMStateDetail	String		True		False
LCMVersion	String		True		False
MaximumDownloadSizeMB	UInt32		False		False
PartialConfigurations	InstanceArray	MSFT_PartialConfiguration	False		False
RebootNodeIfNeeded	Boolean		False		False
RefreshFrequencyMins	UInt32		False		False
RefreshMode	String		False	{Push, Pull, Disabled}	False
ReportManagers	InstanceArray	MSFT_WebReportManager	False		False
ResourceModuleManagers	InstanceArray	{MSFT_FileResourceManager, MSFT_WebResourceManager}	False		False
SignatureValidationPolicy	String		False		False
SignatureValidations	InstanceArray	MSFT_SignatureValidation	False		False
StatusRetentionTimeInDays	UInt32		False		False

Figure 3-4. *Properties of the MSFT_DscMetaConfiguration class*

As you can see in Figure 3-4, not all LCM properties are of simple data types such as String, UInt32, or Boolean values. There are certain properties, such as PartialConfigurations, that can be seen referring to embedded instances of other CIM classes. These classes are called meta configuration extension classes. You can see these extension classes listed in Figure 3-2 as well and they are a part of the DSC CIM namespace. You won't have to directly instantiate or work with these extension classes at any time when using DSC. PowerShell DSC provides better declarative ways to configure the properties represented by these extension classes. You will see this when you look at the list of meta resources in PowerShell DSC. So, we can safely skip any discussion or details around these classes for now.

Tip   You can use the Get-CimClassProperty script provided above to gather details about these extension classes and explain the possible configuration settings for each of those classes.

Table 3-1 provides an overview of the *configurable* LCM properties. For now, use this table as a reference for what each property means. You will see their usage and how to create a meta configuration document for these properties in later chapters.

Table 3-1. *LCM Configuration Settings Overview*

LCM Property	Description	Default Value
ActionAfterReboot	Specifies if the pending configuration should be enacted after a node reboot or not.	ContinueConfiguration
AllowModuleOverwrite	Specifies if the new configuration is allowed to overwrite the modules already existing on the node.	False
CertificateID	Specifies a thumbprint of a certificate to be used for decrypting the secure credentials in a configuration.	NA
ConfigurationDownload Managers	Used only in WMF 4 for specifying a pull server location for the configurations.	NA
ConfigurationID	Unique ID that identifies the configuration file to get from a pull server. Used mostly in WMF 4.0 deployments. For WMF 5.0 and above only deployments, use registration keys and configuration names.	NA
ConfigurationMode	Specifies what actions needs to be taken after configuration enact is complete.	ApplyOnly
ConfigurationMode FrequencyMins	Specifies how often the configuration is checked and applied.	15 minutes
Credential	Specifies the credentials to access configurations and resources stored in a SMB pull share. Applies only to WMF 4.0.	NA
DebugMode	Specifies LCM behavior during a configuration enact for resource module import and debugging of resource scripts.	None
DownloadManagerCustomData	Obsolete in WMF 5.0 and above.	NA

(continued)

Table 3-1. (*continued*)

LCM Property	Description	Default Value
DownloadManagerName	Obsolete in WMF 5.0 and above.	NA
MaximumDownloadSizeMB	The maximum module size in MB that can be downloaded.	500MB
PartialConfigurations	Specifies a reference to the MSFT_PartialConfiguration class settings.	NA
RebootNodeIfNeeded	Specifies that a node should be rebooted automatically if a configuration enact requires so.	False
RefreshFrequencyMins	The time interval, in minutes, at which the LCM checks a pull server to get updated configurations.	30 minutes
RefreshMode	Specifies if the LCM is configured to receive configurations via push, pull, or disabled.	Push
ReportManagers	Obsolete in WMF 5.0 and above.	NA
ResourceModuleManagers	Obsolete in WMF 5.0 and above.	NA
SignatureValidationPolicy	Specifies the current signature validation policy configuration.	NA
SignatureValidations	Specifies an instance of MSFT_SignatureValidation that identifies if configuration and module files need to be signed and validated.	NA

Note   The properties that are listed as obsolete are still supported in PowerShell DSC for backward compatibility.

If you have experience with PowerShell CIM cmdlets and Windows Management Instrumentation (WMI) in general, you may think that you can get values of LCM properties (as an alternative to `Get-DscLocalConfigurationManager`) by creating an instance of the `MSFT_DscMetaConfiguration` class. However, this is not the case. If you want to get the current LCM configuration using CIM, you need to invoke the `GetMetaConfiguration` method in the `MSFT_DSCLocalConfigurationManager` class. This CIM class has many other methods that handle the node and meta configurations. These methods are listed in Figure 3-5.

```
PS C:\> (Get-CimClass -ClassName MSFT_DscLocalConfigurationManager -Namespace root/Microsoft/Windows/DesiredStateConfiguration).CimClassMethods

Name                                ReturnType Parameters                                                                          Qualifiers
----                                ---------- ----------                                                                          ----------
SendConfiguration                   UInt32 {ConfigurationData, force}                                                             {implemented, static}
SendConfigurationApply              UInt32 {ConfigurationData, force}                                                             {implemented, static}
GetConfiguration                    UInt32 {configurationData, configurations}                                                    {implemented, static}
TestConfiguration                   UInt32 {configurationData, InDesiredState, ResourcesInDesiredState, ResourcesNotInDesiredState} {implemented, static}
ApplyConfiguration                  UInt32 {force}                                                                                {implemented, static}
SendMetaConfigurationApply          UInt32 {ConfigurationData, force}                                                             {implemented, static}
GetMetaConfiguration                UInt32 {MetaConfiguration}                                                                    {implemented, static}
RollBack                            UInt32 {configurationNumber}                                                                  {implemented, static}
PerformRequiredConfigurationChecks  UInt32 {Flags}                                                                                {implemented, static}
StopConfiguration                   UInt32 {force}                                                                                {implemented, static}
GetConfigurationStatus              UInt32 {All, configurationStatus}                                                             {implemented, static}
SendConfigurationApplyAsync         UInt32 {ConfigurationData, force, jobId}                                                       {implemented, static}
GetConfigurationResultOutput        UInt32 {jobId, resumeOutputBookmark, output}                                                   {implemented, static}
RemoveConfiguration                 UInt32 {Force, Stage}                                                                         {implemented, static}
ResourceGet                         UInt32 {ModuleName, resourceProperty, ResourceType, configurations}                           {implemented, static}
ResourceSet                         UInt32 {ModuleName, resourceProperty, ResourceType, RebootRequired}                           {implemented, static}
ResourceTest                        UInt32 {ModuleName, resourceProperty, ResourceType, InDesiredState}                           {implemented, static}
EnableDebugConfiguration            UInt32 {BreakAll}                                                                             {implemented, static}
DisableDebugConfiguration           UInt32 {}                                                                                     {implemented, static}
```

Figure 3-5. *CIM methods that are used for node and meta configuration*

As you saw in Chapter 2, the `PSDesiredStateConfiguration` module exports commands that are used in managing node and meta configuration. You also saw in some of the verbose output that those commands internally call some of the CIM methods in the `MSFT_DSCLocalConfigurationManager` class. Table 3-2 provides a mapping between the CIM methods in this class and commands exported by the `PSDesiredStateConfiguration` module.

Table 3-2. *Mapping Between CIM Methods and PowerShell Commands*

CIM Method	PowerShell Command
SendConfiguration	Publish-DscConfiguration
SendConfigurationApply	Start-DscConfiguration
GetConfiguration	Get-DscConfiguration
TestConfiguration	Test-DscConfiguration
ApplyConfiguration	Start-DscConfiguration with -UseExisting
SendMetaConfigurationApply	Set-DscLocalConfigurationManager
GetMetaConfiguration	Get-DscLocalConfigurationManager
RollBack	Restore-DscConfiguration
StopConfiguration	Stop-DscConfiguration
GetConfigurationStatus	Get-DscConfigurationStatus
SendMetaConfigurationApplyAsync	Start-DscConfiguration without -Wait
RemoveConfiguration	Remove-DscConfigurationDocument
ResourceGet	Invoke-DscResource with -Method Get
ResourceSet	Invoke-DscResource with -Method Set
ResourceTest	Invoke-DscResource with -Method Test
EnableDebugConfiguration	Enable-DscDebug
DisableDebugConfiguration	Disable-DscDebug

You will look at invoking these CIM methods directly in Chapter 16.

From Table 3-2, you can infer that the GetMetaConfiguration and SendMetaConfigurationApply CIM methods are used in managing the meta configurations. You saw in Chapter 2 how to configure the LCM using a DSC-style declarative syntax. However, that meta configuration document used a few meta configuration resources such as Settings. Here is that example again:

```
[DscLocalConfigurationManager()]
Configuration metaConfiguration
{
    Node S16-01
    {
        Settings
        {
            ConfigurationModeFrequencyMins = 30
            ConfigurationMode = 'ApplyAndAutoCorrect'
        }
    }
}
```

You know how to gather information about which DSC resources are available using the Get-DscResource cmdlet. This cmdlet returns information only about resources that support node configuration and not meta configuration. So, how do you know what meta resources are available? Each of the DSC resources from either in-box or built-in modules are available as CIM keywords. Similar to this, the meta configuration resources are also exported as CIM keywords, not by the PSDesiredStateConfiguration module but by the PSDesiredStateConfigurationEngine module.

Note   The PSDesiredStateConfigurationEngine module is available only in WMF 5.0 and above. In WMF 4.0, the PSDesiredStateConfiguration module exports the LocalConfigurationManager resource which is used for meta configuration. You can see this listed in the CIM keywords (in Figure 2-5 of Chapter 2) from the PSDesiredStateConfiguration module. This meta resource can't be used for meta configuration properties that are available only in WMF 5.0 and above. However, the meta resources from the PSDesiredStateConfigurationEngine are backward compatible and support configuration of the LCM running on WMF 4.0 system.

You can retrieve the meta resource information in WMF 5.0 and above using the Get-CimKeyword function from Chapter 2. Figure 3-6 shows this list.

```
PS C:\> Get-CimKeyword -ImplementingModule PSDesiredStateConfigurationEngine

Keyword                        ResourceName
-------                        ------------
ConfigurationRepositoryWeb     MSFT_WebDownloadManager
ConfigurationRepositoryShare   MSFT_FileDownloadManager
ResourceRepositoryWeb          MSFT_WebResourceManager
ResourceRepositoryShare        MSFT_FileResourceManager
ReportServerWeb                MSFT_WebReportManager
PartialConfiguration           MSFT_PartialConfiguration
SignatureValidation            MSFT_SignatureValidation
Settings                       MSFT_DSCMetaConfigurationV2
```

Figure 3-6. *Meta configuration resources in WMF 5.0 and above*

In Figure 3-6, if you look at the associated resource names, you will observe that they are CIM classes in the DSC CIM namespace. You can also correlate some of these class names to the configurable LCM properties and their associated CIM embedded class instance names listed in Figure 3-5.

Equipped with this information about how LCM is implemented, let's take a look at how LCM helps in the enact process of both meta and node configurations. Let's start with the local storage location for node and meta configurations.

Configuration Store

In Chapter 2, the component architecture diagram (Figure 2-1) illustrated the configuration store that holds node and meta configuration as a set of MOF files. There is also a partial configuration store but let's postpone that discussion until Chapter 10 where you will dive into DSC partial configurations.

Meta Configurations

On a system with no LCM configuration ever applied, you will not see the meta configuration MOF files in the configuration store. Once you enact any meta configuration, you will see the MetaConfig.mof and MetaConfig.backup.mof files in the C:\Windows\ System32\Configuration directory. Both files contain the same LCM configuration settings. When there is no custom meta configuration present on the system, the Get-DscLocalConfigurationManager PowerShell command or the GetMetaConfiguration CIM method will simply instantiate the MSFT_DSCMetaConfiguration class with default values. The default configuration can be seen in Figure 3-7.

```
PS C:\> Get-DscLocalConfigurationManager
```

```
ActionAfterReboot                  : ContinueConfiguration
AgentId                            : FAA4E364-E887-11E6-9B4D-00155D160625
AllowModuleOverWrite               : False
CertificateID                      :
ConfigurationDownloadManagers      : {}
ConfigurationID                    :
ConfigurationMode                  : ApplyAndMonitor
ConfigurationModeFrequencyMins     : 15
Credential                         :
DebugMode                          : {NONE}
DownloadManagerCustomData          :
DownloadManagerName                :
LCMCompatibleVersions              : {1.0, 2.0}
LCMState                           : Idle
LCMStateDetail                     :
LCMVersion                         : 2.0
StatusRetentionTimeInDays          : 10
SignatureValidationPolicy          : NONE
SignatureValidations               : {}
MaximumDownloadSizeMB              : 500
PartialConfigurations              :
RebootNodeIfNeeded                 : False
RefreshFrequencyMins               : 30
RefreshMode                        : PUSH
ReportManagers                     : {}
ResourceModuleManagers             : {}
PSComputerName                     :
```

Figure 3-7. *Default meta configuration settings*

A successful enact of a meta configuration using the Set-DscLocalConfigurationManager PowerShell command or by invoking the SendMetaConfiguratonApply CIM method will create the MetaConfig.mof and MetaConfig.backup.mof files in the configuration store. Deleting the MetaConfig.mof file will reset the LCM configuration to defaults.

Node Configuration

The state of the meta configuration is like a binary number. It either exists or it doesn't. However, a node configuration has multiple states. This is where the LCM plays a role in managing these states. The component architecture diagram (Figure 2-1) in Chapter 2 illustrates these states as multiple MOF files in the configuration store: Pending.mof, Current.mof, and Previous.mof. The methods in the MSFT_DSCLocalConfigurationManager CIM class or the associated PowerShell commands exported by the PSDesiredStateConfiguration module are what you use to manage these configuration states. Figure 3-8 illustrates these configuration states and the associated PowerShell commands.

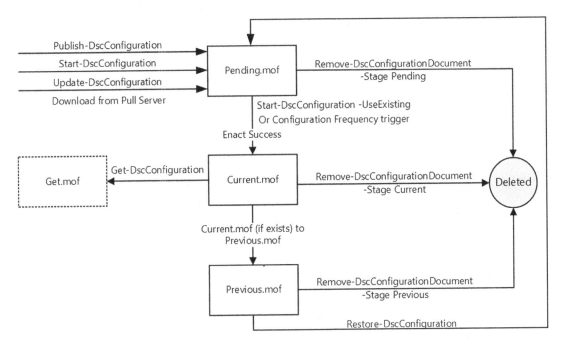

Figure 3-8. *Node configuration states*

Freshly deployed systems will not have any existing DSC configuration in the store. So, when you run the Get-DscConfiguration command, you will see an error message (shown in Figure 3-9) that there is no current configuration.

```
PS C:\> Get-DscConfiguration
Get-DscConfiguration : Current configuration does not exist. Execute Start-DscConfiguration command with -Path parameter to specify a configuration file and create a
current configuration first.
At line:1 char:1
+ Get-DscConfiguration
+ ~~~~~~~~~~~~~~~~~~~~~
    + CategoryInfo          : NotSpecified: (MSFT_DSCLocalConfigurationManager:root/Microsoft/...gurationManager) [Get-DscConfiguration], CimException
    + FullyQualifiedErrorId : MI RESULT 1,Get-DscConfiguration
```

Figure 3-9. *No current configuration error*

You cannot directly set the configuration into the current state. Before that, you need to have the configuration in the pending state so that it can be enacted. There are multiple ways to do so:

- In the push configuration delivery mode,

  - You can use the Publish-DscConfiguration cmdlet to send the configuration as pending.mof into the configuration store and then enact it using the Start-DscConfiguration command with the -UseExisting switch parameter.

  - Using the Start-DscConfiguration PowerShell command will send the configuration as pending.mof and also immediately enact it.

- In the pull configuration delivery mode,

  - LCM will check the pull server for a new or updated configuration and download it as pending.mof. The enact process of the pending configuration usually follows the pending configuration download.

  - The Update-DscConfiguration command can be used to force LCM to check for an updated or new configuration on the pull server. If there is an updated or new configuration available, it will be downloaded as pending.mof and enacted immediately.

As described above, the enact process is usually done automatically (except in the case of Publish-DscConfiguration) after receiving the pending configuration. Once the enact is successful, the pending.mof gets renamed as current.mof.

If the enact process results in a failure, the pending.mof will be left in the configuration store. On systems with WMF 4.0, pending.mof gets deleted in case of enact failure. This bug was fixed in WMF 5.0.

At this point, if you run the Get-DscConfiguration command again, you will see the current state of the resources being configured using DSC. As depicted in Figure 3-8, LCM will copy the current.mof as Get.mof and use it to retrieve the current resource configuration. And this is the reason for error message shown in Figure 3-9 when there is no current configuration or current.mof in the configuration store. The Get.mof is a transient state (therefore the dotted line in Figure 3-8) and you won't see that file in the configuration store once the Get action completes successfully.

If you enact an updated configuration either via pull or push mode, once the enact completes successfully, the current.mof gets copied as previous.mof (and gets overwritten if there is an existing previous.mof file) and pending.mof gets renamed to current.mof. The previous.mof is what gets enacted when you use the Restore-DscConfiguration command.

You can remove any of these configurations from the store using the Remove-DscConfigurationDocument command. If you delete the current configuration or current.mof, LCM will no longer monitor the node for any configuration drift. Monitoring for the drift and for compliance are the next logical things after the node configuration enact is complete. Let's learn about how LCM manages configuration compliance.

Monitoring Configuration Drift

For any configuration management system or tool, it is very important to have the ability to manage configuration compliance. This includes monitoring a configuration for any drift and either reporting or correcting it as needed. PowerShell DSC has built this capability into the LCM.

In WMF 4.0, PowerShell DSC used scheduled tasks to invoke what are called consistency checks, which are used to check if the node configuration is in a desired state or not. However, in WMF 5.0 and above, a WMI provider implemented as the MSFT_DscTimer class in the DSC CIM namespace is used to invoke the consistency checks based on the configuration and refresh frequency intervals configured in LCM.

As you saw in Table 3-1, ConfigurationModeFrequencyMins and RefreshFrequencyMins are used by the LCM to determine when to perform the consistency checks and to check for updated configurations. Let's look a few more details around these two values.

- RefreshFrequencyMins specifies how often the LCM will reach out
  to the pull server to check if there is a new or updated configuration.
  This is applicable only when the RefreshMode setting is configured
  to be pull. If there is current configuration on the node that was
  received from a pull server, the LCM verifies if the checksum on the
  pull server is different from the local checksum for the configuration.
  If so, the LCM initiates a download of the updated configuration
  and any required modules from the pull server. RefreshMode and
  RefreshFrequencyMins aren't methods of validating configuration
  compliance to a desired state; instead, they are methods to ensure
  that the node always has the updated configuration that is being
  placed on the pull server.

- ConfigurationModeFrequencyMins specifies how often the LCM
  validates if the current node configuration is in the desired state
  or not. This validation depends on the configured value of the
  ConfigurationMode property. As you can see from Figure 3-4, this
  property has three possible values: ApplyOnly, ApplyandMonitor,
  and ApplyandAutoCorrect. ApplyandMonitor is the default value.

  - When ConfigurationMode is set to ApplyOnly, no configuration
    drift checks will be performed after the initial configuration enact
    is complete.

  - When ConfigurationMode is set to ApplyandMonitor,
    the LCM will periodically (based on the
    ConfigurationModeFrequencyMins value) trigger a consistency
    check to verify if the current configuration is in the desired state
    or not. If not, the LCM will report this in the event log and to a
    report server if configured in the LCM settings.

  - When ConfigurationMode is set to ApplyandAutoCorrect, the
    consistency check that gets triggered at regular intervals will not
    only check for configuration drift but also correct it automatically
    by reenacting the current configuration.

Note   If there is no current configuration (`current.mof`) on the node, the consistency checks do not get triggered.

In the preceding sections, you looked at several CIM methods in the DSC namespace that are used for managing meta and node configurations. So, is there a CIM method that is used for performing consistency checks as well?

Yes, and it is called `PerformRequiredConfigurationChecks`. This method was listed in Figure 3-5 and some more details are available in Figure 3-10.

```
PS C:\> $cimClass = Get-CimClass -ClassName MSFT_DSCLocalConfigurationManager -Namespace root/Microsoft/Windows/DesiredStateConfiguration

PS C:\> $cimClass.CimClassMethods.Where({$_.Name -eq 'PerformRequiredConfigurationChecks' })

Name                                   ReturnType Parameters Qualifiers
----                                   ---------- ---------- ----------
PerformRequiredConfigurationChecks     UInt32 {Flags}    {implemented, static}
```

Figure 3-10. *The CIM method that is used in consistency checks*

This CIM method takes only one parameter: `Flags`. This accepts an unsigned integer of value 1 or 2 or 4 or 5 or 8. See Table 3-3.

Table 3-3. *Description of Flag Values*

Flag Value	Description
1	Specifies a normal consistency check.
2	Specifies a continuation of a consistency check after a reboot.
4	Specifies that the configuration should be obtained from the pull server. This value should always be combined with 1, for a value of 5.
8	Specifies that the current configuration status be sent to the report server.

You can call this CIM method directly by specifying one of the values in Table 3-3 as an input to the `Flags` property. You will see this as a part of the DSC as a platform discussion in Chapter 16.

I mentioned that the LCM triggers these consistency checks at regular intervals based on what is configured as a value for the `ConfigurationModeFrequencyMins`. But how? In WMF 4.0, two scheduled tasks were registered and configured to run based on the `ConfigurationModeFrequencyMins` value. However, in WMF 5.0 and above, these scheduled tasks do not exist anymore. What, then, triggers these checks?

The answer is in the `DSC_Timer` CIM class in the DSC namespace. Timer events get registered by the WinRM service at the system boot up to trigger these LCM checks. On a system that has the current configuration and the LCM configuration mode set to values other than `ApplyOnly`, you can see the event log messages indicating that the `DscTimer` is performing consistency checks. These event logs will be under `Application and Services Logs\Microsoft\Windows\Desired State Configuration\Operational`. The `DSC_Timer` class is also responsible for restarting the DSC provider from a crash.

Summary

This chapter provided an in-depth understanding of how the LCM is implemented and how it performs the enacting and monitoring processes. This understanding helps with troubleshooting issues that arise out of the enact or overall configuration management process. Use this chapter as a reference while reading subsequent chapters.

## CHAPTER 4

Writing Configurations

So far, you've examined the need for IaC, the role that PowerShell DSC plays in IaC, an overview of DSC architecture and features, and how the LCM (which is the core part of PowerShell DSC) makes it so. Armed with this knowledge, let's go forward and start creating a few configurations to explore PowerShell DSC's declarative syntax. You will start with some very basic examples and make your way towards creating more complex and reusable configurations. You will write more advanced configurations that use secure credentials and configurations that can be transformed into composite resource modules in the next chapter.

Lab Requirements

To try the examples and exercises in this chapter, you will need two or more systems installed with WMF 5.1 or above. I recommend a system with Windows Server 2016. You also need Internet connectivity on one of these systems to find and install custom DSC resource modules from the PowerShell gallery.

What's Not Covered in This Chapter

In this chapter, you will learn the basics of configuration authoring and how to explore DSC resources. With this knowledge and the knowledge that you gained from Chapter 2, it won't be difficult to write your own configuration documents.

There are many in-box DSC resources and many others developed by the community. It is not practical to cover every DSC resource in this chapter or book and I won't do so for a couple of reasons.

© Ravikanth Chaganti 2018
R. Chaganti, *Pro PowerShell Desired State Configuration*, https://doi.org/10.1007/978-1-4842-3483-9_4

Firstly, in the first edition, I described each in-box DSC resource in-depth and showed how to use them in a configuration document. At the time of the first edition, DSC documentation was almost non-existent, so I had to cover those resources in-depth. However, with Microsoft's new documentation strategy and the community contributions towards the documentation, it is no longer difficult to find a quick reference to the in-box resource usage.

The second reason is the open source work that is happening in bug fixing and enhancing the in-box DSC resources as a `PSDscResources` module (more about this later in this chapter) in the gallery. At the time of writing this chapter, this module is at version 2.8.0.0. By the time we release this book and it gets into your hands, I wouldn't be surprised if this module is much updated. So, any in-depth discussion on these in-box resource modules will quickly become stale.

However, all that said, I strongly recommend that you use the methods that you will learn in this chapter to understand the in-box DSC resources and experiment writing a few configurations that use these in-box resources.

Back to Basics

In the "Configuration Authoring" section of Chapter 2, you looked at the language extensions that enable you to author configuration documents in an easy manner. The `Configuration` function and the `Node` and `Import-DscResource` dynamic keywords are examples of these language extensions in PowerShell DSC.

Anatomy of a Configuration Document

Let's look at a sample configuration to understand the anatomy of a DSC configuration document:

```
Configuration ConfigurationName
{
    #Module import using Import-DscResource
    #This has different possible parameters
    Import-DscResource -ModuleName ModuleName
```

```
#Optional Node block with one or more node names
Node @(NodeNameArray) #Or a string literal
{
    #One or more resource instances
    ResourceName ResourceInstanceName
    {
        KeyProperty = Value
        AnotherProperty = AnotherValue
    }
}
}
```

As shown in the above code and from what you saw in Chapter 2, a PowerShell DSC configuration always starts with the Configuration command. Like a function in PowerShell, you need to provide a name. The constraints that apply to naming a PowerShell function apply here as well.

Within the configuration script block, you can use the Import-DscResource keyword to import DSC resource modules. This keyword has certain parameters and can be used in different ways. You will learn more about it later in this chapter.

Note   If you are using any of the in-box resources in a configuration document, you should import the PSDesiredStateConfiguration module using the Import-DscResource keyword. Without it, you will see a warning message when you compile the configuration.

The configuration script block may also contain one or more optional Node blocks that take an array of node names or just a literal string representing a target node. When the Node block is not specified, the compiled configuration is assumed to be for localhost and the generated MOF name will be localhost.mof. There is an advanced use of the Node block that you will see in Chapter 5 when you look at writing complex and reusable configurations.

Inside the Node block or directly inside a Configuration script block (in the absence of a Node block) is a set of one or more resource configurations. Each resource instance configuration starts with a resource keyword followed by a unique name for that resource instance. They are nothing but the resource names shown in the Get-DscResource cmdlet output for any given DSC resource module. Each DSC resource has certain properties that are used to configure it. They are specified as key-value pairs inside the resource instance. Each resource will have one or more key properties and one or more mandatory and/or optional properties. Once again, you can use the Get-DscResource cmdlet to examine, with a few limitations, these resource properties. Of course, there are other better ways that you will learn about later in this chapter.

In Chapter 2, you learned that the configuration resources available on the authoring station are exported as the dynamic keywords and can be used inside the Configuration function to define the desired state of resource configuration. You used the Get-CimKeyword function to list these keywords exported by the PSDesiredStateConfiguration module. The configuration resources exported by this module are the in-box resources. These resources are available on any system that has WMF 5.1 installed and therefore the term *in-box* is used here. However, this list is just a subset of various configurations possible on a system running Windows. This is where you need to either use community-developed custom DSC resource modules or write your own. In Chapter 2, I briefly discussed that you can use the cmdlets in the PowerShellGet PowerShell module to find and install DSC resource modules from the official PowerShell gallery. Let's spend a few minutes exploring how to use these cmdlets and installing some custom DSC resource modules.

Finding and Installing DSC Resource Modules

On systems with WMF 5.1, you can see a list of cmdlets that offer the functionality to interact with the PowerShell gallery. This is shown in Figure 4-1.

```
PS C:\> Get-Command -Module PowerShellGet
```

CommandType	Name	Version	Source
Function	Find-Command	1.1.3.2	PowerShellGet
Function	Find-DscResource	1.1.3.2	PowerShellGet
Function	Find-Module	1.1.3.2	PowerShellGet
Function	Find-RoleCapability	1.1.3.2	PowerShellGet
Function	Find-Script	1.1.3.2	PowerShellGet
Function	Get-InstalledModule	1.1.3.2	PowerShellGet
Function	Get-InstalledScript	1.1.3.2	PowerShellGet
Function	Get-PSRepository	1.1.3.2	PowerShellGet
Function	Install-Module	1.1.3.2	PowerShellGet
Function	Install-Script	1.1.3.2	PowerShellGet
Function	New-ScriptFileInfo	1.1.3.2	PowerShellGet
Function	Publish-Module	1.1.3.2	PowerShellGet
Function	Publish-Script	1.1.3.2	PowerShellGet
Function	Register-PSRepository	1.1.3.2	PowerShellGet
Function	Save-Module	1.1.3.2	PowerShellGet
Function	Save-Script	1.1.3.2	PowerShellGet
Function	Set-PSRepository	1.1.3.2	PowerShellGet
Function	Test-ScriptFileInfo	1.1.3.2	PowerShellGet
Function	Uninstall-Module	1.1.3.2	PowerShellGet
Function	Uninstall-Script	1.1.3.2	PowerShellGet
Function	Unregister-PSRepository	1.1.3.2	PowerShellGet
Function	Update-Module	1.1.3.2	PowerShellGet
Function	Update-ModuleManifest	1.1.3.2	PowerShellGet
Function	Update-Script	1.1.3.2	PowerShellGet
Function	Update-ScriptFileInfo	1.1.3.2	PowerShellGet

Figure 4-1. *Commands in the PowerShellGet module*

Do It Yourself   The version of `PowerShellGet` that comes by default on Windows Server 2016 is 1.0.0.1. There is an updated version of this module available on PowerShell gallery and it can be installed using `Install-Module -Name PowerShellGet -Force`.

While there are many commands in this module, what you are interested for now are only the `Find-Module`, `Find-DscResource`, `Install-Module`, and `Save-Module` cmdlets.

Finding DSC Resources

To find the custom DSC resources published on the PowerShell gallery, you can use either the `Find-Module` or the `Find-DscResource` cmdlet. I say both, because you can!

Note   A few cmdlets in the `PowerShellGet` module such as `Install-Module`, `Find-Module`, and so on require Internet connectivity to be able to download resource modules from the PowerShell gallery.

With the `Find-Module` cmdlet, you can use the `-Includes` parameter with `DscResource` as an argument to list only modules that export DSC resources. Let's see an example:

```
Find-Module -Includes DscResource
```

Figure 4-2 shows partial output from this command.

```
PS C:\> Find-Module -Includes DscResource

Version     Name                           Repository      Description
-------     ----                           ----------      -----------
2.8.0.0     PSDscResources                 PSGallery       This module contains the standard DSC resources..
2.5.0       Carbon                         PSGallery       Carbon is a PowerShell module for automating the
1.1.0.0     SystemLocaleDsc                PSGallery       This DSC Resource allows configuration of the Win
1.1.0.0     xPowerShellExecutionPolicy     PSGallery       This DSC Resources can change the user preference
1.0.0       xInternetExplorerHomePage      PSGallery       This DSC Resources can easily set an URL for the
6.4.0.0     xPSDesiredStateConfiguration   PSGallery       The xPSDesiredStateConfiguration module is a part
5.0.0.0     xNetworking                    PSGallery       Module with DSC Resources for Networking area
1.18.0.0    xWebAdministration             PSGallery       Module with DSC Resources for Web Administration
2.8.0.0     xCertificate                   PSGallery       This module includes DSC resources that simplify
2.0.0.0     xComputerManagement            PSGallery       The xComputerManagement module is originally part
1.1.4.0     PackageManagement              PSGallery       PackageManagement (a.k.a. OneGet) is a new way to
2.16.0.0    xActiveDirectory               PSGallery       The xActiveDirectory module is originally part of
8.0.0.0     xSQLServer                     PSGallery       Module with DSC Resources for deployment and conf
0.3.0.0     xPendingReboot                 PSGallery       This module identifies pending reboots in Windows
2.3.1.0     cChoco                         PSGallery       Chocolatey DSC Resources for use with internal pa
1.3.3       NuGet                          PSGallery       Create Nuget repos, Register Repos, Manage Module
1.6.0.0     xTimeZone                      PSGallery       This DSC Resources can easily set the System Time
2.7.0.0     xWindowsUpdate                 PSGallery       Module with DSC Resources for Windows Update
2.0.0.0     xSmbShare                      PSGallery       Module with DSC Resources for SmbShare area
1.1.0.0     xRemoteDesktopAdmin            PSGallery       Module with DSC Resources for enabling adminsitra
```

Figure 4-2. *Modules containing DSC resources from the PowerShell gallery*

If you run this command on your system, you will see many custom modules from the gallery listed in the output. A few of them are authored by teams at Microsoft and the community together. You can see the author of a module by looking at the Author property of each module listed in the output. This is shown in Figure 4-3.

```
PS C:\> Find-Module -Includes DscResource | Select Name, Author

Name                             Author
----                             ------
PSDscResources                   Microsoft Corporation
Carbon                           Aaron Jensen
SystemLocaleDsc                  Microsoft Corporation
xPowerShellExecutionPolicy       OneScript Team
xInternetExplorerHomePage        OneScript Team
xPSDesiredStateConfiguration     Microsoft Corporation
xNetworking                      Microsoft Corporation
xWebAdministration               Microsoft Corporation
xCertificate                     Microsoft Corporation
xComputerManagement              Microsoft Corporation
PackageManagement                Microsoft Corporation
xActiveDirectory                 Microsoft Corporation
xSQLServer                       Microsoft Corporation
xPendingReboot                   Microsoft Corporation
cChoco                           Chocolatey Software Lawrence Gripper Javy de Koning
NuGet                            Jason
xTimeZone                        Microsoft Corporation
xWindowsUpdate                   Microsoft Corporation
```

Figure 4-3. *Modules and the Author property*

If you need to know what DSC resources a specific module exports, you can take a look at the DSCResources property in the AdditionalMetaData property of the module:

```
Find-Module -Name cWindowsOS | Select -ExpandProperty AdditionalMetaData |
Select -ExpandProperty DSCResources
```

You can search for DSC resources with a specific name using the -DscResource parameter. You can specify more than one resource name an argument.

```
Find-Module -DscResource cDiskImage
```

The -DscResource parameter does not accept the wildcard input and therefore you need to know the complete name of the DSC resource you are looking for.

Finally, if you want to search if a specific DSC resource exists in a given module, you can use -Name and -DscResource parameters together, like so:

```
Find-Module -Name cWindowsOS -DscResource cDiskImage
```

In the second method, using the Find-DscResource, you will more specifically search only for DSC resources published to the PowerShell gallery.

Note   The Find-DscResource module is a wrapper around the Find-Module cmdlet.

Without any parameters, this cmdlet returns a list of all DSC resources available in the gallery. Sample output from this command is shown in Figure 4-4.

```
PS C:\> Find-DscResource

Name                            Version    ModuleName          Repository
----                            -------    ----------          ----------
Archive                         2.8.0.0    PSDscResources      PSGallery
Environment                     2.8.0.0    PSDscResources      PSGallery
Group                           2.8.0.0    PSDscResources      PSGallery
GroupSet                        2.8.0.0    PSDscResources      PSGallery
MsiPackage                      2.8.0.0    PSDscResources      PSGallery
Registry                        2.8.0.0    PSDscResources      PSGallery
Script                          2.8.0.0    PSDscResources      PSGallery
Service                         2.8.0.0    PSDscResources      PSGallery
ServiceSet                      2.8.0.0    PSDscResources      PSGallery
User                            2.8.0.0    PSDscResources      PSGallery
WindowsFeature                  2.8.0.0    PSDscResources      PSGallery
WindowsFeatureSet               2.8.0.0    PSDscResources      PSGallery
WindowsOptionalFeature          2.8.0.0    PSDscResources      PSGallery
WindowsOptionalFeatureSet       2.8.0.0    PSDscResources      PSGallery
WindowsPackageCab               2.8.0.0    PSDscResources      PSGallery
WindowsProcess                  2.8.0.0    PSDscResources      PSGallery
ProcessSet                      2.8.0.0    PSDscResources      PSGallery
Carbon_EnvironmentVariable      2.5.0      Carbon              PSGallery
Carbon_FirewallRule             2.5.0      Carbon              PSGallery
```

Figure 4-4. *DSC resources published to the gallery*

If you observe the difference between Figure 4-4 and Figure 4-2, Find-Module returns the module names that contain the DSC resources whereas Find-DscResource returns the resources within the modules that were found in the gallery.

The -ModuleName parameter can be used to specify the name of a module that contains the resources you are looking for and the -Name parameter for a specific DSC resource within that module. An example of this is shown in Figure 4-5.

```
PS C:\> Find-DscResource -ModuleName xNetworking -Name xHostsFile

Name                          Version   ModuleName                Repository
----                          -------   ----------                ----------
xHostsFile                    5.0.0.0   xNetworking               PSGallery
```

Figure 4-5. *Using both Name and ModuleName parameters*

As you see in Figure 4-5, the `Find-DscResource` cmdlets lists only the most recent and publicly listed version of the DSC resource. Using the `-AllVersions` switch parameter, you can list all available versions of the module and/or resource.

```
PS C:\> Find-DscResource -Name cDiskImage -ModuleName cWindowsOS -AllVersions

Name                          Version   ModuleName                Repository
----                          -------   ----------                ----------
cDiskImage                    1.3.0.0   cWindowsOS                PSGallery
cDiskImage                    1.2       cWindowsOS                PSGallery
cDiskImage                    1.1       cWindowsOS                PSGallery
```

Figure 4-6. *All versions of a DSC resource*

As seen in Figure 4-6, there are multiple versions of this resource available in the gallery. If you want an older version of the module, you can use the `-RequiredVersion` parameter to download a specific version of the resource module.

Do It Yourself   Both `Find-Module` and `Find-DscResource` have many other parameters that I did not show. Take a few minutes to explore these two cmdlets and understand the differences.

Installing DSC Resource Modules

Once you know how to find the resource modules published to the gallery, you can use the `Install-Module` cmdlet to install them on the local system.

You can pipe the output from the `Find-Module` or `Find-DscResource` cmdlets directly into the `Install-Module` cmdlet to download and install the resource module on a local system. This is shown in Figure 4-7. The `-Force` switch parameter suppresses any confirmation prompts.

Note   If this is the first time you are using the `Install-Module` cmdlet on your system, you will receive a prompt to download and install the NuGet provider even when using `-Force` switch. You need to accept the prompt to download the NuGet binary.

```
PS C:\> Find-Module -Name xNetworking | Install-Module -Force

PS C:\> Get-DscResource -Module xNetworking

ImplementedAs    Name                    ModuleName          Version    Properties
-------------    ----                    ----------          -------    ----------
PowerShell       xDefaultGatewayAddress  xNetworking         5.0.0.0    {AddressFamily, InterfaceAlias, Address, Depend...
PowerShell       xDHCPClient             xNetworking         5.0.0.0    {AddressFamily, InterfaceAlias, State, DependsO...
PowerShell       xDnsClientGlobalSetting xNetworking         5.0.0.0    {IsSingleInstance, DependsOn, DevolutionLevel, ...
PowerShell       xDnsConnectionSuffix    xNetworking         5.0.0.0    {ConnectionSpecificSuffix, InterfaceAlias, Depe...
PowerShell       xDNSServerAddress       xNetworking         5.0.0.0    {AddressFamily, InterfaceAlias, Address, Depend...
PowerShell       xFirewall               xNetworking         5.0.0.0    {Name, Action, Authentication, DependsOn...}
PowerShell       xHostsFile              xNetworking         5.0.0.0    {HostName, DependsOn, Ensure, IPAddress...}
PowerShell       xIPAddress              xNetworking         5.0.0.0    {AddressFamily, InterfaceAlias, DependsOn, IPAd...
PowerShell       xNetAdapterBinding      xNetworking         5.0.0.0    {ComponentId, InterfaceAlias, DependsOn, PsDscR...
PowerShell       xNetAdapterLso          xNetworking         5.0.0.0    {Name, Protocol, State, DependsOn...}
PowerShell       xNetAdapterName         xNetworking         5.0.0.0    {NewName, DependsOn, DriverDescription, IgnoreM...
PowerShell       xNetAdapterRDMA         xNetworking         5.0.0.0    {Name, DependsOn, Enabled, PsDscRunAsCredential}
PowerShell       xNetBIOS                xNetworking         5.0.0.0    {InterfaceAlias, Setting, DependsOn, PsDscRunAs...
PowerShell       xNetConnectionProfile   xNetworking         5.0.0.0    {InterfaceAlias, DependsOn, IPv4Connectivity, I...
PowerShell       xNetworkTeam            xNetworking         5.0.0.0    {Name, TeamMembers, DependsOn, Ensure...}
PowerShell       xNetworkTeamInterface   xNetworking         5.0.0.0    {Name, TeamName, DependsOn, Ensure...}
PowerShell       xRoute                  xNetworking         5.0.0.0    {AddressFamily, DestinationPrefix, InterfaceAli...
```

Figure 4-7. *Installing a DSC resource module from the PowerShell gallery*

By default, this cmdlet installs the module at `${env:ProgramFiles}\WindowsPowerShell\Modules` and therefore requires administrator privileges. If you need to install the DSC resource module in the user modules path, you need to specify the `-Scope` parameter with `CurrentUser` as the argument. However, installing modules at the current user module path is only useful if the system is solely used for configuration authoring and not enacting. For enacting, the modules must exist at a system module path such as `${env:ProgramFiles}\WindowsPowerShell\Modules`.

```
Find-Module -Name xNetworking | Install-Module -Scope CurrentUser -Force
```

Before you go on to writing configurations, let's look at one more aspect of the DSC resource modules. Like everything else in this world, code written by me or you or anyone else for that matter is not perfect. There will be bugs and updates that we might have to do frequently. The in-box DSC resource modules are no exception. In WMF 4.0, we had to wait for an OS update to bring the updated in-box resource modules. However, with WMF 5.1 and above, we can simply get updates for these resource modules from the PowerShell gallery. In fact, a subset of the in-box DSC resource modules is available in open source at `https://github.com/PowerShell/PSDscResources`.

I strongly recommend updating the in-box DSC resources to the most recent version on the PowerShell gallery.

Note   The open source `PSDscResources` module does not replace the existing in-box DSC resources but simply provides another version of some of those resources.

Updating In-Box DSC Resource Modules

If you observed the output of the `Find-DscResource` command in Figure 4-2, you saw a module named `PSDscResources`. It contains the updates to in-box DSC resource modules. You can see the in-box resources listed in Figure 4-4 with `PSDscResources` as the module name.

You may think that you can use the `Update-Module` command in the `PowerShellGet` module to download an update to the in-box DSC resources, as a different module of course and not overwrite existing in-box resources. However, the `Update-Module` cmdlet can be used to update modules that are installed using the `Install-Module` cmdlet only. Also, there won't be a module by the name `PSDscResources`; you will see the error message shown in Figure 4-8.

```
PS C:\> Update-Module -Name PSDscResources
Update-Module : Module 'PSDscResources' was not updated because no valid module was found in the module
directory. Verify that the module is located in the folder specified by $env:PSModulePath.
At line:1 char:1
+ Update-Module -Name PSDscResources
+ ~~~~~~~~~~~~~~~~~~~~~~~~~~~~~~~~~~~~
    + CategoryInfo          : InvalidOperation: (PSDscResources:String) [Write-Error], WriteErrorException
    + FullyQualifiedErrorId : ModuleNotInstalledOnThisMachine,Update-Module
```

Figure 4-8. *Update-Module error*

Therefore, you need to use the `Install-Module` cmdlet to update the in-box resource modules for the first time. Once this module from the gallery is installed, you will be able to use the `Update-Module` cmdlet to download any future updates.

```
Install-Module -Name PSDscResources -Force
```

Although partial, you will see two different versions of same resources listed in Figure 4-9.

```
PS C:\> Get-DscResource
```

ImplementedAs	Name	ModuleName	Version	Properties
Binary	File			{DestinationPath, Attributes, Checksum, Content...
Binary	SignatureValidation			{SignedItemType, TrustedStorePath}
PowerShell	PackageManagement	PackageManagement	1.1.4.0	{Name, AdditionalParameters, DependsOn, Ensure...}
PowerShell	PackageManagementSource	PackageManagement	1.1.4.0	{Name, ProviderName, SourceLocation, DependsOn...}
PowerShell	Archive	PSDesiredStateConfiguration	1.1	{Destination, Path, Checksum, Credential...}
PowerShell	Environment	PSDesiredStateConfiguration	1.1	{Name, DependsOn, Ensure, Path...}
PowerShell	Group	PSDesiredStateConfiguration	1.1	{GroupName, Credential, DependsOn, Description...}
Binary	Log	PSDesiredStateConfiguration	1.1	{Message, DependsOn, PsDscRunAsCredential}
PowerShell	Package	PSDesiredStateConfiguration	1.1	{Name, Path, ProductId, Arguments...}
PowerShell	Registry	PSDesiredStateConfiguration	1.1	{Key, ValueName, DependsOn, Ensure...}
PowerShell	Script	PSDesiredStateConfiguration	1.1	{GetScript, SetScript, TestScript, Credential...}
PowerShell	Service	PSDesiredStateConfiguration	1.1	{Name, BuiltInAccount, Credential, Dependencies...
PowerShell	User	PSDesiredStateConfiguration	1.1	{UserName, DependsOn, Description, Disabled...}
PowerShell	WaitForAll	PSDesiredStateConfiguration	1.1	{NodeName, ResourceName, DependsOn, PsDscRunAsC...
PowerShell	WaitForAny	PSDesiredStateConfiguration	1.1	{NodeName, ResourceName, DependsOn, PsDscRunAsC...
PowerShell	WaitForSome	PSDesiredStateConfiguration	1.1	{NodeCount, NodeName, ResourceName, DependsOn...}
PowerShell	WindowsFeature	PSDesiredStateConfiguration	1.1	{Name, Credential, DependsOn, Ensure...}
PowerShell	WindowsOptionalFeature	PSDesiredStateConfiguration	1.1	{Name, DependsOn, Ensure, LogLevel...}
PowerShell	WindowsPackageCab	PSDesiredStateConfiguration	1.1	{Ensure, Name, SourcePath, DependsOn...}
PowerShell	WindowsProcess	PSDesiredStateConfiguration	1.1	{Arguments, Path, Credential, DependsOn...}
PowerShell	Archive	PSDscResources	2.8.0.0	{Destination, Path, Checksum, Credential...}
PowerShell	Environment	PSDscResources	2.8.0.0	{Name, DependsOn, Ensure, Path...}
PowerShell	Group	PSDscResources	2.8.0.0	{GroupName, Credential, DependsOn, Description...}
Composite	GroupSet	PSDscResources	2.8.0.0	{DependsOn, PsDscRunAsCredential, GroupName, En...
PowerShell	MsiPackage	PSDscResources	2.8.0.0	{Path, ProductId, Arguments, Credential...}
Composite	ProcessSet	PSDscResources	2.8.0.0	{DependsOn, PsDscRunAsCredential, Path, Ensure...}
PowerShell	Registry	PSDscResources	2.8.0.0	{Key, ValueName, DependsOn, Ensure...}

Figure 4-9. *Updated in-box resources*

As you know from Chapter 2, the Get-CimKeyword function provides a list of resource names and their associated keywords that you can use in configuration documents. For example, using that function with PSDscResources as the argument to -ImplementingModule parameter will provide the output shown in Figure 4-10.

```
PS C:\Scripts> Get-CimKeyword -ImplementingModule PSDscResources

Keyword                       ResourceName
-------                       ------------
WindowsFeature                MSFT_WindowsFeature
User                          MSFT_UserResource
Service                       MSFT_ServiceResource
Script                        MSFT_ScriptResource
Environment                   MSFT_EnvironmentResource
Registry                      MSFT_RegistryResource
MsiPackage                    MSFT_MsiPackage
Group                         MSFT_GroupResource
Archive                       MSFT_Archive
WindowsOptionalFeature MSFT_WindowsOptionalFeature
WindowsPackageCab             MSFT_WindowsPackageCab
WindowsProcess                MSFT_WindowsProcess
```

Figure 4-10. *Dynamic keywords implemented by the PSDscResources module*

As you can see from Figure 4-10, the keywords listed are same as the resource names listed in Figure 4-9.

If you have any systems that do not have Internet connectivity to download the resource modules from the gallery, you can use the `Save-Module` cmdlet on a system with Internet connectivity and then copy over to the offline systems through a network share or other means.

```
Save-Module -Name PSDscResources -Path C:\Modules -Force
```

Similar to the `Install-Module` cmdlet, you can use the `-RequiredVersion` parameter to download a specific version of the module.

This concludes my brief discussion on finding and installing custom DSC resource modules from the gallery. You will see how to set up your own file share-based repository that works with the `PowerShellGet` cmdlets in Chapter 6; you will also write your own custom resource modules.

Let's start writing configurations!

Your First Configuration

Technically, you've already seen some PowerShell DSC configuration documents and even enacted the configuration using the push method. At the beginning of this chapter, you looked at the anatomy of a configuration document. Let's review it with the help of a real example. In the process, you will learn how the `Import-DscResource` keyword works and how to use the different parameters available with this keyword.

```
Configuration FirstConfiguration
{
    Import-DscResource -ModuleName PSDesiredStateConfiguration
    Node localhost

    {
        Archive FirstArchiveConfiguration
        {
            Path = 'C:\Scripts\test.zip'
            Destination = 'C:\Demo'
            Ensure = 'Present'
```

```
        }
    }
}
```

```
FirstConfiguration
```

When you compile the configuration in this example, it generates a node configuration MOF file. The following is a part of this MOF:

```
instance of MSFT_ArchiveResource as $MSFT_ArchiveResource1ref
{
ResourceID = "[Archive]FirstArchiveConfiguration";
 Path = "C:\\Scripts\\test.zip";
 Ensure = "Present";
 Destination = "C:\\Demo";
 SourceInfo = "::4::5::Archive";
 ModuleName = "PSDesiredStateConfiguration";

ModuleVersion = "1.0";

 ConfigurationName = "FirstConfiguration";

};
instance of OMI_ConfigurationDocument
```

Observe the value of ModuleVersion. It is set to 1.0 whereas the updated version of the Archive resource in PSDscResources module is 2.8.0.0. This is because you have not explicitly mentioned the module version to be used for the module containing the Archive resource. Since the in-box resources and updated OSS resources exist side by side, you need to import the right version of the resource using the Import-DscResource keyword. Therefore, here is the updated configuration document:

```
Configuration FirstConfiguration
{
    Import-DscResource -ModuleName PSDscResources
    Node localhost
    {
        Archive FirstArchiveConfiguration
        {
```

```
            Path = 'C:\Scripts\test.zip'
            Destination = 'C:\Demo'
            Ensure = 'Present'

        }
    }
}
```

FirstConfiguration

Compiling this configuration results in a MOF that reflects the right version of the Archive resource:

```
instance of MSFT_Archive as $MSFT_Archive1ref
{
ResourceID = "[Archive]FirstArchiveConfiguration";
 Path = "C:\\Scripts\\test.zip";
 Ensure = "Present";
 Destination = "C:\\Demo";
 SourceInfo = "::4::5::Archive";
 ModuleName = "PSDscResources";
 ModuleVersion = "2.8.0.0";

 ConfigurationName = "FirstConfiguration";

};
instance of OMI_ConfigurationDocument
```

Therefore, you need to consider PSDscResources as a custom DSC resource module and import it in a configuration document using the Import-DscResource keyword. This applies to every custom DSC resource module that you need to use in a configuration document.

Using the Import-DscResource Keyword

There are different ways to use the Import-DscResource keyword in a configuration document. Table 4-1 shows a list of parameters available with this keyword.

Table 4-1. *Import-DscResource Keyword Parameters*

LCM Property	Description
Name	Specifies the name of the resource to import. You can specify a comma-separated list of resource names.
ModuleName	Specifies the name of the resource module to import. You can specify a comma-separated list of module names.
ModuleVersion	Specifies the required version of the module to be imported.

Unlike the usual PowerShell cmdlets or functions, the `Import-DscResource` does not support positional parameters. Therefore, using named parameters is mandatory. While the parameters appear straightforward, there are some gotchas in the usage.

If you specify the `-Name` parameter, you can only provide a single module name as the argument to the `-ModuleName` parameter. This behavior is shown in Figure 4-11 with an example that fails compilation.

```
PS C:\Scripts> Configuration FirstConfiguration
{
    Import-DscResource -Name xHostsFile, Archive -ModuleName PSDscResources, xNetworking
    Archive FirstArchiveConfiguration
    {
        Path = 'C:\Scripts\test.zip'
        Destination = 'C:\Demo'
        Ensure = 'Present'
    }
}

FirstConfiguration
At line:3 char:62
+ ... rce -Name xHostsFile, Archive -ModuleName PSDscResources, xNetworking
+                                                               ~~~~~~~~~~~~~~~~~~~~~~~~~~~~~~~~~~~~~
Import-DscResource dynamic keyword supports only one module when Name parameter is specified.
    + CategoryInfo          : ParserError: (:) [], ParentContainsErrorRecordException
    + FullyQualifiedErrorId : ImportDscResourceMultipleModulesNotSupportedWithName
```

Figure 4-11. *The argument to ModuleName can only be a single string*

Using the Name parameter without using the ModuleName parameter has performance implications, especially when there are many resource modules installed on the system. The parser, while compiling the configuration, will iterate through all resource modules and find the resource specified. Also, the parser stops searching as soon it finds the first instance of the resource name in a module. This behavior may have unintended consequences if there are multiple resources with the same name and the parser finds the resource that you don't intend to use in the configuration.

Therefore, when you use the -Name parameter, it is recommended that you always use the -ModuleName parameter to make it faster for the parser to find the right module for you.

What if you have multiple versions of the resource module on the system? For example, download an older version of xNetworking resource module using the Install-Module cmdlet. Here is how you do that:

```
Find-Module -Name xNetworking -AllVersions
Install-Module -Name xNetworking -RequiredVersion 4.1.0.0 -Force
```

Once you have a second version of the module installed, try compiling the following resource configuration:

```
Configuration FirstConfiguration
{
    Import-DscResource -Name xHostsFile -ModuleName xNetworking

    xHostsFile HostsFileConfiguration
    {
        IPAddress = '10.0.0.1'
        HostName = 'TestHost10'
    }

}

FirstConfiguration
```

This will result in an error, as shown in Figure 4-12.

```
PS C:\> Configuration FirstConfiguration
{
    Import-DscResource -Name xHostsFile -ModuleName xNetworking

    xHostsFile HostsFileConfiguration
    {
        IPAddress = '10.0.0.1'
        HostName = 'TestHost10'
    }
}
At line:3 char:5
+     Import-DscResource -Name xHostsFile -ModuleName xNetworking
+     ~~~~~~~~~~~~~~~~~~~~~~~~~~~~~~~~~~~~~~~~~~~~~~~~~~~~~~~~~~~~~~
Multiple versions of the module 'xNetworking' were found. You can run 'Get-Module -ListAvailable
-FullyQualifiedName xNetworking' to see available versions on the system, and then use the fully qualified name
'@{ModuleName="xNetworking"; RequiredVersion="Version"}'.
At line:5 char:5
+     xHostsFile HostsFileConfiguration
+     ~~~~~~~~~~~~
Undefined DSC resource 'xHostsFile'. Use Import-DSCResource to import the resource.
    + CategoryInfo          : ParserError: (:) [], ParentContainsErrorRecordException
    + FullyQualifiedErrorId : MultipleModuleEntriesFoundDuringParse
```

Figure 4-12. *Error when there are multiple versions of the same module*

The reason for this is obvious. The parser won't make a decision for you. Unlike the -Name parameter parsing, it won't use the first version or most recent version found on the system. You can certainly use the module specification object as shown in the error message in Figure 4-11 but I recommend using it only when you have multiple modules to import in the configuration. If you have only one module name to import, you should ideally use the -ModuleVersion parameter of the Import-DscResource keyword. Here is a configuration document that uses –ModuleVersion:

Note   Specifying ModuleName and ModuleVersion is always the best practice when authoring configurations. This will ensure that the configuration compiles at a later time in future too, successfully using the version that you specified even when there is an updated module version that might have breaking changes compared to what you used for authoring.

```
Configuration FirstConfiguration
{

    Import-DscResource -ModuleName xNetworking -ModuleVersion 5.0.0.0
```

```
    xHostsFile HostsFileConfiguration
    {
        IPAddress = '10.0.0.1'
        HostName = 'TestHost10'
    }
}

FirstConfiguration
```

Note that you are not using the -Name parameter anymore in the above configuration document. While it is supported, it is not required.

What if you want to import more than one module and also specify a version for each module? There are two ways to do this.

The first method is to use an array of module specification objects and an argument to the -ModuleName parameter. A module specification object is nothing but a hashtable with specific keys in it. Here is an example:

```
Configuration FirstConfiguration
{
    Import-DscResource -ModuleName @{ModuleName='xNetworking';Required
    Version='5.0.0.0'}, @{ModuleName='PSDscResources';
    ModuleVersion='2.8.0.0'}

    xHostsFile HostsFileConfiguration
    {
        IPAddress = '10.0.0.1'
        HostName = 'TestHost10'
    }

    Archive ArchiveConfiguration
    {
        Path = 'C:\Scripts\Test.xip'
        Destination = 'C:\Demo'
        Ensure = 'Present'
    }
}

FirstConfiguration
```

The error message in Figure 4-12 showed the usage of a module specification object. In the example above, you see two variants of this module specification, one that uses RequiredVersion and the second that uses ModuleVersion to specify the version of the module to import. Both specifications are valid.

When I need to specify multiple modules like this in a configuration document, I don't use the module specification object. There is nothing wrong with it, but it is not quite readable. Instead, I prefer what is shown in the following example:

```
Configuration FirstConfiguration
{
    Import-DscResource -ModuleName xNetworking -ModuleVersion 5.0.0.0
    Import-DscResource -ModuleName PSDscResources -ModuleVersion 2.8.0.0

    xHostsFile HostsFileConfiguration
    {
        IPAddress = '10.0.0.1'
        HostName = 'TestHost10'
    }

    Archive ArchiveConfiguration
    {
        Path = 'C:\Scripts\Test.xip'
        Destination = 'C:\Demo'
        Ensure = 'Present'
    }
}

FirstConfiguration
```

This usage of Import-DscResource is more readable even when you have many modules to import.

Note   The module specification object way of using Import-DscResource keyword comes from WMF 4.0 days when there was no explicit support for -ModuleVersion parameter.

Alright. You have seen your first configuration document and what it means to use custom DSC resource modules in a configuration. In the preceding section, you looked at the Import-DscResource keyword usage and its parameters in-depth. So, let's start using some of the in-box DSC resources and learn some more DSC configuration authoring concepts.

Note   All preceding examples use either the in-box resources updated via the PSDscResources module or resources from custom DSC resource modules available on the PowerShell gallery. The examples that use in-box resources may or may not fully work with the PSDesiredStateConfiguration module.

Exploring DSC Resources

As a part of your journey towards mastering configuration authoring, let's look at exploring the properties of a DSC resource and how to know the possible values of any given property within that resource. Yes, the IntelliSense provided by PowerShell ISE and other editors will be helpful in finding the possible properties and auto-completing their values, but learning at the lowest level possible is always better and in this process you will learn about the DSC commands in the PSDesiredStateConfiguration module. Let's dive in. Here's an example:

```
Get-DscResource -Name xHostsFile -Module xNetworking -Syntax
```

The -Syntax switch parameter provides a textual representation of the properties that are available for a DSC resource. Figure 4-13 shows an example of this for the xHostsFile DSC resource.

```
PS C:\> Get-DscResource -Name xHostsFile -Module xNetworking -Syntax
xHostsFile [String] #ResourceName
{
    HostName = [string]
    [DependsOn = [string[]]]
    [Ensure = [string]{ Absent | Present }]
    [IPAddress = [string]]
    [PsDscRunAsCredential = [PSCredential]]
}
```

Figure 4-13. *DSC resource syntax*

In Figure 4-13, the properties that are not enclosed in the square brackets are the mandatory properties. While this representation is good, remember it is just text. Not really the PowerShell way of doing things!

```
Get-DscResource -Name xHostsFile -Module xNetworking | Select-Object
-ExpandProperty Properties
```

This command may be a bit verbose but it gives the DSC resource properties as an object.

As shown in Figure 4-14, by retrieving an object, you can use it in any further automation that you may build.

```
PS C:\> Get-DscResource -Name xHostsFile -Module xNetworking | Select-Object -ExpandProperty Properties

Name                   PropertyType    IsMandatory Values
----                   ------------    ----------- ------
HostName               [string]               True {}
DependsOn              [string[]]            False {}
Ensure                 [string]              False {Absent, Present}
IPAddress              [string]              False {}
PsDscRunAsCredential   [PSCredential]        False {}
```

Figure 4-14. *DSC resource properties as an object*

There is, in fact, a better way to retrieve resource property metadata information. In this case, you inspect the dynamic keywords exported by the DSC resource module and then derive the property metadata. This is the method I prefer to examine the DSC resource properties.

```
Function Get-DscResourceProperty
{
    [CmdletBinding()]
    param (
        [Parameter(Mandatory)]
        [String]
        $ModuleName,

        [Parameter(Mandatory)]
        [String]
        $ResourceName
    )
```

```
[Microsoft.PowerShell.DesiredStateConfiguration.Internal.
DscClassCache]::ClearCache()

    $functionsToDefine = New-Object -TypeName 'System.Collections.Generic.
    Dictionary[string,ScriptBlock]'([System.StringComparer]::
    OrdinalIgnoreCase)

    [Microsoft.PowerShell.DesiredStateConfiguration.Internal.DscClassCache]
    ::LoadDefaultCimKeywords($functionsToDefine)
    $modInfo = Get-Module -Name $ModuleName -ListAvailable
    $schemaFilePath = $null
    $keywordErrors = New-Object -TypeName 'System.Collections.ObjectModel.
    Collection[System.Exception]'
    $foundCimSchema = [Microsoft.PowerShell.DesiredStateConfiguration.
    Internal.DscClassCache]::ImportCimKeywordsFromModule($modInfo,
    $ResourceName, [ref] $SchemaFilePath, $functionsToDefine, $keywordErrors)
    $foundScriptSchema = [Microsoft.PowerShell.DesiredStateConfiguration.
    Internal.DscClassCache]::ImportScriptKeywordsFromModule($modInfo,
    $ResourceName, [ref] $SchemaFilePath, $functionsToDefine )

    $resourceProperties = ([System.Management.Automation.Language.DynamicKe
    yword]::GetKeyword($ResourceName)).Properties
    foreach ($key in $resourceProperties.Keys)
    {
        $resourceProperties.$key | Select Name, TypeConstraint, IsKey,
        Mandatory, Values, Range
    }
}
```

When you use this function, you will see output similar to what is shown in Figure 4-15.

```
PS C:\> Get-DscResourceProperty -ModuleName PSDscResources -ResourceName Service | Format-Table

Name                   TypeConstraint  IsKey Mandatory Values                                       Range
----                   --------------  ----- --------- ------                                       -----
DependsOn              StringArray     False     False {}
PsDscRunAsCredential   MSFT_Credential False     False {}
Name                   String          True       True {}
Ensure                 String          False     False {Present, Absent}
Path                   String          False     False {}
StartupType            String          False     False {Automatic, Manual, Disabled}
BuiltInAccount         String          False     False {LocalSystem, LocalService, NetworkService}
Credential             MSFT_Credential False     False {}
DesktopInteract        Boolean         False     False {}
State                  String          False     False {Running, Stopped, Ignore}
DisplayName            String          False     False {}
Description            String          False     False {}
Dependencies           StringArray     False     False {}
StartupTimeout         UInt32          False     False {}
TerminateTimeout       UInt32          False     False {}
```

Figure 4-15. *DSC resource property metadata*

In Figures 4-13, 4-14 and 4-15, you can see two parameters named DependsOn and PsDscRunAsCredential. These are the common properties that get added to every DSC resource on the system. You will learn about the DependsOn property in this chapter and the PsDscRunAsCredential property in the next chapter.

One difference that you can see between Figures 4-13, Figure 4-14, and Figure 4-15 is the property named IsKey. In PowerShell DSC configuration documents, each resource instance is uniquely identified using a Key property in the resource definition and these key properties are mandatory. From Figure 4-15, the Key property in the Service resource is the Name property. Scripting editors such as PowerShell ISE provide a visual indication of the Key properties as a required property when authoring a configuration document.

Note   You will learn more about the key properties in DSC resource modules in Chapter 6.

An example of this is shown in Figure 4-16.

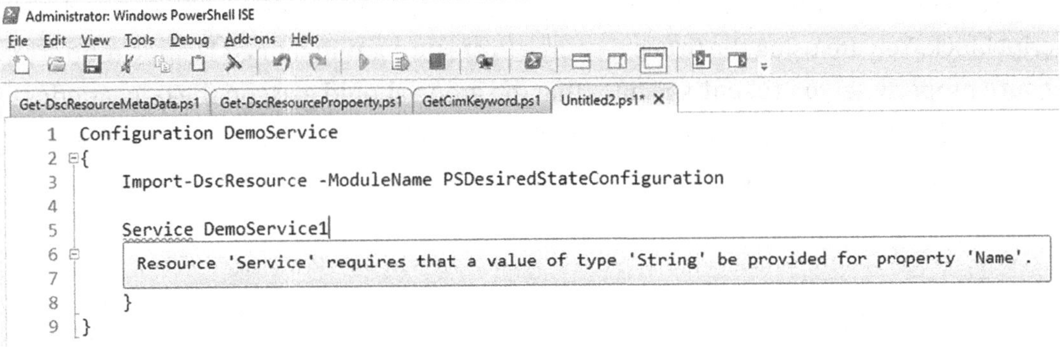

Figure 4-16. *PowerShell ISE indicating the Key property as the first required property*

Multi-Node Configurations

Now that you know the basic anatomy of a configuration document and how to explore the DSC resources and their properties, let's extend your knowledge. It's time to write slightly more useful and complex configurations. You will start with a simple example again but with a common configuration that needs to be applied on multiple nodes:

```
Configuration DemoGroupConfiguration
{
    Import-DscResource -ModuleName PSDscResources

    Node @('S16-01','S16-02')
    {
        User DemoGroup
        {
            GroupName = 'DemoGroup'
            Description = 'Demo Group'
            Ensure = 'Present'
        }
    }
}

DemoGroupConfiguration -OutputPath C:\DemoGroupConfiguration -Verbose
```

In this example, you have two nodes specified as the target nodes within the Node script block. You are using the Group resource to create a group named DemoGroup. The Ensure property set to Present specifies that the group should exist on the target nodes.

Compiling this configuration generates two MOF files that are named S16-01.mof and S16-02.mof. See Figure 4-17.

```
PS C:\> DemoGroupConfiguration -OutputPath C:\DemoGroupConfiguration -Verbose


    Directory: C:\DemoGroupConfiguration


Mode                LastWriteTime         Length Name
----                -------------         ------ ----
-a----        8/14/2017     8:54 PM         1926 S16-01.mof
-a----        8/14/2017     8:54 PM         1926 S16-02.mof
```

Figure 4-17. *Compiled configuration*

You know that you can enact the configurations shown in Figure 4-17 using the Start-DscConfiguration. Figure 4-18 shows the output of this enacting process on both nodes.

```
PS C:\> Start-DscConfiguration -Path .\DemoGroupConfiguration -Wait -Verbose -Force
VERBOSE: Perform operation 'Invoke CimMethod' with following parameters, ''methodName' = SendConfigurationApply,'className
' = MSFT_DSCLocalConfigurationManager,'namespaceName' = root/Microsoft/Windows/DesiredStateConfiguration'.
VERBOSE: Perform operation 'Invoke CimMethod' with following parameters, ''methodName' = SendConfigurationApply,'className
' = MSFT_DSCLocalConfigurationManager,'namespaceName' = root/Microsoft/Windows/DesiredStateConfiguration'.
VERBOSE: An LCM method call arrived from computer S16-JB with user sid S-1-5-21-689661094-3032901192-2251061677-500.
VERBOSE: An LCM method call arrived from computer S16-JB with user sid S-1-5-21-689661094-3032901192-2251061677-500.
VERBOSE: [S16-01]: LCM:  [ Start  Set      ]
VERBOSE: [S16-02]: LCM:  [ Start  Set      ]
VERBOSE: [S16-02]: LCM:  [ End    Set      ]
The PowerShell DSC resource MSFT_GroupResource from module <PSDscResources,2.8.0.0> does not exist at the PowerShell
module path nor is it registered as a WMI DSC resource.
    + CategoryInfo          : InvalidOperation: (root/Microsoft/...gurationManager:String) [], CimException
    + FullyQualifiedErrorId : DscResourceNotFound
    + PSComputerName        : S16-02

VERBOSE: Operation 'Invoke CimMethod' complete.
VERBOSE: [S16-01]: LCM:  [ End    Set      ]
The PowerShell DSC resource MSFT_GroupResource from module <PSDscResources,2.8.0.0> does not exist at the PowerShell
module path nor is it registered as a WMI DSC resource.
    + CategoryInfo          : InvalidOperation: (root/Microsoft/...gurationManager:String) [], CimException
    + FullyQualifiedErrorId : DscResourceNotFound
    + PSComputerName        : S16-01

VERBOSE: Operation 'Invoke CimMethod' complete.
VERBOSE: Time taken for configuration job to complete is 0.539 seconds
```

Figure 4-18. *Enacting the configuration*

As you can see in Figure 4-18, there is an error message that the PSDscResources module does not exist on the target nodes. If you have followed the examples from the beginning and tried everything in order, you will know that you have updated the in-box resources only on the authoring station and not these target nodes. So, the updated resources in the form of the PSDscResources module do not exist on the target nodes, thus the message shown here.

So, how do you install this custom DSC resource module on the target nodes? DSC provides a way for the target nodes to pull missing resource modules from a central repository but you must wait until Chapter 8 to see it. So, for now, you can either install it directly using the Install-Module cmdlet on the target nodes or use PowerShell remoting to install these modules using the Invoke-Command cmdlet. You will use the second method since it is easy and you can do it from the authoring station:

```
Invoke-Command -ComputerName S16-01, S16-02 -ScriptBlock { Install-Module
-Name PSDscResources -RequiredVersion 2.8.0.0 -Force } -Verbose
Invoke-Command -ComputerName S16-01, S16-02 -ScriptBlock { Get-Module -Name
PSDscResources -ListAvailable } -Verbose
```

Note   You may see a couple of prompts to install the NuGet provider.

As shown in Figure 4-19, you now have the required custom DSC resource modules on the target nodes so you can try the enacting process one more time.

```
PS C:\> Invoke-Command -ComputerName S16-01, S16-02 -ScriptBlock { Install-Module -Name PSDscResources -RequiredVersion 2.8.0.0 -Force } -Verbose

PS C:\> Invoke-Command -ComputerName S16-01, S16-02 -ScriptBlock { Get-Module -Name PSDscResources -ListAvailable } -Verbose


    Directory: C:\Program Files\WindowsPowerShell\Modules


ModuleType Version   Name                    ExportedCommands         PSComputerName
---------- -------   ----                    ----------------         --------------
Manifest   2.8.0.0   PSDscResources                                   S16-01
Manifest   2.8.0.0   PSDscResources                                   S16-02
```

Figure 4-19. *Installing modules using PowerShell remoting and Install-Module cmdlet*

As you see in Figure 4-20, the configuration enacting works this time and the group gets created on the target nodes. So, the point that you need to understand through this exercise is that the custom DSC resource modules used in the configuration should exist on the target node before the configuration enacting can be successful.

```
PS C:\> Start-DscConfiguration -Path .\DemoGroupConfiguration -Wait -Verbose -Force
VERBOSE: Perform operation 'Invoke CimMethod' with following parameters, ''methodName' = SendConfigurationApply,'className
' = MSFT_DSCLocalConfigurationManager,'namespaceName' = root/Microsoft/Windows/DesiredStateConfiguration'.
VERBOSE: Perform operation 'Invoke CimMethod' with following parameters, ''methodName' = SendConfigurationApply,'className
' = MSFT_DSCLocalConfigurationManager,'namespaceName' = root/Microsoft/Windows/DesiredStateConfiguration'.
VERBOSE: An LCM method call arrived from computer S16-JB with user sid S-1-5-21-689661094-3032901192-2251061677-500.
VERBOSE: An LCM method call arrived from computer S16-JB with user sid S-1-5-21-689661094-3032901192-2251061677-500.
VERBOSE: [S16-02]: LCM:  [ Start  Set      ]
VERBOSE: [S16-01]: LCM:  [ Start  Set      ]
VERBOSE: [S16-02]: LCM:  [ Start  Resource ] [[Group]DemoGroup]
VERBOSE: [S16-02]: LCM:  [ Start  Test     ] [[Group]DemoGroup]
VERBOSE: [S16-01]: LCM:  [ Start  Resource ] [[Group]DemoGroup]
VERBOSE: [S16-01]: LCM:  [ Start  Test     ] [[Group]DemoGroup]
VERBOSE: [S16-02]:                           [[Group]DemoGroup] Invoking the function Test-TargetResourceOnFullSKU for th
e group DemoGroup.
VERBOSE: [S16-01]:                           [[Group]DemoGroup] Invoking the function Test-TargetResourceOnFullSKU for th
e group DemoGroup.
VERBOSE: [S16-02]:                           [[Group]DemoGroup] A group with the name DemoGroup does not exist.
VERBOSE: [S16-02]: LCM:  [ End    Test     ] [[Group]DemoGroup]   in 5.4430 seconds.
VERBOSE: [S16-02]: LCM:  [ Start  Set      ] [[Group]DemoGroup]
VERBOSE: [S16-02]:                           [[Group]DemoGroup] Begin executing Set functionality on the group DemoGroup.
VERBOSE: [S16-01]:                           [[Group]DemoGroup] A group with the name DemoGroup does not exist.
VERBOSE: [S16-01]: LCM:  [ End    Test     ] [[Group]DemoGroup]   in 5.4070 seconds.
VERBOSE: [S16-01]: LCM:  [ Start  Set      ] [[Group]DemoGroup]
VERBOSE: [S16-01]:                           [[Group]DemoGroup] Begin executing Set functionality on the group DemoGroup.
VERBOSE: [S16-01]:                           [[Group]DemoGroup] Performing the operation "Add" on target "Group: DemoGrou
p".
VERBOSE: [S16-02]:                           [[Group]DemoGroup] Performing the operation "Add" on target "Group: DemoGrou
p".
VERBOSE: [S16-02]:                           [[Group]DemoGroup] Group DemoGroup created successfully.
VERBOSE: [S16-01]:                           [[Group]DemoGroup] Group DemoGroup created successfully.
VERBOSE: [S16-02]:                           [[Group]DemoGroup] End executing Set functionality on the group DemoGroup.
```

Figure 4-20. *The enacting of the configuration*

Now, what if you want to have different resource configurations on target nodes but define all that in the same configuration document? In the preceding example, you created the DemoGroup on target nodes but now you want to remove one of the nodes. How do you specify this resource configuration in a single document?

I mentioned that a Configuration block can have one or more optional Node blocks. You will use that technique now. Here is how you do so:

```
Configuration DemoGroupConfiguration
{
    Import-DscResource -ModuleName PSDscResources

    Node 'S16-01'
    {
        Group DemoGroup
        {
            GroupName = 'DemoGroup'
            Description = 'Demo Group'
            Ensure = 'Present'
        }
    }
```

```
Node 'S16-02'
{
    Group DemoGroup
    {
        GroupName = 'DemoGroup'
        Description = 'Demo Group'
        Ensure = 'Absent'
    }
}
}

DemoGroupConfiguration -OutputPath C:\DemoGroupConfiguration -Verbose
```

As seen in this code, for the node named S16-02 you are setting the Ensure property to 'Absent'. This is a very common pattern that you will see in many in-box and custom DSC resource modules to indicate whether the resource configuration should exist or not. However, it is just one of the ways to design a resource module and not a standard. You will learn more about this in Chapter 6.

```
PS C:\> Start-DscConfiguration -Path .\DemoGroupConfiguration -Wait -Verbose -Force
VERBOSE: Perform operation 'Invoke CimMethod' with following parameters, ''methodName' = SendConfigurationApply,'className' = MSFT_DSCLocalCon
e' = root/Microsoft/Windows/DesiredStateConfiguration'.
VERBOSE: Perform operation 'Invoke CimMethod' with following parameters, ''methodName' = SendConfigurationApply,'className' = MSFT_DSCLocalCon
e' = root/Microsoft/Windows/DesiredStateConfiguration'.
VERBOSE: An LCM method call arrived from computer S16-JB with user sid S-1-5-21-689661094-3032901192-2251061677-500.
VERBOSE: An LCM method call arrived from computer S16-JB with user sid S-1-5-21-689661094-3032901192-2251061677-500.
VERBOSE: [S16-01]: LCM:  [ Start  Set      ]
VERBOSE: [S16-02]: LCM:  [ Start  Set      ]
VERBOSE: [S16-01]: LCM:  [ Start  Resource ]  [[Group]DemoGroup]
VERBOSE: [S16-01]: LCM:  [ Start  Test     ]  [[Group]DemoGroup]
VERBOSE: [S16-02]: LCM:  [ Start  Resource ]  [[Group]DemoGroup]
VERBOSE: [S16-02]: LCM:  [ Start  Test     ]  [[Group]DemoGroup]
VERBOSE: [S16-01]:                            [[Group]DemoGroup] Invoking the function Test-TargetResourceOnFullSKU for the group DemoGroup.
VERBOSE: [S16-02]:                            [[Group]DemoGroup] Invoking the function Test-TargetResourceOnFullSKU for the group DemoGroup.
VERBOSE: [S16-01]:                            [[Group]DemoGroup] A group with the name DemoGroup exists.
VERBOSE: [S16-01]: LCM:  [ End    Test     ]  [[Group]DemoGroup]  in 5.4980 seconds.
VERBOSE: [S16-01]: LCM:  [ Skip   Set      ]  [[Group]DemoGroup]
VERBOSE: [S16-01]: LCM:  [ End    Resource ]  [[Group]DemoGroup]
VERBOSE: [S16-01]: LCM:  [ End    Set      ]
VERBOSE: [S16-01]: LCM:  [ End    Set      ]     in  9.1540 seconds.
VERBOSE: [S16-02]:                            [[Group]DemoGroup] A group with the name DemoGroup exists.
VERBOSE: [S16-02]:                            [[Group]DemoGroup] The value of the Ensure property is expected to be Absent but it is Present.
VERBOSE: [S16-02]: LCM:  [ End    Test     ]  [[Group]DemoGroup]  in 5.5220 seconds.
VERBOSE: [S16-02]: LCM:  [ Start  Set      ]  [[Group]DemoGroup]
VERBOSE: [S16-02]:                            [[Group]DemoGroup] Begin executing Set functionality on the group DemoGroup.
VERBOSE: Operation 'Invoke CimMethod' complete.
VERBOSE: [S16-02]:                            [[Group]DemoGroup] Performing the operation "Remove" on target "Group: DemoGroup".
VERBOSE: [S16-02]:                            [[Group]DemoGroup] Group DemoGroup removed successfully.
VERBOSE: [S16-02]:                            [[Group]DemoGroup] End executing Set functionality on the group DemoGroup.
VERBOSE: [S16-02]: LCM:  [ End    Set      ]  [[Group]DemoGroup]  in 3.4180 seconds.
```

Figure 4-21. *A configuration enact to remove a group*

When you compile the above configuration, it will generate two MOF files, one for each node. When you enact them again with the Start-DscConfiguration cmdlet, you will see that the DemoGroup gets removed from the node named S16-02. Figure 4-21 shows the result of this enact.

While it is easier to combine simple configuration across multiple target nodes in a single configuration document, this is not easily maintainable. Any change for even a single node in the configuration node triggers regeneration of the MOF for each target node mentioned in the document. This is an anti-pattern when it comes to IaC and/or DevOps practices. Therefore, for each node that is being managed using DSC, you should maintain a separate configuration document unless there are nodes that share a resource configuration. PowerShell DSC even provides better ways to share configurations across different nodes. You will see these methods in Chapters 8 and 10 when I discuss the configuration delivery methods and partial configurations.

Parameterized Configurations

In one of the previous examples, you created a group called DemoGroup across multiple target nodes. However, there were resource configuration values such as GroupName and Description hard-coded into the configuration document. This makes the configuration document inflexible and it cannot be reused without changing those values manually. This is where you can parameterize a configuration and implement some reusability. Let's first see an example of how to change that earlier example.

```
Configuration DemoGroupConfiguration
{
    param (
        [Parameter(Mandatory)]
        [String]
        $GroupName,

        [Parameter(Mandatory)]
        [String]
        $Description,
```

```
    [Parameter()]
    [String[]] $Nodes = 'localhost'
)
Import-DscResource -ModuleName PSDscResources

Node $Nodes
{
    Group DemoGroup
    {
        GroupName = $GroupName
        Description = $Description
        Ensure = 'Present'
    }
}
}

DemoGroupConfiguration -OutputPath C:\DemoGroupConfiguration `
    -GroupName 'DemoGroup' `
    -Description 'Demo Group' `
    -Nodes 'S16-01','S16-02'
```

All you did was add a parameter block inside the configuration and add a few parameters to collect the group name, description, and the list of target node names where the configuration needs to get enacted. This is the same as how you define parameters in a function and use them. However, notice how you compile the configuration. The parameters you define in the configuration become parameters to the DemoGroupConfiguration command. Figure 4-22 shows these parameters along with a bunch of other common parameters including -OutputPath that you have been using when compiling configurations.

```
PS C:\> Get-Command -Name DemoGroupConfiguration | Select -ExpandProperty Parameters

Key                      Value
---                      -----
InstanceName             System.Management.Automation.ParameterMetadata
DependsOn                System.Management.Automation.ParameterMetadata
PsDscRunAsCredential     System.Management.Automation.ParameterMetadata
OutputPath               System.Management.Automation.ParameterMetadata
ConfigurationData        System.Management.Automation.ParameterMetadata
GroupName                System.Management.Automation.ParameterMetadata
Description              System.Management.Automation.ParameterMetadata
Nodes                    System.Management.Automation.ParameterMetadata
Verbose                  System.Management.Automation.ParameterMetadata
Debug                    System.Management.Automation.ParameterMetadata
ErrorAction              System.Management.Automation.ParameterMetadata
WarningAction            System.Management.Automation.ParameterMetadata
InformationAction        System.Management.Automation.ParameterMetadata
ErrorVariable            System.Management.Automation.ParameterMetadata
WarningVariable          System.Management.Automation.ParameterMetadata
InformationVariable      System.Management.Automation.ParameterMetadata
OutVariable              System.Management.Automation.ParameterMetadata
OutBuffer                System.Management.Automation.ParameterMetadata
PipelineVariable         System.Management.Automation.ParameterMetadata
```

Figure 4-22. *Configuration command parameters*

Also, in the above example, notice how you use the `Parameter` attribute to specify the `$GroupName` and `$Description` parameters as mandatory parameters. This indicates that you can use other attributes that you generally use in a function definition here in the configuration definition as well.

The above parameterized configuration example is useful only if you want to configure the target nodes in a similar manner. What if you want to implement your multi-node block example using parameterized configurations? For example, based on the role of a target node, you either want the group to get created or removed. How would you implement that?

Think about it and try some implementations. You will revisit this example in the next chapter and see how DSC makes such as scenario very easy to implement with what is called DSC configuration data.

Dependent Resource Configurations

In a real-world scenario, node configurations won't be as simple as what you have seen here. In the real world, when configuring complex target node deployments, you want to ensure that a dependent resource configuration is successful before moving on to another resource configuration. Let's explore how DSC supports this with a simple example.

In the following example, you check for a specific registry value and set it before you can create the setup script that you need. So, you want to create the file configuration only when the registry configuration exists in a desired state.

```
Configuration DependentConfigurationDemo
{
    Import-DscResource -ModuleName PSDscResources -Name Registry

    Node S16-01
    {
        File SetupScript
        {
            DestinationPath = 'C:\Scripts\setup.cmd'
            Contents = 'C:\Windows\System32\Sysprep.exe /oobe /generalize /
            shutdown'
            Type = 'File'
            Ensure = 'Present'
            DependsOn = '[Registry]OOBEInProgress'
        }

        Registry OOBEInProgress
        {
            Key = 'HKEY_LOCAL_MACHINE\SYSTEM\Setup'
            ValueName = 'OOBEInProgress'
            ValueData = 0
            ValueType = 'DWord'
            Ensure = 'Present'
        }
    }
}

DependentConfigurationDemo -OutputPath C:\DependentConfigurationDemo
```

Note   When you compile this configuration, you will see a warning message that you are not importing the PSDesiredStateConfiguration module. At the time of this writing, there is a bug in DSC that prevents importing both of the in-box PSDesiredStateConfiguration and PSDscResources modules you downloaded from the gallery at the same time.

In this example, within the File resource configuration, you use a property called DependsOn. If you refer to the earlier conversation on understanding resource properties, you will understand that the DependsOn and PSDscRunAsCredential properties automatically get added to every DSC resource on the system. The DependsOn property is what you need here to define the dependencies between resource instance configurations on a target node.

When you enact this configuration, since there is a dependency on a registry value's desired state, DSC first enacts Registry resource configuration and then, if successful, proceeds to the File resource configuration. This can be seen in Figure 4-23.

```
PS C:\> Start-DscConfiguration -Path C:\DependentConfigurationDemo -Wait -Force -Verbose
VERBOSE: Perform operation 'Invoke CimMethod' with following parameters, ''methodName' = SendConfigurationApply,'className' = MSFT_DS
e' = root/Microsoft/Windows/DesiredStateConfiguration'.
VERBOSE: An LCM method call arrived from computer S16-JB with user sid S-1-5-21-689661094-3032901192-2251061677-500.
VERBOSE: [S16-01]: LCM:  [ Start  Set      ]
VERBOSE: [S16-01]: LCM:  [ Start  Resource ]    [[Registry]OOBEInProgress]
VERBOSE: [S16-01]: LCM:  [ Start  Test     ]    [[Registry]OOBEInProgress]
VERBOSE: [S16-01]:                                [[Registry]OOBEInProgress] Test-TargetResource is starting for Registry resource with K
VERBOSE: [S16-01]:                                [[Registry]OOBEInProgress] Get-TargetResource is starting for Registry resource with Ke
VERBOSE: [S16-01]:                                [[Registry]OOBEInProgress] The registry key at path HKEY_LOCAL_MACHINE\SYSTEM\Setup exi
VERBOSE: [S16-01]:                                [[Registry]OOBEInProgress] The registry key at path HKEY_LOCAL_MACHINE\SYSTEM\Setup has
VERBOSE: [S16-01]:                                [[Registry]OOBEInProgress] Get-TargetResource has finished for Registry resource with K
VERBOSE: [S16-01]:                                [[Registry]OOBEInProgress] The registry key at path HKEY_LOCAL_MACHINE\SYSTEM\Setup has
VERBOSE: [S16-01]:                                [[Registry]OOBEInProgress] Test-TargetResource has finished for Registry resource with
VERBOSE: [S16-01]: LCM:  [ End    Test     ]    [[Registry]OOBEInProgress]  in 0.2500 seconds.
VERBOSE: [S16-01]: LCM:  [ Skip   Set      ]    [[Registry]OOBEInProgress]
VERBOSE: [S16-01]: LCM:  [ End    Resource ]    [[Registry]OOBEInProgress]
VERBOSE: [S16-01]: LCM:  [ Start  Resource ]    [[File]SetupScript]
VERBOSE: [S16-01]: LCM:  [ Start  Test     ]    [[File]SetupScript]
VERBOSE: [S16-01]:                                [[File]SetupScript] The system cannot find the file specified.
VERBOSE: [S16-01]:                                [[File]SetupScript] The related file/directory is: C:\Scripts\setup.cmd.
VERBOSE: [S16-01]: LCM:  [ End    Test     ]    [[File]SetupScript]  in 0.0000 seconds.
VERBOSE: [S16-01]: LCM:  [ Start  Set      ]    [[File]SetupScript]
VERBOSE: [S16-01]:                                [[File]SetupScript] The system cannot find the file specified.
VERBOSE: [S16-01]:                                [[File]SetupScript] The related file/directory is: C:\Scripts\setup.cmd.
VERBOSE: [S16-01]: LCM:  [ End    Set      ]    [[File]SetupScript]  in 0.0160 seconds.
VERBOSE: [S16-01]: LCM:  [ End    Resource ]    [[File]SetupScript]
VERBOSE: [S16-01]: LCM:  [ End    Set      ]
VERBOSE: [S16-01]: LCM:  [ End    Set      ]     in  0.6090 seconds.
VERBOSE: Operation 'Invoke CimMethod' complete.
VERBOSE: Time taken for configuration job to complete is 0.69 seconds
```

Figure 4-23. *Dependent resource configuration enact*

As you can see in Figure 4-23, even though the `Registry` resource instance configuration is mentioned after the `File` resource instance, using the `DependsOn` property changes the resource enact ordering. In the example above, you defined both `File` and `Registry` resources within the same node block. Within the `File` resource definition, you add the `DependsOn` property and assign it a value to indicate that it depends on the `Registry` resource within the configuration. If you look at the value of the `DependsOn` property, it has a specific syntax. The general syntax is `"[Resource Type] ResourceName"`. So, following that, `"[Registry]OOBEInProgress"` defines that the `File` resource is dependent on the `Registry` resource defined by `OOBEInProgress`.

In WMF 4.0, the resource configuration execution was not necessarily sequential and therefore needed the `DependsOn` definitions to define a proper resource instance enact ordering. However, with WMF 5.0 and above systems, the resource enact is always sequential and goes from top to bottom. Therefore, the `DependsOn` property is needed only when you want to ensure that the subsequent resource enact processes will stop if a dependent resource does not turn into a desired state.

Now, how do you add multiple such dependencies? For example, what if you want to ensure the `setup.cmd` gets created only after configuring multiple registry values to a desired state? The `DependsOn` property is a string array, and therefore, you can add multiple resource definitions to the `DependsOn` value as a comma-separated list. This is shown in the following example:

```
Configuration DependentConfigurationDemo
{
    Import-DscResource -ModuleName PSDscResources -Name Registry

    Node S16-01
    {

        File SetupScript

        {
            DestinationPath = 'C:\Scripts\setup.cmd'
            Contents = 'C:\Windows\System32\Sysprep.exe /oobe /generalize /
            shutdown'
            Type = 'File'
            Ensure = 'Present'
            DependsOn = '[Registry]OOBEInProgress', '[Registry]SetupType'
        }
```

```
    Registry OOBEInProgress
    {
        Key = 'HKEY_LOCAL_MACHINE\SYSTEM\Setup'
        ValueName = 'OOBEInProgress'
        ValueData = 0
        ValueType = 'DWord'
        Ensure = 'Present'
    }

    Registry SetupType
    {
        Key = 'HKEY_LOCAL_MACHINE\SYSTEM\Setup'
        ValueName = 'SetupType'
        ValueData = 0
        ValueType = 'DWord'
        Ensure = 'Present'
    }
    }
}

DependentConfigurationDemo -OutputPath C:\DependentConfigurationDemo
```

The DependsOn property can be used to define only resource instance dependencies within a node's configuration. For dependencies across different nodes, you need to use something called cross-machine synchronization and that is enabled using the in-box DSC resources WaitForAny, WaitForSome, and WaitForAll. You will learn more about these resources in Chapter 11.

Summary

This chapter was intense. I spent several hours reviewing this chapter's content (before even the tech reviewer) and made several revisions to the content to ensure that the flow was proper and that I described the concepts around configuration authoring in an easy way. I started this chapter with a quick introduction to configuration anatomy and showed how to find and install custom DSC resource modules from the official PowerShell gallery. Then I moved on to your first configuration and explained how to use the `Import-DscResource` keyword. Then I showed you DSC resources and their properties, and finally how to create multi-node, parameterized, and dependent configurations. While the goal of this chapter was to only show you how to write some basic to moderately complex configurations, there are some snippets of code that you should review. For example, the `Get-DscResourceProperty` function snippet that you used has tons of internal API calls that are used in the `PSDesiredStateConfiguration` module. It may not be completely relevant at this point in time but do spend some time reading and understanding what's in there. It will certainly help you on your journey towards mastering PowerShell DSC.

In the next chapter, you will delve further into writing complex and reusable configurations. You will learn how to build and share these reusable configurations as resource modules. You will also learn how to use credentials in a configuration document and understand the different methods that enable credentials in a resource configuration.

## CHAPTER 5

Writing Advanced DSC Configurations

In the previous chapter, you learned the basics of configuration authoring and how to write reusable configurations by parameterizing the configuration documents. You used the DependsOn property in a configuration document to define dependencies between resource instances in a configuration. That was all very basic and but a good start.

This chapter will look at the concept of configuration data and why we need it, how we can use configuration data to create flexible and reusable configurations, how to secure sensitive data such as credentials and secure strings in the configuration authoring and enacting process, and many other advanced configuration authoring concepts.

Lab Requirements

To try examples and exercises in this chapter, you will need at minimum two or more systems with Windows Server 2008 R2 or above with WMF 5.1 installed. I recommend a system with Windows Server 2016. The credential encryption requires certificates, so trying the configuration examples that use credentials will require either a certificate authority or self-signed certificates.

Using Credentials in a Configuration

In Chapter 4, you saw some basic examples of DSC configurations. Before you start writing a moderately complex configuration, let's look at a configuration that uses the in-box File resource:

© Ravikanth Chaganti 2018
R. Chaganti, *Pro PowerShell Desired State Configuration*, https://doi.org/10.1007/978-1-4842-3483-9_5

```
Configuration FileCopyConfiguration
{
    Import-DscResource -ModuleName PSDesiredStateConfiguration

    Node S16-01
    {
        File FileCopyDemo
        {
            SourcePath = '\\S16-JB\Share\Unattend.xml'
            DestinationPath = 'C:\Scripts\Unattend.xml'
            Type = 'File'
            Force = $true
        }
    }
}

FileCopyConfiguration
```

In this example, you are copying a file from a remote computer UNC path to a local folder on the target node. By setting the Force property to $true, if the destination folder does not exist, it will be created. Let's enact this configuration and check what happens. See Figure 5-1.

```
PS C:\> Start-DscConfiguration -Path .\FileCopyConfiguration -Verbose -Wait -Force
VERBOSE: Perform operation 'Invoke CimMethod' with following parameters, ''methodName' = SendConfigurationApply,'className' = MSF
T_DSCLocalConfigurationManager,'namespaceName' = root/Microsoft/Windows/DesiredStateConfiguration'.
VERBOSE: An LCM method call arrived from computer S16-JB with user sid S-1-5-21-689661094-3032901192-2251061677-500.
VERBOSE: [S16-01]: LCM: [ Start  Set       ]
VERBOSE: [S16-01]: LCM: [ Start  Resource ] [[File]FileCopyDemo]
VERBOSE: [S16-01]: LCM: [ Start  Test     ] [[File]FileCopyDemo]
VERBOSE: [S16-01]:                          [[File]FileCopyDemo] The system cannot find the path specified.
VERBOSE: [S16-01]:                          [[File]FileCopyDemo] The related file/directory is: C:\Scripts\Unattend.xml.
VERBOSE: [S16-01]:                          [[File]FileCopyDemo] Access is denied.
VERBOSE: [S16-01]:                          [[File]FileCopyDemo] The related file/directory is: \\S16-JB\Share\Unattend.xml.
VERBOSE: [S16-01]:                          [[File]FileCopyDemo] The path cannot point to the root directory or to the root of
a net share.
VERBOSE: [S16-01]:                          [[File]FileCopyDemo] The related file/directory is: \\S16-JB\Share\Unattend.xml.
VERBOSE: [S16-01]: LCM: [ End    Test     ] [[File]FileCopyDemo]  in 0.1250 seconds.
VERBOSE: [S16-01]: LCM: [ Start  Set      ] [[File]FileCopyDemo]
VERBOSE: [S16-01]:                          [[File]FileCopyDemo] The system cannot find the path specified.
VERBOSE: [S16-01]:                          [[File]FileCopyDemo] The related file/directory is: C:\Scripts\Unattend.xml.
VERBOSE: [S16-01]:                          [[File]FileCopyDemo] Access is denied.
VERBOSE: [S16-01]:                          [[File]FileCopyDemo] The related file/directory is: \\S16-JB\Share\Unattend.xml.
VERBOSE: [S16-01]:                          [[File]FileCopyDemo] The path cannot point to the root directory or to the root of
a net share.
VERBOSE: [S16-01]:                          [[File]FileCopyDemo] The related file/directory is: \\S16-JB\Share\Unattend.xml.
VERBOSE: [S16-01]:                          [[File]FileCopyDemo] SourcePath must be accessible for current configuration.
VERBOSE: [S16-01]:                          [[File]FileCopyDemo] The related file/directory is: \\S16-JB\Share\Unattend.xml.
SourcePath must be accessible for current configuration. The related file/directory is: \\S16-JB\Share\Unattend.xml.  The
related ResourceID is [File]FileCopyDemo.
    + CategoryInfo          : InvalidArgument: (:) [], CimException
    + FullyQualifiedErrorId : MI RESULT 4
    + PSComputerName        : S16-01
```

Figure 5-1. *Enact failure with File resource*

As you can see in Figure 5-1, the enact process indicates that the target node is unable to access the remote UNC path. This might need a little bit of investigation. Let's see if the remote node can really access the UNC path or not. You will do this interactively on the remote node, as shown in Figure 5-2.

```
PS C:\> hostname
S16-01

PS C:\> Get-Item -Path \\S16-JB\Share\unattend.xml


    Directory: \\S16-JB\Share


Mode                LastWriteTime         Length Name
----                -------------         ------ ----
-a----        8/9/2017   10:38 AM           1670 unattend.xml
```

Figure 5-2. *Accessing a remote file on the target node*

As seen in Figure 5-2, on the target node you can access the remote file share. So, what is the problem with the configuration enacting process on the remote node? Let's investigate this with a simple DSC configuration that uses a `Script` resource:

```
Configuration DSCRunDemo
{
    Import-DscResource -ModuleName PSDesiredStateConfiguration

    Node S16-01
    {
        Script DSCRunDemo
        {
            SetScript  =
            {
                Write-Verbose -Message $(whoami)
            }

            TestScript =
            {
                return $false
            }
```

```
            GetScript =
            {
                return @{}
            }
        }
    }
}
```

DSCRunDemo

In this example, you are using the Script resource that has GetScript, SetScript, and TestScript properties. Each of these properties takes an arbitrary script block as an argument. However, there are some rules. The script block provided as GetScript must return a hashtable, the argument to TestScript must return a Boolean value, and finally the SetScript argument should do something useful. Without going into too many details here, just understand that these properties are synonymous to the Get-TargetResource, Set-TargetResource, and Test-TargetResource functions in the DSC resource modules, which you will learn more about in Chapter 6 when you look at writing custom DSC resource modules.

For now, understand that when you enact this configuration, the TestScript script block runs first and returns $false, which causes the script block argument provided to SetScript to run. In this example, you just have a simple Write-Verbose statement that prints the output from the whomai.exe command. So, when you enact this configuration, you should see the user context in which DSC is executing. Figure 5-3 shows the output from my lab system.

```
PS C:\> Start-DscConfiguration -Path .\DSCRunDemo -Verbose -Wait -Force
VERBOSE: Perform operation 'Invoke CimMethod' with following parameters, ''methodName' = SendConfigurationApply,'className' = MSF
T_DSCLocalConfigurationManager,'namespaceName' = root/Microsoft/Windows/DesiredStateConfiguration'.
VERBOSE: An LCM method call arrived from computer S16-JB with user sid S-1-5-21-689661094-3032901192-2251061677-500.
VERBOSE: [S16-01]: LCM:  [ Start  Set      ]
VERBOSE: [S16-01]: LCM:  [ Start  Resource ] [[Script]DSCRunDemo]
VERBOSE: [S16-01]: LCM:  [ Start  Test     ] [[Script]DSCRunDemo]
VERBOSE: [S16-01]: LCM:  [ End    Test     ] [[Script]DSCRunDemo]  in 0.2340 seconds.
VERBOSE: [S16-01]: LCM:  [ Start  Set      ] [[Script]DSCRunDemo]
VERBOSE: [S16-01]:                           [[Script]DSCRunDemo] Performing the operation "Set-TargetResource" on target "Execu
ting the SetScript with the user supplied credential".
VERBOSE: [S16-01]:                           [[Script]DSCRunDemo] nt authority\system
VERBOSE: [S16-01]: LCM:  [ End    Set      ] [[Script]DSCRunDemo]  in 0.1250 seconds.
VERBOSE: [S16-01]: LCM:  [ End    Resource ] [[Script]DSCRunDemo]
VERBOSE: [S16-01]: LCM:  [ End    Set      ]
VERBOSE: [S16-01]: LCM:  [ End    Set      ]  in  2.4100 seconds.
VERBOSE: Operation 'Invoke CimMethod' complete.
VERBOSE: Time taken for configuration job to complete is 2.599 seconds
```

Figure 5-3. *Enacting script configuration*

From Figure 5-3, you can see that whoami.exe returned nt authority\system as the
user that DSC is running as. You can infer from the above output that DSC is running as
a LOCAL SYSTEM account and that the account has no permission to read the remote
file share. And this is precisely the reason why the target node was unable to access the
remote UNC share during the configuration enact in the earlier example. So, how do you
resolve this?

The File resource has a property called Credential. This can be used to specify
the credentials required to authenticate and access the remote UNC path. Here is an
example of how to use it:

```
Configuration FileCopyConfiguration
{
    Param
    (
        [Parameter(Mandatory)]
        [pscredential] $Credential
    )
    Import-DscResource -ModuleName PSDesiredStateConfiguration

    Node S16-01
    {
        File FileCopyDemo
        {
            SourcePath   =  '\\S16-JB\Share\Unattend.xml'
            DestinationPath = 'C:\Scripts\Unattend.xml'
            Type  =  'File'
            Credential = $Credential Force = $true
        }
    }
}

FileCopyConfiguration -Credential (Get-Credential)
```

In this updated example, you add a parameter called Credential to the
configuration and use it as the argument to Credential property of File resource. Using
this parameter, you can provide the credentials required to authenticate to the remote
UNC share during the enact process. Figure 5-4 shows what happens when you try to
compile this configuration.

```
PS C:\> FileCopyConfiguration -Credential (Get-Credential)
cmdlet Get-Credential at command pipeline position 1
Supply values for the following parameters:
ConvertTo-MOFInstance : System.InvalidOperationException error processing property 'Credential' OF TYPE 'File': Converting and
storing encrypted passwords as plain text is not recommended. For more information on securing credentials in MOF file, please
refer to MSDN blog: http://go.microsoft.com/fwlink/?LinkId=393729
At line:11 char:9
+    File
At line:341 char:16
+     $aliasId = ConvertTo-MOFInstance $keywordName $canonicalizedValue
+                ~~~~~~~~~~~~~~~~~~~~~~~~~~~~~~~~~~~~~~~~~~~~~~~~~~~~
    + CategoryInfo          : InvalidOperation: (:) [Write-Error], InvalidOperationException
    + FullyQualifiedErrorId : FailToProcessProperty,ConvertTo-MOFInstance
WARNING: It is not recommended to use domain credential for node 'S16-01'. In order to suppress the warning, you can add a proper
ty named 'PSDscAllowDomainUser' with a value of $true to your DSC configuration data for node 'S16-01'.
Compilation errors occurred while processing configuration 'FileCopyConfiguration'. Please review the errors reported in error
stream and modify your configuration code appropriately.
At C:\Windows\system32\WindowsPowerShell\v1.0\Modules\PSDesiredStateConfiguration\PSDesiredStateConfiguration.psm1:3917 char:5
+     throw $ErrorRecord
+     ~~~~~~~~~~~~~~~~~~~
    + CategoryInfo          : InvalidOperation: (FileCopyConfiguration:String) [], InvalidOperationException
    + FullyQualifiedErrorId : FailToProcessConfiguration
```

Figure 5-4. *Error during configuration compile with credentials*

In this case, the configuration does not compile and fails with an error that says converting and storing passwords as plain text is not recommended. While the error message does not tell you the real solution, there are (again) a couple of ways to address this:

- Allowing the PSDscAllowPlainTextPassword key in configuration data

- Using certificates to encrypt passwords in a configuration

The first method should never be used in a production environment. It is meant only for development and test purposes. The second method is the one that should be adopted by all configurations that use credentials and secure strings. Both methods require the use of configuration data in the DSC configuration documents. Let's explore what this is about.

Configuration Data

Some of the earlier examples showed that configuration commands often have a common parameter called ConfigurationData. This is shown again in Figure 5-5.

```
PS C:\> (Get-Command -Name FileCopyConfiguration | Select -ExpandProperty Parameters)['ConfigurationData']

Name             : ConfigurationData
ParameterType    : System.Collections.Hashtable
ParameterSets    : {[__AllParameterSets, System.Management.Automation.ParameterSetMetadata]}
IsDynamic        : False
Aliases          : {}
Attributes       : {__AllParameterSets,
                   Microsoft.PowerShell.DesiredStateConfiguration.ArgumentToConfigurationDataTransformationAttribute,
                   System.Management.Automation.ArgumentTypeConverterAttribute}
SwitchParameter  : False
```

Figure 5-5. *The ConfigurationData parameter in a configuration command*

As shown in Figure 5-5, the `ConfigurationData` parameter in the configuration is a hashtable that can be used to separate environmental data from configuration data. Here is the general syntax of a configuration data hashtable:

```
$configurationData =
@{
    AllNodes = @()
    EnvironmentData = ""
}
```

The value of the `AllNodes` key is an array of hashtables. Each hashtable in this array must contain a key named `NodeName`.

```
$configurationData =
@{
    AllNodes  =
    @(
        @{
            NodeName = 'S16-01'
        },
        @{
            NodeName = 'S16-02'
        }
    )
    EnvironmentData = ''
}
```

> **Note**   The second key in the above example is named `EnvironmentData`.
> But you can name it whatever you want and you can add any number of such
> additional keys with hashtables as their values.

Before I discuss other aspects of the configuration data, let's see a complete example
and build on it as I discuss it in-depth:

```
$configurationData =
@{
    AllNodes  =
    @(
        @{
            NodeName = 'S16-01'
            SourceFile = '\\S16-JB\Share\S16-01.xml'
            DestinationFile = 'C:\Scripts\Unattend.xml'
        },

        @{
            NodeName = 'S16-02'
            SourceFile = '\\S16-JB\Share\S16-02.xml'
            DesitnationFile = 'C:\Scripts\Unattend.xml'
        }
    )
}
Configuration FileCopyConfiguration
{
    Param
    (
        [Parameter(Mandatory)]
        [pscredential] $Credential
    )

    Import-DscResource -ModuleName PSDesiredStateConfiguration

    Node $AllNodes.NodeName
    {
```

```
    File FileCopyDemo
    {
        SourcePath = $Node.SourceFile
        DestinationPath = $Node.Destinationfile
        Type = 'File'
        Credential = $Credential
        Force = $true

    }

  }

}


FileCopyConfiguration -Credential (Get-Credential) -ConfigurationData
$configurationData
```

Don't compile this yet; there are a few things we should discuss in the above example.

In the $configurationData hashtable, you have data defined for two nodes each as a separate hashtable under the AllNodes array. Each node hashtable has the mandatory NodeName key along with other custom keys such as the SourceFile and DestinationFile. You can have any number of such custom keys in each of these hashtables. Observe that you don't have the NonNodeData key in the configuration data. You will come to that in a later section of this chapter.

Now, to access this configuration data inside the resource configuration, you need to first use the $AllNodes automatic variable. The $AllNodes automatic variable provides access to the data you defined within each hashtable.

In a normal configuration document, a target node's computer name follows the Node keyword. But, when you use the configuration data, you use $AllNodes.NodeName. This works like an iterator and provides access to the keys you define inside the AllNodes hashtables. To access the hashtable key values inside the resource instance definition, you need to use the $Node automatic variables. This is roughly equivalent to writing an iterator like foreach ($Node in $AllNodes) { #Do something }.

If you look at the hashtables in the AllNodes array, you have the DestinationFile key with the same value listed in each hashtable. This is redundant and there is, of course, a way to optimize this. Here is an updated example:

```
$configurationData =
@{
    AllNodes =
    @(
        @{
            NodeName = '*'
            DestinationFile = 'C:\Scripts\Unattend.xml'
        },

        @{
            NodeName = 'S16-01'
            SourceFile = '\\S16-JB\Share\S16-01.xml'
        },

        @{
            NodeName = 'S16-02'
            SourceFile = '\\S16-JB\Share\S16-02.xml'
        }
    )
}

Configuration FileCopyConfiguration
{
    Param
    (
        [Parameter(Mandatory)]
        [pscredential] $Credential
    )

    Import-DscResource -ModuleName PSDesiredStateConfiguration

    Node $AllNodes.NodeName
    {
        File FileCopyDemo
        {
            SourcePath = $Node.SourceFile
            DestinationPath = $Node.Destinationfile
```

```
            Type = 'File'
            Credential = $Credential
            Force = $true
        }
    }
}

FileCopyConfiguration -Credential (Get-Credential) -ConfigurationData
$configurationData
```

In this example, you add one more hashtable to the AllNodes array and set the NodeName key to '*'. This indicates that any custom keys defined within this hashtable are available as a property with the $Node automatic variable. Therefore, you can now move the DestinationFile key as well since that is common across all nodes. And that is the exact change you did in this updated example.

Note   If there are keys with the same name in hashtables defined within NodeName='*' and other node specific hashtables, the explicit node hashtables take precedence. This is one way to override a few common settings when needed.

Coming back to the credentials aspect in your file configuration, you haven't specified yet in any of your examples how to deal with credentials.

PowerShell DSC can be forced (again, not recommended) to use plain-text passwords by setting a key called PSDscAllowPlainTextPassword to $true. But where do you add this key? A hint here: this key should be accessible across all nodes defined in the configuration data.

You might have easily guessed it. Yes, it needs to be in the hashtable where NodeName key is set to '*'. *Remember that you cannot have a configuration document with a few nodes with credentials and secure strings encrypted and others not encrypted. So, the* **PSDscAllowPlainTextPassword** *cannot be in any hashtable other than the one with* NodeName *set to* '*'.

Also, if you want to use domain credentials, you may want to set the PSDscAllowDomainUser key to $true as well. This will suppress any warning messages during the compile process if the supplied credentials have a \ format or have an '@' symbol in the user name. Once again, it is not recommended to use domain credentials in a PowerShell DSC configuration document. This is because any user with access to

the C:\Windows\System32\Configuration folder can look at the domain credentials
(encrypted or not) and use them for bad intent such as decrypting the credentials and
using them in any possible way to attack. Or the same encrypted credentials can be used
in another MOF to use the LCM to configure the system for malicious intent.

Here is the complete example:

```
$configurationData    =
@{
    AllNodes  =
    @(
        @{
            NodeName = '*'
            DestinationFile = 'C:\Scripts\Unattend.xml'
            PsDscAllowPlainTextPassword = $true
            PSDscAllowDomainUser = $true
        },
        @{
            NodeName = 'S16-01'
            SourceFile = '\\S16-JB\Share\S16-01.xml'
        },

        @{
            NodeName  =  'S16-02'
            SourceFile = '\\S16-JB\Share\S16-02.xml'
        }
    )
}

Configuration FileCopyConfiguration
{
    Param
    (
        [Parameter(Mandatory)]
        [pscredential] $Credential
    )

    Import-DscResource -ModuleName PSDesiredStateConfiguration
```

```
Node $AllNodes.NodeName
{
    File FileCopyDemo
    {
        SourcePath = $Node.SourceFile
        DestinationPath = $Node.Destinationfile
        Type = 'File'
        Credential = $Credential
        Force = $true
    }
}
}

FileCopyConfiguration -Credential (Get-Credential) -ConfigurationData
$configurationData
```

When you compile this configuration, you will see two MOF files generated, one for each node in the configuration data. This is shown in Figure 5-6.

```
FileCopyConfiguration -Credential (Get-Credential) -ConfigurationData $configurationData
cmdlet Get-Credential at command pipeline position 1
Supply values for the following parameters:


    Directory: C:\FileCopyConfiguration


Mode                LastWriteTime         Length Name
----                -------------         ------ ----
-a----        8/21/2017     3:52 PM          2422 S16-01.mof
-a----        8/21/2017     3:52 PM          2422 S16-02.mof
```

Figure 5-6. *Compiling MOF with configuration data*

The reason why you should not force plain-text passwords in a production environment becomes very clear if you look at the compiled MOF. Here is a snippet from one of the MOF files from my system:

```
/*
@TargetNode='S16-01'
@GeneratedBy=administrator
@GenerationDate=08/21/2017    16:03:18
@GenerationHost=S16-JB
*/
```

```
instance of MSFT_Credential as $MSFT_Credential1ref
{
Password = "P0wer$hell1234";
 UserName = "psdsc\\administrator";

};
```

Enacting this configuration will copy the files from remote UNC share to the target nodes.

Using PSDscRunAsCredential

What if a resource does not provide the Credential property to authenticate to remote resources? This is where the PSDscRunAsCredential property comes in handy.

Note   One thing that I realized while writing this section is that you can't use PSDscRunAsCredential with the File resource to authenticate to a remote share.

In Chapter 4, when exploring DSC resources, you looked at a way to retrieve resource properties. This was done using the Get-DscResourceProperty function provided in one of the examples. Figure 5-7 shows it again.

```
PS C:\> Get-DscResourceProperty -ModuleName PSDesiredStateConfiguration -ResourceName File | Format-Table

Name                  TypeConstraint  IsKey Mandatory Values                                     Range
----                  --------------  ----- --------- ------                                     -----
DependsOn             StringArray     False     False {}
PsDscRunAsCredential  MSFT_Credential False     False {}
DestinationPath       String          True       True {}
Ensure                String          False     False {Present, Absent}
Type                  String          False     False {File, Directory}
SourcePath            String          False     False {}
Contents              String          False     False {}
Checksum              String          False     False {SHA-1, SHA-256, SHA-512, CreatedDate...}
Recurse               Boolean         False     False {}
Force                 Boolean         False     False {}
Credential            MSFT_Credential False     False {}
Attributes            StringArray     False     False {ReadOnly, Hidden, System, Archive}
MatchSource           Boolean         False     False {}
```

Figure 5-7. *File resource properties*

As shown in Figure 5-7, two properties, DependsOn and PSDscRunAsCredential, are added to each DSC resource in the system. You learned about using the DependsOn property in the previous chapter. The PSDscRunAsCredential property can be used to change the user context in which DSC enacts the resource instance configuration. Let's look an updated version of the earlier Script resource example again:

```
$configurationData =
@{
    AllNodes  =
    @(
        @{
            NodeName = 'S16-01' PsDscAllowPlainTextPassword = $true
            PSDscAllowDomainUser = $true
        }
    )
}

Configuration DSCRunDemo
{
    Param
    (
        [Parameter(Mandatory)]
        [pscredential] $Credential
    )

    Import-DscResource -ModuleName PSDesiredStateConfiguration

    Node $AllNodes.NodeName
    {
        Script DSCRunDemo1
        {
            SetScript  =
            {
                Write-Verbose -Message $(whoami)
            }
            TestScript =
            {
```

```
            return $false
        }
        GetScript =
        {
            return @{}
        }
        PSDscRunAsCredential = $Credential
    }
  }
}

DSCRunDemo -configurationData $configurationData -Credential
(Get-Credential)
```

This is similar to what you saw earlier in this chapter except that you use the configuration data and set the PSDscRunAsCredential property in the script resource.

By setting the PSDscRunAsCredential within a resource instance definition, you are instructing DSC to enact that resource instance's configuration in the context of credentials supplied. Figure 5-8 shows what you see when you enact this configuration.

```
PS C:\> Start-DscConfiguration -Path .\DSCRunDemo -Verbose -Wait -Force
VERBOSE: Perform operation 'Invoke CimMethod' with following parameters, ''methodName' = SendConfigurationApply,'className' = MSF
T_DSCLocalConfigurationManager,'namespaceName' = root/Microsoft/Windows/DesiredStateConfiguration'.
VERBOSE: An LCM method call arrived from computer S16-JB with user sid S-1-5-21-689661094-3032901192-2251061677-500.
VERBOSE: [S16-01]: LCM:  [ Start  Set      ]
VERBOSE: [S16-01]: LCM:  [ Start  Resource ] [[Script]DSCRunDemo1]
VERBOSE: [S16-01]: LCM:  [ Start  Test     ] [[Script]DSCRunDemo1]
VERBOSE: [S16-01]: LCM:  [ End    Test     ] [[Script]DSCRunDemo1]  in 0.5480 seconds.
VERBOSE: [S16-01]: LCM:  [ Start  Set      ] [[Script]DSCRunDemo1]
VERBOSE: [S16-01]:                            [[Script]DSCRunDemo1] Performing the operation "Set-TargetResource" on target "Exec
uting the SetScript with the user supplied credential".
VERBOSE: [S16-01]:                            [[Script]DSCRunDemo1] psdsc\administrator
VERBOSE: [S16-01]: LCM:  [ End    Set      ] [[Script]DSCRunDemo1]  in 0.1410 seconds.
VERBOSE: [S16-01]: LCM:  [ End    Resource ] [[Script]DSCRunDemo1]
VERBOSE: [S16-01]: LCM:  [ End    Set      ]
VERBOSE: [S16-01]: LCM:  [ End    Set      ]  in  0.7980 seconds.
VERBOSE: Operation 'Invoke CimMethod' complete.
VERBOSE: Time taken for configuration job to complete is 0.905 seconds
```

Figure 5-8. *Script resource with PSDscRunAsCredential*

See the difference in output between Figure 5-3 and Figure 5-8? In Figure 5-8, you can see that whoami.exe returns psdsc\administrator as the username. So, using this method, you can enforce DSC to use different user credentials and context for enacting a resource instance's configuration.

Let's extend the above example to add one more Script resource but only one instance of the Script resource configured with PSDscRunAsCredential property:

```
$configurationData =
@{
    AllNodes =
    @(
        @{
            NodeName = 'S16-01' PsDscAllowPlainTextPassword = $true
            PSDscAllowDomainUser = $true
        }
    )
}

Configuration DSCRunDemo
{
    Param
    (
        [Parameter(Mandatory)]
        [pscredential] $Credential
    )

    Import-DscResource -ModuleName PSDesiredStateConfiguration

    Node $AllNodes.NodeName
    {
        Script DSCRunDemo1
        {
            SetScript =
            {
                Write-Verbose -Message $(whoami)
            }
            TestScript =
            {
                return $false
            }
```

```
                GetScript =
                {
                    return @{}
                }
                PsDscRunAsCredential = $Credential
        }

        Script DSCRunDemo2
        {
            SetScript  =
            {
                Write-Verbose -Message $(whoami)
            }
            TestScript =
            {
                return $false
            }
            GetScript =
            {
                return @{}
            }
        }
    }
}
}
```

```
DSCRunDemo -ConfigurationData $configurationData -Credential (Get-Credential)
```

Try to compile and enact this configuration. What do you see? An error. This is shown in Figure 5-9.

```
PS C:\> Start-DscConfiguration -Path .\DSCRunDemo -Wait -Force -Verbose
VERBOSE: Perform operation 'Invoke CimMethod' with following parameters, ''methodName' = SendConfigurationApply,'className' = MSF
T_DSCLocalConfigurationManager,'namespaceName' = root/Microsoft/Windows/DesiredStateConfiguration'.
VERBOSE: An LCM method call arrived from computer S16-JB with user sid S-1-5-21-689661094-3032901192-2251061677-500.
VERBOSE: [S16-01]: LCM:  [ Start  Set     ]
VERBOSE: [S16-01]: LCM:  [ End    Set     ]
The resources ('[Script]DSCRunDemo1' and '[Script]DSCRunDemo2') have conflicting values of the following properties:
'PsDscRunAsCredential'. Ensure that their values match.
    + CategoryInfo          : ResourceExists: (root/Microsoft/...gurationManager:String) [], CimException
    + FullyQualifiedErrorId : MI RESULT 11
    + PSComputerName        : S16-01

VERBOSE: Operation 'Invoke CimMethod' complete.
VERBOSE: Time taken for configuration job to complete is 0.211 seconds
```

Figure 5-9. *Conflicting PSDscRunAsCredential values*

This is a compile-time error in Windows Server 2016 before Windows Server version 1709. It is therefore preferred to author and compile configurations on Windows Server version 1709 over earlier versions so you don't have to work around this issue.

If you can't compile on Windows Server 2016 version 1709, the workaround is to either have all resource instances with the same PSDscRunAsCredential value or none at all but keep in mind that this will give a very different end result.

What if all resource instances (same or different) configuration documents require to be run as the same user using PSDscRunAsCredential? For this, you can either add the PSDscRunAsCredential automatic property in all resource instances or specify this as a parameter for the configuration command.

Here is an updated example that does not use PSDscRunAsCredential in the resource instance definition:

```
$configurationData =
@{
    AllNodes =
    @(
        @{
            NodeName = 'S16-01' PsDscAllowPlainTextPassword = $true
            PSDscAllowDomainUser = $true
        }
    )
}

Configuration DSCRunDemo
{
    Import-DscResource -ModuleName PSDesiredStateConfiguration

    Node $AllNodes.NodeName
    {
        Script DSCRunDemo1
        {
            SetScript =
            {
                Write-Verbose -Message $(whoami)
            }
            TestScript =
```

```
        {
            return $false
        }
        GetScript =
        {
            return @{}
        }
    }

    Script DSCRunDemo2
    {
        SetScript =
        {
            Write-Verbose -Message $(whoami)
        }
        TestScript =
        {
            return $false
        }
        GetScript =
        {
            return  @{}
        }
    }
}
}

DSCRunDemo -ConfigurationData $configurationData -PsDscRunAsCredential
(Get-Credential)
```

Observe how you are compiling the configuration in the above example.
PSDscRunAsCredential, similar to ConfigurationData, is another automatic parameter
added to the configuration commands. However, using this parameter with the
configuration command can have unintended consequences since the runas credential
will be used for all resources in the configuration.

Try It   Use the method you saw earlier to investigate the parameters available on a configuration command. Do you see the `PSDscRunAsCredential` parameter?

Therefore, compiling and enacting this will show the same username in both resource instance enact processes. This is shown in Figure 5-10.

```
PS C:\> Start-DscConfiguration -Path .\DSCRunDemo -Wait -Verbose -Force
VERBOSE: Perform operation 'Invoke CimMethod' with following parameters, ''methodName' = SendConfigurationApply,'className' = MSF
T_DSCLocalConfigurationManager,'namespaceName' = root/Microsoft/Windows/DesiredStateConfiguration'.
VERBOSE: An LCM method call arrived from computer S16-JB with user sid S-1-5-21-689661094-3032901192-2251061677-500.
VERBOSE: [S16-01]: LCM:  [ Start  Set     ]
VERBOSE: [S16-01]: LCM:  [ Start  Resource ]    [[Script]DSCRunDemo1]
VERBOSE: [S16-01]: LCM:  [ Start  Test    ]    [[Script]DSCRunDemo1]
VERBOSE: [S16-01]: LCM:  [ End    Test    ]    [[Script]DSCRunDemo1]  in 0.5630 seconds.
VERBOSE: [S16-01]: LCM:  [ Start  Set     ]    [[Script]DSCRunDemo1]
VERBOSE: [S16-01]:                            [[Script]DSCRunDemo1] Performing the operation "Set-TargetResource" on target "Exec
uting the SetScript with the user supplied credential".
VERBOSE: [S16-01]:                            [[Script]DSCRunDemo1] psdsc\administrator
VERBOSE: [S16-01]: LCM:  [ End    Set     ]    [[Script]DSCRunDemo1]  in 0.1560 seconds.
VERBOSE: [S16-01]: LCM:  [ End    Resource ]    [[Script]DSCRunDemo1]
VERBOSE: [S16-01]: LCM:  [ Start  Resource ]    [[Script]DSCRunDemo2]
VERBOSE: [S16-01]: LCM:  [ Start  Test    ]    [[Script]DSCRunDemo2]
VERBOSE: [S16-01]: LCM:  [ End    Test    ]    [[Script]DSCRunDemo2]  in 0.0940 seconds.
VERBOSE: [S16-01]: LCM:  [ Start  Set     ]    [[Script]DSCRunDemo2]
VERBOSE: [S16-01]:                            [[Script]DSCRunDemo2] Performing the operation "Set-TargetResource" on target "Exec
uting the SetScript with the user supplied credential".
VERBOSE: [S16-01]:                            [[Script]DSCRunDemo2] psdsc\administrator
VERBOSE: [S16-01]: LCM:  [ End    Set     ]    [[Script]DSCRunDemo2]  in 0.1090 seconds.
VERBOSE: [S16-01]: LCM:  [ End    Resource ]    [[Script]DSCRunDemo2]
VERBOSE: [S16-01]: LCM:  [ End    Set     ]
VERBOSE: [S16-01]: LCM:  [ End    Set     ]    in  1.3280 seconds.
VERBOSE: Operation 'Invoke CimMethod' complete.
```

Figure 5-10.   *Using PSDscRunAsCredential during MOF compilation*

This concludes our discussion on using configuration data and forcing plain-text credentials in DSC configuration documents. However, this is not a recommended or a secure method, as mentioned, especially when the compiled MOF files are staged on a pull server share or pull service configuration repository. If you remember the DSC feature discussion from Chapter 2, the MOF files (at rest) on the target node (running WMF 5.1 or above) are always encrypted. This should be considered only an obfuscation (through encryption) of configuration MOF files but not a measure towards encrypting credentials in a MOF. The right method to securing credentials in a configuration document is to use certificate-based encryption. Let's dive into that.

Using Certificates to Encrypt Credentials

Securing credentials in PowerShell DSC the right way requires encryption certificates. The error message shown in Figure 4-5 has a link to an article written by PowerShell team about how to secure credentials in PowerShell DSC configuration documents. Here it is for easy reference: http://go.microsoft.com/fwlink/?LinkId=393729.

Before you can start securing credentials in DSC configurations, there are a few prerequisites that must be met:

- You must generate encryption certificates and copy the public keys to the authoring station.

- You must configure the target node LCM to use the certificate to decrypt credentials.

- You must author a configuration document that uses credential encryption.

Generating Encryption Certificates

First and foremost, an encryption certificate is needed for securing credentials. If you have a Certificate Authority (CA) in the infrastructure, this is the most preferred way. However, a self-signed certificate is good enough since this is only credential encryption and not authentication. But be aware that self-signed certificates are a management nightmare. Unlike a complete public key infrastructure (PKI), with self-signed certificates there is management overhead in terms of storing, constraining the usage, and auditing of usage.

Installing and configuring a CA is certainly outside the scope of this chapter (and book!). If you have a CA already, go ahead and ensure that the target nodes where you plan to try the examples have an encryption certificate installed. If not, read on. You will look at creating a self-signed certificate for the purpose of credential encryption.

Note   This section assumes that you have prior understanding of different certificate types and have experience in creating certificates. If you have a certificate authority in your infrastructure, you can skip this section and proceed to next section on configuring the target node LCM to use certificates for credential decryption.

There are two ways you can generate a self-signed certificate.

- Generate the certificate on the authoring station, and copy and install the entire certificate pair on the target node.

- Generate the certificate on the target node, and export and copy only the public key to the authoring station.

The documentation link at the beginning of this section explains these methods in-depth. Therefore, I will not repeat that info here; instead, I will walk you through a function that generates these certificates on the target nodes and copies over the public key and thumbprint to the authoring station. This is the recommended method since the private key stays on the target node.

Note   The following function uses the New-SelfSignedCertificate cmdlet with desired functionality for this example and is available only in Windows Server 2016 and above. If you are trying self-signed certificate generation on a low-level operating system such as Windows Server 2012 R2, you can try the New-SelfSignedCertificateEx function available from the TechNet script center (http://azrs.tk/newSscert).

```
function New-DscCredentialCertificate
{
    [CmdletBinding()]
    param
    (
        [Parameter(Mandatory)] [String]
        $AuthoringStation,

        [Parameter(Mandatory)] [String]
        $PublicKeyPath
    )

    #Generating a new certificate and exporting the public key
    Write-Verbose -Message "Generating a new encryption certificate for
    computer ${env:ComputerName}"
    $certificate = New-SelfSignedCertificate -Type DocumentEncryption
    CertLegacyCsp -DnsName ${env:ComputerName} -HashAlgorithm SHA256
```

```
$null = $certificate | Export-Certificate -FilePath "${env:Temp}\${env:
ComputerName}.cer" -Force

#Copying public key to authoring station
Write-Verbose -Message "Creating a new PS Session to ${AuthoringStation}"
$psSession = New-PSSession -ComputerName $AuthoringStation

try
{
    #Ensure the target path exists on authoring station
    Write-Verbose -Message "Copying public key to ${AuthoringStation}"
    Invoke-Command -Session $psSession -ScriptBlock {
            if (-not (test-Path -Path $using:PublicKeyPath))
            {
                $null = New-Item -Path $using:PublicKeyPath -ItemType
                Directory -Force
            }
    }

    Copy-Item -ToSession $psSession -Path "${env:Temp}\${env:Computer
    Name}.cer" -Destination "${PublicKeyPath}\${env:ComputerName}.cer"
    -Force
}
finally
{
    Remove-PSSession -Session $psSession
}
}
```

I use this function on the DSC target nodes in my lab. This function generates a new encryption certificate, exports the public key, and copies over the public key to the authoring station. Here is how you use it:

```
# AuthoringStation - Computer name of the system where you are authoring
DSC configurations.
# PublicKeyPath - A local folder on the authoring station to copy the
public key files.
```

```
New-DscCredentialCertificate -AuthoringStation S16-JB -PublicKeyPath C:\
PublicKeys -Verbose
```

Figure 5-11 shows this function in action.

```
PS C:\> New-DscCredentialCertificate -AuthoringStation S16-JB -PublicKeyPath C:\PublicKeys -Verbose
VERBOSE: Generating a new encryption certificate for computer S16-01
VERBOSE: Creating a new PS Session to S16-JB
VERBOSE: Copying public key to S16-JB
```

Figure 5-11. *Generating an encryption certificate and copying the public key*

I have run this function on a few systems in my lab and Figure 5-12 shows the copied public keys on the authoring station.

```
PS C:\> Get-ChildItem -Path C:\PublicKeys


    Directory: C:\PublicKeys


Mode                LastWriteTime         Length Name
----                -------------         ------ ----
-a----        8/26/2017   11:56 AM            778 S16-01.cer
-a----        8/26/2017   11:45 AM            778 S16-02.cer
-a----        8/26/2017   11:51 AM            793 S16-PULL-01.cer
-a----        8/26/2017   11:51 AM            793 S16-PULL-02.cer
```

Figure 5-12. *Public keys of DSC target nodes*

Configuring the Target Node LCM to Use Certificates for Decryption

Once a certificate is created (or enrolled using a PKI) on the target node, you can configure the LCM on the target node to use the newly created encryption certificate for any credential decryption. This can be done by creating a meta configuration and enacting it on the target node.

The property that you need to update in the LCM configuration is the CertificateID property. It needs to be configured using the Settings meta resource you saw in Chapter 3. The value for the CertificateID property is the thumbprint of the encryption certificate that you just created on the target node.

Here is how to do this:

```
#Get the certificate thumbprint
$requiredCertificate = Get-ChildItem -Path Cert:\LocalMachine\My |
```

```
                    Where-Object {
                        ($_.Subject -eq "CN=${env:COMPUTERNAME}") -and `
                        ($_.EnhancedKeyUsageList.FriendlyName -contains
                        'Document Encryption')
                    }

#Define meta configuration
[DscLocalConfigurationManager()]
Configuration CertificateConfig
{
    Settings
    {
        CertificateID = $requiredCertificate.Thumbprint
    }
}

#Compile meta configuration
CertificateConfig -OutputPath C:\LCMConfig -verbose

#Enact LCM Configuration
Set-DscLocalConfigurationManager -Path C:\LCMConfig -Force -Verbose
```

The first non-comment statement in this code snippet retrieves the certificate whose subject matches the local computername and the EKU list contains document encryption.

The subsequent statements in the snippet generate the meta configuration, compile it, and enact it. Once the enact is complete, you can verify that the CertificateID property is set to the value of the $requiredCertificate.Thumbprint by using the Get-DscLocalConfigurationManager command. Figure 5-13 shows this from one of the target nodes in my lab.

```
PS C:\> Get-DscLocalConfigurationManager

ActionAfterReboot                : ContinueConfiguration
AgentId                          : 7FE8E864-8101-11E7-B423-00155D87B207
AllowModuleOverWrite             : False
CertificateID                    : E62AAD02E93E8C3082E96AA408032D0325C23FD6
ConfigurationDownloadManagers    : {}
ConfigurationID                  :
ConfigurationMode                : ApplyAndMonitor
ConfigurationModeFrequencyMins   : 15
Credential                       :
DebugMode                        : {NONE}
DownloadManagerCustomData        :
DownloadManagerName              :
LCMCompatibleVersions            : {1.0, 2.0}
LCMState                         : Idle
LCMStateDetail                   :
LCMVersion                       : 2.0
StatusRetentionTimeInDays        : 10
SignatureValidationPolicy        : NONE
SignatureValidations             : {}
MaximumDownloadSizeMB            : 500
PartialConfigurations            :
RebootNodeIfNeeded               : False
RefreshFrequencyMins             : 30
RefreshMode                      : PUSH
ReportManagers                   : {}
ResourceModuleManagers           : {}
PSComputerName                   :
```

Figure 5-13. *LCM settings after configuring CertificateID*

Since the public keys for all nodes are available on the authoring station, the certificate thumbprints needed for the credential and secure string encryption can be retrieved using the following code snippet:

```
foreach ($item in (Get-ChildItem -Path C:\PublicKeys -Filter *.cer))
{
    $cert = [System.Security.Cryptography.X509Certificates.
    X509Certificate2]::new()
    $cert.Import($item.FullName)
    $cert
}
```

This example code will iterate over all available public keys within the C:\PublicKeys folder and retrieve the thumbprint and subject name for each public key. Figure 5-14 shows this example in action.

```
Thumbprint                                Subject
----------                                -------
E62AAD02E93E8C3082E96AA408032D0325C23FD6  CN=S16-01
D8E5C883024F0E5189F8DD5DD88324C2B16551AC  CN=S16-PULL-02
CB4F93FA0A1E26174A35FBD597941297FCD7DDA3  CN=S16-PULL-01
BA3F5815EE05D2D60DF08C6A40F623E9F1E27FC1  CN=S16-02
```

Figure 5-14. *Thumbprints from public keys on the authoring station*

Authoring a Configuration Document to Use Certificates

Now that you have the right infrastructure in place to encrypt the credentials in a configuration document, let's see how to do it. There is, in fact, not much that you don't know. You already learned about the configuration data usage in PowerShell DSC; for credential encryption you just need to implement two additional keys in the node data to let the configuration compiling process know which public key to use for credential encryption.

Here is how the configuration data from one of the earlier examples needs to be changed to enable credential encryption:

```
$configurationData =
@{
    AllNodes  =
    @(
        @{
            NodeName = 'S16-01'
            CertificateFile = 'C:\publicKeys\S16-01.cer'
            Thumbprint = 'E62AAD02E93E8C3082E96AA408032D0325C23FD6'
            PsDscAllowDomainUser = $true
        }
    )
}

Configuration DSCRunDemo
{
    Param
    (
        [Parameter(Mandatory)]
        [psCredential] $Credential
    )
```

```
Import-DscResource -ModuleName PSDesiredStateConfiguration

Node $AllNodes.NodeName
{
    Script DSCRunDemo
    {
        SetScript =
        {
            Write-Verbose -Message $(whoami)
        }
        TestScript =
        {
            return $false
        }
        GetScript =
        {
            return @{}
        }
        PSDscRunAsCredential = $Credential
    }
}
}

DSCRunDemo -configurationData $configurationData -Credential $Credential
```

As you see in this example, within the node data hashtable for S16-01, you specify the CertificateFile key and set it to the path where node's public key is stored. And, the second one you added is the Thumbprint key whose value is the thumbprint value associated with node's public key. This is shown in Figure 5-14.

A node data hashtable, like the one shown in the above example, needs to be specified for every node that needs to receive the encrypted credentials. Let's compile this configuration and take a look at the resulting MOF.

As shown in Figure 5-15, if the credential encryption is successful, you will see the password as encrypted string in the compiled MOF file.

```
/*
@TargetNode='S16-01'
@GeneratedBy=Administrator
@GenerationDate=08/26/2017 21:30:37
@GenerationHost=S16-JB
*/

instance of MSFT_Credential as $MSFT_Credential1ref
{
Password = "-----BEGIN CMS-----\nMIIBmQYJKoZIhvcNAQcDoIIBijCCAYYCAQAxggFBMIIBPQIBADAlMBExDzANl
 UserName = "psdsc\\administrator";

};
```

Figure 5-15. *Encrypted password in the compiled MOF*

Note   CMS encryption is used in DSC v2. The MOF files complied with this encryption can't be used on systems with DSC v1 and vice versa.

This concludes the discussion on securing credentials and secure strings in DSC configurations. There are still a few things you need to know about using configuration data.

Separating Configuration Data from Environment Data

Configuration data forms the basis of separating environmental data from node configuration data. To better understand this, let's look at an example:

```
Configuration WebDBDemo
{
    Import-DscResource -ModuleName PsDscResources -Name Archive
    Import-DscResource -ModuleName PSDesiredStateConfiguration -Name
    WindowsFeature

    Node @('WebServer01', 'WebServer02', 'WebServer03', 'WebServer04')
    {
        WindowsFeature WebServer
```

```
    {
        Name = 'Web-Server'
        IncludeAllSubFeature = $true
        Ensure = 'Present'
    }

    Archive SetupScripts
    {
        Path = '\\S16-JB\Share\Websetup.zip'
        Destination = 'C:\Scripts'
        Force = $true
    }
}

Node @('DBServer01','DBServer02')
{

    WindowsFeature NET35
    {
        Name = 'NET-Framework-Core'
        Source = '\\S16-JB\Share\S160S\Sources\Sxs'
        Ensure = 'Present'
    }

    Archive  SetupScripts
    {
        Path = '\\S16-JB\Share\DBSetupScripts.zip'
        Destination = 'C:\Scripts'
        Force = $true
    }
  }
}
```

In this example, you have node configuration for four nodes that are web servers and two DB servers. For the web server nodes, you have two resources, WindowsFeature and Archive, being configured. And, for the DB server nodes, you are installing the .NET Framework 3.5 from a UNC share and also copying the DB scripts from a zip archive available at a UNC path.

What if some of these nodes are used for a development environment and some in production? What if you want the development servers to deploy the most recent build of web scripts while production gets only the stable build? Each resource across these nodes has some common configuration and some that is very specific to the node. As you might have guessed it, there is still room for optimizing this configuration script and using configuration data here. Let's see what the configuration data might look like in this case.

First, construct the configuration data:

```
@{
AllNodes =
    @(
        @{
            NodeName = '*'
            ScriptDestinationPath = 'C:\Scripts'
            OSSourcePath = '\\S16-JB\Share\S16OS\Sources\Sxs'
        }
        @{
            NodeName = 'WebServer01'
            Role = 'WebServer'
            Environment = 'Production'
        }
        @{
            NodeName = 'WebServer02'
            Role = 'WebServer'
            Environment = 'Production'
        }
        @{
            NodeName = 'WebServer03'
            Role = 'WebServer'
            Environment = 'Development'
        }
        @{
            NodeName = 'WebServer04'
            Role = 'WebServer'
            Environment = 'Development'
        }
```

```
    @{
        NodeName = 'DBServer01'
        Role = 'DBServer'
        Environment = 'Production'
    }
    @{
        NodeName = 'DBServer02'
        Role = 'DBServer'
        Environment = 'Development'
    }
)

EnvironmentData  =
@{
    'WebServer' = @{
        'Production' = @{
            'ScriptsPath' = '\\S16-JB\Share\Websetup-Prod.zip'
        }
        'Development' = @{
            'ScriptsPath' = '\\S16-JB\Share\Websetup-Dev.zip'
        }
    }

    'DBServer' = @{
        'Production' = @{
            'ScriptsPath' = '\\S16-JB\Share\DBsetup-Prod.zip'
        }
        'Development' = @{
            'ScriptsPath' = '\\S16-JB\Share\DBsetup-Dev.zip'
        }
    }
}
}
```

In this configuration data, you define roles for each of the servers and define the data specific to the production and development environments in a hashtable that is associated with the server role within which you have environment-specific settings.

The non-node data named EnvironmentData helps you define the settings that differ from production to development. Since the destination path for the script extraction is same across all environments, you put that property under NodeName='*' so that it is available for all nodes during compilation.

You can save this configuration data hashtable as a PowerShell data file (.psd1) and use it while compiling the configuration.

Tip   If you want to quickly validate if the configuration data hashtable you built is correct or not, you can use the Import-PowerShellDataFile cmdlet in WMF 5.0 and above.

Let's now update the configuration document to use the configuration data:

```
Configuration WebDBDemo
{
    Import-DscResource -ModuleName PsDscResources -Name Archive
    Import-DscResource -ModuleName PSDesiredStateConfiguration
    -Name WindowsFeature

    #Add what is specific to web server role
    Node $AllNodes.Where{$_.Role -eq 'WebServer'}.NodeName
    {
        WindowsFeature WebServer
        {
            Name = 'Web-Server'
            IncludeAllSubFeature = $true
            Ensure = 'Present'
        }
    }

    #Add what is specific to DB server role
    Node $AllNodes.Where{$_.Role -eq 'DBServer'}.NodeName
    {
        WindowsFeature  NET35
        {
            Name = 'NET-Framework-Core'
```

```
        Source = $Node.OSSourcePath
        Ensure = 'Present'
    }
}

#Add configuration that is common across but may have separate
environment data
Node $AllNodes.NodeName
{

    $NodeRole = $Node.Role
    $NodeEnvironment = $Node.Environment

    Archive   SetupScripts
    {
        Path = $ConfigurationData.EnvironmentData.$NodeRole.
        $NodeEnvironment.ScriptsPath
        Destination = $Node.ScriptDestinationPath
        Force = $true
    }
  }
}

WebDBDemo -ConfigurationData C:\Scripts\ConfigurationData.psd1   -Verbose
```

As you can see from this updated configuration document, there are two conditions that check for the role of the nodes and add necessary Windows feature configurations. For the script archive extraction, you use the environment-specific data defined in the configuration data. Notice how the EnvironmentData is accessed. You use the $ConfigurationData parameter passed on as an argument to the configuration script and access EnvironmentData as its property. Since the $Node automatic variable contains the Role and Environment configuration for each node, you can avail those values to get to the right ScriptsPath value for the node.

```
PS C:\> .\Scripts\WebDBConfig.ps1


    Directory: C:\WebDBDemo


Mode                LastWriteTime         Length Name
----                -------------         ------ ----
-a----        11/9/2017   12:36 PM          2688 WebServer01.mof
-a----        11/9/2017   12:36 PM          2688 WebServer02.mof
-a----        11/9/2017   12:36 PM          2686 WebServer03.mof
-a----        11/9/2017   12:36 PM          2686 WebServer04.mof
-a----        11/9/2017   12:36 PM          2666 DBServer01.mof
-a----        11/9/2017   12:36 PM          2664 DBServer02.mof
```

Figure 5-16. *Compiled configurations with configuration data*

Figure 5-16 shows the compiled configurations. You can open any of the generated MOFs to see if the configuration is generated based on the environmental data specified in the configuration data file. Here is a snippet from what is generated on my system:

```
instance of MSFT_RoleResource as $MSFT_RoleResource1ref
{
ResourceID = "[WindowsFeature]WebServer";
 IncludeAllSubFeature = True;
 Ensure = "Present";
 SourceInfo = "C:\\Scripts\\WebDBConfig.ps1::9::9::WindowsFeature";
 Name = "Web-Server";
 ModuleName = "PSDesiredStateConfiguration";

ModuleVersion = "1.0";

 ConfigurationName = "WebDBDemo";

};
instance of MSFT_Archive as $MSFT_Archive1ref
{
ResourceID = "[Archive]SetupScripts";
 Path = "\\\\S16-JB\\Share\\Websetup-Prod.zip";
 Destination = "C:\\Scripts";
 SourceInfo = "C:\\Scripts\\WebDBConfig.ps1::34::9::Archive";
 Force = True;
```

```
ModuleName = "PSDscResources";
ModuleVersion = "2.8.0.0";

ConfigurationName = "WebDBDemo";

};
```

Creating Reusable Configurations

Chapter 4 contained an example where you added parameters to configuration documents. This, in turn, made the configuration document a reusable one. You can compile the configuration with different parameter values to generate MOF documents for different nodes. This is just one method of making DSC configuration documents reusable. You can use the configuration data construct as well to achieve the same goal.

You just saw an example where you achieved some level of reusability by moving the configuration data into a separate data file. In all of the examples so far, you have a single configuration script that defines the configuration that has to be managed on target system(s). So, depending on the number of resources you add to this script, it can become quite big and cumbersome to manage. This is where nested configurations help to simplify authoring complex configuration scripts.

Nested Configurations

Nested configurations (a.k.a composite configurations) are configurations that wrap around other configurations. In this section, you will learn how to create nested configurations and see how this can help take the configuration reusability to a next level. To understand this, you will start with an example. You will begin with the configuration data first:

```
@{
    AllNodes = @(
        @{
            NodeName="*"
            SourcePath = "C:\Temp\Generic-Scripts.zip"
            Destination = "C:\Deployment\Scripts"
        }
```

```
        @{
            NodeName="WebServer01"
            Role = "Web"
            Force = 'False'
        }

        @{
            NodeName="DBServer01"
            Role = "Database"
            Force = 'True'
        }

        @{
            NodeName="WebServer03"
            Force = 'False'
        }
    )

    DBConfig = @{
        SourcePath = "C:\Temp\Database-Scripts.zip"
        ServiceToCheck = "MSSQLSERVER"
    }

    WebConfig  =  @{
        SourcePath = "C:\Temp\WebServer-Scripts.zip"
        ServiceToCheck = "inetsrv"
    }
}
```

You saw the following example earlier, so let's build a nested configuration that uses this configuration data.

You will now build several small configurations to compose a larger nested configuration at the end. The first one you need is a web server configuration. This is simple; you just want to ensure that the Web-Server role is installed.

```
Configuration IIS
{
    Import-DscResource –ModuleName 'PSDesiredStateConfiguration'
```

```
    WindowsFeature WebServer
    {
        Name = 'Web-Server'
        IncludeAllSubFeature = $true
        Ensure  =  'Present'
    }
}
```

If you review the preceding configuration, you'll note that it doesn't have the Node block. The next configuration you need is a service check configuration. Based on the role of the target system, database, or web, you want to enforce a specific service into running state. This code shows how:

```
Configuration ServiceCheck {
    param
    (
        [Parameter(Mandatory)]
        [String] $Name
    )

    Import-DscResource -ModuleName 'PSDesiredStateConfiguration'
    Service $Name
    {
        Name = $Name
        State = 'Running'
    }
}
```

You parameterize this configuration so that it can be reused, based on the role, to provide a different set of input values. The third configuration you require is an Archive resource configuration that takes only the different input parameters and unpacks an archive. Once again, you have the parameters defined on this to make it reusable:

```
Configuration ArchiveUnpack {
    param
    (
        [Parameter(Mandatory)]
        [String]$Source,
```

```
        [Parameter(Mandatory)]
        [String] $Destination,

        [Parameter()]
        [Boolean] $Force = $false
    )

    Import-DscResource –ModuleName 'PSDesiredStateConfiguration'

    Archive Unpack
    {
        Path = $Source
        Destination = $Destination
        Force = $Force
    }
}
```

You can copy these configuration definitions into PS1 files and load them into memory. Once the configuration is loaded into memory, you can use the Get-Command cmdlet to see a list of configurations that are defined in the PS1 file (see Figure 5-17).

```
PS C:\> Get-Command -Name IIS, ArchiveUnpack, ServiceCheck

CommandType     Name                                          Version    Source
-----------     ----                                          -------    ------
Configuration   IIS
Configuration   ArchiveUnpack
Configuration   ServiceCheck
```

Figure 5-17. *Configurations in memory*

From Figure 5-17, you can see that the configuration documents from the PS1 loaded as configuration commands. You will now use these configuration commands in a larger configuration document:

```
Configuration NestedConfiguration {

    Node $AllNodes.NodeName
    {
        Switch ($Node.Role)
```

```
{
    'Web'
    {
        IIS IISInstall { }
        ServiceCheck SvcCheck
        {
            Name = $ConfigurationData.WebConfig.ServiceToCheck
        }

        ArchiveUnpack ExtractZip
        {
            Source = $ConfigurationData.WebConfig.SourcePath
            Destination = $Node.Destination
            Force = $False
        }
    }

    'Database'
    {
        ServiceCheck SvcCheck
        {
            Name = $ConfigurationData.DBConfig.ServiceToCheck
        }

        ArchiveUnpack ExtractZip
        {
            Source = $ConfigurationData.DBConfig.SourcePath
            Destination = $Node.Destination
            Force = $true
        }
    }

    Default
    {
        ArchiveUnpack ExtractZip
```

```
                {
                        Source = $Node.SourcePath
                        Destination = $Node.Destination
                        Force = $true
                }
            }
        }
    }
}
```

When you compile the configuration with the configuration data shown at the beginning of this example, you will see that there are three MOF files generated based on what is defined in the nested configurations.

This example illustrates that you can write individual parameterized configuration documents and then reuse them in a larger configuration document.

Note   With WMF 5.0 and above, you can use the DependsOn property within nested resource configuration. This was not possible in DSC v1.

Nested configurations are good. However, the way you have seen them so far is either packaging them in a PS1 file or just loading them into memory like any other PowerShell function. At some point, these PS1 files become unmanageable. One way to address this is to package these reusable configurations into DSC resource modules. In DSC, this is achieved using *composite resource modules*. Don't confuse them with *composite configurations*. These are modules and not just configurations. You will learn more about this after you understand how to write your own custom DSC resource modules in Chapter 6.

Summary

Through several examples in this chapter, you learned how to write advanced configurations that are reusable. DSC configurations can be parameterized like any PowerShell function and this brings in reusability. The configuration data construct in DSC provides a way to separate the environment data from node data. This helps you create configurations that use either unencrypted or encrypted credentials and also enables another way to create reusable configurations. You looked at wrapping or using configurations inside other configurations. This approach results in nested configurations (a.k.a composite resource configurations). In the next chapter, you will extend this knowledge to build composite resource modules in which nested configurations become a core concept and you'll also write custom DSC resource modules.

CHAPTER 6

Writing Composite and Custom DSC Resource Modules

I ended the previous chapter with a discussion about nested configurations and how they can be packaged as custom DSC resource modules, which are called composite resource modules. Also, in the last few chapters, you looked at how to use in-box and Microsoft- or community-developed custom DSC resource modules in your configuration documents. This collection of custom DSC resource modules available in the PowerShell gallery may or may not be sufficient for all your configuration management needs in your enterprise or IT organization. If not, you have to invest time and resources in writing your own custom DSC resource modules. There are many ways to write custom DSC resource modules. So, in this chapter, you will first look at the composite resource modules and then learn how to create your own custom DSC resource modules.

Lab Requirements

To try the examples and exercises in this chapter, you will need at minimum two or more systems with Windows Server 2008 R2 or above with WMF 5.1 installed. I recommend a system with Windows Server 2016.

© Ravikanth Chaganti 2018
R. Chaganti, *Pro PowerShell Desired State Configuration*, https://doi.org/10.1007/978-1-4842-3483-9_6

Composite Resource Modules

You know how to create nested configurations. Nested configurations let you use parameterized configuration functions inside other configuration documents. With the composite resource modules, you can package these nested configurations as resource modules that can be discovered using the Get-DscResource cmdlet. This requires a special folder structure and naming convention of the module file storing the parameterized configuration.

Let's start with the in-box composite resources and use them as an example to build your own composite resource.

```
Get-DscResource -Module PSDesiredStateConfiguration | Where-Object {
$_.ImplementedAs -eq 'Composite' }
```

Figure 6-1 shows the composite resources available in the in-box PSDesiredStateConfiguration module.

ImplementedAs	Name	ModuleName	Version	Properties
Composite	GroupSet	PSDesiredStateConfiguration	1.1	{DependsOn, PsDscRunAsCredential, GroupName, En...
Composite	ProcessSet	PSDesiredStateConfiguration	1.1	{DependsOn, PsDscRunAsCredential, Path, Credent...
Composite	ServiceSet	PSDesiredStateConfiguration	1.1	{DependsOn, PsDscRunAsCredential, Name, Startup...
Composite	WindowsFeatureSet	PSDesiredStateConfiguration	1.1	{DependsOn, PsDscRunAsCredential, Name, Ensure...}
Composite	WindowsOptionalFeatureSet	PSDesiredStateConfiguration	1.1	{DependsOn, PsDscRunAsCredential, Name, Ensure...}

Figure 6-1. *In-box composite resources*

In WMF 4.0, if you had to install multiple Windows roles and features using a DSC configuration document, you had to put multiple instances of the WindowsFeature resource. Here is an example:

```
Configuration HyperVNode
{
    Import-DscResource -ModuleName PSDesiredStateConfiguration
-ModuleVersion 1.0

    WindowsFeature Hyper-V
    {
        Name = 'Hyper-V'
        IncludeAllSubFeature = $true
        Ensure = 'Present'
    }
```

```
WindowsFeature FailoverCluster
{
    Name = 'Failover-Clustering'
    IncludeAllSubFeature = $true
    Ensure = 'Present'
}

WindowsFeature DataCenterBridging
{
    Name = 'Data-Center-Bridging'
    IncludeAllSubFeature = $true
    Ensure = 'Present'
}

WindowsFeature RSATHyper-V
{
    Name = 'RSAT-Hyper-V-Tools'
    Ensure = 'Present'
}

WindowsFeature RSATClustering
{
    Name = 'RSAT-Clustering'
    IncludeAllSubFeature = $true
    Ensure = 'Present'
}
}
```

This configuration script installs the roles and features needed for a Hyper-V cluster node. This can be really long and complex depending on the number of role and features and any other resource instances that you need to add. You can, of course, implement the role/feature names for a string array parameter in the configuration and use a foreach loop inside the configuration. This will simplify the configuration document to a few lines but this will work if you have similar resource instance such as in the example. However, there are better ways. And then you can use that as a nested configuration inside a large configuration document. However, this does not provide the discoverability available with the Get-DscResource cmdlet.

To enable scenarios like this where you need to install multiple roles and features in a configuration, WMF 5.0 implemented the WindowsFeatureSet in-box composite resource. Using this composite resource, the above configuration document can be simplified to a few lines:

```
Configuration HyperVNode
{
    Import-DscResource -ModuleName PSDesiredStateConfiguration
-ModuleVersion 1.1

    WindowsFeatureSet HyperVClusterNode
    {
        Name = @(
            'Hyper-V',
            'Failover-Clustering',
            'Data-Center-Bridging',
            'RSAT-Hyper-V-Tools',
            'RSAT-Clustering'
        )
        IncludeAllSubFeature = $true
        Ensure = 'Present'
    }
}
```

If you are curious about how the WindowsFeatureSet resource is implemented, take a look at the resource files at C:\Windows\system32\WindowsPowerShell\v1.0\ Modules\PSDesiredStateConfiguration\DSCResources\WindowsFeatureSet. Figure 6-2 shows the folder structure of this DSC resource.

```
tree /F /A (Get-DscResource -Module PSDesiredStateConfiguration -Name
WindowsFeatureSet).ParentPath
```

```
PS C:\> tree /F /A (Get-DscResource -Module PSDesiredStateConfiguration -Name WindowsFeatureSet).ParentPath
Folder PATH listing
Volume serial number is C8D6-C055
C:\WINDOWS\SYSTEM32\WINDOWSPOWERSHELL\V1.0\MODULES\PSDESIREDSTATECONFIGURATION\DSCRESOURCES\WINDOWSFEATURESET
    WindowsFeatureSet.psd1
    WindowsFeatureSet.Schema.psm1

No subfolders exist
```

Figure 6-2. *WindowsFeatureSet DSC resource*

As you can see in Figure 6-2, there are two files within that resource folder. `WindowsFeatureSet.Schema.psm1` contains the logic to generate a nested configuration definition and `WindowsFeatureSet.psd1` is a regular PowerShell module manifest.

Note   Open the `WindowsFeatureSet.Schema.psm1` in your favorite editor and examine the contents of the file. While the PowerShell team chose to implement the logic to generate the nested configuration, it is not necessary for you to implement composite resources the same way.

As you saw in Figure 6-1, there are other in-box composite resources in the `PSDesiredStateConfiguration` module. I suggest that you try out those resources as well.

From your learning so far, you understand that the composite resource modules can simplify the configuration document authoring and enable discoverability for the composite resources. And, you also understand that to be able to package a nested configuration as a composite resource module, you need to package the nested configuration in the form of a `resourceName.Schema.Psm1` file and add a module manifest file.

So, it's time for you to start creating your own composite resource module. For the purpose of this example, you will look at a very simple nested configuration. But I encourage you to experiment with creating of a few more composite resource modules.

Packaging a Composite Resource Module

Let's start with a sample parameterized configuration:

```
Configuration DisableLoopbackCheck
{
    Param
    (
        [Parameter(Mandatory = $true)]
        [Boolean]
        $Enable
    )
```

```
Import-DscResource -ModuleName PSDesiredStateConfiguration
-ModuleVersion 1.1

if ($Enable)
{
    $Ensure = 'Present'
}
else
{
    $Ensure = 'Absent'
}

Registry DefaultDomainName
{
    Key = 'HKEY_LOCAL_MACHINE\SYSTEM\CurrentControlSet\Control\Lsa'
    ValueName = 'DisableLoopbackCheck'
    ValueData = 1
    ValueType = 'DWord'
    Ensure = $Ensure
}
}
```

This configuration updates a registry key using the in-box Registry DSC resource. This is something many SharePoint developers implement on their development systems to allow access to the web server running on the same system using a fully-qualified domain name. Let's say you want to ensure that this configuration is available to all SharePoint developers and they can use it as a part of the larger configuration document that is used to build their development environment. Before you start packaging this configuration document as a composite resource module, let's create the necessary folder structure for the module:

```
New-Item -Path SharePointConfiguration\DSCResources\DisableLoopbackCheck
-ItemType Directory -Force
```

This creates the folder structure shown in Figure 6-3.

```
PS C:\scripts> tree /A /F SharePointConfiguration
Folder PATH listing
Volume serial number is C8D6-C055
C:\SCRIPTS\SHAREPOINTCONFIGURATION
\---DSCResources
    \---DisableLoopbackCheck
```

Figure 6-3. *Folder structure for the composite resource*

Since the configuration in your example is already parameterized, you can save this configuration as DisableLoopbackCheck.Schema.psm1 in the DisableLoopbackCheck folder you created just now. If you are using your own DSC configuration for this exercise, if you have a Node block in the configuration document, make sure you remove it. Composite resources can't contain a Node block since the configuration document where you want to use this composite resource will have the Node script block and the same node name will be passed on to the composite resource as well.

Once this is done, you can generate a module manifest for this resource:

```
$manifestParams = @{
    Path          = '.\SharePointConfiguration\DSCResources\
                     DisableLoopbackCheck\DisableLoopbackCheck.psd1'
    Author        = 'DSCFan'
    GUID          = (New-GUID).Guid
    RootModule    = 'DisableLoopbackCheck.Schema.psm1'
    ModuleVersion = '1.0.0.0'
    CompanyName   = 'The Awesome DSC Inc.'
}

New-ModuleManifest @manifestParams -Verbose
```

To generate the module manifest for the composite resource, you need provide the .Schema.psm1 file as the RootModule. Also, don't forget the ModuleVersion property. This will help you track the version of the composite resource being used in a configuration.

To complete this resource module creation, you need a module manifest for the top-level resource module itself; that is the SharePointConfigurationresource module.

```
$manifestParams = @{
    Path          = '.\SharePointConfiguration\SharePointConfiguration.
                     psd1'
    Author        = 'DSCFan'
    Description   = 'Composite DSC resources for SharePoint development
                     environment.'
    GUID          = (New-GUID).Guid
    ModuleVersion = '1.0.0.0'
    CompanyName   = 'The Awesome DSC Inc.'
}

New-ModuleManifest @manifestParams -Verbose
```

Unlike the resource manifest, you don't need the RootModule specification here for the composite module manifest. Both the top-level folder and the composite resources have the module manifest to ensure that the composite resource can load the Schema. psm1 file and the top-level module manifest ensures that the DSC composite resource in the module is exported.

Once you've generated the manifest, the folder structure will look like Figure 6-4.

```
PS C:\scripts> tree /A /F SharePointConfiguration
Folder PATH listing
Volume serial number is C8D6-C055
C:\SCRIPTS\SHAREPOINTCONFIGURATION
|    SharePointConfiguration.psd1
|
\---DSCResources
    \---DisableLoopbackCheck
            DisableLoopbackCheck.psd1
            DisableLoopbackCheck.schema.psm1
```

Figure 6-4. *Folder structure after manifest creation*

You're ready! Copy the SharePointConfiguration folder to the C:\Program Files\ WindowsPowerShell\Modules folder.

Note   For the compile phase, the module can be in any folder represented by the `$env:PSModulePath`.

Once the resource module is available in the desired modules path, you can use the `Get-DscResource` cmdlet to see if you can discover the composite resource. This is shown in Figure 6-5.

```
PS C:\scripts> Get-DscResource -Module SharePointConfiguration | Format-List


ResourceType    : DisableLoopbackCheck
Name            : DisableLoopbackCheck
FriendlyName    :
Module          : SharePointConfiguration
ModuleName      : SharePointConfiguration
Version         : 1.0.0.0
Path            : C:\Program Files\WindowsPowerShell\Modules\SharePointConfigura
ParentPath      : C:\Program Files\WindowsPowerShell\Modules\SharePointConfigura
ImplementedAs   : Composite
CompanyName     : The Awesome DSC Inc.
Properties      : {DependsOn, PsDscRunAsCredential, Enable}
```

Figure 6-5. *New composite resource in the Get-DscResource output*

Using a Composite Resource in a Configuration

You have already seen how to use a composite resource in a configuration document. It is no different from how to add a regular resource instance to a configuration document. So try it one more time with your new composite DSC resource module. Here is the sample DSC configuration:

```
Configuration SharePointDev
{
    Import-DscResource -ModuleName SharePointConfiguration -Name
DisableLoopbackCheck

    Node localhost
    {
        DisableLoopbackCheck SPLPCheck
        {
            Enable = $true
```

```
        }
    }
}
```

SharePointDev

This is really it. Since the `DisableLoopbackCheck` has only one property (`Enable`), which is the mandatory property, you can compile and enact this. Figure 6-6 shows partial output from the enact.

Note   Check the compiled MOF and see how the composite configuration results into a Registry resource specification. This indicates that the composite resources are compile-time artifacts. Once the compilation is complete, the resource definition gets replaced by the "real" resource that the composite was built upon.

```
PS C:\scripts> Start-DscConfiguration -Path .\SharePointDev -Verbose -Wait
VERBOSE: Perform operation 'Invoke CimMethod' with following parameters, ''methodName' = SendConfig
urationApply,'className' = MSFT_DSCLocalConfigurationManager,'namespaceName' = root/Microsoft/Windo
ws/DesiredStateConfiguration'.
VERBOSE: An LCM method call arrived from computer S16-JB with user sid S-1-5-21-2403796847-13811114
12-2575929524-500.
VERBOSE: [S16-JB]: LCM:  [ Start  Set      ]
VERBOSE: [S16-JB]:                               [DSCEngine] Importing the module C:\Windows\system32\
WindowsPowerShell\v1.0\Modules\PSDesiredStateConfiguration\DscResources\MSFT_RegistryResource\MSFT_
RegistryResource.psm1 in force mode.
VERBOSE: [S16-JB]: LCM:  [ Start  Resource ] [[Registry]DefaultDomainName::[DisableLoopbackCheck]S
PLPCheck]
VERBOSE: [S16-JB]: LCM:  [ Start  Test     ] [[Registry]DefaultDomainName::[DisableLoopbackCheck]S
PLPCheck]
VERBOSE: [S16-JB]:                               [[Registry]DefaultDomainName::[DisableLoopbackCheck]S
PLPCheck] Importing the module MSFT_RegistryResource in force mode.
VERBOSE: [S16-JB]:                               [[Registry]DefaultDomainName::[DisableLoopbackCheck]S
PLPCheck] Found registry key value 'HKLM:\SYSTEM\CurrentControlSet\Control\Lsa\DisableLoopbackCheck
' with type 'DWord' and data '1'
VERBOSE: [S16-JB]: LCM:  [ End    Test     ] [[Registry]DefaultDomainName::[DisableLoopbackCheck]S
PLPCheck]  in 0.1100 seconds.
```

Figure 6-6. *Partial output from the configuration enact*

So far you have learned about creating a new composite resource module and using it in the DSC configuration document.

Composite resources support all common properties for a DSC resource. This includes DependsOn and PSDscRunAsCredential properties. Once the nested configurations are packaged into composite resource modules, they can be published like a custom DSC resource module to either the PowerShell gallery or a local PowerShell module repository. You will learn more about this after you learn how to write custom DSC resource modules.

Custom DSC Resource Modules

What you have seen so far, the composite resource modules, will help you package long and complex configurations into reusable resource modules. However, composite resource modules do not extend the scope of configuration because they do not implement any additional actual resources. A composite resource is just an authoring and compile time artifact. So what if you don't have any existing DSC resource modules for a certain scenario or configuration task? This is where your expertise in creating custom DSC resource modules plays out. In this section, you will explore different types of resource modules and learn how to author a few of them. Towards the end of this chapter, you will learn about publishing these modules to a local PowerShell repository.

Let's examine the different types of DSC resources by looking at the Get-DscResource cmdlet output. This is shown in Figure 6-7.

```
PS C:\> Get-DscResource | Select-Object -Property ImplementedAs -Unique

ImplementedAs
-------------
       Binary
   PowerShell
    Composite
```

Figure 6-7. *Types of DSC resources*

Although there are only three types shown here, there are a few more sub-types. Figure 6-8 shows this classification and Table 6-1 explains them.

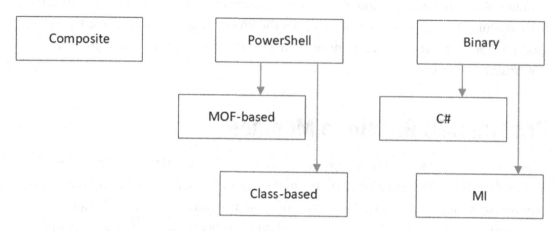

Figure 6-8. *DSC resource classification*

Table 6-1. *An Overview of the Module Types*

Module Type	Sub-Classification	Description
Composite	NA	Composite modules are nested configurations packaged as discoverable and reusable resource modules.
PowerShell	MOF-based	These resources in the PowerShell module are defined using a MOF schema that represents the resource properties and the module implemented as a set of Get, Set, and Test-TargetResource functions.
PowerShell	Class-based	These resources in the PowerShell modules are defined as PowerShell classes. Available only in PowerShell 5.0 and above.
Binary	C#	These resources in the C# modules are implemented as a set of Get, Set, and Test methods in C#.
Binary	Management Infrastructure (MI)	The resources in this type of module are implemented as MI providers written in the native language (C++).

You already know about composite resource modules. They are simply a package of nested configurations.

Desired State Configuration custom resource modules can be written as PowerShell script modules or Binary PowerShell modules (written in C#) or as Management Infrastructure providers.

Of all three, the MI providers are the most complex and, at this time of writing, only providers written in C++ are supported. The built-in `File` and `Log` resource in DSC is an MI provider. The decision to create an MI provider depends on the existing functionality that can be leveraged as a part of the DSC resource. If you already have the required functionality and an MI provider that is used to manage your application settings, extending that functionality to an MI provider for DSC makes sense. Also, if an application or software that you want to manage is written in native code, it may be easier to program such an application configuration using an MI provider than to create a module written either in C# or PowerShell.

The choice between the PowerShell script-based (MOF or Class) resources and the binary resources written in C# depends mostly on your expertise. If you are already proficient in writing PowerShell script modules, you are already equipped to write DSC resources as scripts. However, if your area of expertise is C# and you think that the resource configuration using .NET is more performant than PowerShell, a binary DSC resource could be a better choice.

In this chapter, you will look at authoring MOF- and class-based DSC resources. The `WindowsPackageCab` resource is an example of a class-based DSC resource and rest of the in-box resources are examples of MOF-based DSC resources. To start with, you will look at what a custom DSC resource module really is, its folder structure, and the must-knows. In the later sections, you will look at creating High Quality Resource Modules (HQRM) based on the coding and style guidelines Microsoft has in place.

Note   The HQRM guidelines are evolving, so expect changes to this list.

Towards the end, you will see a Plaster template developed by PowerShell MVP and DSC expert Ben Gelens to see how it makes creation of DSC resource module scaffold. Let's get started.

Before I go into the details of building custom DSC resources (either MOF- or Class-based), it is important to understand the key elements in a DSC resources and the execution flow of a DSC resource. This section introduces these concepts and the subsequent sections build upon this and demonstrate building DSC resources.

Functions in a DSC Resource Script

The DSC MOF- or class-based resources that you need to author have special requirements. These resource scripts must contain the three functions/methods described in Table 6-2. The names of these functions/methods have to be same as shown in the table and they are used in the resource configuration flow. I will discuss more about the execution flow after a brief description of these functions in the resource script.

Table 6-2. *Mandatory Functions in a DSC Resource Script*

Function or Method Name	Description	Input	Output
Get-TargetResource or Get()	This function is used to retrieve the current state of the configuration. For example, by taking the key resource properties as an input, the function should gather the state of the resource on the target system and return all its properties.	The resource properties identified as required/mandatory properties in the schema MOF.	A configuration hash table containing the values of all resource instance properties in the current state or object instance of the DSC resource class.
Set-TargetResource or Set()	This function or method should contain the logic required to perform the configuration change. This function is used to ensure that the resource instance is in the requested state.	The resource properties identified as mandatory/required properties and any other optional properties defined in the schema MOF and class properties.	None.
Test-TargetResource or Test()	This function or method is used to identify if the resource instance is in desired state or not. The output from this function is used to decide if the Set-TargetResource function or Set() method must be called or not.	This function must have the same parameters as the Set-TargetResource function or Set() method.	A Boolean value indicating if the resource instance is in desired state (True) or not (False).

Note   `*-TargetResource` functions are used in the MOF-based custom DSC resource scripts. The `Get`, `Set`, and `Test` methods are used in the class-based DSC resource scripts. For the purpose of creating an easy reading experience, I will refer to both as `Get`, `Set`, and `Test` functions instead of using the full function name or referring to the method names. Where needed, I will explicitly call out the function names or method names.

Let's take a look at how the functions shown in Table 6-2 are used the resource execution flow. Understanding this execution flow is important to enable the right logic in the resource script functions.

DSC Resource Execution Flow

Test and Set are the functions used during the configuration enact process. As described in Table 6-2, Set gets called if and only if Test returns false. Figure 6-9 provides an overview of this in the form of a flow chart.

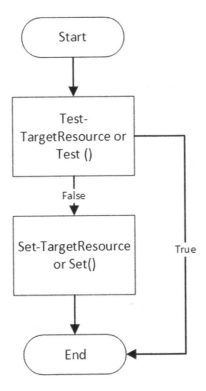

Figure 6-9. *Resource execution flow*

You saw in Table 6-2 that the Test function must return a Boolean value. This function has the same parameters as the Set function. When this function is called, it looks at the current state of the resource instance you are configuring and then returns either true or false. For example, if you are creating a DSC resource to create a virtual machine, you must first check if the VM already exists before you attempt to create one. This is what the Test function in the resource script must check. If it exists and conforms to the desired state, this function/method must return true. It should return false otherwise. The Set function must be executed to create or update the VM configuration if and only if the Test function returns false. So, in essence, how you write Test function decides if your custom DSC resource works as expected or not.

The Set function performs the configuration change required. As this function gets executed only if the resource instance is not in the desired state, the error handling and prerequisite checks can be offloaded to the Test function.

The Get function, unlike the Set and Test, is not a part of the configuration enact process. This is evident from the flow shown in Figure 6-9. However, the Get function is used to retrieve the current state of the resource instance. The Get-DscConfiguration cmdlet uses this function for all resources in a configuration document.

With the above understanding, you can start writing your first MOF-based DSC resource.

MOF-Based DSC Resources

MOF-based resources have existed since version 1 of DSC, which shipped as a part of WMF 4.0. They are called *MOF-based* because the resource requires a schema MOF file that describes the resource properties. The folder structure for a custom DSC resource module is similar to that of a composite resource. Here is bare minimum setup:

```
$env:PSModulePath (folder)
    |- ResourceModuleName (folder)
        |- DSCResources (folder)
            |- ResourceName (folder)
                |- ResourceName.psm1 (file, required)
                |- ResourceName.schema.mof (file, required)
```

Note   Although the module can be within any possible folder represented by $env:PSModulePath during authoring phase, it must be available in the C:\Program Files\WindowsPowerShell\Modules folder during the enact phase.

You will build a custom MOF-based resource for configuring host file entries in Windows OS. In this section, you are not concerned about how and what commands are used in the module-related functions. This section will show how to structure a DSC resource module and what should go into the module file.

The first step in writing a custom DSC resource is to write down the properties of a resource you want to configure.

A hosts file in Windows OS is located at $env:SystemRoot\system32\drivers\etc. This file is a simple text file that takes the host entries as space-separated values. For example, the following string represents host entry: 10.10.10.10 TestHost10.

The DSC resource must be capable of managing these entries. In this example, a hosts file entry is the resource instance you intend to configure. The mandatory input parameters are IPAddress and HostName. So, both parameters can become key properties in the resource schema.

Note   Pertaining to this example, you can implement both IPAddress and HostName as key properties or either of them. This is a design choice. When you implement both properties as key properties, it becomes necessary that each resource instance has a different value for these properties. So, with this design you can't have same IP address mapped to multiple host names or vice versa. I recommend that you play with these different implementations and understand how this design choice changes the behavior of the resource instances.

You also need to use the Ensure property to either add or remove a host entry. The possible values for this property are Present and Absent.

Let's create the folder structure needed for this resource:

```
New-Item -Path ProDSC\DSCResources\HostsFile -Force -ItemType Directory
```

You can now create the schema MOF for the resource.

The Resource Schema File

The schema MOF of a DSC resource defines the properties of a resource. Each MOF file written for a DSC resource must have at minimum one or more properties. Each custom resource class must derive from the OMI_BaseResource class. Also, the ClassVersion and FriendlyName attributes of the class are mandatory. See Table 6-3.

Table 6-3. *Qualifiers in a DSC Schema MOF*

Qualifier	Description	Example
Key	The Key qualifier on a property indicates that the property uniquely identifies the resource instance. Each DSC resource must have at least one Key property.	[Key] String KeyName;
Write	The Write qualifier indicates that a value can be assigned to the property in a configuration script.	[Write] String Description;
Read	The Read qualifier indicates that the property value cannot be assigned or changed in a configuration script. These properties get included when the Get function is invoked.	[Read] String ReadOnlyProperty;
Description	This qualifier is used to provide a description for a property. This is used along with Read, Write, or Key qualifiers. The text specified as description will appear as a tooltip when authoring resource configurations in a script editor like ISE.	[Key, description("Specifies a description for the KeyName")] string KeyName;
Required	This qualifier specifies that the property value is mandatory and cannot be null. Make a note that this is not same as a Key qualifier. The Key qualifier uniquely identifies a resource instance.	[required] string RequireProperty;
ValueMap and Values	Restricts the values that can be assigned to a property to that defined in ValueMap.	[write,ValueMap{"Present", "Absent"},Values{"Present", "Absent"}] string Ensure;

Note   Since the MOF-based resources use a schema file written in MOF syntax, there is a limitation on types of properties you can use. This limitation exists because DSC uses CIM under the covers for data representation.

Table 6-3 shows the basic qualifiers required for creating a DSC resource schema MOF. There are many other standard WMI qualifiers. You usually don't need all that when writing DSC resource schema files. For a complete list of standard qualifiers, refer to http://msdn.microsoft.com/en-us/library/aa393650(v=vs.85).aspx. Make a note of the syntax shown in the example column. The property qualifiers are enclosed in square brackets. The ValueMap and Values qualifiers are used along with the Write qualifier to define a set of valid values for a resource property. The Read property is used to define properties of a resource that cannot be changed or assigned in a configuration script. For example, the VMID is not something you can change or assign while creating a VM. The hypervisor assigns a VMID during the creation of the VM. With the knowledge of these qualifiers, let's look at how to structure the MOF schema file for the HostsFile resource you want to author:

```
[ClassVersion("1.0.0.0"), FriendlyName("HostsFile")]
class HostsFile : OMI_BaseResource
{
    [Key, Description("Specifies the name of the host.")] string HostName;
    [Key, Description("Specifies the IP address associated with the
    hostname.")] string IPAddress;
    [Write, Description("Specifies if the host entry should be present or
    absent."), ValueMap{"Present", "Absent"},Values{"Present", "Absent"}]
    string Ensure;
};
```

In this MOF file, you use a few of the qualifiers shown in Table 6-3. You have also specified the `ClassVersion` and `FriendlyName` attributes that define the version of the DSC resource class you are creating and a friendly name that identifies the DSC resource. The value of `FriendlyName` is what you see in the output of the `Get-DscResource` cmdlet and this is what you use in the configuration documents as well. The value of the `ClassVersion` can be used to uniquely identify the version of a DSC resource although all resources in a module inherit the module version.

Once you have the resource schema file authored, you need to store it as `.Schema.mof`. For instance in the MOF schema you authored in the preceding example, the file name will be `HostsFile.Schema.mof`. Also, make a note that this file needs to be stored with Unicode or ANSI encoding. Using other encoding schemes will result in errors. So, how do you prevalidate a MOF file for errors? You can use `mofcomp.exe` for that.

```
Mofcomp.exe -check HostsFile.Schema.mof
```

Figure 6-10 shows the output from the validation.

```
PS C:\Scripts\ProDSC\DSCResources\HostsFile> mofcomp.exe -check .\HostsFile.Schema.mof
Microsoft (R) MOF Compiler Version 10.0.14393.0
Copyright (c) Microsoft Corp. 1997-2006. All rights reserved.
Parsing MOF file: .\HostsFile.Schema.mof
MOF file has been successfully parsed
Syntax check complete.
WARNING: File .\HostsFile.Schema.mof does not contain #PRAGMA AUTORECOVER.
If the WMI repository is rebuilt in the future, the contents of this MOF file wil
l not be included in the new WMI repository.
To include this MOF file when the WMI Repository is automatically reconstructed,
place the #PRAGMA AUTORECOVER statement on the first line of the MOF file.
Done!
```

Figure 6-10. *MOF validation*

From Figure 6-10, you can see that your schema MOF is valid. Ignore the warning message in the output because it is not related to the syntax you are interested in. There is a PowerShell team module called `xDscResourceDesigner` that can help you test if a schema file is valid or not. You will see it in Chapter 7 briefly.

The Resource Script File

Once you have identified what properties you need and you have created the schema MOF file, you can create the module script that will contain the `Get-TargetResource`, `Set-TargetResource`, and the `Test-TargetResource` functions.

Test-TargetResource

With resource execution flow in mind, let's start with the `Test-TargetResource` function. For your resource, you will have to test if the host entry exists or not in the hosts file and, then, based on the value of the `Ensure` property, you return the necessary `Boolean` value. This function enables the idempotent nature in DSC resources. This means that you can apply the same configuration any number of times. If the current state is same as the desired state, no action will be taken. When writing custom DSC resources, adhering to the idempotent principle is critical. In your example, as discussed, a resource instance is the hosts file entry constructed using the given input parameters, HostName and IPAddress. Once you know if the resource instance exists, you need to look at the value of the Ensure property in the configuration script. Let's look at all the cases arising from this.

Figure 6-11 illustrates this in a flow chart.

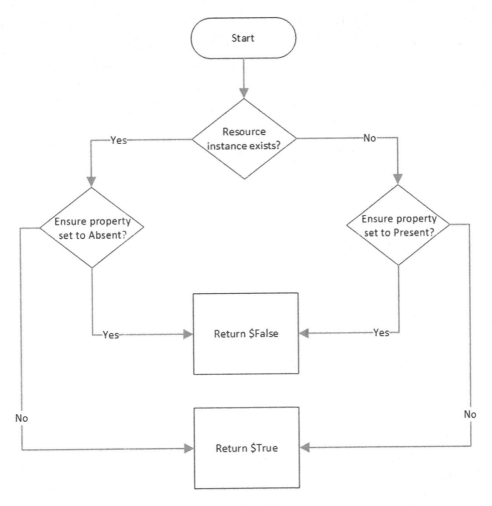

Figure 6-11. *Test-TargetResource execution flow*

If the resource instance exists and the Ensure property is set to Present, you need not do anything. In this case, the Test-TargetResource function exits by returning True. This indicates that there is no need to execute the Set-TargetResource function.

If the resource instance exists and the Ensure property is set to Absent, you need to the remove the instance. In this case, the Test-TargetResource function exists by returning False and the Set-TargetResource function will be used to remove the resource instance.

If the resource does not exist and Ensure is set to Absent, you need not do anything. In this case, the Test-TargetResource function exits by returning True. This indicates that there is no need to execute the Set-TargetResource function.

If the resource instance does not exist and the Ensure property is set to Present, you need to create the instance. In this case, the Test-TargetResource function exists by returning False and the Set-TargetResource function will be used to create the resource instance.

Using what you have learned so far, let's put together the logic for the Test-TargetResource function in your DSC resource. Here is how it should look:

```
function Test-TargetResource
{
    [OutputType([Boolean])]
    param (
        [Parameter(Mandatory = $true)]
        [String]
        $HostName,

        [Parameter(Mandatory = $true)]
        [String]
        $IPAddress,

        [Parameter()]
        [ValidateSet('Present','Absent')]
        [String]
        $Ensure = 'Present'
    )

    Write-Verbose -Message "Checking if the hosts file entry for $HostName
    and $IPAddress exists or not."
```

```
$content = Get-Content "${env:windir}\system32\drivers\etc\hosts"
-ErrorAction SilentlyContinue
$entryExist = ($content -match "^\s*$IPAddress\s+$HostName\s*$")

if ($Ensure -eq 'Present')
{
    if ($entryExist)
    {
        Write-Verbose -Message "Hosts file entry for $HostName and
        $IPAddress exists for the given parameters; nothing to
        configure."
        return $true
    }
    else
    {
        Write-Verbose -Message "Hosts file entry  for $HostName and
        $IPAddress does not exist while it should; it must be added."
        return $false
    }
}
else
{
    if ($entryExist)
    {
        Write-Verbose -Message "Hosts file entry for $HostName and
        $IPAddress exists while it should not; it must be removed."
        return $false
    }
    else
    {
        Write-Verbose -Message "Hosts file entry for $HostName and
        $IPAddress does not exist; nothing to configure."
        return $true
    }
}
}
```

Take a few minutes to understand this code. First and foremost, note that the Test-TargetResource must return a Boolean value and therefore, it is required to mention the output type from this function. In this code, this is done using [OutputType([Boolean])] at the beginning of the function script block.

The way the parameters are declared and so on should not be new. It is worth noting that for all the resource properties marked with the Key qualifier in the schema, you have created mandatory parameters in the PowerShell function. You are using regular expressions to check if the hosts file entry exists for the given input parameters. The $entryExist variable is used to hold a Boolean value from the regular expression matching. Once you have this value, you use the value of the Ensure property to take the right execution path. This was explained earlier in this section and I recommend that you match what we discussed to the code shown above.

Set-TargetResource

As explained earlier, the Set-TargetResource function performs the configuration change. Since this function gets executed only when the resource instance is not in the desired state, you can safely assume that no error checking is needed in this function. In this example, the Test-TargetResourcefunction checks if a hosts file entry exists and relates it to the value of the Ensure property. So, all you need to write within the Set-TargetResource function is to either remove or add the hosts file entry based on the value of the Ensure property.

You can now look at the code required for implementing the Set-TargetResource function. Notice that the parameters of this function are same as that of the Test-TargetResource function.

```
function Set-TargetResource
{
    param
    (
        [Parameter(Mandatory = $true)]
        [String]
        $HostName,

        [Parameter(Mandatory = $true)]
        [String]
        $IPAddress,
```

```
    [Parameter()]
    [ValidateSet('Present','Absent')]
    [String]
    $Ensure = 'Present'
)

$hostEntry = "`n${ipAddress}`t${hostName}"

if ($Ensure -eq 'Present')
{
    Write-Verbose -Message "Creating hosts file entry for $HostName and
    $IPAddress."
    Add-Content -Path "$env:windir\system32\drivers\etc\hosts" -Value
    $hostEntry -Force -Encoding ASCII
}
else
{
    Write-Verbose -Message "Removing hosts file entry for $HostName and
    $IPAddress."
    $content = ((Get-Content "$env:windir\system32\drivers\etc\hosts")
    -notmatch "^\s*$")
    $noMatchContent = ($content -notmatch "^\s*$IPAddress\
    s+$HostName\s*$")
    $noMatchContent | Set-Content "$env:windir\system32\drivers\etc\
    hosts"
}
}
```

The logic here is simple. You check the value of the Ensure property and take the appropriate action.

The final function that you need to write is the Get-TargetResource.

Get-TargetResource

As you saw in Table 6-2, the Get-TargetResource must have all the resource properties marked as Key or Required, in the schema MOF, as the input parameters. For this example, they are the HostName and IPAddress properties of the resource. Also,

I discussed that the output from this function should be a hashtable representing the current state of the resource instance with a 1:1 mapping to the properties defined in the schema MOF. As you can see in the following function script block, you are setting the output type of the function to hashtable.

Let's look at the function definition:

```
function Get-TargetResource
{
    [OutputType([Hashtable])]
    param
    (
        [parameter(Mandatory = $true)]
        [string]
        $HostName,

        [parameter(Mandatory = $true)]
        [string]
        $IPAddress
    )

    $configuration = @{
        HostName = $hostName
        IPAddress = $IPAddress
    }

    Write-Verbose -Message "Checking if hosts file entry exists for
    $HostName and $IPAddress or not."
    if ((Get-Content "$env:windir\system32\drivers\etc\hosts" -ErrorAction
    SilentlyContinue) -match "^\s*$IPAddress\s+$HostName\s*$")
    {
        Write-Verbose -Message "Hosts file entry for $HostName and
        $IPAddress exists."
        $configuration.Add('Ensure','Present')
    }
    else
```

```
{
    Write-Verbose "Hosts file entry for $HostName and $IPAddress does
    not exist."
    $configuration.Add('Ensure','Absent')
}

return $configuration
}
```

This function code is self-explanatory. Note that you do not have the Ensure property as a parameter of this function. The code in this function is almost similar to what you are doing in the Test-TargetResource function. In this function, you set the Ensure property depending on if the resource instance exists or not. So, the hashtable returned from this function has the *current state of the resource instance and not the desired state.*

Note   Using the Write-Verbose cmdlet in each of these functions helps display messages from the resource execution at console. These messages should be written in a way that conveys the task that is being performed by the resource script functions. If you use the Write-Debug cmdlet in the DSC resource script, the debug messages will be logged to the Debug channel of the DSC even logs.

So now you have seen all three functions and implemented the necessary logic to manage the hosts file entries as a DSC resource. You can now package these functions as a PowerShell script module. Remember that you need to add the Export-ModuleMember command at the end of the script module file to export all three functions. Since you only have three functions, you can use * as an argument to the -Function parameter.

```
Export-ModuleMember -Function *-TargetResource
```

The script module with all three functions and the above command can be saved as HostsFile.psm1. For demonstration purposes, I saved both the schema MOF and the script module in the folder structure shown earlier in this section.

Let's generate the module manifest for the top-level module that is ProDSC in this example:

```
$manifestParams = @{
    Path = 'C:\Scripts\ProDSC\ProDSC.psd1'
    Guid = (New-Guid).Guid
    Author = 'DSCFan'
    Company = 'The Awesome DSC Inc.'
    ModuleVersion = "1.0.0.0"
    Description = 'DSC resources from the ProDSC resource module.'
    DscResourcesToExport = @('HostsFile')
}

New-ModuleManifest @manifestParams -Verbose
```

Note   A resource manifest (HostsFile.psd1) is not required.

Notice the ModuleVersion and the DscResourcesToExport keys in the $manifestParams hashtable. This module version is the resource module version and not the individual resource version. The individual resource version is identified using the ClassVersion in the resource schema MOF. The DSCResourcesToExport will tell PowerShell that this module exports DSC resources and what resources it exports. For MOF-based resources, this will help when publishing the resource modules to the PowerShell gallery, which you will learn about towards the end of this chapter. Note that this is not mandatory for the resource module to work but is recommended.

With this, you have all the ingredients for a custom DSC resource. You can now store these files as a DSC resource module. Let's use the script module method to store this DSC resource within any folder represented by $env:PSModulePath. Once you do this, you should be able to see this in the Get-DscResource cmdlet output. This is shown in Figure 6-12.

Note   For authoring and resource discovery, it is OK to have the module located at any path represented by $env:PSModulePath. For the enact process, the module must be available at C:\Program Files\WindowsPowerShell\Modules.

```
PS C:\Scripts> Get-DscResource -Module ProDSC | Format-List


ResourceType   : HostsFile
Name           : HostsFile
FriendlyName   :
Module         : ProDSC
ModuleName     : ProDSC
Version        : 1.0.0.0
Path           : C:\Program Files\WindowsPowerShell\Modules\ProDSC\DSCResources\HostsFile\HostsFile.psd1
ParentPath     : C:\Program Files\WindowsPowerShell\Modules\ProDSC\DSCResources\HostsFile
ImplementedAs  : PowerShell
CompanyName    : The Awesome DSC Inc.
Properties     : {HostName, DependsOn, Ensure, IPAddress...}
```

Figure 6-12. *Custom resource in Get-DscResource*

Here is a sample configuration that uses your newly created DSC resource:

```
Configuration ProDscHosts
{
    param
    (
        [Parameter(Mandatory = $true)]
        [String]
        $HostName,

        [Parameter(Mandatory = $true)]
        [String]
        $IPAddress

    )

    Import-DscResource -ModuleName ProDsc -Name HostsFile -ModuleVersion 1.0.0.0

    Node Localhost
    {
        HostsFile DemoHosts
        {
            HostName = $HostName
            IPAddress = $IPAddress
            Ensure = 'Present'
        }
    }
}

ProDscHosts -HostName 'testServer10' -IPAddress '10.10.10.10' -Verbose
```

183

Writing a configuration document isn't anything new to you anymore. You can compile and enact this configuration and check if it is working as expected.

I will conclude this section on MOF-based DSC resources by mentioning that this type of resource works in both WMF 4.0 and above. Therefore, MOF-based resources are the most implemented or used at the time of writing. If you are targeting the WMF 4.0 platform, ensure that you do not use any PowerShell 5.0 or above specifics in the resource definitions. And, to date, the majority of the modules written by the Microsoft teams or the community so far are MOF-based for backward compatibility reasons.

Another limitation with MOF-based resources is the fact that each resource in the module must have its own PSM1 and schema files. At some point, as the number of resources in the module grows, this becomes a management overhead issue for the resource module author. At least, this is what I have been facing with the large set of MOF-based resources I have written over time.

Class-Based DSC Resources

If you want to create custom DSC resources that work only on PowerShell 5.0 and above, class-based resources offer another choice. PowerShell classes were introduced in PowerShell 5.0 for the purpose of authoring DSC resources. Unlike the MOF-based resources, the class-based resources do not require a schema MOF file. Although you don't need a schema MOF in the class-based resources, you are limited by the CIM data types when it comes to what type of properties can be added to the resource. Configurations with class-based resources get compiled to a CIM MOF representation before the enact. Therefore, the limitation of CIM data types still exists.

For a class-based resource, the folder structure for the resource module is minimal:

```
$env:PSModulePath (folder)
    |- ResourceModuleName (folder)
        |- ResourceModuleName.psm1 (file, required)
        |- ResourceModuleName.psd1 (file, required)
```

As you can see in the above representation, all you need is just a simple folder for the resource module; all resource definitions in a class-based module can be the same PSM1 file. Let's take a look at a skeleton of one such PSM1 file and then you will convert your HostsFile MOF-based resource into a class-based resource:

```
enum Ensure
{
    Absent
    Present
}

[DscResource()]
class HostsFile
{
    [DscProperty(Key)]
    [String]
    $HostName

    [DscProperty(Mandatory = $true)]
    [String]
    $IPAddress

    [DscProperty()]
    [Ensure]
    $Ensure = 'Present'

    [Bool] Test()
    {

    }

    [Void] Set()
    {

    }

    [HostsFile] Get()
    {

    }
}
```

This code snippet shows a skeleton of the DSC class-based resource definition. The [DscResource()] decoration before the class definition indicates that what follows is a DSC resource definition. This attribute and the Class keyword were introduced in PowerShell 5.0. The resource name needs to be specified as the name of the class. Within the class definition are the properties (same as the MOF-based resource) HostName, IPAddress, and Ensure.

The resource properties in a class contain attributes that modify the behavior of the properties. Table 6-4 provides an overview of these attributes.

Table 6-4. *DSC Class-Based Resource Property Attributes*

Attribute	Description
DscProperty(Key)	Specifies the Key property for the resource. This must be a unique key across all instances of the resource in a DSC configuration. HostName is the Key property in your example.
DscProperty(Mandatory)	Specifies the required property for the resource. This is not a key property but mandatory. IPAddress is a required property in your example.
DscProperty()	Specifies a property that can be specified in the resource configuration but not a required property.
DscProperty(NotConfigurable)	Specifies a read-only property in the resource configuration. This is not needed in a resource instance definition but the value for this property will be returned by the Get() method.

For the Ensure property, instead of using the [ValidateSet()] attribute, let's use another PowerShell 5.0 language feature called enums. Using enums, you define a new type called [Ensure] and then added the possible values 'Present' and 'Absent' within that.

What follows the resource property definition is a set of methods equivalent to the Test-TargetResource, Set-TargetResource, and Get-TargetResource functions in MOF-based resources. For the Test() method, the return type is [Bool] and the Get() method should return an instance of the class. The Set() method does not return anything and therefore it is set to [Void].

With this knowledge handy, let's see the full definition of the `HostsFile` class resource:

```
enum Ensure
{
    Absent
    Present
}

[DscResource()]
class HostsFile
{
    [DscProperty(Key)]
    [String]
    $HostName

    [DscProperty(Mandatory = $true)]
    [String]
    $IPAddress

    [DscProperty()]
    [ValidateSet('Present','Absent')]
    [String]
    $Ensure

    [Bool] Test()
    {
        Write-Verbose -Message "Checking if the hosts file entry for
        $($this.HostName) and $($this.IPAddress) exists or not."
        $content = Get-Content "${env:windir}\system32\drivers\etc\hosts"
        -ErrorAction SilentlyContinue
        $entryExist = ($content -match "^\s*$($this.IPAddress)\s+$($this.
        HostName)\s*$")
        if ($this.Ensure -eq [Ensure]::Present)
        {
            if ($entryExist)
            {
```

```
            Write-Verbose -Message "Hosts file entry exists for
            $($this.HostName) and $($this.IPAddress). Nothing to
            configure."
            return $true
        }
        else
        {
            Write-Verbose -Message "Hosts file entry for for $($this.
            HostName) and $($this.IPAddress) does not exist while it
            should; it must be added."
            return $false
        }
    }
    else
    {
        if ($entryExist)
        {
            Write-Verbose -Message "Hosts file entry for for $($this.
            HostName) and $($this.IPAddress) exists while it should
            not; it must be removed."
            return $false
        }
        else
        {
            Write-Verbose -Message "Hosts file entry for for $($this.
            HostName) and $($this.IPAddress) does not exist; nothing to
            configure."
            return $true
        }
    }
}
```

```
[Void] Set()
{
    $hostEntry = "`n$($this.IPAddress)`t$($this.HostName)"

    if ($this.Ensure -eq [Ensure]::Present)
    {
        Write-Verbose -Message "Creating hosts file entry for for
        $($this.HostName) and $($this.IPAddress)"
        Add-Content -Path "${env:windir}\system32\drivers\etc\hosts"
        -Value $hostEntry -Force -Encoding ASCII
    }
    else
    {
        Write-Verbose -Message "Removing hosts file entry for $($this.
        HostName) and $($this.IPAddress)."
        $content = ((Get-Content "${env:windir}\system32\drivers\etc\
        hosts") -notmatch "^\s*$")
        $noMatchContent = $content -notmatch "^\s*$($this.IPAddress)\
        s+$($this.HostName)\s*$"
        $noMatchContent | Set-Content "${env:windir}\system32\drivers\
        etc\hosts"
    }
}

[HostsFile] Get()
{
    Write-Verbose -Message "Checking if hosts file entry for for
    $($this.HostName) and $($this.IPAddress) exists or not"
    if ((Get-Content "${env:windir}\system32\drivers\etc\hosts"
    -ErrorAction SilentlyContinue) -match "^\s*$($this.IPAddress)\
    s+$($this.HostName)\s*$")
```

```
    {
        Write-Verbose -Message "Hosts file entry for $this.HostName and
        $this.IPAddress exists."
        $this.Ensure = [Ensure]::Present
    }
    else
    {
        Write-Verbose "Hosts file entry for for $($this.HostName) and
        $($this.IPAddress) does not exist"
        $this.Ensure = [Ensure]::Absent
    }

    return $this
  }
}
```

As you can see in this code, the logic is same between MOF- and class-based resource definitions. However, look at the way you are referring to the resource properties. Since this is a class-based resource, you need to use the $this variable. $this is the current instance of the class and in this context refers to the DSC resource instance that is currently being configured. You can refer to the individual properties of the resource using $this.<propertyName> notation. Since $Ensure is of property [Ensure], which is a PowerShell enum, you can use the namespace alias qualifier (in C# terminology) :: to access the enumerator values. Therefore, it will be [Ensure]::Present and [Ensure]::Absent for your resource configuration.

In the Get() function, you just return $this because it contains the current instance of the resource and also Get() should return an instance of the DSC resource class.

You can save the above class-based resource definition as the ProDSC.psm1 file. You can now create the module manifest for this resource module:

```
$manifestParams = @{
    Path = 'C:\Scripts\ProDSC\ProDSC.psd1'
    RootModule = 'ProDsc.psm1'
    Guid = (New-Guid).Guid
    Author = 'DSCFan'
```

```
    Company = 'The Awesome DSC Inc.'
    ModuleVersion = "1.0.0.0"
    Description = 'DSC resources from the ProDSC resource module.'
    DscResourcesToExport = @('HostsFile')
}

New-ModuleManifest @manifestParams -Verbose
```

The DscResourcesToExport key is must in class-based resources. You can copy
the folder ProDSC containing ProDsc.psm1 and ProDsc.psd1 to C:\Program Files\
WindowsPowerShell\Modules. You should now be able to discover the HostsFile
resource using the Get-DscResource cmdlet.

The configuration document that you created earlier should work as-is. Try
compiling that document again and enacting it.

Within this resource definition script, if you want to add one more DSC resource,
all you have to do is add another Class definition and the necessary properties and
methods. Here is a skeleton of a resource definition script that contains two class
resource definitions:

```
enum Ensure
{
    Absent
    Present
}

[DscResource()]
class HostsFile
{
    [DscProperty(Key)]
    [String]
    $HostName

    [DscProperty(Mandatory = $true)]
    [String]
    $IPAddress
```

```
    [DscProperty()]
    [Ensure]
    $Ensure = 'Present'

    [Bool] Test()
    {

    }

    [Void] Set()
    {

    }

    [HostsFile] Get()
    {

    }
}

class NewResource
{
    [DscProperty(Key)]
    [String]
    $Property1

    [DscProperty(Mandatory = $true)]
    [String]
    $Property2

    [DscProperty()]
    [Ensure]
    $Ensure = 'Present'

    [Bool] Test()
    {

    }

    [Void] Set()
```

```
    {

    }

    [HostsFile] Get()
    {

    }
}
```

If you want to separate out the class definitions for each resource into a separate PSM1 file, you can do so by creating a folder DSCClassResources at the root of the module and copy each PSM1 with associated PSD1 file into the resource folder under DSCClassResources. Here is what the folder structure would look like:

```
$env:PSModulePath (folder)
    |- ResourceModuleName (folder)
        |- DSCClassResources
            |- Resource1Name
                |- Resource1Name.psm1 (file, required)
                |- Resource1Name.psd1 (file, required)
            |- Resource2Name
                |- Resource2Name.psm1 (file, required)
                |- Resource2Name.psd1 (file, required)
        |- ResourceModuleName.psd1 (file, required)
```

In the root module manifest, you must ensure that the nested resources (Resource1Name and Resource2Name in the above example) mentioned in the NestedModules and the DscResourcesToExport have all the resources in the module.

This concludes our discussion on class-based resources.

The choice between MOF-based and class-based resource modules must be clear now. Class-based resources are for anything that you want to manage on platforms with only PowerShell 5.0 and above. MOF-based resources should be your choice if your module should be able to run on PowerShell 4.0 and above.

In fact, with WMF 5.1 onwards, you can combine MOF- and class-based resources into a single module. This can be used as a way to transition all existing DSC resources created for PowerShell 4.0 to support systems with only WMF 5.1 and above. To make this happen, you need to add a folder called DSCClassResources at the root of the module folder and update the root module manifest to ensure that the DscResourcesToExport key is added. If the module contains multiple resources, you must add the NestedModules key as well. And, as a best practice, you should also define the minimum PowerShell version required for the module in the root module manifest.

There is an example of this right in the in-box DSC resources. This is shown in Figure 6-13.

```
Mode                LastWriteTime         Length Name
----                -------------         ------ ----
d-----         7/16/2016   6:53 PM               DownloadManager
d---s-         7/16/2016   6:53 PM               DSCClassResources
d---s-          8/7/2017   2:47 PM               DSCResources
d---s-         9/11/2017  10:38 PM               en-US
d---s-         7/16/2016   6:53 PM               WebDownloadManager
-a----         7/16/2016   6:50 PM          1145 Disable-DscDebug.cdxml
-a----         7/16/2016   6:50 PM          1440 Enable-DscDebug.cdxml
-a----         7/16/2016   6:50 PM          1366 Get-DscConfiguration.cdxml
-a----         7/16/2016   6:50 PM          1525 Get-DscConfigurationStatus.cdxml
-a----         7/16/2016   6:50 PM          1518 Get-DSCLocalConfigurationManager.cdxml
-a----          8/6/2016   6:22 AM         16202 PSDesiredStateConfiguration.format.ps1xml
-a----         7/16/2016   6:50 PM          5082 PSDesiredStateConfiguration.psd1
-a----         7/16/2016   6:50 PM        200450 PSDesiredStateConfiguration.psm1
-a----         7/16/2016   6:50 PM          3589 PSDesiredStateConfiguration.types.ps1xml
-a----         9/11/2017  10:38 PM           391 PSDesiredStateConfiguration_94b905ff-74b5
-a----         7/16/2016   6:50 PM         11938 PSDscXMachine.psm1
-a----         7/16/2016   6:50 PM          2397 Remove-DscConfigurationDocument.cdxml
-a----         7/16/2016   6:50 PM          1106 Restore-DscConfiguration.cdxml
-a----         7/16/2016   6:50 PM          1441 Stop-DscConfiguration.cdxml
```

Figure 6-13. *Combining MOF- and class-based resources in a single module*

Alright. What you have seen so far will help you quickly write a DSC resource, either a MOF-based or a class-based module, but maybe not with the right quality standards and best practices. In the next few sections, I will review a few DSC resource design patterns and explain quality and coding requirements for building High Quality Resource Modules.

DSC Resource Design Patterns

You have seen that writing a custom DSC resource is as simple as writing a PowerShell script module. In this section, you will explore a few design patterns and see some practical examples. In some cases, you will modify the HostsFile resource created earlier in this section to demonstrate how to implement these patterns, best practices, and guidelines.

Inducing a Reboot After a Configuration Change

When looking at the DSC meta configuration, you saw an LCM property called RebootIfNeeded. This is set, by default, to False. In the default configuration, if the resource configuration requires a reboot, it displays a verbose message that the configuration requires a reboot. When this property is set to True, if a resource configuration requires a reboot, the DSC engine will automatically trigger the reboot. One such DSC resource example is the WindowsFeature resource discussed in Chapter 5. But how does a DSC resource signal a reboot?

A custom DSC resource can signal the LCM to reboot the system by setting a global variable called DSCMachineStatus to $true. This, of course, needs to be done in the Set function. Within this function, after the resource configuration is complete, if you determine that a reboot is needed to complete the configuration, you can signal the LCM on target system by adding the following line:

```
$Global:DSCMachineStatus = $true
```

When the LCM receives this signal and the RebootIfNeeded property is set to True, the target systems restarts to complete the configuration. If you are an administrator, I recommend that you exercise extreme caution before setting the RebootIfNeeded property to True in the LCM meta configuration.

Caution   Ensure that you have the Test function doing the right checks and returning False only when needed. If the resource is inducing a reboot of the target system and the Test function is not written according to the idempotent principles, the target system will end up in an infinite reboot loop.

Localizing Verbose and Debug Messages

In the three functions definitions you wrote for the HostsFile DSC resource, you used the Write-Verbose cmdlet to log messages from the resource execution to the console. This is a good and recommended way of writing custom DSC resources. If you use the Start-DscConfiguration cmdlet with the -Verbose switch parameter, you can see the verbose messages from the resource. This gives the user pushing the configuration an idea about what is happening on the target system. Similarly, you can use the Write-Debug cmdlet in the Set function and other module functions to write log messages to the debug channel of the DSC events.

If you plan on sharing your DSC resources, it is recommended that you localize these messages written either using the verbose/error or debug streams or at least enable the flexibility for someone to add localized messages to the resource. This can be done by using the script internationalization techniques in PowerShell. This is not specific to DSC resources but can be used with any PowerShell modules or scripts.

Tip   I recommend that you read the "About_Data_Sections" and "About_Script_Internationalization" help topics to know more about the string localization in PowerShell.

To start, you first need to create a hashtable that contains all the log message strings. The following is for the HostsFile resource:

```
ConvertFrom-StringData @'
    CheckingHostsFileEntry=Checking if the hosts file entry exists.
    HostsFileEntryFound=Found a hosts file entry for {0} and {1}.
    HostsFileEntryNotFound=Did not find a hosts file entry for {0} and {1}.
    HostsFileShouldNotExist=Hosts file entry exists while it should not.
    HostsFileEntryShouldExist=Hosts file entry does not exist while it should.
    HostsFileEntryDoesNotExist = Hosts file entry does not exist. No action
    needed.
    CreatingHostsFileEntry=Creating a hosts file entry with {0} and {1}.
    RemovingHostsFileEntry=Removing a hosts file entry with {0} and {1}.
'@
```

The ConvertFrom-StringData takes the herestring content and converts it to a hashtable. You now need to store this in a PowerShell data file. You can name this file anything you want but let's call it HostsFile.psd1 for this example. The {0} and {1} in the herestring are used as placeholders for replacing with any values supplied, such as the IPAddress and HostName values in the configuration script. You will see how they are used later in this section. Since these messages are in English and the language culture on my system is set to en-US, let's create a folder named en-US under the resource folder.

For example, if you are using the nested module structure for the DSC custom resource, the folder structure should look similar to what is shown in Figure 6-14. The HostsFile.psd1 file needs to be stored in the en-US folder. If you have localized for any other cultures, create separate .psd1 files for each of the cultures and store them under folders representing each of those cultures.

```
PS C:\Scripts> tree /A /F .\ProDSC
Folder PATH listing
Volume serial number is 8E45-E0C0
C:\SCRIPTS\PRODSC
|   ProDSC.psd1
|   ProDsc.psm1
|
\---en-US
        HostsFile.psd1
```

Figure 6-14. Module folder structure after adding localized strings

---

Note   While I am using the class-based resource here as an example, the concepts that you learn in this section will apply to both types of resources discussed.

You now need to make sure that the resource file (.PSM1) loads this localized data. Here is what I generally add to all the resource definition scripts:

```
if (Test-Path "${PSScriptRoot}\${PSUICulture}")
{
    Import-LocalizedData -BindingVariable LocalizedData -filename
    HostsFile.psd1 `
                    -BaseDirectory "$PSScriptRoot\$PSUICulture"
}
else
{
    #fallback to en-US
    Import-LocalizedData -BindingVariable LocalizedData -filename
    HostsFile.psd1 `
                    -BaseDirectory "$PSScriptRoot\en-US"
}
```

Using this few lines of code, you check if there is a folder named as the value represented by $PSUICulture. If one exists in the module folder, you check if you can load the localized strings from that folder. If not, you fall back to the en-US culture and load the English strings.

This will only load the localized strings. You still have to modify the Write-Verbose and/or Write-Debug commands to ensure that you use the loaded localized strings instead of static message strings. Here is how I modified the class resource script:

```
if (Test-Path "${PSScriptRoot}\${PSUICulture}")
{
    Import-LocalizedData -BindingVariable LocalizedData -filename ProDsc.
    psd1 `
                            -BaseDirectory "${PSScriptRoot}\${PSUICulture}"
}
else
{
    #fallback to en-US
    Import-LocalizedData -BindingVariable LocalizedData -filename ProDsc.
    psd1 `
                            -BaseDirectory "${PSScriptRoot}\en-US"
}

enum Ensure
{
    Absent
    Present
}

[DscResource()]
class HostsFile
{
    [DscProperty(Key)]
    [String]
    $HostName

    [DscProperty(Mandatory = $true)]
    [String]
    $IPAddress
```

```
[DscProperty()]
[ValidateSet('Present','Absent')]
[String]
$Ensure

[Bool] Test()
{
    Write-Verbose -Message $Script:localizedData.CheckingHostsFileEntry
    $content = Get-Content "${env:windir}\system32\drivers\etc\hosts"
    -ErrorAction SilentlyContinue
    $entryExist = ($content -match "^\s*$($this.IPAddress)\s+$($this.
    HostName)\s*$")
    if ($this.Ensure -eq [Ensure]::Present)
    {
        if ($entryExist)
        {
            Write-Verbose -Message ($Script:localizedData.
            HostsFileEntryFound -f $this.HostName, $this.IPAddress)
            return $true
        }
        else
        {
            Write-Verbose -Message ($Script:localizedData.
            HostsFileEntryNotFound -f $this.HostName, $this.IPAddress)
            return $false
        }
    }
    else
    {
        if ($entryExist)
        {
            Write-Verbose -Message ($Script:localizedData.
            HostsFileShouldNotExist -f $this.HostName, $this.IPAddress)
            return $false
        }
        else
```

```
            {
                Write-Verbose -Message $Script:localizedData.
                HostsFileEntryDoesNotExist
                return $true
            }
        }
    }

    [Void] Set()
    {
        $hostEntry = "`n$($this.IPAddress)`t$($this.HostName)"

        if ($this.Ensure -eq [Ensure]::Present)
        {
            Write-Verbose -Message ($Script:localizedData.
            CreatingHostsFileEntry -f $this.HostName, $this.IPAddress)
            Add-Content -Path "${env:windir}\system32\drivers\etc\hosts"
            -Value $hostEntry -Force -Encoding ASCII
        }
        else
        {
            Write-Verbose -Message ($Script:localizedData.
            RemovingHostsFileEntry -f $this.HostName, $this.IPAddress)
            $content = ((Get-Content "${env:windir}\system32\drivers\etc\
            hosts") -notmatch "^\s*$")
            $noMatchContent = $content -notmatch "^\s*$($this.IPAddress)\
            s+$($this.HostName)\s*$"
            $noMatchContent | Set-Content "${env:windir}\system32\drivers\
            etc\hosts"
        }
    }

    [HostsFile] Get()
    {
        Write-Verbose -Message $Script:localizedData.CheckingHostsFileEntry
```

```
    if ((Get-Content "${env:windir}\system32\drivers\etc\hosts"
    -ErrorAction SilentlyContinue) -match "^\s*$($this.IPAddress)\
    s+$($this.HostName)\s*$")
    {
        Write-Verbose -Message ($Script:localizedData.
        HostsFileEntryFound -f $this.HostName, $this.IPAddress)
        $this.Ensure = [Ensure]::Present
    }
    else
    {
        Write-Verbose -Message ($Script:localizedData.
        HostsFileEntryNotFound -f $this.HostName, $this.IPAddress)
        $this.Ensure = [Ensure]::Absent
    }

    return $this
    }
}
```

In this example, observe how the $LocalizedData variable is used along with the
-f formatting operator. The {0} or {1} used in the herestring gets replaced with the
values supplied after the -f operator. For class-based resources, it is important to use the
$script: scope for the $LocalizedData variable.

Adding Help Content

When you author a PowerShell module, you can implement help for each of the
functions as comment-based help. This ensures that the end users can use the Get-Help
cmdlet to understand how your module's functions or cmdlets are used. However, if you
look at the DSC resources, they all contain the same set of functions: Get, Set, and Test.
So, even if you write comment-based help for these functions in your resource, it won't
be of much help. So, how can you include help content for the DSC resources that you
build?

For the DSC resources, the help content should describe how the resource can be
used, with examples describing each possible configuration scenario for the resource.
The ideal place to put this help content is in an About topic. You can author help content
for the DSC resource and store it as a text file with a relevant About topic name.

For example, I put a few examples describing how the HostsFile resource can be used into a text file and named it about_HostsFile.help.txt. Note that the file name must end with .help.txt and should be stored in UTF-8 encoding. Once you create this file, you can store it in a folder named for the language culture. If you are using the nested module structure, this folder must be created at the root of the module. This will enable localization for the About topics for the DSC resource. Figure 6-15 shows an example of this.

Note   Localization of the resource message strings is different from localization for the nested module. For each DSC resource in the nested module, you can create an About topic text file and store in the language culture folder, as shown in Figure 6-15.

```
PS C:\Scripts> tree /F /A .\ProDSC
Folder PATH listing
Volume serial number is 8E45-E0C0
C:\SCRIPTS\PRODSC
|    ProDSC.psd1
|    ProDsc.psm1
|
\---en-US
         about_HostsFile.help.txt
         ProDsc.psd1
```

Figure 6-15.   *DSC resource help text file*

After this help text file is copied to the resource folder, the help text can be accessed using the Get-Help cmdlet.

```
Get-Help About_HostsFile
```

Figure 6-16 shows how the text file content is shown in the output.

```
PS C:\Scripts> Get-Help About_HostsFile
HostsFile [String] #ResourceName
{
    HostName = [String]
    IPAddress = [String]
    [ Ensure = [String] {Absent | Present} ]
}

Properties

HostName  - Name of the server or computer.
IPAddress - IPv4 or IPv6 address of the server or computer.
Ensure    - Set this property to 'Present' to add the hosts file entry. Using 'Abse
nt' will remove the hosts entry, if it exists.
```

Figure 6-16. *Get-Help output*

Granularity in DSC Resources

DSC is fairly new and it will be exciting to learn this technology and implement your own resource and so on. However, when developing or authoring custom DSC resources, ensure that you go to the most granular level of the resource. Let's explore this idea with an example.

A virtual machine as a resource will have many sub-components such as virtual hard disks, virtual network adapters, and so on. So, if you are writing a DSC custom resource for managing virtual machines, it is recommended that you create multiple DSC resources for each manageable component. This simplifies the whole configuration and makes it easy to configure the VM-attached resources in an independent way.

Choosing the Right Key Property

You saw in your example of the HostsFile DSC resource that you chose both HostName and IPAddress as the key properties. Now, let's look at a poor choice of a key property:

```
[ClassVersion("1.0.0.0"), FriendlyName("VMNetworkAdapter")]
class VMNetworkAdapter : OMI_BaseResource
{
    [Key, Description("Specifies the name of the VM.")] string Name;
    [Required, Description("Specifies the name of the VM.")] string VMName;
```

```
    [Required, Description("Specifies the VHDX path for the VM.")] string
    VMSwitch;
    [Write, Description("Specifies if the VM should be present or
    absent."), ValueMap{"Present", "Absent"},Values{"Present", "Absent"}]
    string Ensure;
};
```

This is a very simple example of a schema MOF for a resource that attaches a
network adapter to a VM. You have Name as the key property and a few other required
properties such as VMName and VMSwitch. If you add a network adapter with the same
name to two different VMs, you will end up having a duplicate resource instances
with the same key-value pair. You can work around this by making another property
a key property as well, for example, VMName. Another workaround is to add a dummy
key property that does not necessarily impact any resource configuration. Here is an
example of the second workaround:

```
[ClassVersion("1.0.0.0"), FriendlyName("VMNetworkAdapter")]
class VMNetworkAdapter : OMI_BaseResource
{
[Key, Description("Key property to identify a unique resource instance.")]
string Id;
[Require, Description("Specifies the name of the VM.")] string Name;
[Required, Description("Specifies the name of the VM.")] string VMName;
[Required, Description("Specifies the VHDX path for the VM.")] string
VMSwitch;
[Write, Description("Specifies if the VM should be present or absent."),
ValueMap{"Present", "Absent"},Values{"Present", "Absent"}] string Ensure;
};
```

Single Instance Resources

A single instance resource is a resource that can only be configured once. For example,
there is no need to have multiple instances of a resource that configures the time zone,
since at compilation DSC only checks if the key-value pair across instances of a same
resource is to be unique. It will ignore if two instances of the resource have different
key-value pairs. However, when this configuration gets enacted, the second resource

instance overwrites the configuration done by the first resource instance. In such situations, you should restrict the resource to have only a single instance by using a dummy key property. Taking a cue from the PowerShell team recommendations, name this property as IsSingleInstance and attach a value map that allows only one value. Here is an example from my FailoverClusterDSC module:

```
[ClassVersion("1.0.0.0"), FriendlyName("FailoverClusterQuorum")]
class FailoverClusterQuorum : OMI_BaseResource
{
    [Key, ValueMap{"Yes"}, Values{"Yes"}] String IsSingleInstance;
    [Required, ValueMap{"NodeMajority", "NodeAndDiskMajority",
    "NodeAndFileShareMajority", "DiskOnly"}, Values{"NodeMajority",
    "NodeAndDiskMajority", "NodeAndFileShareMajority", "DiskOnly"}] String
    QuorumType;
    [Write] String Resource;
};
```

Apart from the module authoring or design recommendations you have seen so far, Microsoft has style and coding guidelines for authoring resource modules that you want to submit upstream to DSC resource kit. The style guidelines document for authoring HQRM DSC resource modules is available at http://azrs.tk/dscStyle and the best practices document to implement within these resource modules is available at http://azrs.tk/psbestPractice. The best practices listed at the second link are applicable not just to authoring DSC resource modules but in general for any PowerShell scripts or modules.

Developing HQRM Modules

To contribute DSC resource modules upstream to the PowerShell DSC resource kit or contribute to an official Microsoft DSC resource module, you must author the modules following certain style guidelines and best practices. In this section, I will look at a few of the best practices. I recommend that you do a thorough review of the content at the links provided above for a complete understanding of these HQRM requirements. There is also a DSC resource authoring checklist available at http://azrs.tk/dscCheckList.

Note   Adhering to the style guidelines is mandatory if you submit a resource upstream. Certain style guidelines such as choosing where to place the opening curly bracket either for a function or conditional statement may take some getting used to especially if you are K&R or OTSB kind of person. I was one and I had a tough time adapting AllMan to contribute new resources to the official DSC resource kit.

Adding Examples

Unlike a PowerShell function for which we can attach a multiline comment as inline help, DSC resources do not come with a system that lets us access the help needed for the DSC resources using Get-Help, not unless we add an about_* text file like you saw earlier. To address this, the HQRM guidelines talk about adding examples of DSC resource configurations. These examples should provide a user of the DSC resource insight into how to use different properties of the DSC resource. And, this should be available for each resource in the resource as a separate .PS1 file for easy identification. All of these examples should go into a folder called Examples at the root of the resource module folder.

Adding Tests

One of the other requirements and also a very good practice is to add Pester tests to the resource module. You have not seen this in the example HostsFile module yet. I will discuss this in the next chapter on testing DSC resource modules. For now, understand that it is always a good practice to ensure that the resource module has tests and that these tests are available for both unit and integration testing. These tests should go into a folder called Tests at the root of the resource module folder.

Adding Inline Help for Resource Functions

HQRM guidelines also require that we add inline multi-comment help for each of the resource script functions. Here is an example from one of the resources I contributed to the xNetworking resource module:

```
<#
.SYNOPSIS
    Sets the state of the network adapter RDMA.
.PARAMETER Name
    Specifies the name of network adapter for which RDMA needs
    to be configured.
.PARAMETER Enabled
    Specifies if the RDMA configuration should be enabled or disabled.
    Defaults to $true.
#>
function Set-TargetResource
{
    [CmdletBinding()]
    param
    (
        [Parameter(Mandatory = $true)]
        [System.String]
        $Name,

        [Parameter()]
        [System.Boolean]
        $Enabled = $true
    )

    $configuration = @{
        Name = $Name
    }

    try
    {
        Write-Verbose -Message ($localizedData.GetNetAdapterRDMAMessage -f
        $Name)
```

```
        $netAdapterRdma = Get-NetAdapterRdma -Name $Name -ErrorAction Stop
    }
    catch
    {
        New-InvalidOperationException `
            -Message ($LocalizedData.NetAdapterNotFoundError -f $Name)
    }

    if ($netAdapterRdma)
    {
        Write-Verbose -Message ($localizedData.CheckNetAdapterRDMAMessage
        -f $Name)

        if ($netAdapterRdma.Enabled -ne $Enabled)
        {
            Write-Verbose -Message ($localizedData.SetNetAdapterRDMAMessage
            -f $Name, $Enabled)

            Set-NetAdapterRdma -Name $Name -Enabled $Enabled
        }
    }
}
```

At minimum, the HQRM guidelines require a synopsis of what the function does and a description for each property in the resource schema or class definition.

Adding Helper Modules

The example in this chapter is a trivial one. You just had to check if a hosts file entry existed and based on the value of $Ensure, you had to take an action. There was, however, some level of redundancy in each of the functions in the resource script. You could have ideally moved them all into a set of functions and created a helper module that gets loaded in the resource script. This becomes very critical in larger resource modules with many more related resources. Each of these resources might require some common functionality. For example, in my HyperVDsc resource module at https://github.com/rchaganti/HyperVDsc, there are several resources that manage the VM configuration. Within each of these resource definitions, I have to ensure that a

VM that is attempting to configure exists and exists in the right state for performing the configuration change. When such dependency on a piece of code exists across resources, it is ideal to separate it into a different supporting script or module altogether. And this module can be loaded as a dependency in each resource script. I prefer creating a separate folder for all the helper modules called Modules at the root of the resource module.

With so many additional things added to a resource module, Figure 6-17 shows the folder structure for one of the HQRM modules (NetQoSDSC) I wrote.

```
PS C:\Program Files\WindowsPowerShell\Modules> tree /A NetQosDSC
Folder PATH listing
Volume serial number is 8E45-E0C0
C:\PROGRAM FILES\WINDOWSPOWERSHELL\MODULES\NETQOSDSC
+---DSCResources
|   +---NetAdapterQos
|   |   \---en-US
|   +---NetQosDCBXSetting
|   |   \---en-US
|   +---NetQosFlowControl
|   |   \---en-US
|   +---NetQosPolicy
|   |   \---en-US
|   \---NetQosTrafficClass
|       \---en-US
+---Examples
+---Modules
|   \---NetQosDSC.Helper
|       \---en-US
\---Tests
```

Figure 6-17. *Resource module folder structure (HQRM)*

This may be easy to build when you start working on a new HQRM module but there are better ways to scaffold this. The Plaster project intends to generate the PowerShell module scaffolds based on a template. Ben Gelens, PowerShell MVP and DSC expert, created a Plaster template that generates the folder structure and other files within the module.

> **Note**   There is a Microsoft experimental module called xDscResourceDesigner available at https://github.com/PowerShell/xDSCResourceDesigner. This is not an active project and does not support HQRM or class-based resource module scaffold. However, I still recommend taking a look at it for generating the MOF-based resource modules. You will use a few commands from this module in Chapter 7 when you look at validating DSC resources.

Using Plaster to Generate a HQRM Scaffold

You can download Plaster from the PowerShell gallery using the `Install-Module` cmdlet.

```
Install-Module -Name Plaster -Force
```

Once you have the Plaster module, download Ben's plaster template from http://azrs.tk/dscPlaster. This downloads a zip archive. You can extract the `NewDscHighQualityResourceModule` folder in the zip archive to the local system where the Plaster module is available.

Using `Get-PlasterTemplate` shows the information about the HQRM DSC resource template.

```
Get-PlasterTemplate -Path C:\Scripts\NewDscHighQualityResourceModule
```

The output from this command is shown in Figure 6-18.

```
PS C:\> Get-PlasterTemplate -Path C:\Scripts\NewDscHighQualityResourceModule


Title        : New Dsc High Quality Resource Module
Author       : Ben Gelens
Version      : 0.1.0
Description  : Create a Dsc HQRM Resource Module including a first resource to the root of your workspace
Tags         :
TemplatePath : C:\Scripts\NewDscHighQualityResourceModule
```

Figure 6-18.   *Output from Get-PlasterTemplate*

And a HQRM DSC scaffold can be generated by using the `Invoke-Plaster` command.

```
Invoke-Plaster -TemplatePath C:\Scripts\NewDscHighQualityResourceModule
-DestinationPath C:\Scripts\NewHQRMModule -Force
```

This will invoke the Plaster template, which in turns prompts you for several things like the resource module name, resource details, and so on. This process is interactive and self-explanatory, so I will skip it but show you the result of this run in Figure 6-19.

```
Enter the name of the module (should end with Dsc) (MyHQRMModuleDsc):
Enter the version number of the module (0.1.0.0):
Enter the initial Dsc Resource Friendly Name: HostsFile
Enter the initial Dsc Resource Fully Qualified Name (will be ignored with Class resource) (MSFT_HostsFile):
Destination path: C:\Scripts\NewHQRMModule
   Create  MyHQRMModuleDsc\
   Create  MyHQRMModuleDsc\DSCResources\
   Create  MyHQRMModuleDsc\Tests\
   Create  MyHQRMModuleDsc\Tests\Integration\
   Create  MyHQRMModuleDsc\Tests\Unit\
   Create  MyHQRMModuleDsc\Examples\
   Create  MyHQRMModuleDsc\.vscode\
   Create  MyHQRMModuleDsc\MyHQRMModuleDsc.psd1
   Create  MyHQRMModuleDsc\DSCResources\MSFT_HostsFile\MSFT_HostsFile.psm1
   Create  MyHQRMModuleDsc\DSCResources\MSFT_HostsFile\MSFT_HostsFile.schema.mof
   Create  MyHQRMModuleDsc\Tests\Integration\MSFT_HostsFile.Integration.Tests.ps1
   Create  MyHQRMModuleDsc\Tests\Integration\MSFT_HostsFile.Config.ps1
   Create  MyHQRMModuleDsc\Tests\Unit\MSFT_HostsFile.Tests.ps1
   Create  MyHQRMModuleDsc\Examples\MSFT_HostsFile_Example.ps1
   Create  MyHQRMModuleDsc\README.md
   Create  MyHQRMModuleDsc\appveyor.yml
   Create  MyHQRMModuleDsc\LICENSE
   Create  MyHQRMModuleDsc\.gitignore
   Create  MyHQRMModuleDsc\.codecov.yml
   Create  MyHQRMModuleDsc\.MetaTestOptIn.json
   Create  MyHQRMModuleDsc\.vscode\settings.json
```

Figure 6-19. *Output from Invoke-Plaster*

Once the scaffold generation is complete, you can check the folder structure created by the Plaster template. This is shown in Figure 6-20.

```
C:\SCRIPTS\NEWHQRMMODULE\MYHQRMMODULEDSC
|   .codecov.yml
|   .gitignore
|   .MetaTestOptIn.json
|   appveyor.yml
|   LICENSE
|   MyHQRMModuleDsc.psd1
|   README.md
|
+---.vscode
|       settings.json
|
+---DSCResources
|   \---MSFT_HostsFile
|           MSFT_HostsFile.psm1
|           MSFT_HostsFile.schema.mof
|
+---Examples
|       MSFT_HostsFile_Example.ps1
|
\---Tests
    +---Integration
    |       MSFT_HostsFile.Config.ps1
    |       MSFT_HostsFile.Integration.Tests.ps1
    |
    \---Unit
            MSFT_HostsFile.Tests.ps1
```

Figure 6-20. *Folder structure of the new scaffold*

There are some additional files in the scaffold that you can see, such as `appveyor.yml`. I will discuss this in Chapter 14 when I show you how to implement Continuous Integration for DSC with AppVeyor.

What I have covered in this section is only a small part of the complete style and coding guidelines for the HQRM modules. It is simply not possible to cover it all in a single chapter and some of it doesn't make sense if you don't intend to submit your modules upstream.

Publishing DSC Resource Modules

In the earlier chapters, you used the `Install-Module` cmdlet to download and install the DSC resource modules from the PowerShell gallery on to the authoring station or target nodes when there was no pull server infrastructure. Let's take a look at creating a file share-based internal private PowerShell repository. This can be very useful in scenarios where your target nodes do not have Internet access to download and install the modules directly from the official gallery. I use this method extensively in my lab work to ensure all my target nodes can easily get access to the updated modules as they go out from my source control through a continuous integration pipeline. This is something you will explore in Chapter 14.

Before you can publish to an internal PowerShell repository, you need to create one. The `PowerShellGet` module provides the commands that you need to achieve this task.

Creating a Private Repository

Creating a file-share based internal PowerShell repository is done using the `Register-PSRepository` cmdlet in the `PowerShellGet` module.

```
$localRepository = @{
    Name               = 'ProDscRepo'
    SourceLocation     = '\\S16-JB\ProDSCRepo'
    PublishLocation    = '\\S16-JB\ProDSCRepo'
    InstallationPolicy = 'Trusted'
}

Register-PSRepository @localRepository
```

Once the repository is set up, you can use the `Get-PSRepository` cmdlet to verify that it exists. This is shown in Figure 6-21.

```
PS C:\> Get-PSRepository

Name                 InstallationPolicy   SourceLocation
----                 ------------------   --------------
PSGallery            Untrusted            https://www.powershellgallery.com/api/v2/
ProDscRepo           Trusted              \\S16-JB\ProDSCRepo
```

Figure 6-21. *Registered PowerShell repositories*

Note   The PSGallery repository is registered by default on all WMF 5.0 and above systems. The steps that you performed to register an internal repository must be done all systems that need to publish or download modules.

Publishing a Module to a Private Repository

In this chapter, you built your first DSC resource module. You can try publishing it to the internal private repository you created just now. This is done using the Publish-Module cmdlet. Before using this command, ensure that the module is available within one of the folders represented by $env:PSModulePath.

```
Publish-Module -Name ProDSC -Repository ProDscRepo -Verbose
```

If you're running the Publish-Module or Install-Module cmdlet for the first time, you will receive a prompt to install NuGet.exe. If you click Yes, Nuget.exe will be downloaded and installed on the local system. Once the NuGet install is complete, the module gets packaged and published to the internal repository. Figure 6-22 shows partial output from this process.

```
PS C:\scripts> Publish-Module -Name ProDSC -Repository ProDscRepo -Verbose
VERBOSE: Installing NuGet.exe.
VERBOSE: GET http://go.microsoft.com/fwlink/?LinkID=690216&clcid=0x409 with 0-byte payload
VERBOSE: received 1686528-byte response of content type application/octet-stream
VERBOSE: Repository details, Name = 'ProDscRepo', Location = '\\S16-JB\ProDSCRepo'; IsTrusted = 'T
rue'; IsRegistered = 'True'.
VERBOSE: Repository details, Name = 'ProDscRepo', Location = '\\S16-JB\ProDSCRepo'; IsTrusted = 'T
rue'; IsRegistered = 'True'.
VERBOSE: Publish Location:'\\S16-JB\ProDSCRepo'.
VERBOSE: Module 'ProDSC' was found in 'C:\Program Files\WindowsPowerShell\Modules\ProDSC'.
VERBOSE: Repository details, Name = 'ProDscRepo', Location = '\\S16-JB\ProDSCRepo'; IsTrusted = 'T
rue'; IsRegistered = 'True'.
VERBOSE: Using the provider 'PowerShellGet' for searching packages.
VERBOSE: Using the specified source names : 'ProDscRepo'.
VERBOSE: Getting the provider object for the PackageManagement Provider 'NuGet'.
VERBOSE: The specified Location is '\\S16-JB\ProDSCRepo' and PackageManagementProvider is 'NuGet'.
VERBOSE: Total package yield:'0' for the specified package 'ProDSC'.
VERBOSE: Repository details, Name = 'ProDscRepo', Location = '\\S16-JB\ProDSCRepo'; IsTrusted = 'T
rue'; IsRegistered = 'True'.
```

Figure 6-22. *Publishing a module*

Figure 6-23 shows the repository contents after the module is published.

```
PS C:\scripts> Get-ChildItem -Path \\S16-JB\ProDSCRepo


    Directory: \\S16-JB\ProDSCRepo


Mode                LastWriteTime         Length Name
----                -------------         ------ ----
-a----        2/13/2018  10:41 PM           5870 ProDSC.1.0.0.0.nupkg
```

Figure 6-23. *Repository contents*

Finding and Installing Modules from a Private Repository

At this point, you can use the Find-Module or Find-DscResource cmdlet to see if your newly published module or DSC resource can be seen. Figure 6-24 shows the output from the Find-DscResource cmdlet.

```
PS C:\scripts> Find-DscResource -Repository ProDSCRepo

Name                                  Version    ModuleName
----                                  -------    ----------
HostsFile                             1.0.0.0    ProDSC
```

Figure 6-24. *DSC resource from the internal PowerShell repository*

This DSC resource module can now be installed using the Install-Module cmdlet to download and install. You can, optionally, use the Save-Module cmdlet to save it to a local path.

```
Install-Module -Name ProDSC -Repository ProDSCRepo -Force
Save-Module -Name ProDSC -Repository ProDscRepo -Path C:\scripts\DSCModules
```

As you have seen so far, creating a file-based internal PowerShell repository is quite simple. Any modules that you develop internally can be posted here if sharing with a larger public community is not your goal. However, when you want to share the modules with a larger community, you can publish them to the official PowerShell gallery. To be able to publish to the official gallery, you must have a registered account. Once you have registered and logged into the gallery, you can retrieve the NuGet API key required for the publishing process from the "My Account" page, shown in Figure 6-25.

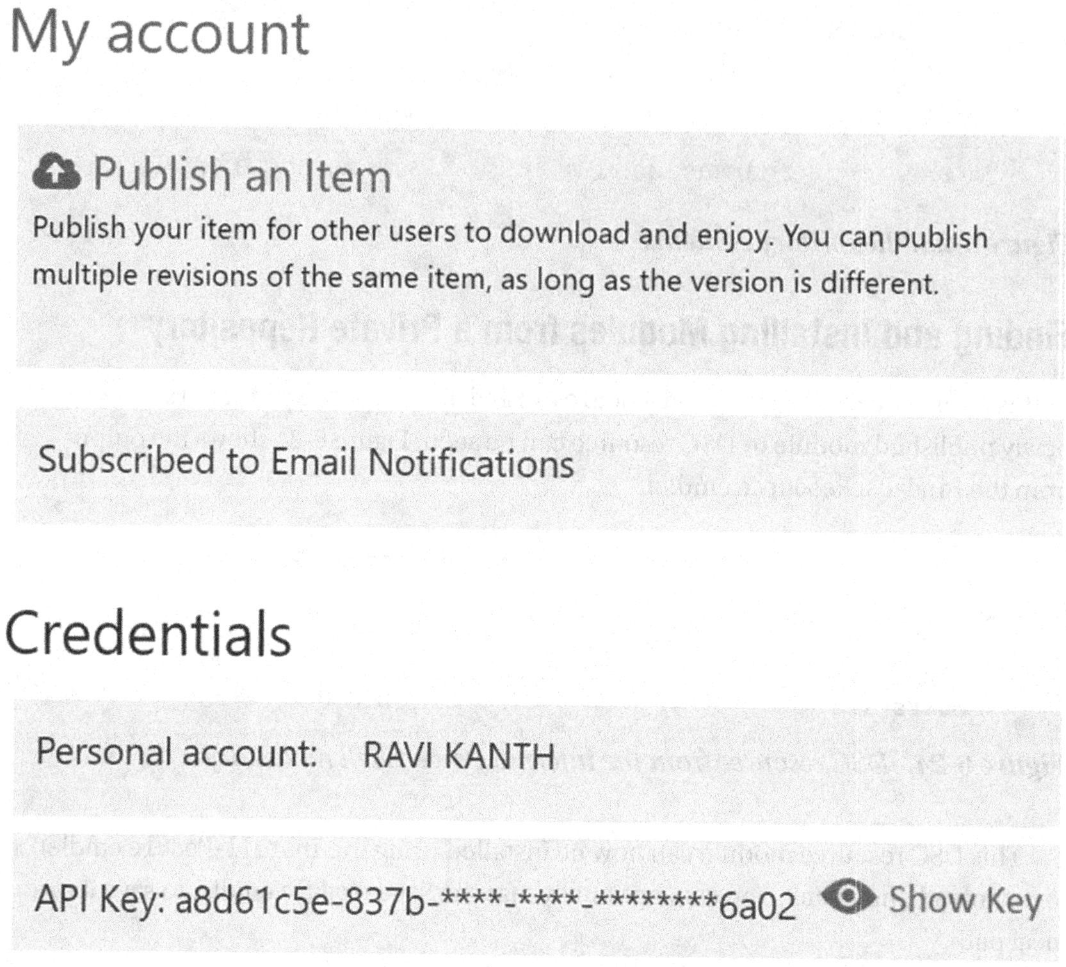

My account

 ## Publish an Item

Publish your item for other users to download and enjoy. You can publish multiple revisions of the same item, as long as the version is different.

Subscribed to Email Notifications

Credentials

Personal account: RAVI KANTH

API Key: a8d61c5e-837b-****_****_********6a02   👁 Show Key

Figure 6-25. *My account page on the PowerShell gallery*

With the API key handy, you can try publishing a module to the gallery using the Publish-Module cmdlet:

```
Publish-Module -Name ProDSC -NuGetApiKey <apiKey>
```

This is it. However, any module that you publish to the official gallery should follow some best practices. These are documented at `http://azrs.tk/pubMod`. These guidelines include using `PSScriptAnalyzer` to ensure that the script code in the module follows coding best practices. You will see this in Chapter 7; you'll also see how to ensure that you perform all these checks as a part of testing the module code.

Summary

This chapter provided detailed content on authoring composite resource modules and custom DSC resource modules. DSC supports developing resource modules as binary modules as well. However, unless there is a specific need to access low-level APIs or the application for which you are writing the DSC resources has the necessary interfaces to configure the application in the form of low-level (accessible as MI APIs) APIs or is written in C#, there is really no need to develop binary resource modules. DSC supports the development of MOF-based and class-based resource modules, which are simply PowerShell modules. MOF-based resource modules work on any system with PowerShell 4.0 and above. The class-based modules work only on PowerShell 5.0 and above. Therefore, choosing between these two types of modules is simple enough. Once you make a choice between MOF- or class-based resources, you can use a Plaster template to help you with the module scaffold generation and start authoring the resource definitions following some of the best practices and guidelines defined in the HQRM guidelines or your own company coding standards. Finally, you learned how to create a local PowerShell module repository and publish the module that you created to that repository. You also learned how similar it is to publish the modules to the official PowerShell gallery. What you did not see in this chapter is information about validating DSC resources. This is available in Chapter 7. You have also not seen how to debug issues with DSC resources, which is the subject of Chapter 12.

CHAPTER 7

Validating DSC Resources

In Chapter 6, you learned how to author DSC resource modules. You also learned how to write MOF-based and class-based DSC resources. To learn these concepts, you created the HostsFile resource, used it in a configuration script, and enacted it. In this entire scenario, you assumed that it worked. It worked, of course, because the code in the examples was tested for basic functionality before putting it in the chapter.

There is a formal way to approach testing of DSC resources and modules. In this chapter, you will learn exactly that. You will learn how to perform basic testing as you start writing the DSC resource script and you will evolve that into a complete set of tests that validate different code paths in the resource script. This will be done using Pester, which is the framework for unit testing and beyond. At the end of this chapter, you should have the necessary knowledge to implement both unit and integration tests for the MOF-based DSC resources. Pester testing for class-based DSC resources is still evolving and there is no standard or method that works across different resources. Therefore, this chapter does not cover class-based resource testing.

Lab Requirements

To try the examples and exercises in this chapter, you will need at minimum two or more systems with Windows Server 2008 R2 or above with WMF 5.1 installed. I recommend a system with Windows Server 2016. The examples and exercises in this chapter require the use of the Pester module and you are expected to know some basics of Pester.

Before you start writing any tests, let's look at some basic validation procedures to ensure that the resources you have authored are syntactically correct and can load as a module. There are multiple small tests that I perform before even writing any configurations that use the newly authored resource module.

© Ravikanth Chaganti 2018

R. Chaganti, *Pro PowerShell Desired State Configuration*, https://doi.org/10.1007/978-1-4842-3483-9_7

Ensuring That the Resource Is Discoverable via Get-DscResource

When the newly authored resource module is copied to the $env:PSModulePath, use the Get-DscResource cmdlet to ensure that the new DSC resource(s) are shown in the output. If the new resource is not available in the Get-DscResource output, it is an indication that one of the module artifacts may not be correct. This includes schema MOF files (for MOF-based resources), resource scripts, the resource manifest (for class-based resources), and the module manifests.

When the new DSC resource is not listed in the Get-DscResource output, commands in the xDscResourceDesigner module can help (for MOF-based resources) figure out what may have gone wrong with the resource module artifacts.

Note   You can try loading the resource script .psm1 files to ensure that they load cleanly with no errors.

Using xDscResourceDesigner for MOF-Based Resources

In Chapter 6, I mentioned the xDscResourceDesigner module a few times but we never really looked at any examples. This module supports generating a scaffold for the MOF-based resources only. It does not implement the HQRM guidelines. So, you have not used xDSCResourceDesigner in the context of scaffolding a new resource but you will use the validation commands from this module to verify the MOF-based resource for the correct syntax. To demonstrate the use of commands from the xDSCResourceDesigner module, I modified the HostsFile MOF-based resource a bit to introduce a bug. This is available as ProDsc-Bug.zip in this chapter's source code. Download this zip archive and extract it to any folder represented by $env:PSModulePath. Run the following command to ensure you have the xDSCResourceDesigner module:

```
Install-Module -Name xDscResourceDesigner -Force
```

This command will install the module from the PowerShell gallery. The commands in this module are shown in Figure 7-1.

```
PS C:\> Get-Command -Module xDSCResourceDesigner

CommandType     Name                              Version    Source
-----------     ----                              -------    ------
Function        Import-xDscSchema                 1.9.0.0    xDSCResourceDesigner
Function        New-xDscResource                  1.9.0.0    xDSCResourceDesigner
Function        New-xDscResourceProperty          1.9.0.0    xDSCResourceDesigner
Function        Test-xDscResource                 1.9.0.0    xDSCResourceDesigner
Function        Test-xDscSchema                   1.9.0.0    xDSCResourceDesigner
Function        Update-xDscResource               1.9.0.0    xDSCResourceDesigner
```

Figure 7-1. *Commands in the xDSCResourceDesigner module*

Within the above set of commands, let's look at the Test-xDscResource command:

Test-xDscResource -Name HostsFile

The Test-xDscResource command searches for the resource at a path represented by the $env:PSModulePath variable and tests the schema and module files. Figure 7-2 shows what you'll see when you try this with the buggy resource module in the ProDsc-Bug.zip.

```
PS C:\> Test-xDscResource -Name HostsFile
Test-ParameterMetaDataIsDscResourceProperty : Property IPAddress has a different
attribute in the schema than in the module.
At C:\Program Files\WindowsPowerShell\Modules\xDSCResourceDesigner\1.9.0.0\xDSCRes
ourceDesigner.psm1:1974 char:23
+ ...        -not (Test-ParameterMetaDataIsDscResourceProperty $SetParameter ...
+              ~~~~~~~~~~~~~~~~~~~~~~~~~~~~~~~~~~~~~~~~~~~~~~~~~~~~~~~~~~~~~~~~~~~~~
    + CategoryInfo          : NotSpecified: (:) [Write-Error], WriteErrorExceptio
   n
    + FullyQualifiedErrorId : SchemaModuleAttributeError,Test-ParameterMetaDataIs
   DscResourceProperty

Test-SetHasExactlyAllNonReadProperties : The functions Set-TargetResource and
Test-TargetResource must take all Key, Required and Write properties. There is an
issue with the parameter IPAddress defined in the schema.
At C:\Program Files\WindowsPowerShell\Modules\xDSCResourceDesigner\1.9.0.0\xDSCRes
ourceDesigner.psm1:1884 char:34
+ ... rror = -not (Test-SetHasExactlyAllNonReadProperties $SetCommandInfo `
+                  ~~~~~~~~~~~~~~~~~~~~~~~~~~~~~~~~~~~~~~~~~~~~~~~~~~~~~~~~~~~~~~~~~
    + CategoryInfo          : NotSpecified: (:) [Write-Error], WriteErrorExceptio
   n
    + FullyQualifiedErrorId : SetAndTestMissingParameterError,Test-SetHasExactlyA
   llNonReadProperties

False
```

Figure 7-2. *Test-xDscResource output*

As shown in Figure 7-2, the schema MOF and the PSM1 do not have a consistent definition of properties. If you open the `HostsFile.Schema.mof` file, you will see that I defined a write qualifier on the `IPAddress` property and the resource script functions have it defined as a mandatory parameter. Let's update the `IPAddress` property in the schema file to define it as a `Key` property and then run the `Test-xDscResource` again. This will return `True`, indicating that the schema and DSC resource script are in good shape.

When working with MOF-based DSC resources, I suggest you use the `Test-xDscResource` command to ensure that the schema and resource scripts have consistent property definitions.

Note   If all you are interested in testing is the schema MOF, you can use the `Test-xDscSchema` command from the `xDscResourceDesigner` module.

Testing for PowerShell Code Guidelines

One of the other tests that I usually perform is to verify if the resource script module is as per the PowerShell coding standards or not. The `PSScriptAnalyzer` module can be used here and it covers a subset of the HQRM style guidelines as well.

To start, install the `PSScriptAnalyzer` module:

```
Install-Module -Name PSScriptAnalyzer -Force
```

Once you have the module installed, you can use the `Invoke-PSScriptAnalyzer` command from this module to test the `HostsFile` resource script for adherence to PowerShell coding standards:

```
Invoke-ScriptAnalyzer -Path (Get-DscResource -Name HostsFile).Path
```

Figure 7-3 shows the results of the script analyzer against the `HostsFile.psm1` file.

```
PS C:\> Invoke-ScriptAnalyzer -Path (Get-DscResource -Name HostsFile).Path
```

RuleName	Severity	ScriptName	Line	Message
PSUseShouldProcessForStateChangingF unctions	Warning	HostsFile. psm1	50	Function 'Set-Ta rgetResource' has verb that could change system state. Therefore, the function has to support 'ShouldProcess'.

Figure 7-3. *Script Analyzer output*

As seen in Figure 7-3, the Set-TargetResource function in the HostsFile resource script impacts the contents of the hosts file on the target node. The suggestion from the script analyzer is to add support for a -WhatIf switch in the Set-TargetResource function. You may choose to implement this support and there is no difference between how you do that for a normal PowerShell function and the Set-TargetResource function in a DSC resource script.

What you have seen so far helps to ensure that resource schema (in case of MOF-based resources) and resource script can be loaded and that they are according to the PowerShell coding guidelines.

When you run the Invoke-ScriptAnalyzer command against the ProDSC module (which you authored in Chapter 6) that contains the class-based resource, you will see a slightly different output. Figure 7-4 shows it.

```
PS C:\> Invoke-ScriptAnalyzer -IncludeDefaultRules -Path 'C:\Program Files\WindowsPowerShell\Modules\ProDSC'
```

RuleName	Severity	ScriptName	Line	Message
PSUseToExportFieldsInManifest	Warning	ProDSC.psd 1	72	Do not use wildcard or $null in this field. Explicitly specify a list for FunctionsToExport.
PSUseToExportFieldsInManifest	Warning	ProDSC.psd 1	75	Do not use wildcard or $null in this field. Explicitly specify a list for CmdletsToExport.
PSUseToExportFieldsInManifest	Warning	ProDSC.psd 1	81	Do not use wildcard or $null in this field. Explicitly specify a list for AliasesToExport.
PSDSCDscExamplesPresent	Information	ProDSC.psm 1	19	No examples found for resource 'HostsFile'
PSDSCDscTestsPresent	Information	ProDSC.psm 1	19	No tests found for resource 'HostsFile'

Figure 7-4. *Suggestions for the class-based resource module*

From Figure 7-4, you can see that your ProDSC resource module is missing examples and tests, which are HQRM requirements and of course a general best practice. Towards the end of Chapter 6 you saw how to add examples. This chapter will give you the information on how to add tests. The other suggestions from Figure 7-4 tell you that the module manifest is using wildcards (*) for FunctionsToExport, CmdletsToExport, and AliasesToExport. This is not needed and therefore the script analyzer is suggesting that the wildcards be replaced with an explicit list of related artifacts to export. In the case of the class-based resource, you do not export any functions or aliases or cmdlets. Therefore, you can simply comment these lines in the module manifest to adhere to the script analyzer recommendations.

You can see a list of rules that the Invoke-ScriptAnalyzer command checks using the Get-ScriptAnalyzerRule command. The rules for DSC are shown in Figure 7-5.

```
PS C:\> Get-ScriptAnalyzerRule | Where SourceName -eq 'PSDSC'
```

RuleName	Severity	Description
PSDSCDscExamplesPresent	Information	Every DSC resource module should contain folder "Examples" with sample configurations for every resource. Sample configurations should have resource name they are demonstrating in the title.
PSDSCDscTestsPresent	Information	Every DSC resource module should contain folder "Tests" with tests for every resource. Test scripts should have resource name they are testing in the file name.
PSDSCReturnCorrectTypesForDSCFuncti ons	Information	Set function in DSC class and Set-TargetResource in DSC resource must not return anything. Get function in DSC class must return an instance of the DSC class and Get-TargetResource function in DSC resource must return a hashtable. Test function in DSC class and Get-TargetResource function in DSC resource must return a boolean.
PSDSCUseIdenticalMandatoryParameter sForDSC	Error	The Get/Test/Set TargetResource functions of DSC resource must have the same mandatory parameters.
PSDSCUseIdenticalParametersForDSC	Error	The Test and Set-TargetResource functions of DSC Resource must have the same parameters.
PSDSCStandardDSCFunctionsInResource	Error	DSC Resource must implement Get, Set and Test-TargetResource functions. DSC Class must implement Get, Set and Test functions.
PSDSCUseVerboseMessageInDSCResource	Information	It is a best practice to emit informative, verbose messages in DSC resource functions. This helps in debugging issues when a DSC configuration is executed.

Figure 7-5. *Script analyzer rules for DSC resource script and modules*

What you have seen so far helps to ensure that the schema files (for MOF-based resources) are valid and the resource scripts follow the PowerShell coding guidelines and DSC module design guidelines (a subset of the HQRM guidelines). However, none of this really validates the logic that went into the Get, Set, and Test functions. There are a few different methods to do this.

- You can simply use the new module in a DSC configuration document, and compile and enact to see if the configuration completes successfully (hopefully!). This is what you did in Chapter 6.

- You can validate each individual function (Get, Set, and Test) using the Invoke-DscResource cmdlet.

- You can write test scripts that use Pester to perform unit and integration testing to validate different code paths in the DSC resource scripts.

The first two methods act on the desired state of the resource. In the first method, you enact a configuration that runs the Test function internally and then calls Set as needed. In the second method, you call individual functions in the context of LCM to ensure that each function works with a given set of resource properties. Let's explore this second method.

Using Invoke-DscResource

WMF 5.0 added the Invoke-DscResource cmdlet within the PSDesiredStateConfiguration module. This was primarily meant for third-party integrations with DSC. For example, other configuration management tools such as Puppet and Chef use this cmdlet to manage DSC configurations on the target nodes. You can use this cmdlet in the context of testing your DSC resource scripts as well. This cmdlet executes the Get, Set, and Test functions in the context of LCM and therefore helps test the resource scripts as if they are being used in a configuration enact process without actually creating a configuration document. This cmdlet can be of great help when debugging resource scripts. When combined with Enable-DscDebug, it will give you the confined scope of debugging through the debugger attachment when compared to a full configuration.

Figure 7-6 shows the `Invoke-DscResource` syntax and Table 7-1 provides an overview of the parameters.

```
PS C:\> Get-Command -Name Invoke-DscResource -Syntax

Invoke-DscResource [-Name] <string> [-Method] <string> -ModuleName <ModuleSpecification> -P
roperty <hashtable> [<CommonParameters>]
```

***Figure 7-6.** Invoke-DscResource parameters*

***Table 7-1.** Overview of Invoke-DscResource Parameters*

Parameter Name	Description
Name	Specifies the name of the DSC resource.
Method	Specifies the name of the resource script method to invoke. The valid values are Get, Set, and Test.
ModuleName	Specifies the name of the DSC resource module. This parameter can also take a module specification hashtable as an argument. For example, @{ModuleName= 'ProDSC';ModuleVersion='1.0.0.0'}.
Property	Specifies a hashtable of key-values pairs for all mandatory and any other optional properties for the resource instance.

Let's look at a few examples.

Invoking the Test Method

Invoking the Test method using the `Invoke-DscResource` cmdlet internally calls the Test function in the resource script.

```
$properties = @{
    HostName  = 'TestServer101'
    IPAddress = '172.16.101.101'
    Ensure = 'Present'
}

Invoke-DscResource -Name HostsFile `
                -Method Test `
```

226

```
                -ModuleName ProDsc `
                -Property $properties `
                -Verbose
```

Figure 7-7 shows the output from this call.

```
VERBOSE: Perform operation 'Invoke CimMethod' with following parameters, ''methodName' = Re
sourceTest,'className' = MSFT_DSCLocalConfigurationManager,'namespaceName' = root/Microsoft
/Windows/DesiredStateConfiguration'.
VERBOSE: An LCM method call arrived from computer S16-JB with user sid S-1-5-21-2403796847-
1381111412-2575929524-500.
VERBOSE: [S16-JB]:                          [DSCEngine] Importing the module C:\Program F
iles\WindowsPowerShell\Modules\ProDSC\ProDSC.psd1 in force mode.
VERBOSE: [S16-JB]: LCM:  [ Start  Test    ] [[HostsFile]DirectResourceAccess]
VERBOSE: [S16-JB]:                          [[HostsFile]DirectResourceAccess] Importing t
he module ProDsc in force mode.
VERBOSE: [S16-JB]:                          [[HostsFile]DirectResourceAccess] Checking if
 the hosts file entry exists.
VERBOSE: [S16-JB]:                          [[HostsFile]DirectResourceAccess] Did not fin
d a hosts file entry for TestHost1 and 172.16.102.101.
VERBOSE: [S16-JB]: LCM:  [ End    Test    ] [[HostsFile]DirectResourceAccess] False in 0.
0310 seconds.
VERBOSE: [S16-JB]: LCM:  [ End    Set     ]  in  0.1560 seconds.
VERBOSE: Operation 'Invoke CimMethod' complete.

InDesiredState
--------------
False
VERBOSE: Time taken for configuration job to complete is 0.277 seconds
```

Figure 7-7. *Test method output*

From Figure 7-7, it is clear that the resource is not in the desired state. The verbose output also tells you that this is a direct resource access, indicating that you are invoking the resource script method directly.

Invoking the Set Method

Since the Test method returned false, you can invoke the Set method to ensure that the resource gets into the desired state.

```
Invoke-DscResource -Name HostsFile `
                -Method Set `
                -ModuleName ProDsc `
                -Property $properties `
                -Verbose
```

```
VERBOSE: Perform operation 'Invoke CimMethod' with following parameters, ''methodName' = Re
sourceSet,'className' = MSFT_DSCLocalConfigurationManager,'namespaceName' = root/Microsoft/
Windows/DesiredStateConfiguration'.
VERBOSE: An LCM method call arrived from computer S16-JB with user sid S-1-5-21-2403796847-
1381111412-2575929524-500.
VERBOSE: [S16-JB]:                              [DSCEngine] Importing the module C:\Program F
iles\WindowsPowerShell\Modules\ProDSC\ProDSC.psd1 in force mode.
VERBOSE: [S16-JB]: LCM:  [ Start  Set     ] [[HostsFile]DirectResourceAccess]
VERBOSE: [S16-JB]:                              [[HostsFile]DirectResourceAccess] Importing t
he module ProDsc in force mode.
VERBOSE: [S16-JB]:                              [[HostsFile]DirectResourceAccess] Creating a
hosts file entry with TestHost1 and 172.16.102.101.
VERBOSE: [S16-JB]: LCM:  [ End    Set     ] [[HostsFile]DirectResourceAccess]  in 0.0160
seconds.
VERBOSE: [S16-JB]: LCM:  [ End    Set     ]  in  0.1250 seconds.
VERBOSE: Operation 'Invoke CimMethod' complete.

RebootRequired
--------------
False
VERBOSE: Time taken for configuration job to complete is 0.249 seconds
```

Figure 7-8. *Set method output*

The Set method output in Figure 7-8 shows that the resource instance is set to the desired state. In this example, the call to the Set method added the hosts file entry.

Invoking the Get Method

You have the resource set to desired using the Set method. Now you can invoke the resource Get method to see the current state of the resource instance.

```
$properties.Remove('Ensure')
Invoke-DscResource -Name HostsFile `
                -Method Get `
                -ModuleName ProDsc `
                -Property $properties
```

This output from the above command can be seen in Figure 7-9.

```
ConfigurationName      :
DependsOn              :
ModuleName             : ProDsc
ModuleVersion          : 1.0.0.0
PsDscRunAsCredential   :
ResourceId             :
SourceInfo             :
Ensure                 : Present
HostName               : TestServer101
IPAddress              : 172.16.101.101
PSComputerName         : localhost
```

Figure 7-9. *Get method output*

What you saw in the preceding section and in the configuration enact method in Chapter 6 help you ensure that the resource instance can be configured essentially acting on the desired state of the resource. However, this type of testing may not always be possible or might not test all possible code paths in a DSC resource script. To address this, you write test scripts to perform unit testing of your DSC resource scripts. Within the unit tests, you mock the functionality needed for the DSC resource script functions so that you don't change the state of the resource instance. This is done using Pester, which is a test framework for PowerShell.

The other type of tests for DSC resource script validations are integration tests. What you saw in Chapter 6, enacting a configuration with your new DSC resource, is an example of an integration test. However, in the ideal test workflow, an integration test must be run only after the unit tests are complete with no errors.

In the subsequent sections, you will see how to author unit and integration tests using Pester.

Authoring Pester Tests for DSC

Pester started as a unit testing framework for PowerShell. At present, it is used as both a unit and operations validation framework. The Pester module (version 3.4.0) is available in-box starting Windows Server 2016. You can install the most recent version of the Pester module (version 4.3.1 at the time of writing) from the PowerShell gallery.

```
Install-Module -Name Pester -SkipPublisherCheck -Force
```

The -SkipPublisherCheck switch parameter is needed since the in-box version of this module is signed by Microsoft but the version from PowerShell gallery is not.

Note   A complete overview of Pester is outside the scope of this book. The Pester wiki on GitHub has a complete and in-depth explanation of the capabilities and the Pester DSL syntax.

At 30,000 feet, here is what a Pester test script looks like:

```
Describe 'Tests that work on numbers' {
    Context 'Tests for adding numbers' {
        It "adds positive numbers" {
            $sum = Add-Numbers 2 3
            $sum | Should Be 5
        }

        It "adds negative numbers" {
            $sum = Add-Numbers (-2) (-3)
            $sum | Should Be (-5)
        }
    }

    Context 'Tests for subtracting numbers' {
        It "subtract positive numbers" {
            $sum = Subtract-Numbers 9 5
            $sum | Should Be 4
        }
    }
}
```

In this code snippet, you see three distinct script blocks:

- Describe is used to define a group of test cases. In the example above, this group tests numerical operations. A test script should contain at least one Describe block. Think of this as a test plan.

- Context is an optional sub-group of test cases. In the above example, all addition tests are grouped into a separate Context within the Describe block. This helps organize tests into logical sub-groups.

- It is used to define an individual test case. There can be many tests cases inside a `Context` block or these tests can be directly inside a `Describe` block.

Within each test case, you are performing an assertion. For example, after you call the `Add-Numbers` function, you assert that the value returned by the function must be equal to a specified value. These assertions are made possible by keywords such as `Should Be` and so on. There are many such assertions available in the overall Pester test framework.

With this understanding, let's look at writing Pester tests for DSC resource scripts.

DSC Resource Unit Tests

Unit testing refers to the testing of individual functions in the DSC resource scripts. In this section, you will look at the Pester unit patterns for DSC resource script functions and implement the tests for one of the patterns.

Note   A set of testing guidelines for the DSC resources is available at `http://azrs.tk/dsctest`.

In the first pattern of writing DSC unit tests, you describe the potential states of a resource instance in the context of each function. Here, the state of a resource instance is more than just absent or present. For example, when you look at the `HostsFile` resource, the following are the potential states of the resource instance:

- **Test-TargetResource**

    - Hosts entry does not exist and it should. Should return `false`.

    - Hosts entry does not exist and it should not. Should return `true`.

    - Hosts entry exists and it should not. Should return `false`.

    - Hosts entry exists and it should. Should return `true`.

- **Get-TargetResource**

    - Hosts entry does not exist and it should return `Ensure` as `Absent`.

    - Hosts entry exists and it should return `Ensure` as `Present`.

- **Set-TargetResource**

    - Hosts entry does not exist and it should. It should be added.

    - Hosts entry exists and it should not. It should be removed.

This is just a subset of the possible states of a `HostsFile` resource instance in the context of each function. The following code snippet shows the bare-bones Pester test script for this pattern:

```
Describe 'Hosts file resource tests'
    Context 'Get-TargetResource' {
        It 'Hosts entry does not exist and it should return Ensure as
        Absent' {
            #Write the test logic here
        }

        It 'Hosts entry exists and it should return Ensure as Present.' {
            #Write the test logic here
        }
    }

    Context 'Set-TargetResource' {
        It 'Hosts entry does not exist and it should. It should be added.' {
            #Write the test logic here
        }

        It 'Hosts entry exists and it should not. It should be removed.' {
            #Write the test logic here
        }
    }

    Context 'Test-TargetResource' {
        It 'Hosts entry does not exist and it should. Should return false.' {
            #Write the test logic here
        }

        It 'Hosts entry does not exist and it should not. Should return
        true.' {
            #Write the test logic here
        }
```

```
    It 'Hosts entry exists and it should not. Should return false.' {
        #Write the test logic here
    }

    It '- Hosts entry exists and it should. Should return true.' {
        #Write the test logic here
    }
  }
}
```

In the second pattern of writing Pester unit tests for DSC resource scripts, you define the potential state of a resource and then test each resource script function in that potential state. This may sound similar to the first pattern but its implementation is different.

The following list describes the potential states:

- A hosts file entry does not exist. It should.

  - Get function should return Ensure as Absent.

  - Test function should return false.

  - Set function should add the hosts file entry.

- A hosts file entry exists as it should.

  - Get function should return Ensure as Present.

  - Test function should return true.

- A hosts file entry exists and it should not.

  - Get function should return Ensure as Present.

  - Test function should return false.

  - Set function should call Set-Content only once.

- A hosts file entry does not exist and it should not.

  - Get function should return Ensure as Absent.

  - Test function should return true.

Do you see how the second pattern differs from the first one? The overall objective does not change, just how you write and organize the tests changes. The bare bones Pester script for this script is as follows:

```
Describe 'Hosts file resource tests' {
    Context 'A hosts file entry does not exist. It should.' {
        It 'Get function should return Ensure as absent.' {

        }

        It 'Test function should return false.' {

        }

        It 'Set function should add the hosts file entry.' {

        }
    }

    Context 'A hosts file entry exists as it should.' {
        It 'Get function should return Ensure as present.' {

        }

        It 'Test function should return true.' {

        }
    }

    Context 'A hosts file entry exists and it should not.' {
        It 'Get function should return Ensure as present.' {

        }

        It 'Test function should return false.' {

        }

        It 'Set function should call Set-Content only once.' {

        }
    }
```

```
Context 'A hosts file entry does not exist and it should not.' {
    It 'Get function should return Ensure as absent.' {

    }

    It 'Test function should return true.' {

    }
  }
}
```

I personally prefer the second pattern because it gives me a clear idea of the resource state I am testing.

Alright! This section, so far, has given you an overview of the two test script patterns for DSC unit testing and provided quick look into the test script for each pattern. However, this is not the end. In the earlier section, I mentioned that the unit tests don't change or act on the desired state of the resource in reality. In unit tests, you validate only the code path and not a real enact of the resource instance configuration. In Pester, this is done using mocking. Mocking in Pester makes it easy to fake dependencies. For example, you used the Get-Content, Set-Content, and Add-Content cmdlets in the HostsFile resource script. These commands help you read and update the hosts file based on the resource instance state. Unlike a real enact, you don't want to make any updates the hosts file while performing unit tests. So, you need to fake these commands using mocking in Pester.

Here is an example of a mock of the Get-Content cmdlet that you can use in the Pester test script:

```
Mock -CommandName Get-Content -MockWith {
    return @(
        '# An example of a host file',
        '',
        '172.16.102.1        Router',
        '127.0.0.1  localhost',
        ''
    )
}
```

In this mock, you are describing the Get-Content cmdlet and also mocking what it returns when invoke. In the DSC resource script for the HostsFile resource, you use Get-Content to read the hosts file on the target node. With -MockWith, when the resource script functions call the Get-Content cmdlet, they receive a mocked object that represents the contents of a hosts file.

This covers the basics that you need to know to start writing your DSC tests. Let's look at the complete test script template and start writing the tests.

Test Template

In Chapter 6, you looked at the Plaster module that you used to scaffold the DSC HQRM module. The scaffold that was generated has the Tests folder and a template test script for the unit tests. This is shown in Figure 7-10.

```
PS C:\scripts> tree /F /A .\NewHQRMModule\ProDSC\Tests
Folder PATH listing
Volume serial number is C8D6-C055
C:\SCRIPTS\NEWHQRMMODULE\PRODSC\TESTS
+---Integration
|       HostsFile.Config.ps1
|       HostsFile.Integration.Tests.ps1
|
\---Unit
        HostsFile.Tests.ps1
```

Figure 7-10. *Tests folder and test templates in the scaffold*

Let's take a look at HostsFile.Tests.ps1.

```
#region HEADER

# Unit Test Template Version: 1.2.0
$script:moduleRoot = Split-Path -Parent (Split-Path -Parent $PSScriptRoot)
if ( (-not (Test-Path -Path (Join-Path -Path $script:moduleRoot -ChildPath
'DSCResource.Tests'))) -or `
    (-not (Test-Path -Path (Join-Path -Path $script:moduleRoot -ChildPath
    'DSCResource.Tests\TestHelper.psm1'))) )
{
    & git @('clone','https://github.com/PowerShell/DscResource.Tests.
    git',(Join-Path -Path $script:moduleRoot -ChildPath '\DSCResource.
    Tests\'))
}
```

```powershell
Import-Module -Name (Join-Path -Path $script:moduleRoot -ChildPath (Join-
Path -Path 'DSCResource.Tests' -ChildPath 'TestHelper.psm1')) -Force

$TestEnvironment = Initialize-TestEnvironment `
    -DSCModuleName 'ProDsc' `
    -DSCResourceName 'HostsFile' `
    -TestType Unit

#endregion HEADER

function Invoke-TestSetup {
    # TODO: Optional init code goes here...
}

function Invoke-TestCleanup {
    Restore-TestEnvironment -TestEnvironment $TestEnvironment

    # TODO: Other Optional Cleanup Code Goes Here...
}

# Begin Testing
try
{
    Invoke-TestSetup

    InModuleScope 'HostsFile' {

        Describe '<Test-name>' {
            BeforeEach {
                # per-test-initialization
            }

            AfterEach {
                # per-test-cleanup
            }

            Context 'Context-description' {
                BeforeEach {
                    # per-test-initialization
                }
```

```
            AfterEach {
                # per-test-cleanup
            }

            It 'Should...test-description' {
                # test-code
            }

            It 'Should...test-description' {
                # test-code
            }
        }

        Context 'Context-description' {
            It 'Should ....test-description' {
                # test-code
            }
        }
    }

    Describe '<Test-name>' {
        Context '<Context-description>' {
            It 'Should ...test-description' {
                # test-code
            }
        }
    }

    # TODO: add more Describe blocks as needed
    }
}
finally
{
    Invoke-TestCleanup
}
```

> **Note**   I removed a few comments that were in the test template and left only what is necessary.

The first few lines in the template above (in the HEADER region) download the DSC resource test helpers from the official PowerShell GitHub repository. Therefore, this requires `git.exe` on the system where you intend to invoke these Pester test scripts. You can get this by installing the Git software from `https://git-scm.com/`. The `TestHelper.psm1` module contains the `Initialize-TestEnvironment` and `Restore-TestEnvironment` among other functions.

The `Initialize-TestEnvironment` function loads the DSC resource scripts into the global scope and makes the resource script functions available for the unit test cases.

The `Invoke-TestSetup` and the `Invoke-TestCleanup` functions defined in the test script help prepare any prerequisites needed for the tests to run and clean up the environment after the tests are complete. These are optional and need not be there in the test script.

The `try-finally` block is where the tests are placed. The `InModuleScope` script block allows you to run the units tests in the context of non-exported code of the DSC resource script. In your case, this is the `HostsFile` module.

The test template script contains a couple of `Describe` blocks. If you look at the first one, it has a few more helper commands such as the `BeforeEach` and `AfterEach`. These commands can be used to define setup and teardown tasks that are performed at the beginning and end of the `It` blocks. For example, in your test script for the `HostsFile` resource, you can use the `BeforeEach` command to create the mocks for `Add-Content` and `Set-Content` cmdlets. This way, these mocks need to be available for each `It` block or test in the script. So, you can define this command within the `Describe` block instead of defining it in each `Context` where it becomes available the `Context` block.

You don't need any command to run after each `It` block and therefore you don't need to use the `AfterEach` command.

HostsFile Unit Tests

With what you have learned so far, let's start putting together this test script incrementally.

Here is how the test script looks with just the initialization code and the BeforeEach in the Describe block:

```
#region HEADER

# Unit Test Template Version: 1.2.0
$script:moduleRoot = Split-Path -Parent (Split-Path -Parent $PSScriptRoot)
if ( (-not (Test-Path -Path (Join-Path -Path $script:moduleRoot -ChildPath
'DSCResource.Tests'))) -or `
    (-not (Test-Path -Path (Join-Path -Path $script:moduleRoot -ChildPath
    'DSCResource.Tests\TestHelper.psm1'))) )
{
    & git @('clone','https://github.com/PowerShell/DscResource.Tests.
    git',(Join-Path -Path $script:moduleRoot -ChildPath '\DSCResource.
    Tests\'))
}

Import-Module -Name (Join-Path -Path $script:moduleRoot -ChildPath (Join-
Path -Path 'DSCResource.Tests' -ChildPath 'TestHelper.psm1')) -Force

$TestEnvironment = Initialize-TestEnvironment `
    -DSCModuleName 'ProDsc' `
    -DSCResourceName 'HostsFile' `
    -TestType Unit

#endregion HEADER

function Invoke-TestCleanup {
    Restore-TestEnvironment -TestEnvironment $TestEnvironment
}

# Begin Testing
try
{
    InModuleScope 'HostsFile' {
        Describe 'Unit tests for the HostsFile resource' {
            BeforeEach {
                Mock -CommandName Add-Content
```

```
            Mock -CommandName Set-Content
        }
    }
}
}
finally
{
    Invoke-TestCleanup
}
```

You don't have any test-subgroups (Context) and test cases (It) yet in the test script. You will start authoring these tests using the second test design pattern you saw earlier.

Context: A Hosts File Entry Does Not Exist. It Should.

Here is what you had in the second pattern as the first state of the HostsFile resource instance:

```
Context 'A hosts file entry does not exist. It should.' {
    It 'Get function should return Ensure as absent.' {

    }

    It 'Test function should return false.' {

    }

    It 'Set function should add the hosts file entry.' {

    }
}
```

Before you define each test case, you need the test parameters that you plan to use with the Get, Set, and Test functions. There is no need to specify the Ensure property since it has a default value set to Present.

```
$testParameters = @{
    HostName  = 'TestServer102'
    IPAddress = '172.16.102.102'
    Verbose   = $true
}
```

You also need a context-specific mock for the Get-Content cmdlet that returns a mocked object representing hosts file content:

```
Mock -CommandName Get-Content -MockWith {
    return @(
        '# An example of a host file',
        '',
        '172.16.102.1        Router',
        '127.0.0.1  localhost',
        ''
    )
}
```

With the test parameters and mock available, you can start writing the test cases (It blocks):

```
Context 'A hosts file entry does not exist. It should.' {
    It 'Get function should return Ensure as absent.' {
        (Get-TargetResource @testParameters).Ensure | Should Be 'Absent'
    }

    It 'Test function should return false.' {
        Test-TargetResource @testParameters | Should Be $false
    }

    It 'Set function should add the hosts file entry.' {
        Set-TargetResource @testParameters
        Assert-MockCalled -CommandName Add-Content
    }
}
```

The first two assertions should self-explanatory. The HostName and IPAddress entry that is specified using $testParameters is not there in the mock object returned by the Get-Content mock function. Therefore, Get-TargetResource is expected to return Ensure as Absent and Test-TargetResource is expected to return $false. In the third test in this context, you use Assert-MockCalled to ensure that the Add-TargetResource indeed attempted to update the content of the hosts file with a new entry.

Let's put these bit and pieces together and see the complete test script.

Note In order to reduce the code snippet length, I have removed the HEADER region from the below example. In the test script that you will run, the commands in the HEADER region are very important.

```
# Begin Testing
try
{
    InModuleScope 'HostsFile' {
        Describe 'Unit tests for the HostsFile resource' {
            BeforeEach {
                Mock -CommandName Add-Content
                Mock -CommandName Set-Content
            }

            Context 'A hosts file entry does not exist. It should.' {
                $testParameters = @{
                    HostName  = 'TestServer102'
                    IPAddress = '172.16.102.102'
                    Verbose   = $true
                }

                Mock -CommandName Get-Content -MockWith {
                    return @(
                        '# An example of a host file',
                        '',
                        '172.16.102.1        Router',
                        '127.0.0.1  localhost',
                        ''

                    )
                }

                It 'Get function should return Ensure as absent.' {
                    (Get-TargetResource @testParameters).Ensure | Should Be
                    'Absent'
                }
```

```
            It 'Test function should return false.' {
                Test-TargetResource @testParameters | Should Be $false
            }

            It 'Set function should add the hosts file entry.' {
                Set-TargetResource @testParameters
                Assert-MockCalled -CommandName Add-Content -Times 1
            }
        }
    }
}
}
finally
{
    Invoke-TestCleanup
}
```

Before invoking this Pester test script, ensure that you have the right folder structure with the MOF-based HostsFile resource. Figure 7-11 shows the required folder structure.

```
PS C:\> Tree /F /A .\scripts\ProDSC
Folder PATH listing
Volume serial number is C8D6-C055
C:\SCRIPTS\PRODSC
|   ProDSC.psd1
|
+---DSCResources
|   \---HostsFile
|           HostsFile.psm1
|           HostsFile.Schema.mof
|
\---Tests
    \---Unit
            HostsFile.Tests.ps1
```

Figure 7-11. Folder structure for the unit testing

It is important to ensure that the resource module folder (ProDSC in this example) is available at the same level as the Tests folder. For the unit tests, you must have a folder called Unit in the Tests folder.

244

Once this folder structure is ready, you can execute the test script using the Invoke-Pester command. You can navigate to the folder containing the test script and run the Invoke-Pester command without any arguments. When this script is executed for the first time, using git.exe, the DSCResources.Tests repository gets cloned locally and the tests in the context block(s) get executed. The output from this is as follows:

```
PS C:\scripts\ProDSC\Tests\Unit> Invoke-Pester

Cloning into 'C:\scripts\ProDSC\DSCResource.Tests'...
remote: Counting objects: 946, done.
remote: Compressing objects: 100% (4/4), done.
Rremote: Total 946 (delta 0), reused 1 (delta 0), pack-reused 942
Receiving objects: 100% (946/946), 340.51 KiB | 253.00 KiB/s, done.
Resolving deltas: 100% (550/550)
Resolving deltas: 100% (550/550), done.
Describing Unit tests for the HostsFile resource
    Context A hosts file entry does not exist. It should.
VERBOSE: Checking if hosts file entry exists for TestServer102 and
172.16.102.102 or not.
VERBOSE: Hosts file entry for TestServer102 and 172.16.102.102 does not
exist.
    [+] Get function should return Ensure as absent. 5s
VERBOSE: Checking if the hosts file entry for TestServer102 and
172.16.102.102 exists or not.
VERBOSE: Hosts file entry  for TestServer102 and 172.16.102.102 does not
exist while it should; it must be added.
    [+] Test function should return false. 179ms
VERBOSE: Creating hosts file entry for TestServer102 and 172.16.102.102.
    [+] Set function should add the hosts file entry. 156ms
Tests completed in 5.34s
Passed: 3 Failed: 0 Skipped: 0 Pending: 0 Inconclusive: 0
```

This is good. Your first three tests in the first context passed, indicating that if a hosts file entry does not exist and if it should, your resource script handles the expected way.

Let's look at the other three contexts and write the tests for each scenario.

Note   When running again, the DSCResource.Tests tests get in scope as well so a lot more tests are actually run then.

Context: A Hosts File Entry Exists As It Should.

Similar to the first context, you will need the test parameters and Get-Content mock here. Since the resource instance state assumes that the hosts file entry exists, the Get-Content should return a mocked object that indicates the same.

```
Context 'A hosts file entry exists as it should.' {

    $testParameters = @{
        HostName  = 'TestServer102'
        IPAddress = '172.16.102.102'
        Verbose   = $true
    }

    Mock -CommandName Get-Content -MockWith {
        return @(
            '# An example of a host file',
            '',
            '127.0.0.1  localhost',
            "$($testParameters.IPAddress)        $($testParameters.
            HostName)",
            ''
        )
    }

    It 'Get function should return Ensure as present.' {
        (Get-TargetResource @testParameters).Ensure | Should Be 'Present'
    }

    It 'Test function should return true.' {
        Test-TargetResource @testParameters | Should Be $true
    }
}
```

In the test parameters, there is no need to specify the Ensure property since it has a default value set to Present.

Context: A Hosts File Entry Exists and It Should Not.

In this context, you test whether the resource script functions can handle the resource state where the hosts file entry exists when it should not. In this case, the Get function should return Ensure set to Present, Test should return $false, and the Set function should remove this entry and should call the Set-Content mock only once.

The test parameters and the Get-Content mock can be same as the second context but the Ensure should be set to Absent.

```
Context 'A hosts file entry exists and it should not.' {

    $testParameters = @{
        HostName  = 'TestServer102'
        IPAddress = '172.16.102.102'
        Ensure    = 'Absent'
        Verbose   = $true
    }

    Mock -CommandName Get-Content -MockWith {
        return @(
            '# An example of a host file',
            '',
            '127.0.0.1  localhost',
            "$($testParameters.IPAddress)            $($testParameters.
            HostName)",
            ''
        )
    }

    It 'Get function should return Ensure as present.' {
        (Get-TargetResource @testParameters).Ensure | Should Be 'Present'
    }

    It 'Test function should return false.' {
        Test-TargetResource @testParameters | Should Be $false
    }
```

```
It 'Set function should call Set-Content only once.' {
    Set-TargetResource @testParameters
    Assert-MockCalled -CommandName Set-Content -Times 1
}
}
```

Context: A Hosts File Entry Does Not Exist and It Should Not.

In this context, you test the state of the HostsFile resource where the hosts file entry does not exist and it should not. In this scenario, you need to test only the Get and Test functions to ensure that Get returns Ensure set to Absent and Test returns $false.

The test parameters will be same as the third context and the Get-Content mock should return the hosts file content that does not contain the entry for specified test parameters.

```
Context 'A hosts file entry does not exist and it should not.' {

    $testParameters = @{
        HostName  = 'TestServer102'
        IPAddress = '172.16.102.102'
        Ensure    = 'Absent'
        Verbose   = $true
    }

    Mock -CommandName Get-Content -MockWith {
        return @(
            '# An example of a host file',
            '',
            '127.0.0.1  localhost',
            ''
        )
    }

    It 'Get function should return Ensure as absent.' {
        (Get-TargetResource @testParameters).Ensure | Should Be 'Absent'
    }
```

```
    It 'Test function should return true.' {
        Test-TargetResource @testParameters | Should Be $true
    }
}
```

Here is the final test script that contains test cases for all potential resource states:

```
#region HEADER

# Unit Test Template Version: 1.2.0
$script:moduleRoot = Split-Path -Parent (Split-Path -Parent $PSScriptRoot)
if ( (-not (Test-Path -Path (Join-Path -Path $script:moduleRoot -ChildPath
'DSCResource.Tests'))) -or `
        (-not (Test-Path -Path (Join-Path -Path $script:moduleRoot
        -ChildPath 'DSCResource.Tests\TestHelper.psm1'))) )
{
    & git @('clone','https://github.com/PowerShell/DscResource.Tests.git',
    (Join-Path -Path $script:moduleRoot -ChildPath '\DSCResource.Tests\'))
}

Import-Module -Name (Join-Path -Path $script:moduleRoot -ChildPath (Join-
Path -Path 'DSCResource.Tests' -ChildPath 'TestHelper.psm1')) -Force

$TestEnvironment = Initialize-TestEnvironment `
    -DSCModuleName 'ProDsc' `
    -DSCResourceName 'HostsFile' `
    -TestType Unit

#endregion HEADER

function Invoke-TestCleanup {
    Restore-TestEnvironment -TestEnvironment $TestEnvironment
}

# Begin Testing
try
{
```

```powershell
InModuleScope 'HostsFile' {
    Describe 'Unit tests for the HostsFile resource' {
        BeforeEach {
            Mock -CommandName Add-Content
            Mock -CommandName Set-Content
        }

        Context 'A hosts file entry does not exist. It should.' {
            $testParameters = @{
                HostName  = 'TestServer102'
                IPAddress = '172.16.102.102'
                Verbose   = $true
            }

            Mock -CommandName Get-Content -MockWith {
                return @(
                    '# An example of a host file',
                    '',
                    '172.16.102.1         Router',
                    '127.0.0.1  localhost',
                    ''
                )
            }

            It 'Get function should return Ensure as absent.' {
                (Get-TargetResource @testParameters).Ensure | Should Be
                'Absent'
            }

            It 'Test function should return false.' {
                Test-TargetResource @testParameters | Should Be $false
            }

            It 'Set function should add the hosts file entry.' {
                Set-TargetResource @testParameters
                Assert-MockCalled -CommandName Add-Content -Times 1
            }
        }
```

```
Context 'A hosts file entry exists as it should.' {

    $testParameters = @{
        HostName  = 'TestServer102'
        IPAddress = '172.16.102.102'
        Verbose   = $true
    }

    Mock -CommandName Get-Content -MockWith {
        return @(
            '# An example of a host file',
            '',
            '127.0.0.1  localhost',
            "$($testParameters.IPAddress)
             $($testParameters.HostName)",
            ''
        )
    }

    It 'Get function should return Ensure as present.' {
        (Get-TargetResource @testParameters).Ensure | Should Be
        'Present'
    }

    It 'Test function should return true.' {
        Test-TargetResource @testParameters | Should Be $true
    }
}

Context 'A hosts file entry exists and it should not.' {

    $testParameters = @{
        HostName  = 'TestServer102'
        IPAddress = '172.16.102.102'
        Ensure    = 'Absent'
        Verbose   = $true
    }
```

```
Mock -CommandName Get-Content -MockWith {
    return @(
        '# An example of a host file',
        '',
        '127.0.0.1  localhost',
        "$($testParameters.IPAddress)
         $($testParameters.HostName)",
        ''

    )
}

It 'Get function should return Ensure as present.' {
    (Get-TargetResource @testParameters).Ensure | Should Be
    'Present'
}

It 'Test function should return false.' {
    Test-TargetResource @testParameters | Should Be $false
}

It 'Set function should call Set-Content only once.' {
    Set-TargetResource @testParameters
    Assert-MockCalled -CommandName Set-Content -Times 1
}
}

Context 'A hosts file entry does not exist and it should not.' {

    $testParameters = @{
        HostName  = 'TestServer102'
        IPAddress = '172.16.102.102'
        Ensure    = 'Absent'
        Verbose   = $true
    }

    Mock -CommandName Get-Content -MockWith {
        return @(
            '# An example of a host file',
            '',
```

```
                    '127.0.0.1  localhost',
                    ''

                )
            }

            It 'Get function should return Ensure as absent.' {
                (Get-TargetResource @testParameters).Ensure | Should Be
                'Absent'
            }

            It 'Test function should return true.' {
                Test-TargetResource @testParameters | Should Be $true
            }
        }
    }
}
}
finally
{
    Invoke-TestCleanup
}
```

Here is the output from the final test script:

```
PS C:\scripts\ProDSC\Tests\Unit> Invoke-Pester -CodeCoverage C:\scripts\
ProDSC\DSCResources\HostsFile\HostsFile.psm1

Describing Unit tests for the HostsFile resource
   Context A hosts file entry does not exist. It should.
VERBOSE: Checking if hosts file entry exists for TestServer102 and
172.16.102.102 or not.
VERBOSE: Hosts file entry for TestServer102 and 172.16.102.102 does not
exist.
   [+] Get function should return Ensure as absent. 707ms
VERBOSE: Checking if the hosts file entry for TestServer102 and
172.16.102.102 exists or not.
VERBOSE: Hosts file entry  for TestServer102 and 172.16.102.102 does not
exist while it should; it must be added.
```

[+] Test function should return false. 81ms
VERBOSE: Creating hosts file entry for TestServer102 and 172.16.102.102.
    [+] Set function should add the hosts file entry. 89ms
   Context A hosts file entry exists as it should.
VERBOSE: Checking if hosts file entry exists for TestServer102 and
172.16.102.102 or not.
VERBOSE: Hosts file entry for TestServer102 and 172.16.102.102 exists.
    [+] Get function should return Ensure as present. 130ms
VERBOSE: Checking if the hosts file entry for TestServer102 and
172.16.102.102 exists or not.
VERBOSE: Hosts file entry for TestServer102 and 172.16.102.102 exists for
the given parameters; nothing to configure.
    [+] Test function should return true. 75ms
   Context A hosts file entry exists and it should not.
VERBOSE: Checking if hosts file entry exists for TestServer102 and
172.16.102.102 or not.
VERBOSE: Hosts file entry for TestServer102 and 172.16.102.102 exists.
    [+] Get function should return Ensure as present. 269ms
VERBOSE: Checking if the hosts file entry for TestServer102 and
172.16.102.102 exists or not.
VERBOSE: Hosts file entry for TestServer102 and 172.16.102.102 exists while
it should not; it must be removed.
    [+] Test function should return false. 115ms
VERBOSE: Removing hosts file entry for TestServer102 and 172.16.102.102.
    [+] Set function should call Set-Content only once. 83ms
   Context A hosts file entry does not exist and it should not.
VERBOSE: Checking if hosts file entry exists for TestServer102 and
172.16.102.102 or not.
VERBOSE: Hosts file entry for TestServer102 and 172.16.102.102 does not
exist.
    [+] Get function should return Ensure as absent. 408ms
VERBOSE: Checking if the hosts file entry for TestServer102 and
172.16.102.102 exists or not.
VERBOSE: Hosts file entry for TestServer102 and 172.16.102.102 does not
exist; nothing to configure.

```
[+] Test function should return true. 544ms
Tests completed in 2.51s
Passed: 10 Failed: 0 Skipped: 0 Pending: 0 Inconclusive: 0
```

What you have covered in this test script is a subset of what can be possible within unit testing. Pester can also be used to retrieve the code coverage percentage with regards to the tests in the Pester script. For any test script, you can add the -CodeCoverage parameter with path(s) to the script files as an argument.

Here is how you can do so for the HostsFile resource.

```
Invoke-Pester -CodeCoverage C:\scripts\ProDSC\DSCResources\HostsFile\
HostsFile.psm1
```

The returned output (partial) is shown in Figure 7-12.

```
Tests completed in 2.51s
Passed: 10 Failed: 0 Skipped: 0 Pending: 0 Inconclusive: 0

Code coverage report:
Covered 100.00 % of 39 analyzed commands in 1 file.
```

Figure 7-12. *Code coverage test*

As shown in Figure 7-12, you have 100% code coverage, which is very good. In a larger resource script, this may not always be possible.

DSC Integration Tests

The unit tests you have seen so far help you test different code paths and the behavior within the resource script without actually enacting any configuration. It is equally important to perform integration tests that verify an actual enact and then validate if the configuration enact brought the system to the desired state or not. The earlier methods you saw where you enacted configuration were manual. You enacted the configuration either as a configuration script or used the Invoke-DscResource cmdlet to invoke the Set function in the resource script.

The integration test script helps you automate these validations. The Plaster template that you generated in Chapter 6 has the template scripts for the integration tests as well. You can see this in Figure 7-10.

Here is the integration test script from the template that was generated in Chapter 6:

```
$script:DSCModuleName      = 'ProDsc'
$script:DSCResourceName    = 'HostsFile'

#region HEADER
# Integration Test Template Version: 1.1.1
[String] $script:moduleRoot = Split-Path -Parent (Split-Path -Parent
$PSScriptRoot)
if ( (-not (Test-Path -Path (Join-Path -Path $script:moduleRoot -ChildPath
'DSCResource.Tests'))) -or `
        (-not (Test-Path -Path (Join-Path -Path $script:moduleRoot -ChildPath
        'DSCResource.Tests\TestHelper.psm1'))) )
{
    & git @('clone','https://github.com/PowerShell/DscResource.Tests.
    git',(Join-Path -Path $script:moduleRoot -ChildPath '\DSCResource.
    Tests\'))
}

Import-Module -Name (Join-Path -Path $script:moduleRoot -ChildPath (Join-
Path -Path 'DSCResource.Tests' -ChildPath 'TestHelper.psm1')) -Force
$TestEnvironment = Initialize-TestEnvironment `
    -DSCModuleName $script:DSCModuleName `
    -DSCResourceName $script:DSCResourceName `
    -TestType Integration

#endregion

# Using try/finally to always cleanup.
try
{
    #region Integration Tests
    $configFile = Join-Path -Path $PSScriptRoot -ChildPath
    "$($script:DSCResourceName).config.ps1"
    . $configFile

    Describe "$($script:DSCResourceName)_Integration" {
        It 'Should compile and apply the MOF without throwing' {
```

```
            {
                & "$($script:DSCResourceName)_Config" -OutputPath $TestDrive
                Start-DscConfiguration -Path $TestDrive `
                    -ComputerName localhost -Wait -Verbose -Force
            } | Should not throw
        }

        It 'Should be able to call Get-DscConfiguration without throwing' {
            { Get-DscConfiguration -Verbose -ErrorAction Stop } | Should
            Not throw
        }

        It 'Should be in the desired state' {
            {Test-DscConfiguration} | Should be $true
        }
    }
    #endregion

}
finally
{
    Restore-TestEnvironment -TestEnvironment $TestEnvironment
}
```

Once again, I removed all the comments from the template and kept only what is necessary. As you can see, this is mostly similar to the unit test template. In the try-finally block, you are required to compile a configuration script, enact that configuration, and then validate the result of that enact. The configurations to be tested will be specified in a separate config.ps1 file, as seen in Figure 7-10.

Here is the configuration that contains the HostsFile resource instances:

```
Configuration HostsFile_Config
{
    param
    (
        [Parameter()]
        [System.String[]]
        $NodeName = 'localhost'
```

```
)

Import-DSCResource -ModuleName ProDsc -ModuleVersion 1.0.0.0

Node $NodeName
{
    HostsFile HostEntry
    {
        HostName  = 'TestServer10'
        IPAddress = '172.16.100.10'
        Ensure    = 'Present'
    }
}
}
```

Now, when you run the integration test shown above, it compiles the configuration and enacts it. After the enact is complete, you check if the Get-DscConfiguration runs successfully or not. Figure 7-13 shows partial output from the integration test run.

```
PS C:\Source\ProDSC\ProDsc\Tests\Integration> Invoke-Pester
```

```
WARNING: There is no operation running currently. Stop will return without any action.
Describing HostsFile_Integration
VERBOSE: Perform operation 'Invoke CimMethod' with following parameters, ''methodName' = SendConfigurationAp
  root/Microsoft/Windows/DesiredStateConfiguration'.
VERBOSE: An LCM method call arrived from computer S16-JB with user sid S-1-5-21-2403796847-1381111412-257592
VERBOSE: [S16-JB]: LCM:  [ Start  Set      ]
VERBOSE: [S16-JB]:                          [DSCEngine] Importing the module C:\Source\ProDSC\ProDsc\DscRe
VERBOSE: [S16-JB]: LCM:  [ Start  Resource ] [[HostsFile]HostEntry]
VERBOSE: [S16-JB]: LCM:  [ Start  Test     ] [[HostsFile]HostEntry]
VERBOSE: [S16-JB]:                          [[HostsFile]HostEntry] Importing the module HostsFile in force
VERBOSE: [S16-JB]:                          [[HostsFile]HostEntry] Checking if the hosts file entry for Te
VERBOSE: [S16-JB]:                          [[HostsFile]HostEntry] Hosts file entry  for TestServer10 and
VERBOSE: [S16-JB]: LCM:  [ End    Test     ] [[HostsFile]HostEntry]  in 0.1520 seconds.
VERBOSE: [S16-JB]: LCM:  [ Start  Set      ] [[HostsFile]HostEntry]
VERBOSE: [S16-JB]:                          [[HostsFile]HostEntry] Importing the module HostsFile in force
VERBOSE: [S16-JB]:                          [[HostsFile]HostEntry] Creating hosts file entry for TestServe
VERBOSE: [S16-JB]: LCM:  [ End    Set      ] [[HostsFile]HostEntry]  in 0.0200 seconds.
```

Figure 7-13. *Integration test output*

This brings us to the end of this chapter. What you saw at the end is just a simple integration test. It does not have any operational validations after the resource is in the desired state. For example, after a host entry is added, you may want to try out name resolution to ensure that the entry added to the hosts file indeed is effective. This type of test is called an operational validation test. You should create comprehensive integration test scripts to ensure that you cover the operational aspects as well.

In fact, before you start development of any DSC resource scripts, ideally you should have the tests written first. This is called test-driven development (TDD). With the concepts you learned in this chapter and in Chapter 6, you may work backwards to ensure that you have tests written first and then write the resource scripts that will make the tests pass. TDD is not always easy, but it is certainly a recommended practice in the world of DevOps and IaC.

Summary

In this chapter, you learned how to perform validation of your custom DSC resource modules to ensure that they are functional and are designed as per Microsoft's coding guidelines. Testing is an essential part of continuous integration and delivery, and it helps you ensure that the code you write has no obvious bugs and works as expected. In this chapter, you wrote both unit and integration tests. In Chapter 1, you looked at the concept of a release pipeline to help you take the code from source control to production in an automated manner. What you learned in Chapter 6 and in this chapter become the foundation of building this release pipeline. You will implement this release pipeline that uses the tests defined here in Chapters 14 and 15.

PART II

Advanced DSC Concepts

After learning the basics of DSC, you move on to learning more advanced features such as configuration delivery methods, DSC monitoring, and reporting methods.

You look at some of the new features in DSC such as partial configurations and cross-node synchronization. Partial configurations help us with delegated configuration management, and cross-node synchronization lets us create an orchestration-like configuration experience with DSC.

You extend your knowledge of writing custom DSC resources and testing them to debugging DSC resource module issues in Chapter 12. Debugging is an essential skill for troubleshooting any DSC resource script issues that arise due to buggy code or the environment in which the DSC resource is being used.

Finally, you conclude this section by looking at how DSC secures MOF files at rest on the target nodes, how to enable signing of DSC configurations and resource modules, and how to delegate access to DSC operations using WMI namespace permissions and Just Enough Administration (JEA) endpoints.

CHAPTER 8

Configuration Delivery Methods

In Chapter 2, the DSC architecture and feature overview, you briefly looked at different configuration delivery methods in DSC. With WMF 5.0 and above, DSC supports push, pull, mixed, and disabled refresh modes. The RefreshMode property of the DSC LCM configuration takes only Push, Pull, and Disabled as the valid values. The mixed mode does not exist as a possible value and in reality can be used only with partial configurations. In this chapter, I will discuss a few more concepts around the push model and move towards the other configuration refresh modes.

Lab Requirements

To try the examples and exercises in this chapter, you will need at minimum two or more systems with Windows Server 2008 R2 or above with WMF 5.1 or above installed. I recommend a system with Windows Server 2016. The HTTPS pull service and credential encryption requires certificates and therefore these will require either a certificate authority or self-signed certificates. You will need at least three nodes to try out the pull mode configuration delivery.

Push Mode

The first DSC configuration delivery model I discussed was the push model. This is the default mode for the LCM. All of the examples in earlier chapters used the push mode. In the push mode, the configuration MOF gets pushed to the target node and gets enacted.

© Ravikanth Chaganti 2018
R. Chaganti, *Pro PowerShell Desired State Configuration*, https://doi.org/10.1007/978-1-4842-3483-9_8

The DSC LCM is in push refresh mode be default and hence requires no additional meta-configuration if the goal is just basic configuration delivery. In one of the push methods, this is done using the `Start-DscConfiguration` cmdlet, which stages the pending configuration and enacts it immediately.

Stage and Enact

Another way to push a configuration is to use `Publish-DscConfiguration` to stage the pending configuration and then use the `-UseExisting` switch parameter with the `Start-DscConfiguration` cmdlet to enact the pending configuration. Let's take a look at this.

Here is the configuration file you will compile, stage, and enact:

```
Configuration WebServerConfiguration
{
    Import-DscResource -ModuleName PSDesiredStateConfiguration
    -ModuleVersion 1.1

    Node @('S16-01','S16-02','CNODE05')
    {
        WindowsFeature WebServer
        {
            Name = 'Web-Server'
            Ensure = 'Present'
        }
    }
}

WebServerConfiguration
```

When you compile this, you will see three MOF files generated, each with the name of a node. See Figure 8-1.

```
         Directory: C:\scripts\WebServerConfiguration


Mode                LastWriteTime         Length Name
----                -------------         ------ ----
-a----        12/8/2017   12:31 PM           1910 S16-01.mof
-a----        12/8/2017   12:31 PM           1910 S16-02.mof
-a----        12/8/2017   12:31 PM           1912 CNODE05.mof
```

Figure 8-1. *Compiled MOF files for each node*

Now you can stage these MOFs as pending configurations on the target nodes using the `Publish-DscConfiguration` cmdlet. See Figure 8-2.

```
PS C:\scripts> Get-Command -Name Publish-DscConfiguration -Syntax

Publish-DscConfiguration [-Path] <string> [[-ComputerName] <string[]>] [-Force] [-Credenti
al <pscredential>] [-ThrottleLimit <int>] [-WhatIf] [-Confirm] [<CommonParameters>]

Publish-DscConfiguration [-Path] <string> -CimSession <CimSession[]> [-Force] [-ThrottleLi
mit <int>] [-WhatIf] [-Confirm] [<CommonParameters>]
```

***Figure 8-2.** Publish-DscConfiguration command parameters*

The parameters for this command are more or less similar to what you saw with the `Start-DscConfiguration` cmdlet. When you point this command to a path (using the `-Path` parameter) containing all compiled MOF files, it will iterate over all files at the path and try to connect to the target nodes with the same name as the MOF file and stage the MOF as a pending configuration. While the NetBIOS name works, it may be a good idea to use the FQDN of the target node. If you want to stage the configuration on only one of the target nodes, you can use the `-ComputerName` parameter or the `-CimSession` parameter. Let's try this to stage a pending configuration on one of the nodes. See Figure 8-3 also.

```
Publish-DscConfiguration -Path .\WebServerConfiguration -ComputerName
S16-01 -Verbose
```

Note   The argument to the `-ComputerName` parameter should match one of the file names at the path specified.

```
PS C:\scripts> Publish-DscConfiguration -Path .\WebServerConfiguration -ComputerName S16-01 -Verbose

VERBOSE: Perform operation 'Invoke CimMethod' with following parameters, ''methodName' = SendConfigura
tion,'className' = MSFT_DSCLocalConfigurationManager,'namespaceName' = root/Microsoft/Windows/DesiredS
tateConfiguration'.
VERBOSE: An LCM method call arrived from computer S16-JB with user sid S-1-5-21-689661094-3032901192-2
251061677-500.
VERBOSE: [S16-01]: LCM:  [ Start  Set      ]
VERBOSE: [S16-01]:                          [] Configuration document successfully saved to pending
state.
VERBOSE: [S16-01]: LCM:  [ End    Set      ]
VERBOSE: Operation 'Invoke CimMethod' complete.
VERBOSE: Publish-DscConfiguration finished in 0.677 seconds.
```

***Figure 8-3.** Staging a configuration as pending.mof*

If the target node LCM is configured to use the pull refresh mode (which you will see in the next section) or has a pending configuration already, you can use the -Force switch with the Publish-DscConfiguration cmdlet. If the target node is in pull refresh mode, it will be set to push mode after using -Force with the Publish-DscConfiguration cmdlet.

Once the staging is complete, you can enact this configuration using the -UseExisting switch parameter of the Start-DscConfiguration cmdlet.

```
Start-DscConfiguration -ComputerName S16-01 -UseExisting -Wait -Verbose
```

While you can use this method (stage and enact) with normal node configurations, this is useful especially in managing partial configuration fragments. You will look at partial configurations in Chapter 10.

The way you use -CimSession or -ComputerName and -Force is same across the Start-DscConfiguration and Publish-DscConfiguration cmdlets. The -Wait and -Verbose parameters are common too and I recommend using them when staging or enacting a configuration. The verbose stream of messages from the DSC resources modules can be useful in identifying what is happening behind the scenes and what might be causing an enact failure.

Background Enact

The Start-DscConfiguration cmdlet has additional parameters such as -JobName and -ThrottleLimit. Let's see where these parameters are useful. When dealing with a larger number of target systems, it does not make a lot of sense to wait at the console for the configuration change to complete or look at the verbose stream of messages from the configuration resources. So, this is where the -JobName parameter plays a role.

Note   You can simply remove the -Wait parameter to run the configuration as a background job. It is not mandatory to use the -JobName parameter to start the configuration enact process as a background job. However, the -JobName parameter makes it easy to identify the configuration job and access the state of the configuration job(s).

When using the -JobName parameter, the Start-DscConfiguration cmdlet starts the configuration enact process as a background job and returns a job object. This job object can be used to monitor the job progress and receive the output from the configuration change process. This job object is a PowerShell configuration job object and you can examine it by listing out its members.

Let's start with a configuration script that helps explain this:

```
Configuration ScriptDemo
{
    Node ('S16-1', 'S16-2')
    {
        Script ScriptDemo
        {
            GetScript = {
                @{
                    GetScript = $GetScript
                    SetScript = $SetScript
                    TestScript = $TestScript
                    Result = 'TestScript'
                }
            }

            SetScript = {
                Write-Verbose 'Sleeping for 50 seconds'
                Start-Sleep 50
                Write-Verbose 'Completed Script task'
            }

            TestScript = {
                $false
            }
        }
    }
}

ScriptDemo
```

This configuration document uses the Script resource that just waits for some time. Apart from that, what you are doing in the SetScript script block is writing some verbose messages. The following code snippet shows how to use the -JobName parameter:

```
$ConfigJob = Start-DscConfiguration -JobName scriptjob -Path .\ScriptDemo
-Verbose
```

That is simple. This starts the configuration enact process for all MOF files that exist under the ScriptDemo folder. The $ConfigJob property becomes a container job for all the configuration jobs started for every target system MOF in the ScriptDemo folder. This is shown in Figure 8-4.

```
PS C:\scripts> $ConfigJob = Start-DscConfiguration -JobName scriptjob -Path .\ScriptDemo -Verbose
VERBOSE: Time taken for configuration job to complete is 0.124 seconds

PS C:\scripts> $ConfigJob

Id    Name       PSJobTypeName    State     HasMoreData    Location     Command
--    ----       -------------    -----     -----------    --------     -------
69    scriptjob  Configuratio...  Failed    True           S16-1,S16-2  $ConfigJob = Start-Dsc...
```

Figure 8-4. _Starting an enact as a background job_

The ChildJobs property of the $ConfigJob object provides a list of jobs started for each MOF in the ScriptDemo directory.

```
PS C:\scripts> $ConfigJob.ChildJobs

Id    Name    PSJobTypeName    State     HasMoreData    Location    Command
--    ----    -------------    -----     -----------    --------    -------
70    Job70   Configuratio...  Failed    True           S16-1       $ConfigJob = Start-Dsc...
71    Job71   Configuratio...  Failed    True           S16-2       $ConfigJob = Start-Dsc...
```

Figure 8-5. _Child jobs started for the configuration enact_

As you can see in the child job status from Figure 8-5, all jobs have failed. To find out why, you need to look at the properties of the job object. Let's examine this using the Get-Member cmdlet. See Figure 8-6.

```
TypeName: System.Management.Automation.ContainerParentJob

Name            MemberType      Definition
----            ----------      ----------
ChildJobs       Property        System.Collections.Generic.IList[System.Management.Automation.Job] ChildJobs {get;}
Command         Property        string Command {get;}
Debug           Property        System.Management.Automation.PSDataCollection[System.Management.Automation.DebugRecord] Debug {get;set;}
Error           Property        System.Management.Automation.PSDataCollection[System.Management.Automation.ErrorRecord] Error {get;set;}
Finished        Property        System.Threading.WaitHandle Finished {get;}
HasMoreData     Property        bool HasMoreData {get;}
Id              Property        int Id {get;}
Information     Property        System.Management.Automation.PSDataCollection[System.Management.Automation.InformationRecord] Information {get;set;}
InstanceId      Property        guid InstanceId {get;}
JobStateInfo    Property        System.Management.Automation.JobStateInfo JobStateInfo {get;}
Location        Property        string Location {get;}
Name            Property        string Name {get;set;}
Output          Property        System.Management.Automation.PSDataCollection[psobject] Output {get;set;}
Progress        Property        System.Management.Automation.PSDataCollection[System.Management.Automation.ProgressRecord] Progress {get;set;}
PSBeginTime     Property        System.Nullable[datetime] PSBeginTime {get;}
PSEndTime       Property        System.Nullable[datetime] PSEndTime {get;}
PSJobTypeName   Property        string PSJobTypeName {get;}
StartParameters Property        System.Collections.Generic.List[System.Management.Automation.Runspaces.CommandParameterCollection] StartParameters {get;set;}
StatusMessage   Property        string StatusMessage {get;}
Verbose         Property        System.Management.Automation.PSDataCollection[System.Management.Automation.VerboseRecord] Verbose {get;set;}
Warning         Property        System.Management.Automation.PSDataCollection[System.Management.Automation.WarningRecord] Warning {get;set;}
State           ScriptProperty  System.Object State (get=$this.JobStateInfo.State.ToString();)
```

Figure 8-6. *Background job properties*

The Debug, Error, Output, Verbose, and Warning properties each correspond to an output stream from the configuration. The following code snippet shows how to access the values from these output streams:

```
Get-Job -Name Job70 | Select Debug, Error, Output, Verbose, Warning
Get-Job -Name Job71 | Select Debug, Error, Output, Verbose, Warning
```

Note   You are using the child job names from Figure 8-5 and not the job name specified with the Start-DscConfiguration cmdlet.

```
PS C:\scripts> Get-Job -Name Job70 | Select Debug, Error, Output, Verbose, Warning


Debug   : {}
Error   : {HRESULT 0x80070035}
Output  : {}
Verbose : {Perform operation 'Invoke CimMethod' with following parameters, ''methodName' =
          SendConfigurationApply,'className' = MSFT_DSCLocalConfigurationManager,'namespaceName' =
          root/Microsoft/Windows/DesiredStateConfiguration'., Operation 'Invoke CimMethod' complete.}
Warning : {}



PS C:\scripts> Get-Job -Name Job71 | Select Debug, Error, Output, Verbose, Warning


Debug   : {}
Error   : {HRESULT 0x80070035}
Output  : {}
Verbose : {Perform operation 'Invoke CimMethod' with following parameters, ''methodName' =
          SendConfigurationApply,'className' = MSFT_DSCLocalConfigurationManager,'namespaceName' =
          root/Microsoft/Windows/DesiredStateConfiguration'., Operation 'Invoke CimMethod' complete.}
Warning : {}
```

Figure 8-7. *Different output streams from the child jobs*

From Figure 8-7, you can see that that there was an error. However, it is in hexadecimal format. You can infer the meaning of this hex code by using the `winrm helpmsg` command. See Figure 8-8.

```
PS C:\scripts> winrm helpmsg 0x80070035
The network path was not found.

PS C:\scripts>
```

Figure 8-8. *WinRM error message*

Ok, you now know what went wrong. You had the wrong node names: S16-1 and S16-2 instead of S16-01 and S16-02! Fix that, compile, and run the enact again. See Figure 8-9.

Note   You can see the error message from the job by using the `Receive-Job` cmdlet or by retrieving the `$ConfigJob.ChildJobs[0].Error.Exception` value. The goal of the above exercise is to show you the different streams of messages available after an enact.

```
PS C:\scripts> Get-Job -Name scriptjob -IncludeChildJob

Id    Name         PSJobTypeName    State       HasMoreData    Location         Command
--    ----         -------------    -----       -----------    --------         -------
72    scriptjob    Configuratio... Completed    True           S16-01,S16-02    $ConfigJ...
73    Job73        Configuratio... Completed    True           S16-01           $ConfigJ...
74    Job74        Configuratio... Completed    True           S16-02           $ConfigJ...
```

Figure 8-9. *Child jobs in the running state*

Once the jobs are complete, you can see the verbose output by receiving the jobs using the `Receive-Job` cmdlet. See Figure 8-10.

```
Get-Job -Name scriptjob -IncludeChildJob | Receive-Job -Keep -Verbose
```

```
PS C:\scripts> Get-Job -Name scriptjob -IncludeChildJob | Receive-Job -Keep -Verbose

VERBOSE: Perform operation 'Invoke CimMethod' with following parameters, ''methodName' = SendConfigura
tionApply,'className' = MSFT_DSCLocalConfigurationManager,'namespaceName' = root/Microsoft/Windows/Des
iredStateConfiguration'.
VERBOSE: An LCM method call arrived from computer S16-JB with user sid S-1-5-21-689661094-3032901192-2
251061677-500.
VERBOSE: [S16-01]: LCM:  [ Start  Set       ]
VERBOSE: [S16-01]: LCM:  [ Start  Resource ] [[Script]ScriptDemo]
VERBOSE: [S16-01]: LCM:  [ Start  Test      ] [[Script]ScriptDemo]
VERBOSE: [S16-01]: LCM:  [ End    Test      ] [[Script]ScriptDemo]  in 0.0620 seconds.
VERBOSE: [S16-01]: LCM:  [ Start  Set       ] [[Script]ScriptDemo]
VERBOSE: [S16-01]:                            [[Script]ScriptDemo] Performing the operation "Set-Targe
tResource" on target "Executing the SetScript with the user supplied credential".
VERBOSE: [S16-01]:                            [[Script]ScriptDemo] Sleeping for 50 seconds
VERBOSE: [S16-01]:                            [[Script]ScriptDemo] Completed Script task
VERBOSE: [S16-01]: LCM:  [ End    Set       ] [[Script]ScriptDemo]  in 50.0360 seconds.
VERBOSE: [S16-01]: LCM:  [ End    Resource ] [[Script]ScriptDemo]
VERBOSE: [S16-01]: LCM:  [ End    Set       ]
VERBOSE: [S16-01]: LCM:  [ End    Set       ]   in  50.4570 seconds.
VERBOSE: Operation 'Invoke CimMethod' complete.
VERBOSE: Perform operation 'Invoke CimMethod' with following parameters, ''methodName' = SendConfigura
tionApply,'className' = MSFT_DSCLocalConfigurationManager,'namespaceName' = root/Microsoft/Windows/Des
iredStateConfiguration'.
VERBOSE: An LCM method call arrived from computer S16-JB with user sid S-1-5-21-689661094-3032901192-2
251061677-500.
VERBOSE: [S16-02]: LCM:  [ Start  Set       ]
```

Figure 8-10. *Verbose output stream from the background jobs*

By default, the Receive-Job cmdlet clears the values of output streams associated with each job object. If you want to retain those values in the job object for later use, you need to use the -Keep switch parameter with the Receive-Job cmdlet.

Throttling an Enact

The -ThrottleLimit parameter of Start-DscConfiguration and other DSC commands governs how many concurrent operations are performed within the CIM session established by the cmdlet. For example, in the preceding example, there were two target systems where the configuration was being enacted. The two configuration jobs you saw in Figure 8-9 executed concurrently. This is a much smaller set and you need not worry about resource consumption or limitations on the system from where the configuration is being pushed. However, if you are pushing a configuration to hundreds if not thousands of target systems, you need to ensure that these configuration jobs are throttled so that none of them fails for lack of resources on the system pushing the configuration.

Note   You can use throttling without background jobs by specifying the -Wait parameter. But this is counterintuitive and I don't recommend doing so.

The default value for the -ThrottleLimit parameter is 32. However, if 0 is provided as an argument to this parameter, an optimum throttle limit is calculated based on the number of CIM cmdlets running on the local computer. The following is an example of this parameter in action.

To understand the difference, add a few more nodes to the earlier configuration document and compile again. You will first enact the configuration on all four target nodes using background jobs. See Figure 8-11.

```
PS C:\scripts> Start-DscConfiguration -JobName scriptjob -Path .\ScriptDemo -Verbose

Id      Name            PSJobTypeName    State        HasMoreData    Location          Command
--      ----            -------------    -----        -----------    --------          -------
78      scriptjob       Configuratio... Running      True           S16-01,S16-02,S16... Start-Ds...
VERBOSE: Time taken for configuration job to complete is 0.064 seconds
```

Figure 8-11. *Starting all jobs at once without throttling*

Now, let's set ThrottleLimit to 2 and try this again. See Figure 8-12.

```
PS C:\scripts> Start-DscConfiguration -JobName scriptjob -Path .\ScriptDemo -Verbose -ThrottleLimit 2

Id      Name            PSJobTypeName    State        HasMoreData    Location          Command
--      ----            -------------    -----        -----------    --------          -------
83      scriptjob       Configuratio... Running      True           S16-01,S16-02,S16... Start-Ds...
VERBOSE: Time taken for configuration job to complete is 50.809 seconds
```

Figure 8-12. *Starting enact jobs with ThrottleLimit*

As you can see from Figures 8-11 and 8-12, there is a difference in behavior around how the jobs are started. In the first case, all jobs start simultaneously and it took only few milliseconds to start all of them. However, with throttling in place, the Start-DscConfiguration cmdlet waited for the first two nodes' background jobs to complete before starting the remaining two. So the total time taken to invoke the jobs was 50.809 seconds since there was a 50 seconds sleep in the SetScript of the configuration document.

The CimSession parameter is useful in cases when the WinRM is not running on the default HTTP port or is using HTTPS only. For a DSC enact to work, whether the target node is local or remote, you must have the WinRM service running and the WinRM listeners configured. The default port numbers for WinRM listeners are 5895 (HTTP) and 5896 (HTTPS). So if you changed the default HTTP port number, you need to use -CimSession to specify a CIM Session with WinRM port set to a custom port number using a CIM session option. If the target node has HTTPS listeners only, then you must use the CimSession parameter while enacting.

Let's conclude this discussion on the push mode of configuration delivery by listing out the pros and cons of this model.

The push mode is simple and easy. It does not require any infrastructure services such as a central shared location to host the configurations and so on. However, the push model is not scalable. Pushing a configuration to hundreds if not thousands of systems would take a long time and can be limited based on the resources available on the system where the Start-DscConfiguration cmdlet is being run. Of course, this is where I said the ThrottleLimit parameter would help, but it increases the overall time it takes to complete configuration enact. Another drawback with the push mode is that enacting configurations that use custom DSC resource modules is a two-step process. You need to first ensure all target nodes have the custom DSC resource modules and then enact the configuration. Of course, as you'll see later in the chapter, starting with WMF 5.0 you can configure the LCM to download the custom DSC resource modules from a pull server or pull share in push mode as well.

Also, one of the important reasons why the pull mode is preferred is that for push you need to be able to reach the target (routing and firewall configurations). The Windows firewall blocks, by default, traffic originating from a different subnet. Pushing to a node that is not in the same domain as the management station will require you to authenticate to the target node.

This is where the pull mode of configuration delivery helps. Using the pull model, you can solve the scalability, configuration, and resource module distribution problems just discussed. And, the target node reachability and authentication issues do not arise; the pull client is configured to retrieve the configurations in a secure manner.

In the following sections, you will look at the pull mode of configuration delivery, different methods of configuring the pull model, and configuring target systems as pull clients.

Pull Mode

In pull model, the LCM initiates the connection by looking for new or updated configurations and/or resource modules. Figure 8-13 depicts an overview of this process. It also depicts the components involved in the pull mode for configuration delivery.

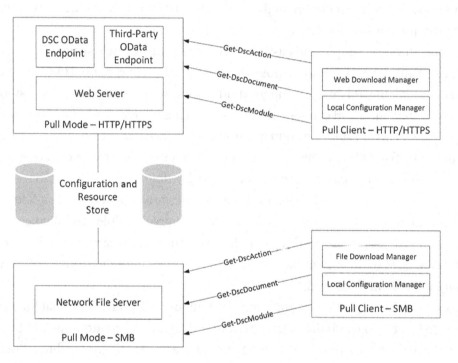

Figure 8-13. *Pull mode in DSC*

Before I go into the details of the flow of a configuration in the pull model, let's look into the details of setting up a pull service and configuring a pull client. DSC supports two types of pull servers:

- oData-based pull service

- SMB-based pull service

Each method has pros and cons. You will look at each of them in-depth and learn the configuration steps involved.

Note   Yet another way to use pull configuration delivery is to configure the DSC LCM as a pull client of the Azure Automation DSC pull service or any other service that implements the pull server protocol. You will look into this in Chapter 17.

oData-based (HTTP/HTTPS) Pull Service

On Windows Server OS, Windows Management Framework 4.0 and above includes a feature called Windows PowerShell Desired State Configuration Service. This is the official name but you will find that many in the community simply refer to this as *DSC pull service*. So, I too shall stick to this short form. Using this feature, you can configure either an HTTP or HTTPS endpoint for the pull service. This feature implements the required support for setting up an oData-based pull service. Installing this feature alone does not ensure that you have a functional pull service but requires a bunch of additional steps be performed.

Note   The Windows PowerShell Desired State Configuration Service Windows feature is available only on systems running Windows Server 2012 and above. Although WMF 4.0 and 5.x are supported on Windows Server 2008 R2, the pull service feature is not available. This chapter assumes that you are setting up the DSC pull service on either Windows Server 2012 or Windows Server 2012 R2.

The easiest method to configure the DSC pull service is to use the custom DSC resource, xDSCWebService, written by the Windows PowerShell team at Microsoft. This is a part of the xPSDesiredStateConfiguration module.

This resource module will take care of configuring the pull server by creating the necessary IIS sites and configuring the right web application settings and so on. This DSC resource also supports both HTTP and HTTPS endpoints for the pull service. Once the pull service is installed and configured, you will see a folder named DSCService at the path $env:ProgramFiles\WindowsPowerShell and another folder named PullServer at the path $pshome\modules\PSDesiredStateConfiguration.

The pull service in WMF 5.0 and above can be configured to implement a registration key-based authentication. In this method, a registration key is used during one-time pull client registration. In the absence of the registration keys, the LCM uses the configuration IDs to identify itself with a pull server, which used to be the only method in the WMF 4.0 pull service. You will see both methods in this section.

Pull Server: HTTPS

Let's first look at creating an HTTPS endpoint for a pull server with registration keys for authentication. The following configuration document installs the DSC Service feature and then configures the pull server. You will see a detailed explanation of this later in this section.

```
$certificateThumbPrint = (Get-ChildItem -Path Cert:\LocalMachine\My |
Where-Object { $_.Subject -eq 'CN=S16-Pull-02.psdsc.lab' }).Thumbprint
$registrationkey = ([guid]::NewGuid()).Guid

Configuration PullServerHTTPS
{
    param
    (
        [Parameter()]
        [String]
        $NodeName = 'localhost',

        [Parameter(Mandatory = $true)]
        [String]
        $certificateThumbPrint,

        [Parameter(Mandatory = $true)]
        [String]
        $RegistrationKey
    )

    Import-DSCResource -ModuleName xPSDesiredStateConfiguration -Name x
    DSCWebService -ModuleVersion 8.0.0.0
    Import-DscResource -ModuleName PSDesiredStateConfiguration
    -ModuleVersion 1.1

    Node $NodeName
    {
        WindowsFeature DSCServiceFeature
        {
            Ensure = 'Present'
            Name   = 'DSC-Service'
        }
```

```
    xDscWebService PSDSCPullServer
    {
        Ensure                  = 'Present'
        EndpointName            = 'PSDSCPullServer'
        Port                    = 8080
        PhysicalPath            = "$env:SystemDrive\inetpub\
                                    PSDSCPullServer"
        CertificateThumbPrint   = $certificateThumbPrint
        ModulePath              = "$env:PROGRAMFILES\WindowsPowerShell\
                                    DscService\Modules"
        ConfigurationPath       = "$env:PROGRAMFILES\WindowsPowerShell\
                                    DscService\Configuration"
        State                   = 'Started'
        RegistrationKeyPath     = "$env:PROGRAMFILES\WindowsPowerShell\
                                    DscService"
        AcceptSelfSignedCertificates = $true
        UseSecurityBestPractices = $true
        DependsOn               = '[WindowsFeature]DSCServiceFeature'
    }

    File RegistrationKeyFile
    {
        Ensure          = 'Present'
        Type            = 'File'
        DestinationPath = "$env:ProgramFiles\WindowsPowerShell\
                            DscService\RegistrationKeys.txt"
        Contents        = $RegistrationKey
    }
  }
}

PullServerHTTPS -RegistrationKey $registrationkey -certificateThumbPrint
$certificateThumbPrint
```

In this code snippet, the xDSCWebservice resource instance is what configures the pull server to be functional, so make sure you have downloaded the resource module to the authoring station as well as the node that will be configured as a pull server.

There are a few things you need to understand here. The EndpointName and Port properties become a part of the URL that will be used to configure the LCM as a pull client.

Configuration and Resource Module Path

The xDSCWebService properties ModulePath and ConfigurationPath define where the compiled configuration MOF files should be staged and where the resource module zip files should be stored so that the DSC LCM pull clients can retrieve them from the pull server. This path should be accessible to the pull server. There is a specific naming convention in which the configuration MOF and module zip files should be stored at this path. You will look at this in later sections.

Registration Key

Starting with WMF 5.0, the LCM can register with an oData-based REST pull server using a shared secret, which is the registration key. The RegistrationKeyPath in the xDSCWebService specifies where the RegistrationKeys.txt is present. Once again, this path needs to be accessible from the pull server. The RegistrationKeys.txt can contain one or more GUIDs that act as the shared secret(s) between the pull service and the client. The registration key is used only once. It allows the pull server to insert a row in the database containing the AgentId. Once the pull server database is updated with the AgentId, the LCM is free to communicate with the pull server and uses its AgentId as the identifier, which serves as the key.

Pull Service Security

Creating an HTTPS endpoint requires a certificate bound to the IIS site. If you already have an Active Directory CA or other means for generating a certificate, you can retrieve the thumbprint of that certificate installed on the node and use it with the above configuration document. If not, you can create a self-signed certificate and install it on the node. It is possible to create an HTTP endpoint by specifying AllowUnecryptedTraffic as the argument to the CertificateThumbprint property. You will see this in the HTTP endpoint section. This certificate needs be a web server certificate that is capable of server authentication and not the client authentication certificate.

```
New-SelfSignedCertificate -DnsName S16-Pull-02.psdsc.lab -Type
SSLServerAuthentication -CertStoreLocation Cert:\LocalMachine\My
```

The AcceptSelfSignedCertificates property in the xDSCWebService configures IIS to accept self-signed certificates. If you are using a PKI for your certificate infrastructure, you can safely set this property to $false.

The UseSecurityBestPractices property will enforce the security best practice configuration on the pull server. This includes changing the Schannel protocol settings to enable only TLS 1.1 and TLS 1.2 protocols. The rest of the protocols such as SSL 2.0, SSL 3.0, TLS 1.0, PCT 1.0, and Multi-Protocol Unified Hello will be disabled. You need to plan for this if you want to run pull services on a node that is shared among other web applications. The security settings may break older or legacy applications that depend on protocols such as SSL 2.0.

The DSC pull service available in WMF 5.0 and above does not support encryption at rest. This means anyone who has access to the pull service configuration path can read the MOF files. It is highly recommended that any secure strings and credentials used in the configuration MOF be encrypted using certificates.

Now that you understand the basics of the above configuration document and the meaning of some of those properties, let's compile the configuration and enact it.

```
PS C:\> Start-DscConfiguration -Path .\PullServerHTTPS -Wait -Verbose -Force
VERBOSE: Perform operation 'Invoke CimMethod' with following parameters, ''methodName' = SendConfigurationApply,'className' = MSFT_DSCLocalConfigurationManager,'namespaceNa
me' = root/Microsoft/Windows/DesiredStateConfiguration'.
VERBOSE: An LCM method call arrived from computer S16-PULL-02 with user sid S-1-5-21-689661094-3032901192-2251061677-500.
VERBOSE: [S16-PULL-02]: LCM:  [ Start  Set      ]
VERBOSE: [S16-PULL-02]: LCM:  [ Start  Resource ]  [[WindowsFeature]DSCServiceFeature]
VERBOSE: [S16-PULL-02]: LCM:  [ Start  Test     ]  [[WindowsFeature]DSCServiceFeature]
VERBOSE: [S16-PULL-02]:                             [[WindowsFeature]DSCServiceFeature] The operation 'Get-WindowsFeature' started: DSC-Service
VERBOSE: [S16-PULL-02]:                             [[WindowsFeature]DSCServiceFeature] The operation 'Get-WindowsFeature' succeeded: DSC-Service
VERBOSE: [S16-PULL-02]: LCM:  [ End    Test     ]  [[WindowsFeature]DSCServiceFeature]  in 1.3370 seconds.
VERBOSE: [S16-PULL-02]: LCM:  [ Skip   Set      ]  [[WindowsFeature]DSCServiceFeature]
VERBOSE: [S16-PULL-02]: LCM:  [ End    Resource ]  [[WindowsFeature]DSCServiceFeature]
VERBOSE: [S16-PULL-02]: LCM:  [ Start  Resource ]  [[xDSCWebService]PSDSCPullServer]
VERBOSE: [S16-PULL-02]: LCM:  [ Start  Test     ]  [[xDSCWebService]PSDSCPullServer]
VERBOSE: [S16-PULL-02]:                             [[xDSCWebService]PSDSCPullServer] Check Ensure
VERBOSE: [S16-PULL-02]:                             [[xDSCWebService]PSDSCPullServer] The Website PSDSCPullServer is not present
VERBOSE: [S16-PULL-02]: LCM:  [ End    Test     ]  [[xDSCWebService]PSDSCPullServer]  in 1.1560 seconds.
VERBOSE: [S16-PULL-02]: LCM:  [ Start  Set      ]  [[xDSCWebService]PSDSCPullServer]
VERBOSE: [S16-PULL-02]:                             [[xDSCWebService]PSDSCPullServer] Create the IIS endpoint
VERBOSE: [S16-PULL-02]:                             [[xDSCWebService]PSDSCPullServer] Setting up endpoint at - https://S16-PULL-02:8080/PSDSCPullServer.svc
VERBOSE: [S16-PULL-02]:                             [[xDSCWebService]PSDSCPullServer] Verify that the certificate with the provided thumbprint exists in CERT:\LocalMachine\M
Y\
VERBOSE: [S16-PULL-02]:                             [[xDSCWebService]PSDSCPullServer] Checking IIS requirements
VERBOSE: [S16-PULL-02]:                             [[xDSCWebService]PSDSCPullServer] Delete the App Pool if it exists
VERBOSE: [S16-PULL-02]:                             [[xDSCWebService]PSDSCPullServer] Remove the site if it already exists
VERBOSE: [S16-PULL-02]:                             [[xDSCWebService]PSDSCPullServer] Create the bin folder for deploying custom dependent binaries required by the endpoint
VERBOSE: [S16-PULL-02]:                             [[xDSCWebService]PSDSCPullServer] Adding App Pool
VERBOSE: [S16-PULL-02]:                             [[xDSCWebService]PSDSCPullServer] Set App Pool Properties
VERBOSE: [S16-PULL-02]:                             [[xDSCWebService]PSDSCPullServer] Add and Set Site Properties
VERBOSE: [S16-PULL-02]:                             [[xDSCWebService]PSDSCPullServer] p11
VERBOSE: [S16-PULL-02]:                             [[xDSCWebService]PSDSCPullServer] Enabling firewall exception for port 8080
```

***Figure 8-14.** Enacting a pull service configuration*

Figure 8-14 shows only partial output from the enact process. The verbose output provides the endpoint URL that you must use in configuring the LCM as a pull client. This is an oData endpoint. You can open it in a browser to ensure that it is functional.

```xml
<?xml version="1.0" encoding="utf-8" ?>
- <service xml:base="https://s16-pull-02:8080/PSDSCPullServer.svc/" xmlns="http://www.w3.org/2007/app"
    xmlns:atom="http://www.w3.org/2005/Atom">
  - <workspace>
      <atom:title>Default</atom:title>
    - <collection href="Configurations">
        <atom:title>Configurations</atom:title>
      </collection>
    - <collection href="Modules">
        <atom:title>Modules</atom:title>
      </collection>
    - <collection href="Action">
        <atom:title>Action</atom:title>
      </collection>
    - <collection href="Module">
        <atom:title>Module</atom:title>
      </collection>
    - <collection href="StatusReport">
        <atom:title>StatusReport</atom:title>
      </collection>
    - <collection href="Node">
        <atom:title>Node</atom:title>
      </collection>
    - <collection href="Reports">
        <atom:title>Reports</atom:title>
      </collection>
    - <collection href="Nodes">
        <atom:title>Nodes</atom:title>
      </collection>
  </workspace>
</service>
```

Figure 8-15. *Response from a functional pull service endpoint*

Figure 8-15 confirms that you have a functional pull service. Let's now move on to configuring the LCM as a pull client. This can be verified using the Invoke-RestMethod cmdlet as well.

```
#Following type definition is required only when using self-signed
certificates
Add-Type @"
using System.Net;
using System.Security.Cryptography.X509Certificates;
public class TrustAllCertsPolicy : ICertificatePolicy {
    public bool CheckValidationResult(
        ServicePoint srvPoint, X509Certificate certificate,
        WebRequest request, int certificateProblem) {
        return true;
    }
}
"@
$AllProtocols = [System.Net.SecurityProtocolType]'Ssl3,Tls,Tls11,Tls12'
[System.Net.ServicePointManager]::SecurityProtocol = $AllProtocols
```

```
[System.Net.ServicePointManager]::CertificatePolicy = New-Object
TrustAllCertsPolicy
```

```
(Invoke-RestMethod -Uri https://S16-Pull-02:8080/PSDSCPullServer.svc
-UseBasicParsing).service.workspace.collection
```

Pull Client Configuration with an HTTPS Pull Service and Registration Keys

Unlike the push mode, to be able to pull configurations and resource modules from a central location like the pull service you just implemented, the DSC LCM must be made aware of the pull service endpoint and what configurations to look for in that central configuration repository. This is done by using the ConfigurationRepositoryWeb and ResourceRepositoryWeb meta resources.

Here is an example of the LCM pull client configuration to fetch the configuration MOF and resource modules from the oData pull service endpoint:

```
[DSCLocalConfigurationManager()]
configuration oDataHTTPSPullClient
{
    param
    (
        [Parameter()]
        [String]
        $NodeName = 'localhost',

        [Parameter(Mandatory = $true)]
        [String]
        $RegistrationKey,

        [Parameter(Mandatory = $true)]
        [String]
        $PullSvcEndpoint,

        [Parameter(Mandatory = $true)]
        [String[]]
        $ConfigNames
    )
```

```
    Node $NodeName
    {
        Settings
        {
            RefreshMode         = 'Pull'
        }

        ConfigurationRepositoryWeb HTTPSPullSvc
        {
            ServerURL           = $PullSvcEndpoint
            RegistrationKey     = $RegistrationKey
            ConfigurationNames  = $ConfigNames
        }

        ResourceRepositoryWeb HTTPSPullSvc
        {
            ServerURL           = $PullSvcEndpoint
            RegistrationKey     = $RegistrationKey
        }
    }
}

oDataHTTPSPullClient -RegistrationKey '5a81ccf0-ae70-4ddf-8c3b-
6e9fb54a3979' -PullSvcEndpoint 'https://s16-pull-02.psdsc.lab:8080/
PSDSCPullServer.svc/' -ConfigNames @('OSConfig')
```

Note   When using self-signed certificates, for the registration to be complete successfully, the server authentication certificate used for the pull service should be trusted on the pull client. This trusted certificate should exist in `Cert:\Localhost\Root`. You will see how to force an unsecure connection with an HTTP pull server endpoint later in this chapter.

In this code, the `Settings` meta resource has just one property configured and it is `RefreshMode` set to Pull. Followed by that, the `ConfigurationRepositoryWeb` and `ResourceRepositoryWeb` meta resources point to the pull service endpoint. In both `ConfigurationRepositoryWeb` and `ResourceRepositoryWeb`, a `ServerURL` property points to the pull server REST endpoint and the `RegistrationKey` property points to the value that was used in the configuration of pull server endpoint. The argument to `RegistrationKey` must match one of the values used in configuring the pull service.

The `ConfigurationNames` property in the `ConfigurationRepositoryWeb` meta resource tells the LCM on the pull client what configuration MOF to pull from the server. Although this property accepts an array of configuration names, for a normal node configuration, only one configuration name is allowed. Multiple configuration names are used in the context of partial configurations, which is the subject of Chapter 10.

With this, let's compile and enact this meta configuration.

```
PS C:\scripts> Set-DscLocalConfigurationManager -Path .\oDataHTTPSPullClient -Force -Verbose
VERBOSE: Performing the operation "Start-DscConfiguration: SendMetaConfigurationApply" on target "MSFT_DSCLocalConfigurationManager".
VERBOSE: Perform operation 'Invoke CimMethod' with following parameters, ''methodName' = SendMetaConfigurationApply,'className' = MSFT_DSCLocalConfigurationManager,
'namespaceName' = root/Microsoft/Windows/DesiredStateConfiguration'.
VERBOSE: An LCM method call arrived from computer S16-JB with user sid S-1-5-21-689661094-3032901192-2251061677-500.
WARNING: There is no operation running currently. Stop will return without any action.
VERBOSE: An LCM method call arrived from computer S16-JB with user sid S-1-5-21-689661094-3032901192-2251061677-500.
VERBOSE: [S16-02]: LCM:  [ Start  Set      ]
VERBOSE: [S16-02]: LCM:  [ Start  Resource ]  [MSFT_DSCMetaConfiguration]
VERBOSE: [S16-02]: LCM:  [ Start  Set      ]  [MSFT_DSCMetaConfiguration]
VERBOSE: [S16-02]: LCM:  [ End    Set      ]  [MSFT_DSCMetaConfiguration]  in 0.0150 seconds.
VERBOSE: [S16-02]: LCM:  [ End    Resource ]  [MSFT_DSCMetaConfiguration]
VERBOSE: [S16-02]:                              [] Registration of the Dsc Agent with the server https://s16-pull-02.psdsc.lab:8080/PSDSCPullServer.svc was successful
.
VERBOSE: [S16-02]:                              [] Registration of the Dsc Agent with the server https://s16-pull-02.psdsc.lab:8080/PSDSCPullServer.svc was successful
.
VERBOSE: [S16-02]: LCM:  [ End    Set      ]
VERBOSE: [S16-02]: LCM:  [ End    Set      ]  in  6.5260 seconds.
VERBOSE: Operation 'Invoke CimMethod' complete.
VERBOSE: Set-DscLocalConfigurationManager finished in 25.459 seconds.
```

Figure 8-16. *The LCM registered as pull client*

As shown in Figure 8-16, you have a pull client registered with the oData-based pull service. At this point in time, if you look at `Cert:\Localmachine\My` path, you will see that there is a new self-signed certificate associated with the pull server URL in the meta configuration. With an on-premises pull server, this certificate is not used. This is used with the Azure Automation DSC pull service, which you will see in Chapter 17. However, if you do not use the client authentication certificate, you can specify an already installed client authentication certificate's thumbprint as a value of the `CertificateID` property of the `ConfigurationRepositoryWeb`. This requires server side configuration as well to ensure that this certificate is trusted.

It is possible to configure a pull service in WMF 5.0 and above systems without using the registration keys. You just remove the `RegistrationKeyPath` property from the `xDscWebService` resource configuration in the above `PullServerHTTPS` configuration and remove the `File` resource instance that creates the registration keys file. When doing so, the target node LCM is allowed to use Configuration IDs only, which is the "old, WMF4" way of doing a DSC pull, instead of named configurations.

Here is the modified configuration for creating the pull server without registration keys:

```
$thumbprint = (Get-ChildItem -Path Cert:\LocalMachine\My | Where-Object {
$_.Subject -eq 'CN=S16-Pull-01.psdsc.lab' }).Thumbprint


Configuration PullServerHTTPS
{
    param
    (
        [Parameter()]
        [String]
        $NodeName = 'localhost',

        [Parameter(Mandatory = $true)]
        [String]
        $certificateThumbPrint
    )

    Import-DSCResource -ModuleName xPSDesiredStateConfiguration -Name x
    DSCWebService -ModuleVersion 8.0.0.0
    Import-DscResource -ModuleName PSDesiredStateConfiguration -Module
    Version 1.1

    Node $NodeName
    {
        WindowsFeature DSCServiceFeature
        {
            Ensure = 'Present'
            Name   = 'DSC-Service'
        }

        xDscWebService PSDSCPullServer
        {
            Ensure                     = 'Present'
            EndpointName               = 'PSDSCPullServer'
            Port                       = 8080
```

```
            PhysicalPath                = "$env:SystemDrive\inetpub\
                                            PSDSCPullServer"
            CertificateThumbPrint    = $certificateThumbPrint
            ModulePath               = "$env:PROGRAMFILES\WindowsPowerShell\
                                            DscService\Modules"
            ConfigurationPath        = "$env:PROGRAMFILES\WindowsPowerShell\
                                            DscService\Configuration"
            State                    = 'Started'
            AcceptSelfSignedCertificates = $true
            UseSecurityBestPractices = $true
            DependsOn                = '[WindowsFeature]DSCServiceFeature'
        }
    }
}

PullServerHTTPS -certificateThumbPrint $thumbprint
```

Note   Do not compile and enact this configuration yet. Complete the next section on using named configurations and then try converting them to configuration IDs.

Staging and Enacting Configurations with Configuration Names

Now that you have the pull server and client successfully set up, let's create a simple configuration and place it on the pull server so that the DSC LCM in pull mode can download and enact it. Here is a simple configuration that you will compile and store.

In the pull client configuration above, you already configured the configuration name as OSConfig. So, let's create one with the same name.

```
configuration WebServerConfig
{
    Import-DscResource -ModuleName PSDesiredStateConfiguration
    -ModuleVersion 1.1

    node OSConfig
    {
```

```
    WindowsFeature Web-Server
    {
        Name = 'Web-Server'
        Ensure = 'Present'
    }
  }
}

WebServerConfig -OutputPath .\OSConfig -Verbose
```

Note   Observe in this code listing that the name of the configuration function is not OSConfig. It is not necessary to call it with the same name as the configuration name in the meta configuration. The MOF file name, however, should match.

Make sure the nodename in the above configuration document is same as the configuration name mentioned in the meta configuration. Once verified, you need to create a checksum of this MOF file and store both the MOF and checksum on the pull server. This checksum file is needed for the LCM on the pull client to understand if anything changed with the node configuration. So, every time you update the node configuration and compile it, you must create the checksum as well so that the target node can identify that something has changed and will re-download and enact the updated configuration.

This is done using the New-DscChecksum command. Figure 8-17 shows how to use this command.

```
PS C:\scripts\OSConfig> New-DscChecksum -Path .\OSConfig.mof

PS C:\scripts\OSConfig> dir


    Directory: C:\scripts\OSConfig


Mode                LastWriteTime         Length Name
----                -------------         ------ ----
-a----        12/9/2017     5:13 PM           1862 OSConfig.mof
-a----        12/9/2017     5:17 PM             64 OSConfig.mof.checksum
```

Figure 8-17. *Checksum for the node configuration MOF*

Note   If the argument to `-Path` is a folder containing multiple MOF files, a checksum will be generated for each MOF at the path.

The node configuration MOF and checksum files can now be moved to the pull server. You need to store them at the path represented by the `ConfigurationPath` property in the pull server example earlier.

```
Copy-Item .\OSConfig\* -Destination 'C:\Program Files\WindowsPowerShell\
DscService\Configuration'
```

Once the files are placed on the pull server, you can either wait for the consistency check to trigger or use the `Update-DscConfiguration` cmdlet to force a check on the pull server. Trigger this command on the target node that is configured as a pull client.

```
Update-DscConfiguration -Wait -Verbose
```

```
PS C:\> Update-DscConfiguration -ComputerName S16-02 -Wait -Verbose
VERBOSE: Perform operation 'Invoke CimMethod' with following parameters, ''methodName' = PerformRequiredConfigurationChecks,'className' = MSFT_DSCLocalConfiguration
Manager,'namespaceName' = root/Microsoft/Windows/DesiredStateConfiguration'.
VERBOSE: An LCM method call arrived from computer S16-JB with user sid S-1-5-21-689661094-3032901192-2251061677-500.
VERBOSE: [S16-02]:                            [] Executing Get-Action with configuration (null)'s checksum: 3ffc54a0e6dae84a25161be000e631c23e12600985b70202da011721
3d10c375.
VERBOSE: [S16-02]:                            [] Executing Get-Action with configuration 's checksum returned result status: GetConfiguration.
VERBOSE: [S16-02]:                            [] Checksum is different. LCM will execute GetConfiguration to pull configuration .
VERBOSE: [S16-02]:                            [] Executing GetConfiguration succeeded. Configuration  was pulled from server.
VERBOSE: [S16-02]:                            [] Applying the new configuration(s) pulled.
VERBOSE: [S16-02]: LCM:  [ Start  Resource ]  [[WindowsFeature]Web-Server]
VERBOSE: [S16-02]: LCM:  [ Start  Test     ]  [[WindowsFeature]Web-Server]
VERBOSE: [S16-02]:                            [[WindowsFeature]Web-Server] The operation 'Get-WindowsFeature' started: Web-Server
VERBOSE: [S16-02]:                            [[WindowsFeature]Web-Server] The operation 'Get-WindowsFeature' succeeded: Web-Server
VERBOSE: [S16-02]: LCM:  [ End    Test     ]  [[WindowsFeature]Web-Server]  in 7.6430 seconds.
VERBOSE: [S16-02]: LCM:  [ Start  Set      ]  [[WindowsFeature]Web-Server]
VERBOSE: [S16-02]:                            [[WindowsFeature]Web-Server] Installation started...
VERBOSE: [S16-02]:                            [[WindowsFeature]Web-Server] Continue with installation?
VERBOSE: [S16-02]:                            [[WindowsFeature]Web-Server] Prerequisite processing started...
VERBOSE: [S16-02]:                            [[WindowsFeature]Web-Server] Prerequisite processing succeeded.
VERBOSE: [S16-02]:                            [[WindowsFeature]Web-Server] Installation succeeded.
VERBOSE: [S16-02]:                            [[WindowsFeature]Web-Server] Successfully installed the feature Web-Server.
VERBOSE: [S16-02]: LCM:  [ End    Set      ]  [[WindowsFeature]Web-Server]  in 119.8200 seconds.
VERBOSE: [S16-02]: LCM:  [ End    Resource ]  [[WindowsFeature]Web-Server]
VERBOSE: Operation 'Invoke CimMethod' complete.
VERBOSE: Time taken for configuration job to complete is 133.583 seconds
```

Figure 8-18. *A configuration enact in pull mode*

Figure 8-18 shows that the pull client on the target node checks the pull server for a configuration. Since this is the first time you are enacting this, there is no existing checksum to compare against. So the configuration gets downloaded and enacted.

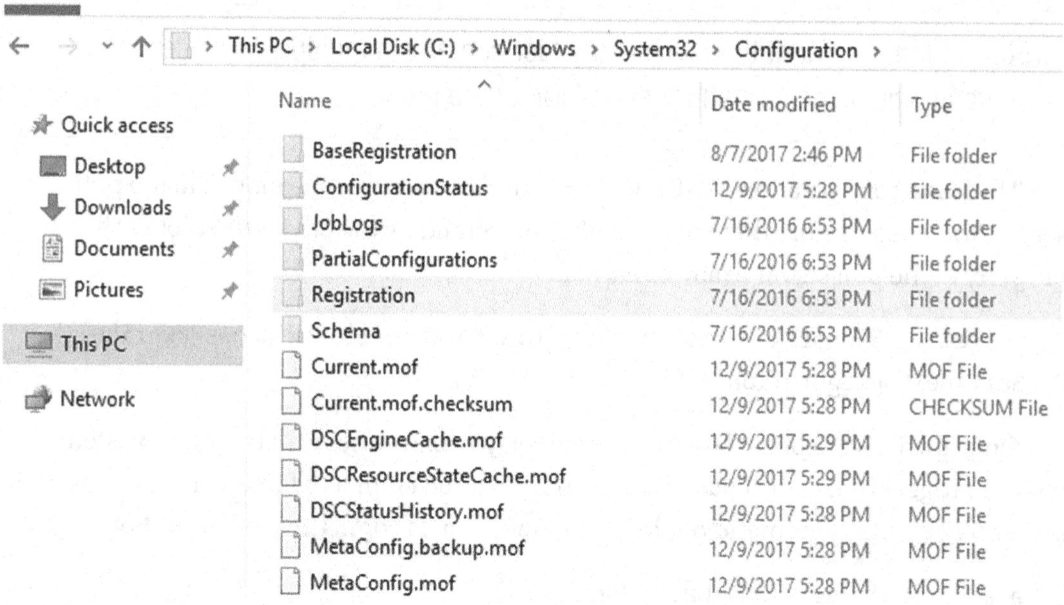

Figure 8-19. *The configuration store after the enact*

As shown in Figure 8-19, the configuration store after the enact consists of the current.mof and the current.mof.checksum files. So, every time a consistency check gets triggered, the local checksum will be compared against what is available on the pull server for downloading any updated configuration.

Pull Client Configuration with HTTPS Pull Service Configuration IDs

In the absence of the registration keys, the LCM uses the ConfigurationId meta property to identify itself to the pull server and retrieve the right configuration files.

Note   The following meta configuration document, although it uses ConfigurationId, can be used to on-board the LCM to a pull server that uses registration keys.

```
[DSCLocalConfigurationManager()]
configuration oDataHTTPSPullClient
{
    param
    (
```

```
    [Parameter()]
    [String]
    $NodeName = 'localhost',

    [Parameter(Mandatory = $true)]
    [String]
    $ConfigurationID,

    [Parameter(Mandatory = $true)]
    [String]
    $PullSvcEndpoint
)

Node $NodeName
{
    Settings
    {
        RefreshMode     = 'Pull'
        ConfigurationID = $ConfigurationID
    }

    ConfigurationRepositoryWeb HTTPSPullSvc
    {
        ServerURL           = $PullSvcEndpoint
    }

    ResourceRepositoryWeb HTTPSPullSvc
    {
        ServerURL           = $PullSvcEndpoint
    }
}
}

oDataHTTPSPullClient -ConfigurationID 'af7250ef-83fb-4cfd-b09b-
0f43fe012a50' -PullSvcEndpoint 'https://s16-pull-01.psdsc.lab:8080/
PSDSCPullServer.svc'
```

In this meta configuration, you have set the ConfigurationID property in the
Settings meta resource. The pull client node gets identified using this configuration ID.
Now you can compile and enact this meta configuration.

289

```
PS C:\OSConfig> Set-DscLocalConfigurationManager -Path .\oDataHTTPSPullClient -Verbose
VERBOSE: Performing the operation "Start-DscConfiguration: SendMetaConfigurationApply" on target "MSFT_DSCLocalConfigurationManager".
VERBOSE: Perform operation 'Invoke CimMethod' with following parameters, ''methodName' = SendMetaConfigurationApply,'className' = MSFT_DSCLocalConfigurationManager,
'namespaceName' = root/Microsoft/Windows/DesiredStateConfiguration'.
VERBOSE: An LCM method call arrived from computer S16-J8 with user sid S-1-5-21-689661094-3032901192-2251061677-500.
VERBOSE: [S16-01]: LCM:  [ Start  Set      ]
VERBOSE: [S16-01]: LCM:  [ Start  Resource ]  [MSFT_DSCMetaConfiguration]
VERBOSE: [S16-01]: LCM:  [ Start  Set      ]  [MSFT_DSCMetaConfiguration]
VERBOSE: [S16-01]: LCM:  [ End    Set      ]  [MSFT_DSCMetaConfiguration] in 0.0310 seconds.
VERBOSE: [S16-01]: LCM:  [ End    Resource ]  [MSFT_DSCMetaConfiguration]
VERBOSE: [S16-01]: LCM:  [ End    Set      ]
VERBOSE: [S16-01]: LCM:  [ End    Set      ]      in  0.0310 seconds.
VERBOSE: Operation 'Invoke CimMethod' complete.
VERBOSE: Set-DscLocalConfigurationManager finished in 0.168 seconds.
```

Figure 8-20. *LCM meta configuration with a pull server with no registration keys*

Observe the difference between what is shown in Figure 8-20 and Figure 8-16. In Figure 8-16, you can see that the LCM pull client registers with the pull server whereas in Figure 8-20 there is no such registration.

With this, let's try the `Update-DscConfiguration` cmdlet to see if the node can download the configuration MOF from the pull server.

```
PS C:\> Update-DscConfiguration -ComputerName S16-01 -Wait -Verbose
VERBOSE: Perform operation 'Invoke CimMethod' with following parameters, ''methodName' = PerformRequiredConfigurationChecks,'className' = MSFT_DSCLocalConfiguration
Manager,'namespaceName' = root/Microsoft/Windows/DesiredStateConfiguration'.
VERBOSE: An LCM method call arrived from computer S16-J8 with user sid S-1-5-21-689661094-3032901192-2251061677-500.
VERBOSE: [S16-01]:                            [] Executing Get-Action with configuration af7250ef-83fb-4cfd-b09b-0f43fe012a50's checksum: .
VERBOSE: [S16-01]:                            [] Executing Get-Action with configuration af7250ef-83fb-4cfd-b09b-0f43fe012a50's checksum failed. Please check the av
ailability of pull server.
The attempt to 'get an action' from server
https://s16-pull-01.psdsc.lab:8080///PSDSCPullServer.svc/Action(ConfigurationId='af7250ef-83fb-4cfd-b09b-0f43fe012a50')/GetAction failed because a valid
configuration af7250ef-83fb-4cfd-b09b-0f43fe012a50 cannot be found.
    + CategoryInfo          : ResourceUnavailable: (root/Microsoft/...gurationManager:string) [], CimException
    + FullyQualifiedErrorId : WebDownloadManagerGetActionConfigurationNotFound,Microsoft.PowerShell.DesiredStateConfiguration.Commands.GetDscActionCommand
    + PSComputerName        : S16-01

VERBOSE: Operation 'Invoke CimMethod' complete.
VERBOSE: Time taken for configuration job to complete is 5.652 seconds
```

Figure 8-21. *Update-DscConfiguration failure*

As shown in the error in Figure 8-21, there is no configuration MOF associated with the configuration ID specified in the node meta configuration. That's right; you have not staged any configuration MOF yet on the pull server. So, let's do so. You will use the same configuration document (OSConfig) example seen earlier. Compile the configuration MOF. Once you have the compiled MOF, you need to rename the MOF file to a format similar to *configurationID*.mof.

From the meta configuration example you just saw, the `ConfigurationID` is 'af7250ef-83fb-4cfd-b09b-0f43fe012a50' and therefore the MOF in this case will be renamed to af7250ef-83fb-4cfd-b09b-0f43fe012a50.MOF. Once you have this MOF, you can generate the checksum and copy both files to the pull server configuration path specified in the configuration document.

Once the configuration staging on the pull server is complete, download and enact it using the `Update-DscConfiguration` cmdlet.

```
PS C:\> Update-DscConfiguration -ComputerName S16-01 -Wait -Verbose
VERBOSE: Perform operation 'Invoke CimMethod' with following parameters, ''methodName' = PerformRequiredConfigurationChecks,'className' = MSFT_
Manager,'namespaceName' = root/Microsoft/Windows/DesiredStateConfiguration'.
VERBOSE: An LCM method call arrived from computer S16-JB with user sid S-1-5-21-689661094-3032901192-2251061677-500.
VERBOSE: [S16-01]:                          [] Executing Get-Action with configuration af7250ef-83fb-4cfd-b09b-0f43fe012a50's checksum: .
VERBOSE: [S16-01]:                          [] Executing Get-Action with configuration 's checksum returned result status: GetConfiguration.
VERBOSE: [S16-01]:                          [] Checksum is different. LCM will execute GetConfiguration to pull configuration .
VERBOSE: [S16-01]:                          [] Executing GetConfiguration succeeded. Configuration  was pulled from server.
VERBOSE: [S16-01]:                          [] Applying the new configuration(s) pulled.
VERBOSE: [S16-01]: LCM:  [ Start  Resource ]  [[WindowsFeature]Web-Server]
VERBOSE: [S16-01]: LCM:  [ Start  Test     ]  [[WindowsFeature]Web-Server]
VERBOSE: [S16-01]:                          [[WindowsFeature]Web-Server] The operation 'Get-WindowsFeature' started: Web-Server
VERBOSE: [S16-01]:                          [[WindowsFeature]Web-Server] The operation 'Get-WindowsFeature' succeeded: Web-Server
```

Figure 8-22. *Configuration download and enact*

Note   If there is no existing pull server in the infrastructure and this is a greenfield deployment, you should always prefer to implement the pull server with registration keys.

As seen in Figure 8-22, the pull client downloads the configuration document from the pull server and starts an enact.

Pull Server: HTTP

The oData-based pull server endpoint can be configured to use the less-secure HTTP protocol as well. To configure this, all you really need to do is set the CertificateThumbprint property in the xDSCWebService to AllowUnencryptedTraffic instead of assigning it a certificate thumbprint. Also, you need to set the UseSecurityBestPractices property to $false since you won't be using certificates.

Here is an example of a pull server configuration that deploys an HTTP endpoint:

```
$registrationkey = ([guid]::NewGuid()).Guid

Configuration PullServerHTTP
{
    param
    (
        [Parameter()]
        [String]
        $NodeName = 'localhost',

        [Parameter(Mandatory = $true)]
        [String]
        $certificateThumbPrint,
```

```
        [Parameter(Mandatory = $true)]
        [String]
        $RegistrationKey
    )

    Import-DSCResource -ModuleName xPSDesiredStateConfiguration -Name
    xDSCWebService -ModuleVersion 8.0.0.0
    Import-DscResource -ModuleName PSDesiredStateConfiguration -Module
    Version 1.1

    Node $NodeName
    {
        WindowsFeature DSCServiceFeature
        {
            Ensure = 'Present'
            Name   = 'DSC-Service'
        }

        xDscWebService PSDSCPullServer
        {
            Ensure                  = 'Present'
            EndpointName            = 'PSDSCPullServer'
            Port                    = 8080
            PhysicalPath            = "$env:SystemDrive\inetpub\
                                        PSDSCPullServer"
            CertificateThumbPrint   = $certificateThumbPrint
            ModulePath              = "$env:PROGRAMFILES\WindowsPowerShell\
                                        DscService\Modules"
            ConfigurationPath       = "$env:PROGRAMFILES\WindowsPowerShell\
                                        DscService\Configuration"
            State                   = 'Started'
            RegistrationKeyPath     = "$env:PROGRAMFILES\WindowsPowerShell\
                                        DscService"
            AcceptSelfSignedCertificates = $true
            UseSecurityBestPractices = $false
            DependsOn               = '[WindowsFeature]DSCServiceFeature'
        }
    }
```

```
    File RegistrationKeyFile
    {
        Ensure          = 'Present'
        Type            = 'File'
        DestinationPath = "$env:ProgramFiles\WindowsPowerShell\
                          DscService\RegistrationKeys.txt"
        Contents        = $RegistrationKey
    }
  }
}

PullServerHTTP -RegistrationKey $registrationkey -certificateThumbPrint
'AllowUnencryptedTraffic'
```

Compiling and enacting this configuration will configure the HTTP endpoint.

Pull Client Configuration with an HTTP Pull Service

To register the LCM pull client with the HTTP pull service endpoint, use the following
meta configuration document. This isn't any different from the pull client registration
example you saw earlier. This will fail for a reason. Compile and enact the configuration
to see why.

```
[DSCLocalConfigurationManager()]
configuration oDataHTTPPullClient
{
    param
    (
        [Parameter()]
        [String]
        $NodeName = 'localhost',

        [Parameter(Mandatory = $true)]
        [String]
        $RegistrationKey,

        [Parameter(Mandatory = $true)]
        [String]
        $PullSvcEndpoint,
```

```
        [Parameter(Mandatory = $true)]
        [String]
        $ConfigNames
    )

    Node $NodeName
    {
        Settings
        {
            RefreshMode      = 'Pull'
        }

        ConfigurationRepositoryWeb HTTPPullSvc
        {
            ServerURL          = $PullSvcEndpoint
            RegistrationKey    = $RegistrationKey
            ConfigurationNames = $ConfigNames
        }

        ResourceRepositoryWeb HTTPPullSvc
        {
            ServerURL          = $PullSvcEndpoint
            RegistrationKey    = $RegistrationKey
        }
    }
}

oDataHTTPPullClient -NodeName 'S16-01' -RegistrationKey '32549046-1f4f-
4787-93c0-84cb6387f756' -PullSvcEndpoint 'http://S16-PULL-01:8080/
PSDSCPullServer.svc' -ConfigNames 'OSConfig'
```

Let's compile and enact this meta configuration.

```
VERBOSE: Performing the operation "Start-DscConfiguration: SendMetaConfigurationApply" on target "MSFT_DSCLocalConfigurationManager".
VERBOSE: Perform operation 'Invoke CimMethod' with following parameters, ''methodName' = SendMetaConfigurationApply,'className' = MSFT_DSCLocalConfigurationManager,
'namespaceName' = root/Microsoft/Windows/DesiredStateConfiguration'.
VERBOSE: An LCM method call arrived from computer S16-JB with user sid S-1-5-21-689661094-3032901192-2251061677-500.
VERBOSE: [S16-01]: LCM:  [ Start  Set      ]
VERBOSE: [S16-01]: LCM:  [ Start  Resource ]  [MSFT_DSCMetaConfiguration]
VERBOSE: [S16-01]: LCM:  [ Start  Set      ]  [MSFT_DSCMetaConfiguration]
VERBOSE: [S16-01]: LCM:  [ End    Set      ]  [MSFT_DSCMetaConfiguration]  in 0.0310 seconds.
VERBOSE: [S16-01]: LCM:  [ End    Resource ]  [MSFT_DSCMetaConfiguration]
VERBOSE: [S16-01]: LCM:  [ End    Set      ]
Registration of the Dsc Agent with the server http://S16-PULL-01:8080/PSDSCPullServer.svc failed. The underlying error is: Cannot register at
http://S16-PULL-01:8080/PSDSCPullServer.svc. Registering over HTTP is not allowed. To ensure security in registration, use an HTTPS address for the ServerUrl in
the ConfigurationRepository of the LocalConfigurationManager resource for this device. If you understand the security implications of using HTTP and want to allow
its use on this device, set AllowUnsecureConnection property to true in the ConfigurationRepository of the LocalConfigurationManager resource for this device. .
    + CategoryInfo          : InvalidResult: (root/Microsoft/...gurationManager:String) [], CimException
    + FullyQualifiedErrorId : UnsecureRegistrationNotAllowed,Microsoft.PowerShell.DesiredStateConfiguration.Commands.RegisterDscAgentCommand
    + PSComputerName        : S16-01

VERBOSE: Operation 'Invoke CimMethod' complete.
VERBOSE: Set-DscLocalConfigurationManager finished in 0.741 seconds.
```

Figure 8-23. *LCM configuration enact failure*

In Figure 8-23, you can see that the LCM enact failed because pull client registration over HTTP is not allowed. As mentioned in the error message, to be able to force the LCM to use pull protocol over HTTP, you need to add the `AllowUnsecureConnection` property to the meta configuration. Here is the updated meta configuration:

```
[DSCLocalConfigurationManager()]
configuration oDataHTTPPullClient
{
    param
    (
        [Parameter()]
        [String]
        $NodeName = 'localhost',

        [Parameter(Mandatory = $true)]
        [String]
        $RegistrationKey,

        [Parameter(Mandatory = $true)]
        [String]
        $PullSvcEndpoint,

        [Parameter(Mandatory = $true)]
        [String]
        $ConfigNames
    )
```

```
Node $NodeName
{
    Settings
    {
        RefreshMode      = 'Pull'
    }

    ConfigurationRepositoryWeb HTTPPullSvc
    {
        ServerURL           = $PullSvcEndpoint
        Registra/tionKey    = $RegistrationKey
        ConfigurationNames  = $ConfigNames
        AllowUnsecureConnection = $true
    }

    ResourceRepositoryWeb HTTPPullSvc
    {
        ServerURL           = $PullSvcEndpoint
        RegistrationKey     = $RegistrationKey
        AllowUnsecureConnection = $true
    }
}
}
```

```
oDataHTTPPullClient -NodeName 'S16-01' -RegistrationKey '32549046-1f4f-
4787-93c0-84cb6387f756' -PullSvcEndpoint 'http://S16-PULL-01:8080/
PSDSCPullServer.svc' -ConfigNames 'OSConfig'
```

Compile and enact this configuration to force the LCM pull client to use the HTTP protocol.

Try It   With the knowledge gained in this section, try on-boarding the LCM as a pull client using the WMF 4.0 method. Try this with both HTTPS and HTTP endpoints of the pull server. Hint: You need to use the `LocalConfigurationManager` meta resource.

Whether you use HTTP or HTTPS, the way you stage configuration MOF files and download and enact using the `Update-DscConfiguration` cmdlet does not change.

So far you have looked at creating oDATA-based pull service endpoints that either use HTTP or HTTPS. This approach has certain advantages but the configuration of these endpoints is relatively complex and requires a separate service deployed for the same. The pull service can also be deployed to support SMB file share. The next section shows how to configure this.

SMB-Based Pull Service

The process of configuring a SMB-based pull server is much simpler. In fact, you just create a SMB share for storing the configuration MOF files and resource modules. All you need to do is identify a system that will host the SMB file share, create the file share, and assign appropriate permissions. Once you have a system identified for hosting the file share, you can use the `New-SmbShare` cmdlet to create a file share for storing the configuration and modules.

```
New-SmbShare -Name SMBpull -Path C:\SMBPull -ReadAccess Everyone
-Description "SMB Share for Pull Mode"
```

This is really it! You just configured the pull service over SMB! Okay, there is more. What you created is really a staging area for the configuration and resource modules. But, when using the SMB mode, you need not do anything on the server that is hosting the file share but configure the target system to look at the SMB file share for any configuration and required modules. Also, notice that in the above command you have given read access to everyone. This gives all systems configured as pull clients access to the SMB file share where the configuration and modules are stored. Is this really a best practice? Not necessarily. You will see a better method a bit later.

Pull Client Configuration

To use the DSC LCM as a pull client with an SMB pull server, you need to use the `ConfigurationRepositoryShare` and `ResourceRepositoryShare` meta resources. Here is an example of this meta configuration:

```
[DSCLocalConfigurationManager()]
configuration SMBPullClient
```

```powershell
{
    param
    (
        [Parameter()]
        [String]
        $NodeName = 'localhost',

        [Parameter(Mandatory = $true)]
        [String]
        $ConfigurationID,

        [Parameter(Mandatory = $true)]
        [String]
        $PullSvcSMBShare
    )

    Node $NodeName
    {
        Settings
        {
            RefreshMode     = 'Pull'
            ConfigurationID = $ConfigurationID
        }

        ConfigurationRepositoryShare SMBPullSvc
        {
            SourcePath = $PullSvcSMBShare
        }

        ResourceRepositoryShare SMBPullSvc
        {
            SourcePath = $PullSvcSMBShare
        }
    }
}

SMBPullClient -ConfigurationID '32549046-1f4f-4787-93c0-84cb6387f756'
-PullSvcSMBShare '\\s16-pull-01\SMBpull'
```

As shown in this meta configuration document, you use the
ConfigurationRepositoryShare and ResourceRepositoryShare meta resources and set
the SourcePath property to the UNC path where you are staging the configuration MOF
files. And, also note that the ConfigurationID property in the Settings meta resource is
specified. There is no registration supported with an SMB pull server and therefore you
need to use the configuration ID.

Let's compile and enact this meta configuration using the Set-
DscLocalConfigurationManager cmdlet. Once the LCM is configured, use the Update-
DscConfiguration cmdlet to download and enact the node configuration.

Note   Before the enact, ensure you have named the configuration MOF files
appropriately in the ConfigurationID.mof format and staged them on the SMB pull
share.

In the example you just tried, gave everyone read access to the SMB share
configured as the pull server. However, that is not a good practice. To support
a secure way of pulling configurations and resource modules from a SMB pull
share, ConfigurationRepositoryShare and ResourceRepositoryShare support
the Credential property. This can be used to supply the credentials needed for
authenticating to the SMB pull share from the DSC LCM. To use the Credential
property in these meta resources, you need to use certificates. You learned how to
use certificates to encrypt credentials in Chapter 5. So, here is the meta configuration
example that configures credentials for ConfigurationRepositoryShare and
ResourceRepositoryShare:

```
$cert = [System.Security.Cryptography.X509Certificates.
X509Certificate2]::new()
$certFile = 'C:\publicKeys\S16-01.cer'
$cert.Import($certFile)

$configData = @{
    AllNodes = @(
        @{
            NodeName = 'S16-01'
            CertificateFile = $certFile
            Thumbprint = $cert.Thumbprint
```

```
                PsDscAllowDomainUser = $true
        }
    )
}

[DSCLocalConfigurationManager()]
configuration SMBPullClient
{
    param
    (
        [Parameter()]
        [String]
        $NodeName = 'localhost',

        [Parameter(Mandatory = $true)]
        [String]
        $ConfigurationID,

        [Parameter(Mandatory = $true)]
        [String]
        $PullSvcSMBShare,

        [Parameter(Mandatory = $true)]
        [psCredential]
        $SmbCredential
    )

    Node $AllNodes.NodeName
    {
        Settings
        {
            RefreshMode     = 'Pull'
            ConfigurationID = $ConfigurationID
            CertificateID = $cert.Thumbprint
        }

        ConfigurationRepositoryShare SMBPullSvc
        {
```

```
        SourcePath = $PullSvcSMBShare
        Credential = $SmbCredential
    }

    ResourceRepositoryShare SMBPullSvc
    {
        SourcePath = $PullSvcSMBShare
        Credential = $SmbCredential
    }
  }
}

SMBPullClient -ConfigurationID '32549046-1f4f-4787-93c0-84cb6387f756' `
            -PullSvcSMBShare '\\s16-pull-01\SMBpull' `
            -SmbCredential (Get-Credential -Message 'Enter credentials to
            access SMB share ...') `
            -ConfigurationData $configData
```

After you enact this meta configuration on the pull client, the DSC LCM will be able to use the credentials to authenticate to the SMB pull share.

Note   The initial release of WMF 5.0 had a bug that prevented using credentials for the SMB pull share. This was later fixed in a patch release.

This concludes the discussion on oData and SMB pull service configuration. You learned how to create both HTTPS- and HTTP-based endpoints using the DSC pull service feature in WMF 5.0 and above. With the oData endpoints, you can use either pull client registration with configuration names or configuration IDs to stage and download the configuration MOF files. The SMB pull server, due to its very nature of implementation, won't be accessible over the Internet.

Let's now move on to learning about staging resource modules.

Staging Resource Modules

In the code snippets for pull service (oData) configuration, you specified the ModulePath property. The argument to this represents where on the pull server (oData) the resource modules are staged. For the SMB pull server configuration, you simply point the SourcePath property of the ResourceRepositoryShare meta resource to a UNC path where the resource modules are staged. You already saw a few examples earlier of configuring the LCM to either use ResourceRepositoryWeb or ResourceRepositoryShare.

Note   Mixing of different types (oData and SMB) of configuration and resource repositories is supported only with partial configurations. You will see this in Chapter 10.

The format in which the modules are packaged is same irrespective of whether you use the oData pull service (HTTPS or HTTP) or SMB pull server. Before you look at the packaging the resource modules, here's a configuration document that has a few custom DSC resources:

```
Configuration HostsFile
{
    Import-DscResource -ModuleName xNetworking -Name xHostsFile
    -ModuleVersion 5.3.0.0
    Import-DscResource -ModuleName PSDesiredStateConfiguration
    -ModuleVersion 1.1

    xHostsFile HostFileEntry
    {
        HostName = 'Test10'
        IPAddress = '192.171.182.10'
        Ensure = 'Present'
    }
}

HostsFile
```

In this configuration document, you use the xHostsFile resource from the xNetworking DSC resource module. I used the 5.3.0.0 version so I have the Import-DscResource dynamic keyword in the document and I specified these parameters.

Now, you already know how to compile and stage the configuration MOF files for a given pull server scenario. You are using ConfigurationID instead of registration keys so you named the compiled MOF file as .mof and staged it along with the checksum file.

Let's enact the following meta configuration on the target node:

```
$cert = [System.Security.Cryptography.X509Certificates.
X509Certificate2]::new()
$certFile = 'C:\publicKeys\S16-01.cer'
$cert.Import($certFile)

$configData = @{
    AllNodes = @(
        @{
            NodeName = 'S16-01'
            CertificateFile = $certFile
            Thumbprint = $cert.Thumbprint
            PsDscAllowDomainUser = $true
        }
    )
}

[DSCLocalConfigurationManager()]
configuration SMBPullClient
{
    param
    (
        [Parameter()]
        [String]
        $NodeName = 'localhost',

        [Parameter(Mandatory = $true)]
        [String]
        $ConfigurationID,

        [Parameter(Mandatory = $true)]
        [String]
        $PullSvcSMBShare,

        [Parameter(Mandatory = $true)]
        [psCredential]
        $SmbCredential
    )
```

```
Node $AllNodes.NodeName
{
    Settings
    {
        RefreshMode     = 'Pull'
        ConfigurationID = $ConfigurationID
        CertificateID = $cert.Thumbprint
    }

    ConfigurationRepositoryShare SMBPullSvc
    {
        SourcePath = $PullSvcSMBShare
        Credential = $SmbCredential
    }

    ResourceRepositoryShare SMBPullSvc
    {
        SourcePath = $PullSvcSMBShare
        Credential = $SmbCredential
    }
}
}

SMBPullClient -ConfigurationID '32549046-1f4f-4787-93c0-84cb6387f756' `
            -PullSvcSMBShare '\\s16-pull-01\SMBpull' `
            -SmbCredential (Get-Credential -Message 'Enter credentials to
            access SMB share ...') `
            -ConfigurationData $configData
```

As discussed earlier, you have the ResourceRepositoryShare meta resource for the custom DSC resource module download. However, you have not packaged and staged the resource modules yet. Anyway, let's go ahead and download/enact the configuration and see what happens.

```
PS C:\> Update-DscConfiguration -ComputerName S16-01 -Verbose -Wait
VERBOSE: Perform operation 'Invoke CimMethod' with following parameters, ''methodName' = PerformRequir
edConfigurationChecks,'className' = MSFT_DSCLocalConfigurationManager,'namespaceName' = root/Microsoft
/Windows/DesiredStateConfiguration'.
VERBOSE: An LCM method call arrived from computer S16-JB with user sid S-1-5-21-689661094-3032901192-2
251061677-500.
VERBOSE: [S16-01]:                        [] Executing Get-Action with configuration 32549046-1f4f
-4787-93c0-84cb6387f756's checksum: 72E14664057B307EF9F1BDB7AEF7FA15ECF7455A5AE7B57E9A99CFC11159F7CB.
VERBOSE: [S16-01]:                        [] Executing Get-Action with configuration 's checksum r
eturned result status: GETCONFIGURATION.
VERBOSE: [S16-01]:                        [] Checksum is different. LCM will execute GetConfigurat
ion to pull configuration .
VERBOSE: [S16-01]:                        [] Executing GetConfiguration failed. Configuration  is
not pulled.
The file \\s16-pull-01\SMBpull\xNetworking_5.3.0.0.zip is not found.
    + CategoryInfo         : ObjectNotFound: (\\s16-pull-01\S...ing_5.3.0.0.zip:String) [], CimExce
   ption
    + FullyQualifiedErrorId : DSCFileFileNotFound,Microsoft.PowerShell.DesiredStateConfiguration.Dow
   nloadManager.FileGetModuleCommand
    + PSComputerName       : S16-01

VERBOSE: Operation 'Invoke CimMethod' complete.
VERBOSE: Time taken for configuration job to complete is 0.734 seconds
```

Figure 8-24. *Pull configuration failure*

Figure 8-24 shows an error that the custom DSC resource module could not be found. As you saw in Chapter 3, the LCM knows the exact version of the module that it needs from the compiled MOF file. For each resource that you use in the configuration document, the compiled MOF includes the version of the module that was used on the authoring station at the compile time.

Figure 8-24 shows the path \s16-pull-01\SMBPull\xNetworking_5.3.0.0.zip as the file that was not found. This should ring some bells about what the LCM was expecting. Yes, this is how the resource module needs to be packaged.

The format for packaging the resource module is modulename_moduleversion. zip. Therefore, the package name for the module that you are importing in the node configuration will be xNetworking_5.3.0.0.zip. This format for naming module packages helps us have multiple versions of the same module available on the pull server. Before you start packaging the module, let's step back and see how the module is stored on the authoring station.

```
PS C:\> tree /A /F 'C:\Program Files\WindowsPowerShell\Modules\xNetworking'
Folder PATH listing
Volume serial number is 8E45-E0C0
C:\PROGRAM FILES\WINDOWSPOWERSHELL\MODULES\XNETWORKING
\---5.3.0.0
    |   xNetworking.psd1
    |
    +---DSCResources
    |   +---MSFT_xDefaultGatewayAddress
    |   |   |   MSFT_xDefaultGatewayAddress.psm1
    |   |   |   MSFT_xDefaultGatewayAddress.schema.mof
    |   |   |   README.md
    |   |   |
    |   |   \---en-US
    |   |           MSFT_xDefaultGatewayAddress.strings.psd1
    |   |
    |   +---MSFT_xDhcpClient
    |   |   |   MSFT_xDhcpClient.psm1
    |   |   |   MSFT_xDhcpClient.schema.mof
    |   |   |   README.md
    |   |   |
    |   |   \---en-US
    |   |           MSFT_xDhcpClient.strings.psd1
    |   |
```

Figure 8-25. *Module structure (partial output)*

As shown in Figure 8-25, when you download the custom DSC resource modules from the PowerShell gallery, they are downloaded (by default) to the C:\Program Files\ WindowsPowerShell\Modules folder. Within the module folder, each version of the module is contained in its own folder. On my authoring station, I have only version 5.3.0.0 of the xNetworking module. All module files are under this folder named 5.3.0.0. Now, when it comes to packaging this module for distribution to pull clients, you should package only the module files under the version folder. Figure 8-26 shows the folder structure.

```
PS C:\> tree /A /F C:\ModulesForPull\xNetworking
Folder PATH listing
Volume serial number is 8E45-E0C0
C:\MODULESFORPULL\XNETWORKING
|   xNetworking.psd1
|
+---DSCResources
|   +---MSFT_xDefaultGatewayAddress
|   |   |   MSFT_xDefaultGatewayAddress.psm1
|   |   |   MSFT_xDefaultGatewayAddress.schema.mof
|   |   |   README.md
|   |   |
|   |   \---en-US
|   |           MSFT_xDefaultGatewayAddress.strings.psd1
|   |
|   +---MSFT_xDhcpClient
|   |   |   MSFT_xDhcpClient.psm1
|   |   |   MSFT_xDhcpClient.schema.mof
|   |   |   README.md
|   |   |
|   |   \---en-US
|   |           MSFT_xDhcpClient.strings.psd1
|   |
```

Figure 8-26. *Folder structure for pull server distribution*

Let's package this folder as a zip file and name it as **xNetworking_5.3.0.0.zip**. You also need a checksum of this package. See Figure 8-27.

```
PS C:\ModulesForPull> New-DscChecksum -Path .\xNetworking_5.3.0.0.zip .

PS C:\ModulesForPull> dir


    Directory: C:\ModulesForPull


Mode                LastWriteTime         Length Name
----                -------------         ------ ----
d-----       12/10/2017     2:30 PM                xNetworking
-a----       12/10/2017     2:33 PM         118660 xNetworking_5.3.0.0.zip
-a----       12/10/2017     2:34 PM             64 xNetworking_5.3.0.0.zip.checksum
```

Figure 8-27. *Module package and checksum*

Once both the module package and package checksum are available, you can stage them on the pull server for download by the download manager that is a part of the LCM. I used an SMB pull server for both configurations and resources, so I have the configuration MOF and resources staged at the same location. See Figure 8-28.

Figure 8-28. *Staged configuration MOF and module packages*

Now that you have the MOF and module packaged staged on the server, enact the configuration by using the `Update-DscConfiguration` cmdlet. It should work this time. See Figure 8-29.

```
PS C:\> Update-DscConfiguration -ComputerName S16-01 -Wait -Verbose
VERBOSE: Perform operation 'Invoke CimMethod' with following parameters, ''methodName' = PerformRequir
edConfigurationChecks,'className' = MSFT_DSCLocalConfigurationManager,'namespaceName' = root/Microsoft
/Windows/DesiredStateConfiguration'.
VERBOSE: An LCM method call arrived from computer S16-JB with user sid S-1-5-21-689661094-3032901192-2
251061677-500.
VERBOSE: [S16-01]:                          [] Executing Get-Action with configuration 32549046-1f4f
-4787-93c0-84cb6387f756's checksum: 72E146640457B307EF9F1BDB7AEF7FA15ECF7455A5AE7B57E9A99CFC11159F7CB.
VERBOSE: [S16-01]:                          [] Executing Get-Action with configuration 's checksum r
eturned result status: GETCONFIGURATION.
VERBOSE: [S16-01]:                          [] Checksum is different. LCM will execute GetConfigurat
ion to pull configuration .
VERBOSE: [S16-01]:                          [] Executing GetConfiguration succeeded. Configuration
was pulled from server.
VERBOSE: [S16-01]:                          [] Applying the new configuration(s) pulled.
VERBOSE: [S16-01]: LCM:  [ Start  Resource ] [[xHostsFile]HostFileEntry]
VERBOSE: [S16-01]: LCM:  [ Start  Test     ] [[xHostsFile]HostFileEntry]
VERBOSE: [S16-01]:                          [[xHostsFile]HostFileEntry] Looking up host entry for Te
st10.
VERBOSE: [S16-01]:                          [[xHostsFile]HostFileEntry] Testing host entry for Test1
0.
VERBOSE: [S16-01]: LCM:  [ End    Test     ] [[xHostsFile]HostFileEntry]  in 0.2350 seconds.
VERBOSE: [S16-01]: LCM:  [ Start  Set      ] [[xHostsFile]HostFileEntry]
VERBOSE: [S16-01]:                          [[xHostsFile]HostFileEntry] Looking up host entry for Te
```

Figure 8-29. *Resource module download from pull server*

What if you want to overwrite the resource module on the target node with what is being downloaded from the pull server? You need to set the `AllowModuleOverwrite` to `$true` in the DSC LCM Settings meta resource. This is needed when you want to update the resource module without updating the module version number.

This concludes our discussion about the pull mode and various ways to implement and use pull services in DSC. The final valid setting for the `RefreshMode` property in the LCM Settings meta resource is `Disabled`. So, what about the disabled mode?

Disabled Mode

Starting with WMF 5.0, DSC enabled a new refresh mode called Disabled. The following meta configuration shows how to use this:

```
[DSCLocalConfigurationManager()]
configuration DisabledRefreshmode
{
    param
    (
        [Parameter()]
        [String]
        $NodeName = 'localhost'
    )

    Node $NodeName
    {
        Settings
        {
            RefreshMode      = 'Disabled'
        }
    }
}

DisabledRefreshmode -NodeName 'S16-01'
```

When you enact this meta configuration, the `RefreshMode` of the LCM gets set to `Disabled`, as shown in Figure 8-30.

```
PS C:\> Get-DscLocalConfigurationManager -CimSession S16-01


ActionAfterReboot                   : ContinueConfiguration
AgentId                             : 7FE8E864-8101-11E7-B423-00155D87B207
AllowModuleOverWrite                : False
CertificateID                       :
ConfigurationDownloadManagers       : {}
ConfigurationID                     :
ConfigurationMode                   : ApplyAndMonitor
ConfigurationModeFrequencyMins      : 15
Credential                          :
DebugMode                           : {NONE}
DownloadManagerCustomData           :
DownloadManagerName                 :
LCMCompatibleVersions               : {1.0, 2.0}
LCMState                            : Idle
LCMStateDetail                      :
LCMVersion                          : 2.0
StatusRetentionTimeInDays           : 10
SignatureValidationPolicy           : NONE
SignatureValidations                : {}
MaximumDownloadSizeMB               : 500
PartialConfigurations               :
RebootNodeIfNeeded                  : False
RefreshFrequencyMins                : 30
RefreshMode                         : Disabled
```

Figure 8-30. *Disabled refresh mode in the LCM*

When the DSC LCM is set to the disabled refresh mode, the LCM will not
run any consistency checks and you can run only DSC cmdlets such as Set-
DscLocalConfigurationManager, Get-DscConfiguration, Stop-DscConfiguration, and
Invoke-DscResource. You used Invoke-DscResource in Chapter 6 when learning how to
write new DSC resource modules.

So, what is the use of the disabled refresh mode when there are so many restrictions?
Remember, the DSC is not just a configuration management tool set. It is a configuration
management platform. The already popular configuration management tools such
as Chef, Puppet, and others are expected to leverage the DSC for configuration
management on Windows OS. When you have a third-party equivalent of the LCM
sitting on the same system managing a configuration based on its own policies, you
don't want the LCM to get in its way and start doing consistency checks on a periodic
basis. That does not make sense. Disabling any document processing by setting the LCM
RefreshMode is the right way here.

Try It   With the LCM set to the `Disabled` refresh mode, try enacting a configuration MOF via push mode (`Start-DscConfiguration`). What do you see?

Using Resource Repositories with Push Mode

Starting with WMF 5.0, it is now possible to use a central resource repository for downloading custom resource modules for a configuration enact in push mode. Here is a meta configuration example for the same:

```
[DSCLocalConfigurationManager()]
Configuration PushClient
{
    param
    (
        [Parameter()]
        [String]
        $NodeName = 'localhost',

        [Parameter(Mandatory = $true)]
        [String]
        $PullSvcEndpoint
    )

    Node $NodeName
    {
        Settings
        {
            RefreshMode      = 'Push'
        }

        ResourceRepositoryWeb oDATAPullSvc
        {
```

```
            ServerURL = $PullSvcEndpoint
            AllowUnsecureConnection = $true
        }
    }
}

PushClient  -PullSvcEndpoint 'http://S16-PULL-01:9090/PSDSCPullServer.svc'
```

Try It   Using the knowledge gained so far, try configuring a DSC LCM on the
target node in the push refresh mode with the above meta configuration to pull the
resource modules from a central repository.

How Configuration and Resource Modules Are Downloaded

This brings us to the end of this chapter. You learned how to configure and use a pull
client and how to download configuration MOF and resource module packages from the
central repositories. But what happens behind the scenes? You saw this at a very high
level in Figure 8-13.

In each of the pull models (HTTPS/HTTP and SMB), different
download managers get used. For the HTTPS/HTTP pull clients, the
WebDownloadManager gets used. This module is present at $PSHOME\Modules\
PSDesiredStateConfiguration\DownloadManager\WebDownloadManager. The SMB
pull clients use the FileDownloadManager module that is located at $PSHOME\Modules\
PSDesiredStateConfiguration\DownloadManager\DSCFileDownloadManager. Each of
these modules has cmdlets that have common names.

- **Get-DscAction** is used by the pull client to understand if the
  configuration on the pull server is different from that on the target
  system.

- **Get-DscDocument** is used by the pull client to retrieve the
  configuration document from the pull server.

- **Get-DscModule** is used by the pull client to retrieve the dependent modules and unpack them on the target system to enact the configuration specified in the configuration document.

Note   It is not necessary to use the cmdlets in the download manager modules manually anytime. They are meant for the pull client to function. And, it is good to understand their purpose so if you experience debugging or troubleshooting issues with pull client configurations, you know where to start from.

These are commands you saw in Figure 8-13 as the pull client workflow in both HTTP/HTTPS and SMB modes.

Summary

This has been one lengthy chapter! You learned about the different refresh modes possible in DSC and looked at push and pull modes in-depth. You saw the different types of pull service implementations that are supported within DSC and looked at how to configure and use them. When using pull mode, the configuration MOF files and resource modules need to be packaged in a certain format for staging. The naming convention for the configuration MOF depends on the version of the pull server protocol. You have, so far, used the pull service only as way to download configurations and resource modules. However, the LCM pull client reports the configuration status information back to the pull service when using oData-based pull servers. You will see this in the next chapter about reporting DSC configurations.

CHAPTER 9

Reporting, Monitoring, and Correcting a Configuration

In the configuration management processes, after the configuration is enacted, the most important step is to monitor the target systems for configuration drift and enact status for pull clients. IT and application administrators prefer quick fixes to the issues that arise in day-to-day operations. Over time in the life cycle of target systems and the applications running on those systems, there is a probability of a configuration drifting away from the original configuration. In an ideal world, all changes on the target system must go through the designated configuration management system. This helps prevent configuration drift. However, this is certainly not the case in many IT organizations. And, when a disaster strikes with a target system that has drifted away from the baseline configuration, it may take more than few hours to restore services offered to the end users.

DSC provides interfaces to monitor and report on a configuration from the target systems and also a method to auto-correct configuration drift. In this chapter, you will take a look at the internals of configuration management using DSC, monitoring and correcting the configuration on target systems, and finally, reporting on the configuration from target systems using built-in methods.

In earlier chapters, you looked at how the configuration can be pushed to target systems or how the pull clients on the target nodes can pull the configuration from a pull server. In Chapter 3, you looked at what happens when a configuration is pushed or pulled from a configuration life cycle point of view (Figure 3-8). Towards the end of Chapter 3, you briefly looked at monitoring the configuration state in DSC. In this chapter, you'll take an in-depth look at monitoring and learn how to report and correct configuration drift. But first let's review how the LCM monitors DSC configurations after an enact.

© Ravikanth Chaganti 2018
R. Chaganti, *Pro PowerShell Desired State Configuration*, https://doi.org/10.1007/978-1-4842-3483-9_9

Lab Requirements

To try the examples and exercises in this chapter, you will need at minimum two or more systems with Windows Server 2008 R2 or above with WMF 5.1 or above installed. I recommend a system with Windows Server 2016. The HTTPS pull service and credential encryption requires certificates, so you will need either a certificate authority or self-signed certificates. You will also need at least three nodes to try out the examples in this chapter.

Let's start this chapter with an overview of how the DSC consistency checks happen at regular intervals.

DSC Consistency Check Workflow

In WMF 4.0, PowerShell DSC scheduled tasks to invoke *consistency checks*, which were used to check if the node configuration was in the desired state or not. However, in WMF 5.0 and above, a WMI provider implemented as the `MSFT_DscTimer` class in the DSC CIM namespace is used to invoke the consistency checks based on the configuration and refresh frequency intervals configured in the LCM. The `ConfigurationModeFrequencyMins` specifies how often the LCM validates if the current node configuration is in the desired state or not. This validation depends on the configured value of the `ConfigurationMode` property. This property has three possible values: `ApplyOnly`, `ApplyAndMonitor`, and `ApplyAndAutoCorrect`. `ApplyAndMonitor` is the default value. The flow chart in Figure 9-1 depicts what is described above.

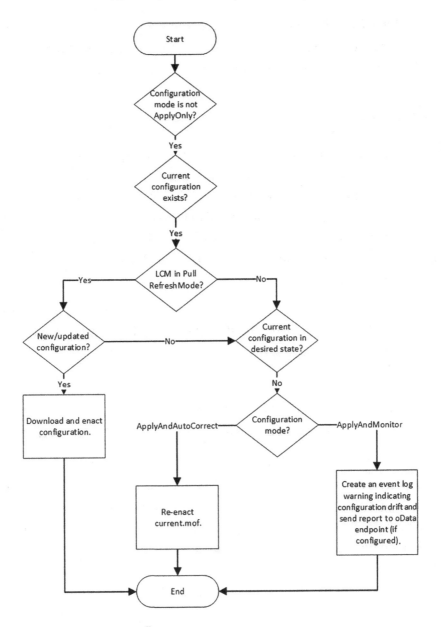

Figure 9-1. *Consistency run flow*

As shown in Figure 9-1, no consistency checks will be performed if the LCM is set to the ApplyOnly configuration mode. Also, consistency checks will not be triggered if there is no existing current configuration on the node. If the configuration mode is set to ApplyAndMonitor or ApplyAndAutoCorrect, LCM will check the refresh mode setting and then act upon the configuration drift, if any. If there is a drift and the configuration

317

mode is set to ApplyAndAutoCorrect, the current configuration on the node (current. mof) gets re-enacted. If the ConfigurationMode is set to ApplyAndMonitor, then an entry gets created in the DesiredStateConfiguration event log.

DSC Event Logs

Desired State Configuration event logs can be found under Application and Services Logs\Microsoft\Windows\Desired State Configuration. By default, only operational and admin logs are enabled. The operational logs do not provide much information about the resource execution. The analytic and debug logs provider deeper insights into what happens when a configuration is enacted or when a consistency check is performed. These logs are not enabled by default. To enable these logs, you can follow the steps mentioned below.

Note   You need to "show analytic and debug logs" in the view section of the event viewer to make these logs visible.

```
wevtutil.exe set-log 'Microsoft-Windows-Dsc/Analytic' /q:true /e:true
wevtutil.exe set-log 'Microsoft-Windows-Dsc/Debug' /q:true /e:true
```

These commands enable the Debug and Analytic channels for DSC logs. The event log messages from the three channels (Operational, Analytic, and Debug) can be accessed using the Get-WinEvent cmdlet. As you can see in the following example, Microsoft-Windows-Dsc is the primary log channel and you can retrieve the log messages by appending the Operational, Analytic, or Debug channel to the primary log. The Analytic channel contains messages that identify errors occurred and the verbose and messages from the LCM. The Debug channel can be used for troubleshooting and debugging purposes.

```
Get-WinEvent -LogName 'Microsoft-Windows-Dsc/Operational'
```

```
PS C:\Scripts> Get-WinEvent -LogName "Microsoft-Windows-Dsc/Operational" -ComputerName S16-01


    ProviderName: Microsoft-Windows-DSC

TimeCreated                   Id LevelDisplayName Message
-----------                   -- ---------------- -------
12/16/2017 12:44:22 PM      4270 Information      The local configuration manager was shut down.
12/16/2017 12:43:06 PM      4343 Information      The DscTimer has successfully run LCM method P
12/16/2017 12:43:06 PM      4266 Information      Job {8F829154-E230-11E7-8A8A-00155D87B207} : .
12/16/2017 12:43:06 PM      4264 Information      Job {8F829154-E230-11E7-8A8A-00155D87B207} : .
12/16/2017 12:43:06 PM      4262 Information      Job {8F829154-E230-11E7-8A8A-00155D87B207} : .
12/16/2017 12:43:06 PM      4263 Information      Job {8F829154-E230-11E7-8A8A-00155D87B207} : .
12/16/2017 12:43:06 PM      4261 Information      Job {8F829154-E230-11E7-8A8A-00155D87B207} : .
12/16/2017 12:43:06 PM      4508 Information      Job {8F829154-E230-11E7-8A8A-00155D87B207} : .
12/16/2017 12:43:06 PM      4513 Information      Job {8F829154-E230-11E7-8A8A-00155D87B207} : C
12/16/2017 12:43:06 PM      4251 Information      Job {8F829154-E230-11E7-8A8A-00155D87B207} : .
12/16/2017 12:43:06 PM      4257 Information      Job {8F829154-E230-11E7-8A8A-00155D87B207} : .
12/16/2017 12:43:06 PM      4115 Information      Job {8F829154-E230-11E7-8A8A-00155D87B207} : .
12/16/2017 12:43:06 PM      4222 Information      Job {8F829154-E230-11E7-8A8A-00155D87B207} : .
```

Figure 9-2.   DSC event logs

Each time a consistency check runs or a configuration is either pulled or pushed, DSC generates these messages. Each of these activities can be grouped under a single operation. Within these DSC logs, the Message property contains the information relevant to identify or group messages pertaining to a specific operation. To be specific, the Job ID, which is a GUID, as shown in Figure 9-2, uniquely identifies a DSC operation. You can use this information to group the log messages pertaining to a single operation.

Since you are interested in log messages from all three channels, you can use the Get-WinEvent cmdlet to construct an array containing all event log messages.

```
$AllDscLogs = Get-WinEvent -LogName 'Microsoft-windows-dsc/operational',
'Microsoft-Windows-Dsc/Analytic','Microsoft-Windows-Dsc/Debug' -Oldest
```

Note   You may not see any analytic or debug logs if no enact or consistency checks were performed after enabling these logs.

In the above command, you use the -Oldest switch parameter. This is because the event logs store the newest messages at the top. By using the -Oldest parameter, you can get the messages from oldest to newest. The Properties attribute of an event log object contains the values of event properties published by the providers. In fact, the Properties attribute returns an object array of type System.Diagnostics.Eventing. Reader.EventProperty. In this array, the first element contains the GUID of the job. So, the following code provides the JobID of all DSC activities:

```
$AllDscLogs.ForEach{$_.Properties[0].Value} | Select-Object -Unique
```

319

You already know that the JobID can be used to group a set of DSC operations. You can use the Group-Object cmdlet for this purpose.

```
$AllDscLogs | Group-Object { $_.Properties[0].Value }
```

```
PS C:\Scripts> $AllDscLogs | Group-Object { $_.Properties[0].Value }

Count Name                    Group
----- ----                    -----
  145                         {System.Diagnostics.Eventing.Reader.EventLogRecord, System.Dia
   37 DscTimerConsistencyOpe... {System.Diagnostics.Eventing.Reader.EventLogRecord, System.Dia
   11 {BB1E79A1-E235-11E7-B4... {System.Diagnostics.Eventing.Reader.EventLogRecord, System.Dia
   36 5                       {System.Diagnostics.Eventing.Reader.EventLogRecord, System.Dia
  146 1                       {System.Diagnostics.Eventing.Reader.EventLogRecord, System.Dia
   10 {BB1E79A0-E235-11E7-B4... {System.Diagnostics.Eventing.Reader.EventLogRecord, System.Dia
   10 {A2AE3882-E233-11E7-B4... {System.Diagnostics.Eventing.Reader.EventLogRecord, System.Dia
    9 {8A39B58D-E231-11E7-B4... {System.Diagnostics.Eventing.Reader.EventLogRecord, System.Dia
   11 {8A39B58C-E231-11E7-B4... {System.Diagnostics.Eventing.Reader.EventLogRecord, System.Dia
   10 {71C6DC43-E22F-11E7-B4... {System.Diagnostics.Eventing.Reader.EventLogRecord, System.Dia
   11 {59579DAC-E22D-11E7-B4... {System.Diagnostics.Eventing.Reader.EventLogRecord, System.Dia
   10 {59579DAB-E22D-11E7-B4... {System.Diagnostics.Eventing.Reader.EventLogRecord, System.Dia
   10 {40EBE065-E22B-11E7-B4... {System.Diagnostics.Eventing.Reader.EventLogRecord, System.Dia
   11 {28790E16-E229-11E7-B4... {System.Diagnostics.Eventing.Reader.EventLogRecord, System.Dia
   10 {28790E15-E229-11E7-B4... {System.Diagnostics.Eventing.Reader.EventLogRecord, System.Dia
   10 {10039C38-E227-11E7-B4... {System.Diagnostics.Eventing.Reader.EventLogRecord, System.Dia
```

Figure 9-3. *Logs grouped by job ID*

Each set of the DSC operations shown in Figure 9-3 contains the log messages from all three DSC event log channels. You can retrieve the messages in each group by selecting the Message property of the event log record.

```
$DSCOperations[0].Group.Message
```

```
PS C:\> $DSCoperations = $AllDscLogs | Group-Object { $_.Properties[0].Value }

PS C:\> $DSCoperations[0].Group.Message
The local configuration manager was shut down.
The local configuration manager started.
The local configuration manager was shut down.
The local configuration manager started.
The local configuration manager was shut down.
The local configuration manager started.
The local configuration manager was shut down.
The local configuration manager started.
The local configuration manager was shut down.
The local configuration manager started.
The local configuration manager was shut down.
The local configuration manager started.
The local configuration manager was shut down.
The local configuration manager started.
```

Figure 9-4. *Logs from a single DSC operation*

Once you have the events grouped by a specific DSC operation, similar to what is shown in Figure 9-4, it is easy to filter it for errors or any such criteria. This can be done using the Where-Object cmdlet.

```
$AllDscLogs | Group-Object { $_.Properties[0].Value } | Where-Object {
$_.Group.LevelDisplayName -eq "Warning" }
```

What you have seen so far is a slightly difficult or maybe tedious way of retrieving event logs and making sense of them. This is still not a clean approach. The PowerShell team wrote an open source module called xDSCDiagnotics, which is available on the PowerShell gallery, to investigate DSC event logs in an easy-to-understand manner. Let's take a look at it now:

```
Install-Module -Name xDSCDiagnostics -Force
Get-Command -Module xDscDiagnostics
```

```
PS C:\> Install-Module -Name xDSCDiagnostics -Force

PS C:\> Get-Command -Module xDscDiagnostics

CommandType     Name                               Version    Source
-----------     ----                               -------    ------
Alias           Get-xDscDiagnosticsZip             2.6.0.0    xDscDiagnostics
Function        Get-XDscConfigurationDetail        2.6.0.0    xDscDiagnostics
Function        Get-xDscDiagnosticsZipDataPoint    2.6.0.0    xDscDiagnostics
Function        Get-xDscOperation                  2.6.0.0    xDscDiagnostics
Function        New-xDscDiagnosticsZip             2.6.0.0    xDscDiagnostics
Function        Trace-xDscOperation                2.6.0.0    xDscDiagnostics
Function        Unprotect-xDscConfiguration        2.6.0.0    xDscDiagnostics
Function        Update-xDscEventLogStatus          2.6.0.0    xDscDiagnostics
```

Figure 9-5. *xDSCDiagnostics module*

The Get-xDSCOperation command in this module can be used to retrieve the newest 10 DSC operations from a target node; see Figure 9-5. If you would like to see more items in the output, you can use the -Newest parameter and specify an integer argument, as shown in Figure 9-6.

```
PS C:\> Get-xDscOperation -ComputerName S16-01

ComputerName  SequenceId  TimeCreated            Result   JobID                                      AllEvents
------------  ----------  -----------            ------   -----                                      ---------
S16-01        1           12/16/2017 3:14:23 PM  Success                                             {@{Message=; TimeC...
S16-01        2           12/16/2017 3:13:06 PM  Success                                             {@{Message=; TimeC...
S16-01        3           12/16/2017 3:13:06 PM  Success   83e6af91-e245-11e7-8a8a-00155d87b207       {@{Message=Operati...
S16-01        4           12/16/2017 2:58:07 PM  Success                                             {@{Message=Operati...
S16-01        5           12/16/2017 2:58:07 PM  Success   6b72acd8-e243-11e7-8a8a-00155d87b207       {@{Message=Operati...
S16-01        6           12/16/2017 2:58:06 PM  Success   6b72acd7-e243-11e7-8a8a-00155d87b207       {@{Message=Operati...
S16-01        7           12/16/2017 2:52:47 PM  Success   adad759b-e242-11e7-8a8a-00155d87b207       {@{Message=Operati...
S16-01        8           12/16/2017 2:43:06 PM  Success   53079761-e241-11e7-8a8a-00155d87b207       {@{Message=Operati...
S16-01        9           12/16/2017 2:35:20 PM  Success   3d74df63-e240-11e7-8a8a-00155d87b207       {@{Message=Operati...
S16-01        10          12/16/2017 2:32:59 PM  Success   e945f7f0-e23f-11e7-8a8a-00155d87b207       {@{Message=Operati...
```

Figure 9-6. *Get DSC operations*

The Trace-xDSCOperation command can be used to dig into a specific job and retrieve the details of the DSC operation; see Figure 9-7.

```
PS C:\> Trace-xDscOperation -ComputerName S16-01 -SequenceID 7 -JobId adad759b-e242-11e7-8a8a-00155d87b207
WARNING: XDscDiagnostics : The Analytic log is not enabled. To enable it, please run the following command:
        Update-xDscEventLogStatus -Channel Analytic -Status Enabled
For more help on this cmdlet run Get-Help Update-xDscEventLogStatus
WARNING: XDscDiagnostics : The Debug log is not enabled. To enable it, please run the following command:
        Update-xDscEventLogStatus -Channel Debug -Status Enabled
For more help on this cmdlet run Get-Help Update-xDscEventLogStatus

ComputerName  EventType    TimeCreated            Message
------------  ---------    -----------            -------
S16-01        OPERATIONAL  12/16/2017 2:52:47 PM  Operation Get-DscLocalConfigurationManager started by user sid S-1-5-21-(
S16-01        OPERATIONAL  12/16/2017 2:52:47 PM  Operation Get-DscLocalConfigurationManager completed successfully.
```

Figure 9-7. *Trace DSC operations*

As you can see in the above output, I don't have the Analytics and Debug logs enabled on the target node. When you need to debug a DSC operational issue, you should enable these logs. You already saw a way to do this using wevtutil.exe. The xDSCDiagnostics module provides a method to do this as well.

```
Update-xDscEventLogStatus -ComputerName S16-01 -Channel Analytic -Status Enabled
Update-xDscEventLogStatus -ComputerName S16-01 -Channel Debug -Status Enabled
```

When needed, you can package these logs into a zip file and share it with others who may be looking to debug a certain DSC issue. The New-xDscDiagnosticsZip command can be used for that purpose. For adding different types of log and other inventory information in this zip file, you can use the -IncludedDatapoint parameter. A list of available data points can be retrieved using the Get-xDscDiagnosticsZipDataPoint command.

Configuration Reporting

The PSDesiredStateConfiguration module has cmdlets that can be used for configuration reporting. Let's look at these commands. The first one is something you have been using all along. It is the Get-DscConfiguration cmdlet. This cmdlet gets the current state of the node configuration as reported by the DSC resource's Get method.

Here is a simple example of a File resource configuration that I use to create a file-based flag to be used in the OS deployment process:

```
Configuration OSConfig
{
    Import-DscResource -ModuleName PSDesiredStateConfiguration
    File ScriptFlag
    {
        DestinationPath = 'C:\OSDeployment.tag'
        Type = 'File'
        Contents = ''
        Ensure = 'Present'
    }
}

OSConfig
```

When you enact this configuration on any node, a 0-byte file named OSDeployment.tag gets created at C:. Once the enact is complete, if you run the Get-DSCConfiguration cmdlet, it returns the current state of the File resource on that node.

```
PS C:\Scripts> Get-DscConfiguration -CimSession S16-01


ConfigurationName        : OSConfig
DependsOn                :
ModuleName               : PSDesiredStateConfiguration
ModuleVersion            :
PsDscRunAsCredential     :
ResourceId               : [File]ScriptFlag
SourceInfo               :
Attributes               : {archive}
Checksum                 :
Contents                 :
CreatedDate              : 12/15/2017 2:15:30 PM
Credential               :
DestinationPath          : C:\OSDeployment.tag
Ensure                   : present
Force                    :
MatchSource              :
ModifiedDate             : 12/15/2017 2:15:30 PM
Recurse                  :
Size                     : 0
SourcePath               :
SubItems                 :
Type                     : file
PSComputerName           : S16-01
CimClassName             : MSFT_FileDirectoryConfiguration
```

Figure 9-8. *Current state if the file resource*

As shown in Figure 9-8, Get-DscConfiguration retrieves the current state of the node configuration. In this example, there is only one resource instance. However, if there are multiple resources in the configuration document, this cmdlet will return the current state of each of those resource instances. Understand that this is the current state and not necessarily the desired state. For this example, the desired state is that the file should exist with no contents (0 bytes in size). So, what if you open the file in Notepad and add some random contents to it?

```
PS C:\Scripts> Get-DscConfiguration -CimSession S16-01


ConfigurationName    : OSConfig
DependsOn            :
ModuleName          : PSDesiredStateConfiguration
ModuleVersion       :
PsDscRunAsCredential :
ResourceId          : [File]ScriptFlag
SourceInfo          :
Attributes          : {archive}
Checksum            :
Contents            :
CreatedDate         : 12/15/2017 2:15:30 PM
Credential          :
DestinationPath     : C:\OSDeployment.tag
Ensure              : present
Force               :
MatchSource         :
ModifiedDate        : 12/15/2017 2:29:59 PM
Recurse             :
Size                : 20
SourcePath          :
SubItems            :
Type                : file
PSComputerName      : S16-01
CimClassName        : MSFT_FileDirectoryConfiguration
```

Figure 9-9. *Current state of the file resource after modification*

Observe the size of the file shown in Figure 9-9 and compare it what is shown in Figure 9-8. This indicates a configuration drift and that Get-DscConfiguration only tells you the current state of configuration. So, how do you know if the node configuration is in the desired state or not? The Test-DscConfiguration cmdlet helps out here.

```
PS C:\Scripts> Test-DscConfiguration -ComputerName S16-01
False

PS C:\Scripts> |
```

Figure 9-10. *Desired state test*

As shown in Figure 9-10, the Test-DscConfiguration cmdlet returns $false. From Chapter 6, you know that the Test-TargetResource function in a resource module returns false only when the resource is not in the desired state and the Test-DscConfiguration cmdlet calls the Test-TargetResource function.

Let's add one more resource instance to the example and enact again.

```
Configuration OSConfig
{
    Import-DscResource -ModuleName PSDesiredStateConfiguration
-ModuleVersion 1.1

    File ScriptFlag
    {
        DestinationPath = 'C:\OSDeployment.tag'
        Type = 'File'
        Contents = ''
        Ensure = 'Present'
    }

    File ScriptsFolder
    {
        DestinationPath = 'C:\Scripts'
        Type = 'Directory'
        Ensure = 'Present'
    }
}

OSConfig
```

When you enact this updated configuration, it will set the file to 0 bytes and create a folder (if it doesn't already exist) called Scripts at C:. Let's once again modify the contents of the OSDeployment.tag file to create a configuration drift and then check the Test-DscConfiguration command.

What do you see? It still returns only False as the output and does not tell you exactly which resource out of all resource instances in the configuration is not in the desired state. This is where the -Detailed switch parameter on this cmdlet helps.

```
PS C:\Scripts> Test-DscConfiguration -ComputerName S16-01 -Detailed

PSComputerName  ResourcesInDesiredState    ResourcesNotInDesiredState   InDesiredState
--------------  -----------------------    --------------------------   --------------
S16-01          {[File]ScriptsFolder}      {[File]ScriptFlag}           False
```

Figure 9-11. *Resources not in desired state*

In Figure 9-11, using the -Detailed switch parameter tells you that one of the instances of the File resource is not in the desired state. This was not possible before WMF 5.0. This is a good enhancement, but it still does not tell you *why* the resource is not in the desired state. A future release of DSC might include this enhancement.

Testing for Desired State Against a Reference Configuration

Another enhancement in WMF 5.0 is the ability to test a remote node against a reference MOF. In the earlier two examples, you tested the current configuration (current.mof) for the desired state. What if there is no current configuration at all on the node and you only want to test if the resources on a node are in the desired state or not without enacting any configuration? Or what if you want to check the potential outcome of running a configuration on a node?

The Test-DscCconfiguration cmdlet provides two different methods to do this.

Note   If the reference configuration includes any custom DSC resource modules, those modules must be present on the target nodes before running the Test-DscConfiguration cmdlet with either -Path or -ReferenceConfiguration parameters. This won't work even when you have the LCM configured as a pull client and ResourceRepositoryWeb or ResourceRepositoryShare are configured to download the missing resource modules.

Using the Path Parameter

Using the Path parameter with this cmdlet is similar to how you use it with other DSC cmdlets such as Start-DscConfiguration. You can store multiple compiled MOF files each having the format *ComputerName.mof* within a folder and that folder path can be specified as an argument to -Path.

The following example will iterate over this path and connect to each target node and perform the desired state checks:

```
Configuration OSConfig
{
    Import-DscResource -ModuleName PSDesiredStateConfiguration
    Node S16-01
    {
        File ScriptFlag
        {
            DestinationPath = 'C:\OSDeployment.tag'
            Type = 'File'
            Contents = ''
            Ensure = 'Present'
        }

        File ScriptsFolder
        {
            DestinationPath = 'C:\Scripts'
            Type = 'Directory'
            Ensure = 'Present'
        }

        File Script
        {
            DestinationPath = 'C:\Scripts\DeployApp.ps1'
            Type = 'File'
            Contents = 'Start-AppDeploy -Name MyApp'
            Ensure = 'Present'
        }
    }

    Node S16-02
    {
        File AppFlag
        {
            DestinationPath = 'C:\AppDeploy.tag'
            Type = 'File'
```

```
        Contents = ''
        Ensure = 'Present'
    }

    File AppFolder
    {
        DestinationPath = 'C:\MyApp'
        Type = 'Directory'
        Ensure = 'Present'
    }
  }
}

OSConfig
```

Compiling this configuration produces two MOF files, one for each node. Let's now try the Test-DscConfiguration cmdlet with the -Path parameter; see Figure 9-12.

```
Test-DscConfiguration -Path .\OSConfig
```

```
PS C:\Scripts> Test-DscConfiguration -Path .\OSConfig

PSComputerName  ResourcesInDesiredState       ResourcesNotInDesiredState      InDesiredState
--------------  -----------------------       --------------------------      --------------
S16-02                                        {[File]AppFlag, [File]AppFo... False
S16-01          {[File]ScriptsFolder}         {[File]ScriptFlag, [File]Sc... False
```

Figure 9-12. *Using the Path parameter with Test-DscConfiguration*

This method is useful when you have multiple target nodes each with a different configuration. But if you want to test a single reference configuration across multiple target nodes, the best approach is to use the -ReferenceConfiguration parameter.

Using the ReferenceConfiguration Parameter

Using the -ReferenceConfiguration parameter, a single MOF file can be tested for the desired state across multiple target nodes. Let's take one of the MOF files from the above example and use that MOF file path as the argument to the -ReferenceConfiguration parameter:

```
Test-DscConfiguration -ReferenceConfiguration .\OSConfig\S16-02.mof
-ComputerName S16-01, S16-02
```

329

When using -ReferenceConfiguration, you can supply the target node names using the -ComputerName parameter. In the absence of the –ComputerName parameter, the reference configuration will be tested against the local system. See Figure 9-13.

```
PS C:\Scripts> Test-DscConfiguration -ReferenceConfiguration .\OSConfig\S16-02.mof -ComputerName S16-01, S16-02

PSComputerName  ResourcesInDesiredState           ResourcesNotInDesiredState     InDesiredState
--------------  -----------------------           --------------------------     --------------
S16-02                                            {[File]AppFlag, [File]AppFo... False
S16-01                                            {[File]AppFlag, [File]AppFo... False
```

Figure 9-13. *Testing target nodes using the ReferenceConfiguration parameter*

So far, you've seen how to get the current state and verify the target node's desired state against a current configuration or a reference configuration. Let's now check how to review the configuration run history using the Get-DscConfigurationStatus command.

Reviewing the Configuration Run History

Starting with WMF 5.0, DSC keeps a history of configuration runs. This status history can be retrieved using the Get-DscConfigurationStatus cmdlet. This cmdlet returns instances of the MSFT_DSCConfigurationStatus CIM class in the root/Microsoft/ Windows/DesiredStateConfiguration namespace.

Let's use the GetCimClassProperty.ps1 script from Chapter 2 to inspect this class.

As seen in Figure 9-14, several properties are returned by the Get-DscConfigurationStatus cmdlet. Table 9-1 provides high-level description of each property.

```
PS C:\Scripts> .\GetCimClassProperty.ps1 -ClassName MSFT_DSCConfigurationStatus -Namespace root/Microsoft/Windows/DesiredStateConfiguration | ft

Name                         CimType      EmbeddedInstanceOf              IsReadyOnly AllowedValues                          IsKey
----                         -------      ------------------              ----------- -------------                          -----
DurationInSeconds            UInt32                                       True                                               False
Error                        String                                      True                                               False
HostName                     String                                      True                                               False
IPV4Addresses                StringArray                                  True                                               False
IPV6Addresses                StringArray                                  True                                               False
JobID                        String                                      True                                               False
LCMVersion                   String                                      True                                               False
Locale                       String                                      True                                               False
MACAddresses                 StringArray                                  True                                               False
MetaConfiguration            Instance     MSFT_DSCMetaConfiguration       True                                               False
MetaData                     String                                      True                                               False
Mode                         String                                      True        {Push, Pull, Disabled}                 False
NumberOfResources            UInt32                                       True                                               False
RebootRequested              Boolean                                      True                                               False
ResourcesInDesiredState      InstanceArray MSFT_ResourceInDesiredState    True                                               False
ResourcesNotInDesiredState   InstanceArray MSFT_ResourceNotInDesiredState True                                               False
StartDate                    DateTime                                     True                                               False
Status                       String                                      True        {Success, Failure, Aborted, InProgress} False
Type                         String                                      True        {Initial, Consistency, Reboot, ReadOnly...} False
```

Figure 9-14. *Properties of the MSFT_DSCConfigurationStatus class*

Table 9-1. *Properties from a Configuration Run Status*

Property Name	Description
DurationInSeconds	Specifies how long the configuration run took to complete.
Error	Specifies any error during the configuration run.
HostName	Specifies the name of the host where the configuration ran.
IPV4Addresses	Specifies the IPv4 address of the host where the configuration ran.
IPV6Addresses	Specifies the IPv6 address of the host where the configuration ran.
JobID	Specifies the unique ID assigned to the configuration.
LCMVersion	Version of the LCM used at the time of the configuration run.
Locale	Locale information at the time of the configuration run.
MACAddresses	MAC addresses on the host where the configuration ran.
MetaConfiguration	Snapshot of the LCM configuration settings at the time of the configuration run.
MetaData	Meta data from the configuration document. Includes details such as author name, compilation date, and time.
Mode	Specifies the refresh mode in which the configuration was run.
NumberOfResources	Number of resources in the configuration.
RebootRequested	Specifies if a reboot was requested during or after the configuration run.
ResourcesInDesiredState	Resources that are in the desired state.
ResourcesNotInDesiredState	Resources that are not in the desired state.
StartDate	Start date and time of the configuration run.
Status	Status of the configuration run.
Type	Type of the configuration run. This includes Initial, Consistency, Reboot, ReadOnly, and Local Configuration Manager.

By default, without any parameters, the Get-DscConfigurationStatus cmdlet returns only the status of the last configuration run. See Figure 9-15.

```
PS C:\Scripts> Get-DscConfigurationStatus -CimSession S16-01 | Format-List *

PSShowComputerName         : True
DurationInSeconds          : 0
Error                      :
HostName                   : S16-01
IPV4Addresses              : {172.16.102.92, 127.0.0.1}
IPV6Addresses              : {fe80::2cc3:29ac:86c5:4879%2, ::2000:0:0:0, ::1, ::2000:0:0:0}
JobID                      : {4627605A-E22A-11E7-8A8A-00155D87B207}
LCMVersion                 : 2.0
Locale                     : en-US
MACAddresses               : {00-15-5D-87-B2-07, 00-00-00-00-00-00-00-E0}
MetaConfiguration          : MSFT_DSCMetaConfiguration
MetaData                   : Author: Administrator; Name: OSConfig; Version: 2.0.0; GenerationDate: 12/15/2017 14:41:38; GenerationHost: S16-PULL-01;
Mode                       : Pull
NumberOfResources          : 2
RebootRequested            : False
ResourcesInDesiredState    : {[File]ScriptFlag, [File]ScriptsFolder}
ResourcesNotInDesiredState :
StartDate                  : 12/16/2017 11:58:06 AM
Status                     : Success
Type                       : Consistency
PSComputerName             : S16-01
CimClass                   : root/Microsoft/Windows/DesiredStateConfiguration:MSFT_DSCConfigurationStatus
CimInstanceProperties      : {DurationInSeconds, Error, HostName, IPV4Addresses...}
CimSystemProperties        : Microsoft.Management.Infrastructure.CimSystemProperties
```

Figure 9-15. *Last configuration run status*

Using the -All switch parameter, you can see a complete list of configuration runs on the node. This list can be huge based on the values of StatusRetentionTimeInDays in the LCM meta configuration. The default value is 10 days.

Try It   From what you learned in Chapter 3 about updating the meta configuration, try changing the retention time in days to 15.

You can see the status history get accumulated as DSCStatusHistory.mof in the C:\ Windows\System32\Configuration folder. In this MOF file, you will see a set of DSC_ ConfigurationStatusData class instances each representing a configuration run. Each of these instances has a JobID and there will be associated status files in the C:\Windows\ System32\Configuration\ConfigurationStatus folder. Depending when the initial configuration was applied on the target node and the number of consistency checks run on the node (assuming that the LCM ConfigurationMode is not set to ApplyOnly), there may be many MOF and JSON files each having the job ID in their file name. What you see in the output of the Get-DscConfigurationStatus cmdlet is a collection of data retrieved from these MOF and JSON files. When the LCM is busy, the Get-DscConfigurationStatus cmdlet cannot be used but these JSON files can be monitored. If you have large configurations, Get-Content -Wait can be your friend. Using the Select-String cmdlet on these files is a very useful in debugging as well.

The status history from this command can be quite useful in understanding how the configuration changes were happening on a given node. However, these status reports are stored only for a few days, per the StatusRetentionTimeInDays meta property. After the retention period is over, the older JSON and MOF files get deleted. But what if you want to retain these status files for a long time for compliance purposes? This is where the DSC reporting service is helpful.

DSC Reporting Endpoint

In Chapter 8, you learned how to create a DSC pull service endpoint using the DSC Service Windows feature. This section extends that to add a reporting endpoint. The process is very similar except for a few settings that you need to configure and the files you copy to the IIS endpoint directories. The report service endpoint requires DSC Service and Windows Authentication features. Unlike WMF 4.0, where there was a different configuration for a reporting service endpoint, WMF 5.0 offers a pull service and a reporting service using the same endpoint.

So, if you have already deployed a pull service endpoint, you can use the following LCM meta configuration document to configure a report server for a target node:

```
[DSCLocalConfigurationManager()]
Configuration oDataHTTPSPullClient
{
    param
    (
        [Parameter()]
        [String[]]
        $NodeName = 'localhost',

        [Parameter(Mandatory = $true)]
        [String]
        $RegistrationKey,
```

```
        [Parameter(Mandatory = $true)]
        [String]
        $PullSvcEndpoint,

        [Parameter(Mandatory = $true)]
        [String[]]
        $ConfigNames
    )

    Node $NodeName
    {
        Settings
        {
            RefreshMode         = 'Pull'
        }

        ConfigurationRepositoryWeb HTTPSPullSvc
        {
            ServerURL           = $PullSvcEndpoint
            RegistrationKey     = $RegistrationKey
            ConfigurationNames  = $ConfigNames
        }

        ResourceRepositoryWeb HTTPSPullSvc
        {
            ServerURL           = $PullSvcEndpoint
            RegistrationKey     = $RegistrationKey
        }

        ReportServerWeb HTTPSReport
        {
            ServerURL = $PullSvcEndpoint
            RegistrationKey = $RegistrationKey
        }
    }
}
```

```
$nodes = @('S16-01','S16-02')
oDataHTTPSPullClient -NodeName $nodes -RegistrationKey '713c4332-f12c-
4008-9435-3329b97a27a8' -PullSvcEndpoint 'https://s16-pull-01:8080/
PSDSCPullServer.svc/' -ConfigNames @('OSConfig')
```

This meta configuration example uses the pull refresh mode on the target nodes. Starting with WMF 5.0, you can even have the target nodes in push mode send their configuration run status to a report server. The following meta configuration provides an example:

```
[DSCLocalConfigurationManager()]
configuration oDataHTTPSReportClient
{
    param
    (
        [Parameter()]
        [String[]]
        $NodeName = 'localhost',

        [Parameter(Mandatory = $true)]
        [String]
        $RegistrationKey,

        [Parameter(Mandatory = $true)]
        [String]
        $PullSvcEndpoint
    )

    Node $NodeName
    {
        Settings
        {
            RefreshMode        = 'Push'
        }

        ReportServerWeb HTTPSReport
        {
            ServerURL = $PullSvcEndpoint
```

```
            RegistrationKey = $RegistrationKey
        }
    }
}
```

```
$nodes = @('S12R2-01','S12R2-02')
oDataHTTPSReportClient -NodeName $nodes -RegistrationKey '713c4332-
f12c-4008-9435-3329b97a27a8' -PullSvcEndpoint 'https://s16-pull-01:8080/
PSDSCPullServer.svc/'
```

When you compile and enact the meta configuration document shown above, the LCM on nodes S16-01, S16-02, S12R2-01, and S12R2-02 gets configured to send their configuration run statuses to the report server endpoint.

Note   There is no ReportServerShare, unlike ResourceRepositoryShare and ConfigurationRepositoryShare. If you need centralized reporting, it is mandatory that you deploy a DSC pull service and use it as ReportServerWeb.

When you browse to a pull service endpoint in a browser, it returns the possible routes available in the endpoint as an XML document. You saw this in Chapter 8. One such method is Reports.

You can use the Invoke-RestMethod cmdlet to query this report's endpoint and gather the status information for all configuration runs from a given target node. Here is a helper function for that:

```
function Get-DscReport
{
    param
    (
        [Parameter(Mandatory = $true)]
        [String[]]
        $NodeName,

        [Parameter(Mandatory = $true)]
        [ValidateNotNullOrEmpty()]
        [String]
        $ReportEndpoint,
```

```
        [Parameter()]
        [Switch]
        $UseTLS12
    )

    if ($UseTLS12)
    {
        [Net.ServicePointManager]::SecurityProtocol = [Net.
SecurityProtocolType]::Tls12
    }

    foreach ($node in $NodeName)
    {
        $agentId = (Get-DscLocalConfigurationManager -CimSession $node).
        AgentId

        $requestUri = "$ReportEndpoint/Nodes(AgentId='$agentId')/Reports"

        $nodeReport = (Invoke-RestMethod -Uri $requestUri -UseBasicParsing
        -Headers @{Accept = 'application/json';ProtocolVersion = '2.0'}).
        Value
        return $nodeReport
    }
}
```

Note in this helper function that if you have deployed a pull service endpoint
with security best practices (refer to Chapter 8), the xDSCWebServiceDSC resource
will configure the pull service endpoint to use TLS1.2. However, Invoke-RestMethod
does not use TLS 1.2 by default. What is shown in this function is a workaround for
that. Therefore, if you have deployed a HTTPS pull service endpoint with security best
practices, supply the -UseTLS12 switch parameter with the Get-DscReport function. To
retrieve a node's configuration run history, you need to know the AgentId of the node.
AgentId is a read-only property of the DSC LCM. This property contains a GUID and
it needs to be supplied to the Reports method to retrieve the node's configuration run
status. The Get-DscReport function retrieves the AgentId for each target node in the
$NodeName array using the Get-DSCLocalConfigurationManager cmdlet.

Note   At present, there is no way (out of the box) to retrieve a list of all nodes
registered with a DSC pull service endpoint or report service endpoint. You must
know the agent ID before you can retrieve the node status reports. That said, you
can use Ben's `DscPullServerAdmin` module to get a list of Agent IDs registered
with the pull server. This module is available at `https://github.com/`
`bgelens/DSCPullServerAdmin`.

Let's see the `Get-DscReport` function in action.

```
$reports = Get-DscReport -NodeName S16-01, S16-02 -ReportEndpoint 'https://
s16-pull-01:8080/PSDSCPullServer.svc' -UseTLS2
```

The `$reports` variable contains an array of configuration run history objects from
each node. See Figure 9-16.

```
PS C:\> $reports[0]


JobId                 : 046ae360-e23b-11e7-8a8a-00155d87b207
OperationType         : Consistency
RefreshMode           : Pull
Status                : Success
ReportFormatVersion   : 2.0
ConfigurationVersion  : 2.0.0
StartTime             : 2017-12-16T13:58:06.138
EndTime               : 2017-12-16T13:58:06.138
RebootRequested       : False
Errors                : {}
StatusData            : {{"StartDate":"2017-12-16T13:58:06.1380000+05:30","IPV6Address(
                        ionInSeconds":"0","JobID":"{046AE360-E23B-11E7-8A8A-00155D87B2(
                        9D47C0300C","MetaData":"Author: Administrator; Name: OSConfig;
                        -01;","RebootRequested":"False","Status":"Success","IPV4Addres:
                        "Type":"Consistency","HostName":"S16-01","ResourcesInDesiredSt;
                        "DurationInSeconds":"0","InstanceName":"ScriptFlag","StartDate'
                        .1","RebootRequested":"False","ResourceId":"[File]ScriptFlag",'
                        ::File","ModuleName":"PSDesiredStateConfiguration","DurationIn:
                        06.5910000+05:30","ResourceName":"File","ModuleVersion":"1.1",'
                        e":"OSConfig","InDesiredState":"True"}],"MACAddresses":["00-15-
                        4C9-E171-11E7-8A8A-00155D87B207","ConfigurationDownloadManager:
                        r.svc/","ResourceId":"[ConfigurationRepositoryWeb]HTTPSPullSvc'
                        toryWeb"}],"ActionAfterReboot":"ContinueConfiguration","LCMCom|
                        egistrationKey":"","ServerURL":"https://s16-pull-01:8080/PSDSCI
                        o":"::37::9::ResourceRepositoryWeb"}],"ReportManagers":[{"Regi:
                        esourceId":"[ReportServerWeb]HTTPSReport","SourceInfo":"::43::!
                        imumDownloadSizeMB":"500","ConfigurationMode":"ApplyAndMonitor'
```

Figure 9-16. *Partial output of one of the report objects*

Accessing $report[0].StatusData and converting it from JSON to a PowerShell object provides output similar to Get-DscConfigurationStatus; see Figure 9-17.

```
PS C:\> $reports[0].StatusData | ConvertFrom-Json

StartDate                 : 2017-12-16T13:58:06.1380000+05:30
IPV6Addresses             : {fe80::2cc3:29ac:86c5:4879%2, ::2000:0:0:0, ::1, ::2000:0:0:0}
DurationInSeconds         : 0
JobID                     : {046AE360-E23B-11E7-8A8A-00155D87B207}
CurrentChecksum           : CF9E7D118C2F1E1AC927620AAEC7659E3FD15C63FB8629183B345A9D47C0300C
MetaData                  : Author: Administrator; Name: OSConfig; Version: 2.0.0; GenerationDate: 12/
RebootRequested           : False
Status                    : Success
IPV4Addresses             : {172.16.102.92, 127.0.0.1}
LCMVersion                : 2.0
NumberOfResources         : 2
Type                      : Consistency
HostName                  : S16-01
ResourcesInDesiredState   : {@{SourceInfo=::4::5::File; ModuleName=PSDesiredStateConfiguration; Durati
                            StartDate=2017-12-16T13:58:06.5910000+05:30; ResourceName=File; ModuleVers
                            ConfigurationName=OSConfig; InDesiredState=True}, @{SourceInfo=::12::5::Fi
                            DurationInSeconds=0.016; InstanceName=ScriptsFolder; StartDate=2017-12-16T
                            RebootRequested=False; ResourceId=[File]ScriptsFolder; ConfigurationName=C
MACAddresses              : {00-15-5D-87-B2-07, 00-00-00-00-00-00-00-E0}
MetaConfiguration         : @{AgentId=DF0E94C9-E171-11E7-8A8A-00155D87B207; ConfigurationDownloadManag
                            LCMCompatibleVersions=System.Object[]; LCMState=Idle; ResourceModuleManage
                            StatusRetentionTimeInDays=10; LCMVersion=2.0; MaximumDownloadSizeMB=500; C
                            RebootNodeIfNeeded=False; SignatureValidationPolicy=NONE; RefreshMode=Pull
                            AllowModuleOverwrite=False; ConfigurationModeFrequencyMins=15; SignatureVa
Locale                    : en-US
Mode                      : Pull
```

Figure 9-17. *Partial output from the status data property*

So, how does the LCM client send this information to the report service endpoint? After every consistency check run, the DSC LCM, if a report server endpoint is configured using the ReportServerWeb meta resource, calls the SendReport method. For example, on my target node, it will invoke https://s16-pull-01:8080/ PSDSCPullServer.svc/Nodes(AgentId='DF0E94C9-E171-11E7-8A8A-00155D87B207')/ SendReport. As a part of this request, the LCM client also sends the snapshot of the configuration run status object.

There is no graphical dashboard or way to visualize which of the nodes registered with the report server are in the desired state. This is available in the Azure Automation DSC service. You will review this service in Chapter 17.

Summary

DSC provides detailed telemetry of configuration runs on a target node. This can be retrieved using the commands available in the `PSDesiredStateConfiguration` module, Desired State Configuration event logs, and by querying the report service endpoint when the target node LCM is configured to send the status reports to a report server. While these methods provide very rich information that can be used for troubleshooting and debugging purposes, DSC does not provide a graphical dashboard to visualize the node status. However, given the data that is available in the different methods you saw in this chapter, it would not be too hard to build a graphical representation of that in tools like Power BI or by some other means. There are third-party solutions available in this space as well.

CHAPTER 10

Partial Configurations

One of the features introduced in WMF 5.0 is partial configurations. Chapter 2 featured a very brief overview of this feature. Partial configurations can help in an IT organization where multiple individuals are responsible for the configuration of the infrastructure. Partial configurations enable delegation of configuration management tasks and separation of the common configuration from node-specific configurations. By saying *common configuration*, I refer to the baseline configuration that applies to a subset of the nodes in an infrastructure. Each administrator responsible for his/her configuration can author and manage it independent of what other administrators author, thereby eliminating any human errors involved in updating a single configuration document.

This chapter goes in-depth into partial configurations and provides a walk-through of how partial configurations can be built and used. You will look at preparing the necessary infrastructure to start enacting partial configurations. You will also see an updated configuration life cycle that presents a complete view of configuration management including partial configurations.

Lab Requirements

To try the examples and exercises in this chapter, you will need at minimum a Windows Server 2008 R2 or above system with WMF 5.1 installed. I recommend a system with Windows Server 2016. You will need Windows Server 2016 and SQL Server 2014 installation media to try the partial configuration examples in this chapter. You must also have certificates for encrypting credentials in the configuration documents. You can do this using self-signed certificates as well. You can use Chapter 5 as a reference for this. You will also need a domain controller since the examples use partial configurations to join an existing domain.

© Ravikanth Chaganti 2018
R. Chaganti, *Pro PowerShell Desired State Configuration*, https://doi.org/10.1007/978-1-4842-3483-9_10

Introduction

You have seen an overview of partial configurations already. There are two reasons why you might want to implement partial configurations: incremental configurations and delegated configuration management.

Incremental Configurations

Let's look at deploying a SQL Server instance using DSC. Assume that you already have the OS installed and you plan on using DSC to perform the post-OS deployment tasks such domain join and SQL install and configuration.

What you see in Figure 10-1 represents the complete and incremental configuration of the target system. You start by enacting the network configuration and domain join as soon as the OS deployment is complete. This OS configuration can be a single configuration script. Once this is done, you can start installing the SQL prerequisites and finally, complete the SQL install and instance configuration. Optionally, once the SQL instance configuration is complete, you can apply firewall rules as a part of OS and SQL hardening.

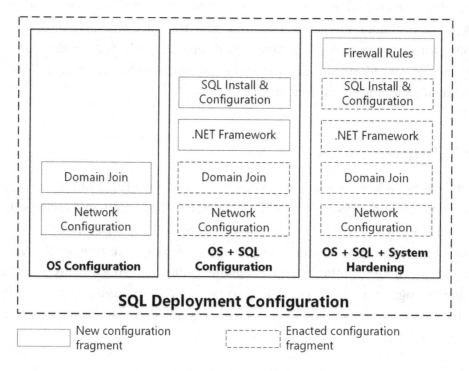

Figure 10-1. *Incremental configuration of SQL Server*

Now, if you build these configurations as individual documents and enact one after another, DSC will have no knowledge of the previously enacted configurations and therefore won't be able to monitor any drift within those configurations. Prior to WMF 5.0, the only way to ensure that each configuration was monitored for drift was to combine all configurations into a single document and enact.

With the partial configurations feature, you can now let the DSC LCM know that you are enacting partial configurations and enact one fragment at a time as long as there are no dependencies defined between those partial fragments. You will look into this with an example later in this chapter.

So, when using partial configurations in this approach, you can use an external orchestrator script to configure the LCM and enact partial configurations one at a time. This method may be useful when all fragments of the system configuration are not ready yet but you still want to complete your part of the configuration and hand over the system to the next person responsible. Since all configuration fragments are not available during initial enact, you need to configure the LCM only with available configuration fragments and enact. Whenever a new fragment is available, it can be updated in the meta configuration and then enacted using the push or pull mode.

While the incremental approach of using partial configurations may sound somewhat useful, the real use case for partial configurations is in delegated configuration management.

Delegated Configuration Management

In a real-world scenario, the SQL deployment discussed above will typically be handled by multiple administrators from many different teams. With the earlier release, all of these teams had to update the same configuration script. While collaboration is good, it creates much room for errors. DSC partial configurations allow delegated control and ownership in such a scenario. Figure 10-2 illustrates this.

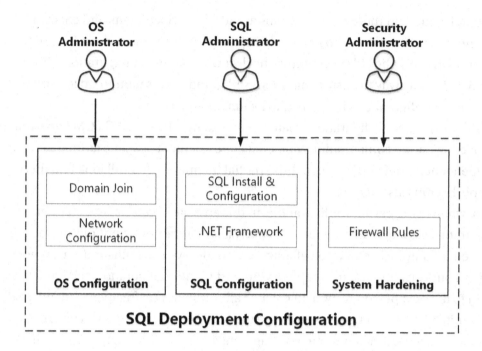

Figure 10-2. *Delegated ownership of configurations*

In this approach, one of the administrators will configure the DSC LCM with what to expect as a part of the partial configurations. And, as soon as any of the administrators involved in the node configurations send their configuration fragment, it will be enacted based on the dependency resolution. Every team owns its configuration and manages it independent of others. In fact, with partial configurations, it is possible for these different teams to have their own DSC pull server for delivering configurations to the target systems or push the configuration when they are ready. Therefore, partial configurations are supported in a mixed refresh mode.

Getting Started

I mentioned that the DSC LCM needs to be aware of the partial configuration fragments it must expect. This is the starting point before you can start enacting partial configuration fragments. In Chapter 3, you saw how to configure a node meta configuration using the DSC declarative syntax. Let's look at the LCM settings that are related to partial configurations.

Note   A few examples or figures in this chapter use scripts from earlier chapters.

The DSC partial configuration settings in DSC meta configurations are instances of the MSFT_PartialConfiguration class. Let's verify this.

You saw this in Chapter 3. And, as you can see in Figure 10-3, the PartialConfiguration meta resource is mapped as the MSFT_PartialConfiguration CIM class.

```
PS C:\> Get-CimKeyword -ImplementingModule PSDesiredStateConfigurationEngine

Keyword                         ResourceName
-------                         ------------
ConfigurationRepositoryWeb      MSFT_WebDownloadManager
ConfigurationRepositoryShare    MSFT_FileDownloadManager
ResourceRepositoryWeb           MSFT_WebResourceManager
ResourceRepositoryShare         MSFT_FileResourceManager
ReportServerWeb                 MSFT_WebReportManager
PartialConfiguration            MSFT_PartialConfiguration
SignatureValidation             MSFT_SignatureValidation
Settings                        MSFT_DSCMetaConfigurationV2
```

Figure 10-3. *Partial configuration meta resource to CIM class mapping*

As seen in Figure 10-4, there are several properties, except ResourceId and SourceInfo, available within this meta resource. Table 10-1 provides a brief overview of these properties.

```
PS C:\Scripts> .\GetCimClassProperty.ps1 -ClassName MSFT_PartialConfiguration -Namespace root/Microsoft/Windows/DesiredStateConfiguration | ft

Name                  CimType     EmbeddedInstanceOf IsReadyOnly AllowedValues           IsKey
----                  -------     ------------------ ----------- -------------           -----
ResourceId            String                         False                               False
SourceInfo            String                         False                               False
ConfigurationSource   StringArray                    False                               False
DependsOn             StringArray                    False                               False
Description           String                         False                               False
ExclusiveResources    StringArray                    False                               False
RefreshMode           String                         False       {Push, Pull, Disabled}  False
ResourceModuleSource  StringArray                    False                               False
```

Figure 10-4. *Partial configuration CIM class properties*

Table 10-1. *Properties in Partial Configuration Meta Resource*

Property Name	Description
RefreshMode	Partial configurations are supported in both pull and push modes. Or you can use a mix of both modes when implementing partial configurations. Disabled refresh mode is not supported with partial configurations.
ConfigurationSource	This property is required when using partial configurations in pull mode. Using this, you can configure the source (Pull SMB share or REST Server) from which the fragment can be downloaded. When using the pull mode for partial configurations in the meta configuration, it is important to specify the pull source using the ConfigurationRepositoryWeb and/or ConfigurationRepositoryShare meta resources.
Description	Description of the partial configuration.
ResourceModuleSource	Specifies the source for resource module location. When using this, the meta configuration must have ResourceRepositoryWeb and/or ResourceRepositoryShare meta resources.
ExclusiveResources	Specifies the DSC resources that are explicitly locked for this partial configuration fragment. No other partial configurations can use the resources listed as ExclusiveResources.

In the subsequent sections, you will use these properties in the meta configuration documents to make the DSC LCM aware of partial configurations. Let's start with the push refresh mode for partial configurations:

```
[DscLocalConfigurationManager()]
Configuration LCMConfiguration
{
    Settings
    {
        CertificateID = '1DAEA5189FA2D927151C96C5F43F3DA13114573D'
        RebootNodeIfNeeded = $true
        ActionAfterReboot = 'ContinueConfiguration'
    }
```

```
    PartialConfiguration OSConfig
    {
        RefreshMode = 'Push'
        Description = 'OS configuration fragment for Windows feature,
                    host network, and domain join'
    }

    PartialConfiguration   SQLConfig
    {
        RefreshMode = 'Push'
        Description = 'SQL configuration fragment for SQL instance install
                    and configuration.'
    }

    PartialConfiguration FirewallConfig
    {
        RefreshMode = 'Push'
        Description = 'Firewall configuration fragment for OS and SQL
                    instance hardnening.'
    }
}
```

LCMConfiguration

This example shows the common LCM settings along with three instances of the partial configuration meta resource. This example uses certificate-based credential encryption and therefore the CertificateID property of the Settings meta resource is used.

Note   If you do not have certificates for credential encryption, you should change the configuration data to use plain-text passwords. You learned about this in Chapter 5. However, this is not recommended in production environments.

You can enact this meta configuration and verify that the LCM configuration reflects these settings.

While this meta configuration document has three configuration fragments, it is always possible to add one at a time. However, when you do that, ensure that you don't overwrite the existing LCM configuration. Instead, you should keep adding new fragments to the existing meta configuration. However, I don't recommend this approach of changing the meta configuration for each fragment, mainly because it can lead to LCM misconfiguration due to human error and can also create a dependency on an administrator to configure the LCM before another administrator can enact their configuration fragment. Instead, as shown in the above meta configuration, add all instances of the partial configuration meta resources at once (at least the configuration fragments that have no dependencies). As you will see in later examples, partial configurations with no dependencies can be enacted without all fragments being in place. This is what enables the first approach towards using partial configurations: incremental configurations.

So, how do you achieve an incremental configuration enact? Before we go there, let's take a look at three configuration documents that you will enact in an incremental manner.

OS Configuration

Here is the OS configuration fragment that you will enact on the target node:

```
$confgData = @{
    AllNodes = @(
        @{
            NodeName = 'localhost'
            PSDscAllowDomainUser = $true
            CertificateFile = 'C:\PublicKeys\sqldb.cer'
            Thumbprint = '1DAEA5189FA2D927151C96C5F43F3DA13114573D'
        }
    )
}

configuration OSConfig
{
    Param
    (
        [Parameter(Mandatory)]
        [pscredential]
        $Credential,
```

```
    [Parameter(Mandatory)]
    [string]
    $OSImageDriveLetter
)

Import-DscResource -ModuleName xComputerManagement -Name xComputer
-ModuleVersion 3.1.0.0
Import-DscResource -ModuleName xNetworking -Name xIPAddress,
xDefaultGatewayAddress, xDnsServerAddress -ModuleVerison 5.3.0.0

Import-DscResource -ModuleName 'PSDesiredStateConfiguration'

Node $AllNodes.NodeName
{
    WindowsFeature 'NetFramework35'
    {
        Name = 'NET-Framework-Core'
        Source = "${OSImageDriveLetter}\Sources\Sxs"
        Ensure = 'Present'
    }

    xIPAddress   NodeIPAddress
    {
        InterfaceAlias = 'Ethernet'
        IPAddress = '172.16.102.39/24'
        AddressFamily = 'IPv4'
    }

    xDefaultGatewayAddress NodeDefaultGateway
    {
        Address        = '172.16.102.1'
        InterfaceAlias = 'Ethernet'
        AddressFamily  = 'IPv4'
        DependsOn = '[xIPAddress]NodeIPAddress'
    }
```

```
        xDnsServerAddress   NodeDnsServerAddress
        {
            Address        = '172.16.102.91'
            InterfaceAlias = 'Ethernet'
            AddressFamily  = 'IPv4'
            DependsOn = '[xIPAddress]NodeIPAddress'
        }

        xComputer RenameAndDomainHJoin
        {
            Name = 'SQLDB'
            DomainName = 'psdsc.lab'
            Credential = $Credential
            DependsOn = '[xDnsServerAddress]NodeDnsServerAddress'
        }
    }
}

OSConfig -configurationData $confgData -Credential (Get-Credential)
-osImageDriveLetter 'D:'
```

There are several custom DSC resources being used in this configuration fragment. You need to ensure that these custom DSC resource modules are available on the node where you need to enact this configuration. You install the .NET 3.5 Framework core, configure host IPv4 settings, and finally add the target node to the Active Directory domain. This configuration assumes that the OS ISO image is mounted as a drive for installing the .NET Framework feature from the media source. You use configuration data that specifies the public key of the target node certificate to use for encryption of passwords.

Note   Ensure that you change the IPv4 settings in the above configuration document to reflect your own lab environment.

The .NET 3.5 Framework core is not needed if you plan to deploy SQL Server 2016 or SQL Server 2017. For those versions of SQL, you can remove the WindowsFeature resource instance from the above configuration. And, it also means that there is no need to locally mount the OS ISO as a drive.

SQL Configuration

The next fragment is the SQL install and instance configuration:

```
$confgData = @{
    AllNodes = @(
        @{
            NodeName = 'localhost'
            PSDscAllowDomainUser = $true
            CertificateFile = 'C:\PublicKeys\sqldb.cer'
            Thumbprint = '1DAEA5189FA2D927151C96C5F43F3DA13114573D'
        }
    )
}

Configuration SQLConfig
{
    [CmdletBinding()]
    param
    (
        [Parameter(Mandatory)]
        [psCredential]
        $SqlInstallCredential,

        [Parameter()]
        [psCredential]
        $SqlAdministratorCredential = $SqlInstallCredential,

        [Parameter(Mandatory)]
        [psCredential]
        $SqlServiceCredential,

        [Parameter()]
        [psCredential]
        $SqlAgentServiceCredential = $SqlServiceCredential,

        [Parameter(Mandatory)]
        [String]
```

```
        $SqlInstallerDriverLetter
    )

    Import-DscResource -ModuleName xSQLServer -ModuleVersion 9.0.0.0

    Node $AllNodes.NodeName
    {
        xSQLServerSetup 'InstallDefaultInstance'
        {
            InstanceName          = 'MSSQLSERVER'
            Features              = 'SQLENGINE'
            SQLCollation          = 'SQL_Latin1_General_CP1_CI_AS'
            SQLSvcAccount         = $SqlServiceCredential
            AgtSvcAccount         = $SqlAgentServiceCredential
            SQLSysAdminAccounts   = $SqlAdministratorCredential.UserName
            InstallSharedDir      = 'C:\Program Files\Microsoft SQL Server'
            InstallSharedWOWDir   = 'C:\Program Files (x86)\Microsoft
                                     SQL Server'
            InstanceDir           = 'C:\Program Files\Microsoft SQL Server'
            SourcePath            = $SqlInstallerDriverLetter
            UpdateEnabled         = 'False'
            ForceReboot           = $false

            PsDscRunAsCredential = $SqlInstallCredential
        }
    }
}

$SqlInstallCredential = Get-Credential -Message 'Enter SQL Install account
credentials ...'
$SqlServiceCredential = Get-Credential -Message 'Enter SQL service account
credentials ...'

SQLConfig -SqlInstallCredential $SqlInstallCredential -SqlServiceCredential
$SqlServiceCredential -SqlInstallerDriverLetter 'E:' -ConfigurationData
$confgData -Verbose
```

Within this SQL configuration fragment, you install SQL Server and configure the default instance. Since this configuration requires specifying credentials for SQL setup account, administrator, and service accounts, you have configuration data that specifies the public key of the target node certificate to use for the encryption of passwords.

Firewall Configuration

Finally, the firewall configuration allows inbound communication on TCP port 1433 for the SQL database engine. This is something very trivial; on a real production system, you may have many more such rules hardening the SQL and OS configuration.

```
Configuration FirewallConfig
{
    Import-DSCResource -ModuleName xNetworking -Name xFirewall
    -ModuleVersion 5.3.0.0

    Node Localhost
    {
        xFirewall Firewall
        {
            Name                = 'SQLDBEngineFWRule'
            DisplayName         = 'Firewall Rule SQL Database Engine
                                  inbound'
            Group               = 'SQL Firewall Rule Group'
            Ensure              = 'Present'
            Enabled             = 'True'
            Profile             = ('Domain', 'Private')
            Direction           = 'Inbound'
            LocalPort           = '1433'
            Protocol            = 'TCP'
            Description         = 'Firewall Rule SQL Database Engine
                                  inbound - TCP 1433'
        }
    }
}

FirewallConfig
```

In all of the above configuration fragments, notice the name of the configuration function. It is the same as what you had in the LCM meta configuration for each configuration fragment. This is necessary to ensure that the LCM meta resource configuration for each partial configuration fragment matches the right configuration function in the fragment.

On the authoring station, ensure that the custom DSC resource modules for these configurations are available, compile the configurations, and keep the MOF ready (he process that you are already familiar with). See Figure 10-5.

```
PS C:\> Start-DscConfiguration -Path C:\OSConfig -Verbose -Wait
VERBOSE: Perform operation 'Invoke CimMethod' with following parameters, ''methodName' = SendConfigur
ationApply,'className' = MSFT_DSCLocalConfigurationManager,'namespaceName' = root/Microsoft/Windows/D
esiredStateConfiguration'.
VERBOSE: An LCM method call arrived from computer WIN-M90ER0KH8N4 with user sid S-1-5-21-1102856324-5
99673247-239348776-500.
VERBOSE: [WIN-M90ER0KH8N4]: LCM:  [ Start  Set     ]
VERBOSE: [WIN-M90ER0KH8N4]: LCM:  [ End    Set     ]
The only way DSC Partial Configurations can be used in Push mode is if the Publish-DscConfiguration
Cmdlet is used. No other push cmdlet is supported. To avoid this error, either set a
metaconfiguration without partial configurations, or use the Publish-DscConfiguration cmdlet to
deploy your partial configuration.
    + CategoryInfo          : NotImplemented: (root/Microsoft/...gurationManager:String) [], CimExc
   eption
    + FullyQualifiedErrorId : MI RESULT 7
    + PSComputerName        : localhost

VERBOSE: Operation 'Invoke CimMethod' complete.
VERBOSE: Time taken for configuration job to complete is 0.255 seconds
```

Figure 10-5. *Compiled configuration fragment MOF*

Before you can enact these configurations, the custom DSC resource modules need to exist on the target node. So, copy them over to the $env:ProgramFiles\ WindowsPowerShell\Modules folder, or if you have a pull server configured, add the ResourceModuleSource property in the partial configuration settings pointing to instances of ResourceRepositoryWeb and/or ResourceRepositoryShare.

You can copy the compiled configuration fragments to the target node also so that each of them can be enacted locally.

Enacting a Partial Configuration: Push Mode

How do you generally enact a configuration in push mode? Or in another words, how do you push a configuration to a target node? You use the Start-DscConfiguration cmdlet. So, let's start there.

As seen in Figure 10-6, for partial configurations in push mode, you first need to use the `Publish-DscConfiguration` cmdlet to place the configuration fragment in the partial configuration store. See Figure 10-7.

```
Publish-DscConfiguration -Path .\OSConfig -Verbose
```

```
PS C:\Scripts\SQlDB> tree /F /A
Folder PATH listing
Volume serial number is 00000094 8E45:E0C0
C:.
|   FirewallConfig.ps1
|   OSConfig.ps1
|   SqlConfig.ps1
|
+---FirewallConfig
|       localhost.mof
|
+---OSConfig
|       localhost.mof
|
\---SQLConfig
        localhost.mof
```

Figure 10-6. *Using Start-DscConfiguration to push the configuration fragment*

```
PS C:\Configurations> Start-DscConfiguration -Path .\OSConfig -Wait -Verbose
VERBOSE: Perform operation 'Invoke CimMethod' with following parameters, ''methodName' = SendConfigur
ationApply,'className' = MSFT_DSCLocalConfigurationManager,'namespaceName' = root/Microsoft/Windows/D
esiredStateConfiguration'.
VERBOSE: An LCM method call arrived from computer WIN-M90ER0KH8N4 with user sid S-1-5-21-1102856324-5
99673247-239348776-500.
VERBOSE: [WIN-M90ER0KH8N4]: LCM:  [ Start  Set      ]
VERBOSE: [WIN-M90ER0KH8N4]: LCM:  [ End    Set      ]
The only way DSC Partial Configurations can be used in Push mode is if the Publish-DscConfiguration
Cmdlet is used. No other push cmdlet is supported. To avoid this error, either set a
metaconfiguration without partial configurations, or use the Publish-DscConfiguration cmdlet to
deploy your partial configuration.
    + CategoryInfo          : NotImplemented: (root/Microsoft/...gurationManager:String) [], CimExc
   eption
    + FullyQualifiedErrorId : MI RESULT 7
    + PSComputerName        : localhost

VERBOSE: Operation 'Invoke CimMethod' complete.
VERBOSE: Time taken for configuration job to complete is 0.784 seconds
```

Figure 10-7. *Publishing a configuration to a partial configuration store*

These published configuration fragments can be seen in the `C:\Windows\System32\Configuration\PartialConfigurations` folder. Once the fragment is available in the partial configuration store, it can be enacted using the `Start-DscConfiguration` cmdlet. You need to use the `-UseExisting` switch parameter instead of `-Path`.

```
Start-DscConfiguration -UseExisting -Wait -Verbose
```

Since you configured the LCM to reboot the node if needed, once you enact this configuration, the target node will reboot after the domain join configuration.

Note   You can also wait for the consistency check to get triggered to get the configuration enacted.

You may now repeat the publish and enact steps you just tried for the rest of the configuration fragments, SQLConfig and FirewallConfig, and this will complete the SQL DB instance configuration and system hardening.

Partial Configuration Dependencies

Similar to resource instance dependencies in a node configuration, you can define dependencies between different fragments of a node configuration. This is done using the DependsOn property of the PartialConfiguration meta resource.

```
[DscLocalConfigurationManager()]
Configuration LCMConfiguration
{
    Settings
    {
        CertificateID = '1DAEA5189FA2D927151C96C5F43F3DA13114573D'
        RebootNodeIfNeeded = $true
        ActionAfterReboot = 'ContinueConfiguration'
    }

    PartialConfiguration OSConfig
    {
        RefreshMode = 'Push'
        Description = 'OS configuration fragment for Windows feature,
                        host network, and domain join'
    }

    PartialConfiguration   SQLConfig
    {
        RefreshMode = 'Push'
```

```
        Description = 'SQL  configuration fragment for SQL instance install
                       and configuration.'
        DependsOn = '[PartialConfiguration]OSConfig'
    }

    PartialConfiguration FirewallConfig
    {
        RefreshMode = 'Push'
        Description = 'Firewall configuration fragment for OS and SQL
                       instance hardnening.'
        DependsOn = '[PartialConfiguration]SQLConfig'
    }
}
```

LCMConfiguration

When there are dependencies between different fragments, all dependent fragments must exist in the partial configuration store before the dependent fragments can be enacted. So, looking at the above meta configuration example, SQLConfig depends on OSConfig and FirewallConfig depends on SQLConfig.

In this scenario, only the OSConfig fragment can be enacted independently. What happens if you try to publish and enact the SQLConfig fragment? See Figure 10-8.

```
PS C:\Configurations> Publish-DscConfiguration -Path .\OSConfig -Verbose
VERBOSE: Perform operation 'Invoke CimMethod' with following parameters, ''methodName' = SendConfigur
ation,'className' = MSFT_DSCLocalConfigurationManager,'namespaceName' = root/Microsoft/Windows/Desire
dStateConfiguration'.
VERBOSE: An LCM method call arrived from computer WIN-M90ER0KH8N4 with user sid S-1-5-21-1102856324-5
99673247-239348776-500.
VERBOSE: [WIN-M90ER0KH8N4]: LCM:  [ Start  Set      ]
VERBOSE: [WIN-M90ER0KH8N4]: LCM:  [ End    Set      ]      Saved configuration document into the parti
al configuration store.
VERBOSE: [WIN-M90ER0KH8N4]: LCM:  [ End    Set      ]
VERBOSE: Operation 'Invoke CimMethod' complete.
VERBOSE: Publish-DscConfiguration finished in 0.318 seconds.
```

Figure 10-8. *Failure in enacting a dependent fragment*

This can be resolved by publishing the OSConfig fragment and then retrying the enact with Start-DscConfiguration cmdlet.

If you publish all fragments at once and enact, all partial configurations get converged into a single pending configuration and get enacted. Since you configured the node to continue configuration after reboot, the SQL install will start after the domain join.

The push mode for configuration is good for smaller deployments but does not scale well. Also, when using delegated configuration management, it may not be prudent to give every application or configuration owner local administrator permissions on the target node for them to be able to push configurations.

You learned this earlier and have seen the pull mode for configuration delivery in Chapter 8. Partial configurations can be used in pull mode as well.

Enacting a Partial Configuration: Pull Mode

There are certain LCM configuration requirements and configuration naming requirements when delivering partial configurations in pull mode.

Note   This section assumes that you already have a REST-based or SMB share-based pull server endpoint configured. The example in this section uses a REST-based pull configuration.

```
[DscLocalConfigurationManager()]
Configuration LCMConfiguration
{
    Settings
    {
        CertificateID = '1DAEA5189FA2D927151C96C5F43F3DA13114573D'
        RebootNodeIfNeeded = $true
        ActionAfterReboot = 'ContinueConfiguration'
    }

    ConfigurationRepositoryWeb S16Pull01
    {
        ServerURL = 'http://S16-PULL-01:8080/PSDSCPullServer.svc'
        RegistrationKey = '4867cdea-9dde-48a0-8416-2daa89471991'
        AllowUnsecureConnection = $true
        ConfigurationNames = @('OSConfig','SQLConfig','FirewallConfig')
    }
```

```
    ResourceRepositoryWeb S16Pull01
    {
        ServerURL = 'http://S16-PULL-01:8080/PSDSCPullServer.svc'
        RegistrationKey = '4867cdea-9dde-48a0-8416-2daa89471991'
        AllowUnsecureConnection = $true
    }

    PartialConfiguration OSConfig
    {
        RefreshMode = 'Pull'
        Description = 'OS configuration fragment for Windows feature, host
                      network, and domain join'
        ConfigurationSource = '[ConfigurationRepositoryWeb]S16Pull01'
    }

    PartialConfiguration SQLConfig
    {
        RefreshMode = 'Pull'
        Description = 'SQL configuration fragment for SQL instance install
                      and configuration.'
        ConfigurationSource = '[ConfigurationRepositoryWeb]S16Pull01'
        DependsOn = '[PartialConfiguration]OSConfig'
    }

    PartialConfiguration FirewallConfig
    {
        RefreshMode = 'Pull'
        Description = 'Firewall  configuration fragment for OS and SQL
                      instance hardnening.'
        ConfigurationSource = '[ConfigurationRepositoryWeb]S16Pull01'
        DependsOn = '[PartialConfiguration]OSConfig'
    }
}

LCMConfiguration
```

In this meta configuration, the three partial configurations are configured to pull the fragments from a REST-based pull server. Unlike the push example, you pull the required resource modules as well from the same pull server. This is configured using the ResourceRepositoryWeb meta resource.

If you keenly observe the partial configuration instances in the meta configuration and compare the properties used to Table 10-1, you will see that the ResourceModuleSource is not used although you are using a pull server for this purpose too. This property is not mandatory, unlike the ConfigurationSource property of the partial configuration resource. The LCM will look up the configured ResourceRepositoryWeb or ResourceRepositoryShare for the required resource modules.

Once you have this meta configuration enacted, you can compile and copy over the MOF and resource module files to the DSC pull service path. This process is no different from what you practiced in Chapter 8. For partial configurations, you just need to name the fragments as <configuration-fragment-name>.mof and place it on the pull server with its associated checksum.

Once you have the necessary files (configuration fragments and resource modules) placed on the pull server, you can use the Update-DscConfiguration cmdlet to force the target node check with the pull server for updated configurations. This triggers the module and configuration fragment download to the target node and the enact process.

Enacting a Partial Configuration: Mixed Mode

Like any other node configuration, partial configurations can also be enacted in mixed refresh mode.

```
[DscLocalConfigurationManager()]
Configuration LCMConfiguration
{
    Settings
    {
        CertificateID = '1DAEA5189FA2D927151C96C5F43F3DA13114573D'
        RebootNodeIfNeeded  = $true
        ActionAfterReboot = 'ContinueConfiguration'
    }
```

```
ConfigurationRepositoryWeb    S16Pull01
{
    ServerURL = 'http://S16-PULL-01:8080/PSDSCPullServer.svc'
    RegistrationKey = '4867cdea-9dde-48a0-8416-2daa89471991'
    AllowUnsecureConnection = $true
    ConfigurationNames = @('SQLConfig','FirewallConfig')
}

ResourceRepositoryWeb    S16Pull01
{
    ServerURL = 'http://S16-PULL-01:8080/PSDSCPullServer.svc'
    RegistrationKey = '4867cdea-9dde-48a0-8416-2daa89471991'
    AllowUnsecureConnection  = $true
}

PartialConfiguration    OSConfig
{
    RefreshMode = 'Push'
    Description = 'OS configuration fragment for Windows feature, host
                   network, and domain join'
}

PartialConfiguration    SQLConfig
{
    RefreshMode = 'Pull'
    Description = 'SQL configuration fragment for SQL instance install
                   and configuration.'
    ConfigurationSource = '[ConfigurationRepositoryWeb]S16Pull01'
    DependsOn = '[PartialConfiguration]OSConfig'
}

PartialConfiguration FirewallConfig
{
    RefreshMode = 'Pull'
    Description = 'Firewall configuration fragment for OS and SQL
                   instance hardnening.'
```

```
        ConfigurationSource = '[ConfigurationRepositoryWeb]S16Pull01'
        DependsOn = '[PartialConfiguration]OSConfig'
    }
}
```

LCMConfiguration

This meta configuration is more or less similar to the pull mode example. However, for the OSConfig fragment, you change the refresh mode to push. This configuration has no dependencies and hence can be enacted independently. You have already seen the process of enacting in both cases, push and pull. So, for the OSConfig, you use the Publish-DscConfiguration cmdlet followed by the Start-DscConfiguration cmdlet. For the pull mode, you simply call the Update-DscConfiguration cmdlet once the required files are placed on the pull server and all dependent configurations in push mode are already enacted.

Exclusive Resource Reservation

One of the features associated with partial configurations is resource reservations in each fragment. Consider the example in this chapter. As a part of the delegated configuration control, you want to restrict who can use the WindowsFeature DSC resource to install features and roles. This may be to prevent any other administrator from installing whatever roles and features they want and ensure that it will be done exclusively using the OS configurations.

This is what the ExclusiveResources property of the PartialConfiguration meta resource is used for. To be able to use it, you need to set the meta configuration. Here is how it looks:

```
[DscLocalConfigurationManager()]
Configuration LCMConfiguration
{
    Settings
    {
        CertificateID = '1DAEA5189FA2D927151C96C5F43F3DA13114573D'
        RebootNodeIfNeeded = $true
        ActionAfterReboot = 'ContinueConfiguration'
    }
```

```
ConfigurationRepositoryWeb S16Pull01
{
    ServerURL = 'http://S16-PULL-01:8080/PSDSCPullServer.svc'
    RegistrationKey = '4867cdea-9dde-48a0-8416-2daa89471991'
    AllowUnsecureConnection = $true
    ConfigurationNames = @('OSConfig','SQLConfig','FirewallConfig')
}

ResourceRepositoryWeb S16Pull01
{
    ServerURL = 'http://S16-PULL-01:8080/PSDSCPullServer.svc'
    RegistrationKey = '4867cdea-9dde-48a0-8416-2daa89471991'
    AllowUnsecureConnection = $true
}

PartialConfiguration OSConfig
{
    RefreshMode = 'Pull'
    Description = 'OS configuration fragment for Windows feature, host
                  network, and domain join'
    ExclusiveResources = 'WindowsFeature'
    ConfigurationSource = '[ConfigurationRepositoryWeb]S16Pull01'
}

PartialConfiguration SQLConfig
{
    RefreshMode = 'Pull'
    Description = 'SQL configuration fragment for SQL instance install
                  and configuration.'
    ConfigurationSource = '[ConfigurationRepositoryWeb]S16Pull01'
    DependsOn = '[PartialConfiguration]OSConfig'
}

PartialConfiguration FirewallConfig
{
    RefreshMode = 'Pull'
    Description = 'Firewall configuration fragment for OS and SQL
                  instance hardnening.'
```

```
        ConfigurationSource = '[ConfigurationRepositoryWeb]S16Pull01'
        DependsOn = '[PartialConfiguration]OSConfig'
    }
}
```

LCMConfiguration

In this updated meta configuration, you reserve the WindowsFeature resource only to the OSConfig fragment. Now, if any other configuration fragment tries to configure an instance of that reserved resource, it will result in an error. Let's see that in action.

Here is the modified SQLConfig fragment that tries to install a web server role:

```
$confgData = @{
    AllNodes = @(
        @{
            NodeName = 'localhost' PSDscAllowDomainUser = $true
            CertificateFile = 'C:\PublicKeys\sqldb.cer'
            Thumbprint = '1DAEA5189FA2D927151C96C5F43F3DA13114573D'
        }
    )
}

Configuration SQLConfig
{
    [CmdletBinding()]
    param
    (
        [Parameter(Mandatory)]
        [psCredential]
        $SqlInstallCredential,

        [Parameter()]
        [psCredential]
        $SqlAdministratorCredential = $SqlInstallCredential,

        [Parameter(Mandatory)]
        [psCredential]
        $SqlServiceCredential,
```

```
    [Parameter()]
    [psCredential]
    $SqlAgentServiceCredential = $SqlServiceCredential,

    [Parameter(Mandatory)]
    [ValidateNotNullorEmpty()]
    [String]
    $SqlInstallerDriverLetter
)

Import-DscResource -ModuleName xSQLServer

Node $AllNodes.NodeName
{
    WindowsFeature WebServer
    {
        Name   = 'Web-Server'
        Ensure = 'Present'
    }

    xSQLServerSetup 'InstallDefaultInstance'
    {
        InstanceName         = 'MSSQLSERVER'
        Features             = 'SQLENGINE'
        SQLCollation         = 'SQL_Latin1_General_CP1_CI_AS'
        SQLSvcAccount        = $SqlServiceCredential
        AgtSvcAccount        = $SqlAgentServiceCredential
        SQLSysAdminAccounts  = $SqlAdministratorCredential.UserName
        InstallSharedDir     = 'C:\Program  Files\Microsoft SQL Server'
        InstallSharedWOWDir  = 'C:\Program Files (x86)\Microsoft
                                 SQL Server'
        InstanceDir          = 'C:\Program  Files\Microsoft SQL Server'
        SourcePath           = $SqlInstallerDriverLetter
        UpdateEnabled        = 'False'
        ForceReboot          = $false
        PsDscRunAsCredential = $SqlInstallCredential
    }
  }
}
```

```
$SqlInstallCredential = Get-Credential -Message 'Enter SQL Install account
credentials ...'
$SqlServiceCredential = Get-Credential -Message 'Enter SQL service account
credentials ...'

SQLConfig -SqlInstallCredential $SqlInstallCredential -SqlServiceCredential
$SqlServiceCredential -SqlInstallerDriverLetter 'E:' -ConfigurationData
$confgData -Verbose
```

When you compile this MOF, publish it to the partial configuration store, and enact it, the LCM will throw an error that one of the partial configuration fragments is invalid and the failing fragment will be discarded from the configuration enact process. This is shown in Figure 10-9.

```
PS C:\> Publish-DscConfiguration -Path C:\Configurations\SQLConfig

PS C:\> Start-DscConfiguration -UseExisting -Wait -Verbose
VERBOSE: Perform operation 'Invoke CimMethod' with following parameters, ''methodName' = ApplyConfigu
ration,'className' = MSFT_DSCLocalConfigurationManager,'namespaceName' = root/Microsoft/Windows/Desir
edStateConfiguration'.
VERBOSE: An LCM method call arrived from computer WIN-M90ER0KH8N4 with user sid S-1-5-21-1102856324-5
99673247-239348776-500.
VERBOSE: [WIN-M90ER0KH8N4]:                          [] Starting consistency engine.
WARNING: [WIN-M90ER0KH8N4]:                          [] The partial configuration [PartialConfigura
tion]SQLConfig depends on another partial configuration that does not exist. This partial configurati
on will not be set until it finds the partial configuration that it depends on.
One or more partial configurations failed to apply. No configuration could be created.  LCM failed
to start desired state configuration manually.
    + CategoryInfo          : ObjectNotFound: (root/Microsoft/...gurationManager:String) [], CimExc
   eption
    + FullyQualifiedErrorId : MI RESULT 6
    + PSComputerName        : localhost

VERBOSE: Operation 'Invoke CimMethod' complete.
VERBOSE: Time taken for configuration job to complete is 4.758 seconds
```

Figure 10-9. *Error with exclusive resources*

Partial Configuration Life Cycle

In Chapter 3, you saw the life cycle of a node configuration document. You can represent partial configurations as well in the same manner. Figure 10-10 illustrates this.

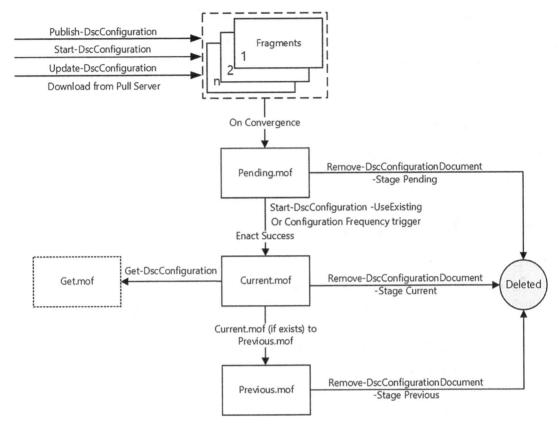

Figure 10-10. *Partial configuration life cycle*

Figure 10-10 is very much self-explanatory. All configuration fragments first land in the partial configuration store represented by `$env:SystemDrive\Windows\System32\Configuration\PartialConfigurations`. This is the location where all fragments get stored irrespective of the refresh mode.

When either the consistency check gets triggered or an administrator runs a command to explicitly start the enact process, the partial configuration fragments are validated and converged into a pending configuration (`pending.mof`) for the enact.

The rest of the life cycle stays as is and does not change. Unlike the pending, current, and previous documents, there is no command to remove the partial configuration fragments. If you delete one manually, if the fragment is configured to pull, it will be pulled during the next consistency check and enacted.

What if you delete all of the fragments that were received in the push refresh mode and then use `Start-DscConfiguration` with the `-UseExisting` switch? What do you expect to happen?

Try it before you read the next line!

The `current.mof` gets enacted in this case. If you delete the `current.mof` too, the LCM will complain that the partial fragments are not available.

Limitations

Partial configurations come with a lot of baggage. You need to understand this before planning to implement partial configurations.

Exclusive Resource Reservations

The exclusive resource reservation may be an interesting feature to restrict who can configure what resource instances, but it can be a huge road-block in certain scenarios. Consider this example from former PowerShell MVP Steven Murawski. In this example, consider the `xWebAdministration` resource as exclusively reserved for only the web team and that xSQLServer is locked only to the DBA team. All is well until the DBA team needs to configure reporting services, but they can't since they are barred from using `xWebAdminstration`. The DBA team may work around this by creating their own custom resource and continue to modify the web configuration. For the web team, these reporting services configurations never existed in their inventory and audit. So, this becomes a compliance issue.

Resource Naming Conflicts

If you have read the life cycle section carefully, I mentioned that the partial fragments are validated and enacted. So, consider a scenario where two different fragments carry the same resource configuration with same instance name. In a single node configuration document, this conflict will be seen at compile time. However, with partial configurations, this is not the case. The validation only happens only at the enact time. Figure 10-11 shows an example of one such error.

```
PS C:\> Start-DscConfiguration -UseExisting -Wait -Verbose
VERBOSE: Perform operation 'Invoke CimMethod' with following parameters, ''methodName' =
ApplyConfiguration,'className' = MSFT_DSCLocalConfigurationManager,'namespaceName' = root
/Microsoft/Windows/DesiredStateConfiguration'.
VERBOSE: An LCM method call arrived from computer SQLDB with user sid S-1-5-21-689661094-
3032901192-2251061677-500.
VERBOSE: [SQLDB]:                                  [] Starting consistency engine.
The resources ('[WindowsFeature]NetFramework35' and '[WindowsFeature]NetFramework35')
have conflicting values of the following properties: 'ModuleName, PsDscRunAsCredential,
Source'. Ensure that their values match.  Merging of partial configurations failed. LCM
failed to start desired state configuration manually.
    + CategoryInfo          : ResourceExists: (root/Microsoft/...gurationManager:String
 ) [], CimException
    + FullyQualifiedErrorId : MI RESULT 11
    + PSComputerName        : localhost

VERBOSE: Operation 'Invoke CimMethod' complete.
VERBOSE: Time taken for configuration job to complete is 0.341 seconds
```

Figure 10-11. *Resource conflicts during an enact*

Summary

Partial configurations promote collaboration and enable delegated control over the node configurations. You can use partial configurations in either push or pull mode or mixed refresh mode. All or most of the knowledge that you gained through the earlier chapters around node configurations is applicable to partial configurations as well. However, remember the limitations or drawbacks of using partial configuration without proper planning. If reusability is the goal, using composite resources or configurations can be a better option.

CHAPTER 11

Cross-Node Synchronization

In the previous chapter on partial configurations, you looked at the incremental approach to applying configuration fragments. With partial configurations, all fragments are limited to a single target node. But, what if you need to orchestrate dependencies between multiple resources across different nodes? For example, if you are building a failover cluster, you will have to wait for all participating nodes to first get the failover cluster feature installed and then proceed to creating the cluster and joining other nodes into the newly created cluster. With or without partial configurations, you can do this in an orchestrated manner using an orchestration script. The whole purpose of this orchestration script is to ensure that the target nodes come into a desired state with respect to all dependencies and then ensure that the cluster gets created. With partial configuration fragments, you can configure some resource instances that don't have any internal or external dependencies independently and simultaneously while all other dependent configuration happens at the end in a serial manner. Once again, you can use an orchestration script that stitches all this together.

However, this approach requires some heavy lifting within the orchestration script. You need to know how to make sense of dependencies in the configuration document and how to monitor the target nodes' resources for the desired state. You need to build error handling into the orchestration script so that it can recover and resume from the point of failure.

© Ravikanth Chaganti 2018
R. Chaganti, *Pro PowerShell Desired State Configuration*, https://doi.org/10.1007/978-1-4842-3483-9_11

If you have ever used Microsoft-developed DSC resource modules such as
xActiveDirectory and xFailoverCluster, you might have seen resources such
as xWaitForADDomain and xWaitForCluster. These resources helped wait for any
dependent resources to be in a desired state before proceeding to the final configuration
on a given node. Take a look at this example:

```
$certFile = 'C:\PublicKeys\AD.cer'
$thumbprint = $(
    $cert = [System.Security.Cryptography.X509Certificates.
            X509Certificate2]::new()
    $cert.Import($certFile)
    $cert.Thumbprint
)

$configData = @{
    AllNodes = @(
        @{
            NodeName = 'localhost'
            CertificateFile = $certFile
            Thumbprint = $thumbprint
            PSDscAllowDomainUser = $true
        }
    )
}

Configuration CreateADDomain
{
    param
    (
        [Parameter(Mandatory = $true)]
        [String]
        $DomainName,

        [Parameter(Mandatory = $true)]
        [pscredential]
        $DomainCredential,
```

```
    [Parameter(Mandatory = $true)]
    [pscredential]
    $SafemodeAdministratorCredential,

    [Parameter(Mandatory = $true)]
    [pscredential]
    $FirstUserCredential
)

Import-DscResource -ModuleName xActiveDirectory -ModuleVersion 2.16.0.0
Import-DscResource –ModuleName PSDesiredStateConfiguration
-ModuleVersion 1.1
Node $AllNodes.NodeName
{
    WindowsFeature ADDS
    {
        Ensure = 'Present'
        Name = 'AD-Domain-Services'
    }

    WindowsFeature ADDSMgmt
    {
        Ensure = 'Present'
        Name = 'RSAT-ADDS'
        DependsOn = '[WindowsFeature]ADDS'
    }

    xADDomain FirstDS
    {
        DomainName = $DomainName
        DomainAdministratorCredential = $DomainCredential
        SafemodeAdministratorPassword = $SafemodeAdministratorCredential
        DependsOn = '[WindowsFeature]ADDSMgmt'
    }

    xWaitForADDomain FirstDSWait
    {
        DomainName = $DomainName
```

```
                DomainUserCredential = $DomainCredential
                DependsOn = '[xADDomain]FirstDS'
            }

        xADUser FirstUser
        {
            DomainName = $DomainName
            DomainAdministratorCredential = $DomainCredential
            UserName = $FirstUserCredential.Username
            Password = $FirstUserCredential
            Ensure = 'Present'
            DependsOn = '[xWaitForADDomain]FirstDSWait'
        }
    }
}

CreateADDomain -configurationData $confgData `
            -DomainCredential (Get-Credential -Message 'Enter new
            domain administrator credentials ...') `
            -SafemodeAdministratorCredential (Get-Credential -Message
            'Enter safe mode administrator credentials ...') `
            -FirstUserCredential (Get-Credential -Message 'Enter first
            user credentials ...')
```

Note This example requires a reboot to complete the DS configuration. You must set the LCM configuration property`RebootNodeIfNeeded` in the Settings meta resource to `$true`.

This example installs the necessary Windows features for creating an Active Directory domain and then proceeds to create the first domain controller itself. Before creating the first user in that domain, you need to wait for the domain to be available. This is where you use the `xWaitforADDomain` resource. You are waiting here for the domain to become functionally available, which in this case will be installed on the same node by the xADDomain resource, before the `FirstUser` resource configuration can proceed. The `DependsOn` automatic property in the resource instance is only a way to specify dependencies between resource instances on the same node but not across different nodes. In this scenario, this would work for multiple nodes as well, as the xWaitForADDomain resource checks on a functional level. But what if such a resource does not exist? How do you achieve cross-node configuration dependency in DSC?

With WMF 5.0, Microsoft introduced a new feature called cross-node synchronization in DSC. At the surface, you see three DSC resources that help you wait for dependencies to be in a desired state before proceeding to finalizing the configuration. But, behind the scenes, there is something more interesting. You will go there but let's first see what these three resources are and how to use them.

Lab Requirements

To try the examples and exercises in this chapter, you will need at minimum Windows Server 2008 R2 or above system with WMF 5.1 installed. I recommend a system with Windows Server 2016. Since cross-node synchronization involves more than one system, depending on the type of resource example, you will need three or four systems to try out the examples.

Getting Started

As mentioned, there are three inbox DSC resources in the PSDesiredStateConfiguration module that make cross-node dependency and synchronization possible.

As shown in Figure 11-1, WaitForAll, WaitForAny, and WaitForSome are the three resources that help in cross-node synchronization. Table 11-1 provides a brief overview of these resources.

```
PS C:\> Get-DscResource -Module PSDesiredStateConfiguration -Name WaitFor*

ImplementedAs   Name          ModuleName                    Version   Properties
-------------   ----          ----------                    -------   ----------
PowerShell      WaitForAll    PSDesiredStateConfiguration   1.1       {NodeName, ResourceName, DependsOn, PsDscRunAsC...
PowerShell      WaitForAny    PSDesiredStateConfiguration   1.1       {NodeName, ResourceName, DependsOn, PsDscRunAsC...
PowerShell      WaitForSome   PSDesiredStateConfiguration   1.1       {NodeCount, NodeName, ResourceName, DependsOn...}
```

Figure 11-1. *The WaitForX resources in the PSDesiredStateConfiguration module*

In Table 11-1, pay attention to the highlighted phrases in the descriptions. Each resource is designed for a specific purpose. If you only need to check one target node for resource state dependency, you can use any of these three resources for that purpose. However, beyond that, you need to specifically choose between them based on the scenario that you plan to implement.

Table 11-1. *Overview of the WaitForX Resources*

Resource Name	Description
WaitForAll	Wait for one or more resources on ***all specified target nodes*** to appear in the desired state.
WaitForAny	Wait for one or more resources on ***any one of the specified target nodes*** to appear in the desired state.
WaitForSome	Wait for one or more resources on some of the ***specified number of target nodes*** to appear in the desired state. The count of nodes to be in the desired state is specified using the NodeCount property.

These resources share common properties. Table 11-2 provides a list of these properties.

Table 11-2. *WaitForX DSC Resource Properties*

Property Name	Description	Applies to
NodeName	Specifies an array of one or more nodes to monitor for the resource's desired state.	All resources
ResourceName	Specifies a resource ID on target nodes to monitor for the desired state.	All resources
RetryIntervalSec	Specifies the interval (in seconds) between retries while waiting for the resource(s) to be in the desired state. Default value is 1.	All resources
RetryCount	Specifies the number of retries while waiting for the resource(s) to be in the desired state. Default value is 0. The default value means that the WaitForX resource will wait only for the value defined in the RetryIntervalSec property and will not retry after that.	All resources
NodeCount	Specifies the minimum number of target nodes to be in the desired state.	WaitForSome only
ThrottleLimit	Number of machines to connect simultaneously.	All

Prerequisites for Using Cross-Node Synchronization

Before you proceed to the examples, understand that the target nodes must have a configuration enact in progress or an enacted configuration that contains the resource instance configuration with the same names as mentioned in the ResourceName property.

Note If there is no current or pending configuration on the target node, the WaitForX enact results in an access denied error.

Here is an example of what happens when the target node does not meet this first prerequisite with a resource instance that you want to monitor:

```
Configuration WaitErrorDemo
{
    Import-DscResource -ModuleName PSDesiredStateConfiguration

    Node localhost
    {
        WaitForAny AudioService
        {
            NodeName = 'CNODE01'
            ResourceName = '[Service]AudioService'
        }
    }
}

WaitErrorDemo
```

When you enact this configuration, assuming that the pending or enacted configuration exists for the Service resource, you'll see the results shown in Figure 11-2.

```
PS C:\> Start-DscConfiguration -Path .\WaitErrorDemo -Wait -Verbose -Force
VERBOSE: Perform operation 'Invoke CimMethod' with following parameters, ''methodName' = SendConfigurationApply,'classN
ame' = MSFT_DSCLocalConfigurationManager,'namespaceName' = root/Microsoft/Windows/DesiredStateConfiguration'.
VERBOSE: An LCM method call arrived from computer S16-JB with user sid S-1-5-21-689661094-3032901192-2251061677-500.
VERBOSE: [S16-JB]: LCM:  [ Start  Set      ]
VERBOSE: [S16-JB]: LCM:  [ Start  Resource ]  [[WaitForAny]AudioService]
VERBOSE: [S16-JB]: LCM:  [ Start  Test     ]  [[WaitForAny]AudioService]
VERBOSE: [S16-JB]:                            [[WaitForAny]AudioService] Remote resource '[Service]AudioService' is not
 ready.
VERBOSE: [S16-JB]: LCM:  [ End    Test     ]  [[WaitForAny]AudioService]  in 1.8280 seconds.
VERBOSE: [S16-JB]: LCM:  [ Start  Set      ]  [[WaitForAny]AudioService]
VERBOSE: [S16-JB]: LCM:  [ End    Set      ]  [[WaitForAny]AudioService]  in 0.8130 seconds.
PowerShell DSC resource MSFT_WaitForAny  failed to execute Set-TargetResource functionality with error message:
Resource '[Service]AudioService' on machine(s) 'CNODE01' is not ready.
    + CategoryInfo          : InvalidOperation: (:) [], CimException
    + FullyQualifiedErrorId : ProviderOperationExecutionFailure
    + PSComputerName        : localhost

VERBOSE: [S16-JB]: LCM:  [ End    Set      ]
The SendConfigurationApply function did not succeed.
    + CategoryInfo          : NotSpecified: (root/Microsoft/...gurationManager:String) [], CimException
    + FullyQualifiedErrorId : MI RESULT 1
    + PSComputerName        : localhost

VERBOSE: Operation 'Invoke CimMethod' complete.
VERBOSE: Time taken for configuration job to complete is 3.144 seconds
```

Figure 11-2. *Error during the enact of the configuration*

Try This   Create and enact a configuration document that contains the AudioService resource instance on the target node and then try the above example again. What do you see in the verbose output?

The WaitForAll Resource

Going back to the earlier example of failover clustering, you would need to wait for all participating nodes in a cluster to get the failover clustering feature installed. The WaitForAll resource is a perfect fit here. See Figure 11-3.

```
PS C:\> Get-DscResource -Name WaitForAll -Syntax
WaitForAll [String] #ResourceName
{
    NodeName = [string[]]
    ResourceName = [string]
    [DependsOn = [string[]]]
    [PsDscRunAsCredential = [PSCredential]]
    [RetryCount = [UInt32]]
    [RetryIntervalSec = [UInt64]]
    [ThrottleLimit = [UInt32]]
}
```

Figure 11-3. *WaitForAll resource syntax*

Note   For the following example, you must use four domain-joined systems that will become a part of a failover cluster when the configuration enact completes.

Within the failover cluster example you are going to see now, you need two different configuration documents: one for the node where you create the cluster and another for rest of the nodes.

Cluster Nodes Configuration

The following configuration shows what you need on the target nodes to become a part of the failover cluster:

```
Configuration ClusterFeature
{
    param
    (
        [Parameter(Mandatory)]
        [String[]]
        $Nodes
    )

    Import-DscResource -Module PSDesiredStateConfiguration

    Node $Nodes
    {
        WindowsFeature FailoverCluster
        {
```

```
            Name = 'Failover-Clustering'
            IncludeAllSubFeature = $true
            Ensure = 'Present'
        }
    }
}

ClusterFeature -Node 'CNODE02','CNODE03','CNODE04'
```

This is a simple example. You have one resource instance and it is the
WindowsFeature resource to install the failover-clustering feature.

Creating a Cluster Configuration

On one of the nodes, you will have to wait for the rest of the nodes to have the failover-
clustering Windows feature installed before you can create the failover cluster. The
configuration document for this purpose should have the WaitForAll resource.

```
$certFile = 'C:\PublicKeys\CNODE01.cer'
$thumbprint = $(
    $cert = [System.Security.Cryptography.X509Certificates.
    X509Certificate2]::new()
    $cert.Import($certFile)
    $cert.Thumbprint
)

$configData = @{
    AllNodes = @(
        @{
            NodeName = 'CNODE01'
            CertificateFile = $certFile
            Thumbprint = $thumbprint
            PSDscAllowDomainUser = $true
        }
    )
}

Configuration CreateCluster
{
```

```powershell
param
(
    [Parameter(Mandatory)]
    [pscredential]
    $Credential,

    [Parameter(Mandatory)]
    [String]
    $ClusterName,

    [Parameter(Mandatory)]
    [String]
    $ClusterIPAddress,

    [Parameter(Mandatory)]
    [String[]]
    $ClusterNodes
)

Import-DscResource -ModuleName FailoverClusterDsc -Name
FailoverCluster, FailoverClusterNode, FailoverClusterResourceParameter
Import-DscResource -ModuleName PSDesiredStateConfiguration

Node $AllNodes.NodeName
{
    WindowsFeature FailoverCluster
    {
        Name = 'Failover-Clustering'
        IncludeAllSubFeature = $true
        Ensure = 'Present'
    }

    WindowsFeature FailoverClusterMgmt
    {
        Name = 'RSAT-Clustering'
        IncludeAllSubFeature = $true
        Ensure = 'Present'
        DependsOn = '[WindowsFeature]FailoverCluster'
    }
```

```
    WaitForAll FCFeature
    {
        NodeName = $ClusterNodes
        ResourceName = '[WindowsFeature]FailoverCluster'
        RetryIntervalSec = 30
        RetryCount = 10
    }

    FailoverCluster CreateCluster
    {
        ClusterName = $ClusterName
        StaticAddress = $ClusterIPAddress
        NoStorage = $true
        Ensure = 'Present'
        PsDscRunAsCredential = $Credential
        DependsOn = '[WaitForAll]FCFeature'
    }

    foreach ($clusterNode in $clusterNodes)
    {
        FailoverClusterNode $clusterNode
        {
            NodeName = $clusterNode
            ClusterName = 'S2D4NCluster'
            PsDscRunAsCredential = $Credential
            Ensure = 'Present'
            DependsOn = '[FailoverCluster]CreateCluster'
        }
    }
}
}

CreateCluster -Credential (Get-Credential) -ConfigurationData $configData
-ClusterName 'S2D4NCluster' -ClusterIPAddress '172.16.102.45' -ClusterNodes
'CNODE02','CNODE03','CNODE04'
```

Look at how you are using the `WaitForAll` resource in this configuration document. You have the `ResourceName` property to set to the `WindowsFeature` resource instance from the cluster node configuration. Notice how the value of `ResourceName` matches the resource instance name used in the cluster node configuration. This is very important. If there is a mismatch, the `WaitForAll` resource will always exit with a *resource not ready* error. The `NodeName` property is set to a list of participating nodes except the node where the cluster will be created.

Note Make sure you have the `FailoverClusterDSC` resource module downloaded from the PowerShell gallery and that it is available on both the authoring station and the node where the cluster creation configuration needs to be enacted.

Let's compile these configurations. See Figure 11-4.

```
PS C:\> CreateCluster -Credential (Get-Credential) -ConfigurationData $configData -ClusterName 'S2D4NCluster' -ClusterIPAddr
cmdlet Get-Credential at command pipeline position 1
Supply values for the following parameters:


    Directory: C:\CreateCluster


Mode                LastWriteTime         Length Name
----                -------------         ------ ----
-a----        12/2/2017     4:47 PM        13134 CNODE01.mof


PS C:\> ClusterFeature -Node 'CNODE02','CNODE03','CNODE04'


    Directory: C:\ClusterFeature


Mode                LastWriteTime         Length Name
----                -------------         ------ ----
-a----        12/2/2017     4:47 PM         1974 CNODE02.mof
-a----        12/2/2017     4:47 PM         1974 CNODE03.mof
-a----        12/2/2017     4:47 PM         1974 CNODE04.mof
```

Figure 11-4. *Compiled node configurations*

You first enact the node configuration (containing the `FailoverCluster` resource) with the -`Verbose` and -`Wait` switch parameters. Wait for a few seconds and in a second PowerShell console window, or whatever other place you prefer, start the configuration enact on rest of the nodes.

Note This order is important if you want to really see the `WaitForAll` resource in action.

As seen in Figure 11-5 (partial output only), the `WaitForAll` resource starts checking the `[WindowsFeature]FailoverCluster` resource instance on all of the nodes specified using `NodeName`. It will wait until all nodes come to the desired state for this specific resource instance or wait until a timeout is reached.

```
VERBOSE: [CNODE01]:                                [[WindowsFeature]FailoverClusterMgmt] Prerequisite processing succeeded.
VERBOSE: [CNODE01]:                                [[WindowsFeature]FailoverClusterMgmt] Installation succeeded.
VERBOSE: [CNODE01]:                                [[WindowsFeature]FailoverClusterMgmt] Successfully installed the feature RSAT-Clustering.
VERBOSE: [CNODE01]: LCM:  [ End    Set      ]      [[WindowsFeature]FailoverClusterMgmt]  in 92.7530 seconds.
VERBOSE: [CNODE01]: LCM:  [ End    Resource ]      [[WindowsFeature]FailoverClusterMgmt]
VERBOSE: [CNODE01]: LCM:  [ Start  Resource ]      [[WaitForAll]FCFeature]
VERBOSE: [CNODE01]: LCM:  [ Start  Test     ]      [[WaitForAll]FCFeature]
VERBOSE: [CNODE01]:                                [[WaitForAll]FCFeature] Remote resource '[WindowsFeature]FailoverCluster' is not ready.
VERBOSE: [CNODE01]: LCM:  [ End    Test     ]      [[WaitForAll]FCFeature]  in 4.3280 seconds.
VERBOSE: [CNODE01]: LCM:  [ Start  Set      ]      [[WaitForAll]FCFeature]
VERBOSE: [CNODE01]:                                [[WaitForAll]FCFeature] Remote resource '[WindowsFeature]FailoverCluster' is not ready. Retrying after 30 second(s)
VERBOSE: [CNODE01]:                                [[WaitForAll]FCFeature] Remote resource '[WindowsFeature]FailoverCluster
' is not ready. Retrying after 30 second(s)
```

Figure 11-5. *WaitForAll in action: Resource not ready*

Figure 11-6 shows that the `WaitForAll` resource waits until the failover clustering feature is installed on all monitored target nodes before starting the cluster creation.

```
VERBOSE: [CNODE01]:                                [[WaitForAll]FCFeature] Remote resource '[WindowsFeature]FailoverCluster' is not ready.
VERBOSE: [CNODE01]: LCM:  [ End    Test     ]      [[WaitForAll]FCFeature]  in 0.5940 seconds.
VERBOSE: [CNODE01]: LCM:  [ Start  Set      ]      [[WaitForAll]FCFeature]
VERBOSE: [CNODE01]:                                [[WaitForAll]FCFeature] Remote resource '[WindowsFeature]FailoverCluster' is not ready. Retrying after 30 second(s)
VERBOSE: [CNODE01]:                                [[WaitForAll]FCFeature] Remote resource '[WindowsFeature]FailoverCluster' is not ready. Retrying after 30 second(s)
VERBOSE: [CNODE01]:                                [[WaitForAll]FCFeature] Remote resource '[WindowsFeature]FailoverCluster' is ready
VERBOSE: [CNODE01]: LCM:  [ End    Set      ]      [[WaitForAll]FCFeature]  in 60.0550 seconds.
VERBOSE: [CNODE01]: LCM:  [ End    Resource ]      [[WaitForAll]FCFeature]
VERBOSE: [CNODE01]: LCM:  [ Start  Resource ]      [[FailoverCluster]CreateCluster]
VERBOSE: [CNODE01]: LCM:  [ Start  Test     ]      [[FailoverCluster]CreateCluster]
VERBOSE: [CNODE01]:                                [[FailoverCluster]CreateCluster] Cluster does not exist while it should.
VERBOSE: [CNODE01]: LCM:  [ End    Test     ]      [[FailoverCluster]CreateCluster]  in 21.9210 seconds.
VERBOSE: [CNODE01]: LCM:  [ Start  Set      ]      [[FailoverCluster]CreateCluster]
VERBOSE: [CNODE01]:                                [[FailoverCluster]CreateCluster] Creating cluster.
VERBOSE: [CNODE01]:                                [[FailoverCluster]CreateCluster] No nodes specified. Creating a 1 node cluster on cnode01.
VERBOSE: [CNODE01]:                                [[FailoverCluster]CreateCluster] Adding static network 172.16.102.0/24.
```

Figure 11-6. *WaitForAll in action: resource is ready*

It is hard to have a good example for the WaitForX resources that applies to a generic scenario for a book like this. As with everything else, there is more than one way to achieve things with DSC, and one way might work better than the other depending on your specific situation and scenario. An alternate method is where the cluster nodes join the cluster on their own by using a functional resource validating the presence of the cluster instead of depending on WaitForX resources.

This concludes the example and discussion around the `WaitForAll` resource. For the next two resources, you won't see such a detailed example but you'll see how they can be used.

The WaitForAny Resource

The WaitForAny resource, shown in Table 11-1, can be used in a similar way as the WaitForAll resource except that the configuration will proceed even when one of the nodes being monitored achieves the desired state. Consider the example illustrated in Figure 11-7.

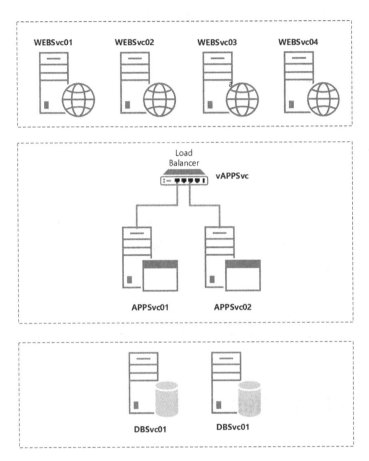

Figure 11-7. *Multi-tier application architecture*

As shown in Figure 11-7, a typical mulit-tier web application deployment has a front-end tier, an application tier, and the database tier. Each tier has one or more instances based on the need for high availability and redundancy. In this example, there are two application servers in the app tier behind a load balancer represented by virtual application instance called vAPPSvc.

If you were to configure this web application deployment using DSC, you would have to wait for the virtual application service instance to come up before the web server configuration could be modified. However, you just need to wait for one of the application servers to get deployed because the load balancer may already be configured to include the deployed application servers. This is where the WaitForAny resource comes handy. Here is a hypothetical example of what this resource configuration might look like:

```
WaitForAny ApplicationVApp
{
    NodeName = @('APPSvc01','APPSvc02')
    ResourceName = '[cAppService]AppServerInstall'
    RetryIntervalSec = 30
    RetryCount = 10
}
```

Note   As mentioned, this is just a hypothetical example and does not include a complete configuration document or any custom DSC resource modules created for the purpose of this example.

The above snippet is similar to what you saw with the WaitForAll example. By design, it will wait for any of the nodes to achieve the desired state and then proceed to the dependent configuration.

The WaitForSome Resource

With the WaitForSome resource, you can specify the number of nodes where the resource should achieve the desired state before the dependent configuration on the local node can be processed. This is done by adding the NodeCount property to the WaitForSome resource instance.

Here is another hypothetical example of how to use this resource:

```
WaitForSome ApplicationVApp
{
    NodeName = @('APPSrv01','APPSrv02')
    NodeCount = 1
    ResourceName = '[cAppService]AppServerInstall'
```

```
    RetryIntervalSec = 30
    RetryCount = 10
}
```

This example is similar to what you saw with the WaitForAny example except for the NodeCount property. By specifying the NodeCount as 1, you are specifying that the any dependent configuration on the local node should wait for one node to achieve the desired state before proceeding further.

What Happens Behind the Scenes?

You just saw examples for each of the resources that enable you to perform cross-node synchronization. However, how exactly do they work? What goes on behind the scenes?

The answer is in the resource module script (PSM1) files. If you follow the code in these scripts, you will see that these resources internally invoke the GetResourceState method in the MSFT_DSCProxy class in the root/Microsoft/Windows/DesiredStateConfigurationProxy namespace. See Figure 11-8.

```
Get-CimClass -Namespace root/Microsoft/Windows/DesiredStateConfigurationProxy
-ClassName MSFT_DscProxy |
    Select-Object -ExpandProperty CimClassMethods
```

```
PS C:\scripts> Get-CimClass -Namespace root/Microsoft/Windows/DesiredStateConfigurationProxy -ClassName MSFT_DscProxy |
    Select-Object -ExpandProperty CimClassMethods

Name                ReturnType Parameters                Qualifiers
----                ---------- ----------                ----------
GetResourceState       UInt32 {ConfigurationData, state} {Description, implemented, static}
```

Figure 11-8. *GetResourceState method*

Figure 11-9 shows the parameters available on this method.

```
PS C:\scripts> Get-CimClass -Namespace root/Microsoft/Windows/DesiredStateConfigurationProxy -ClassName MSFT_DscProxy |
    Select-Object -ExpandProperty CimClassMethods |
    Select-Object -ExpandProperty Parameters

Name              CimType Qualifiers            ReferenceClassName
----              ------- ----------            ------------------
ConfigurationData UInt8Array {ID, In, Octetstring}
state             Boolean {ID, Out}
```

Figure 11-9. *GetResourceState method parameters*

This method has only one input parameter: ConfigurationData. This is an Octet string or, in other words, a Base64-encoded string. You need to encode the resource ID that you specify as a value to the ResourceName property of any of the WaitForX resources and invoke theGetResourceState method.

Here is the excerpt from the resource module code that invokes this method. I modified it a bit to add some variables to try.

```
$resourceId = '[WindowsFeature]FailoverCluster'
$buf = [Text.Encoding]::Unicode.GetBytes($resourceId)
$data = [System.Convert]::ToBase64String($buf)

$computerName = 'S16-JB'

$result = Invoke-WSManAction -ResourceURI http://schemas.microsoft.com/
wbem/wsman/1/wmi/root/microsoft/windows/DesiredStateConfigurationProxy/
MSFT_DscProxy `
                -action GetResourceState -ComputerName $computerName
                -valueset @{ConfigurationData = "$data" } `
                -Authentication None
$result.State
```

Note   The broadcast resolving stops at the router so if you have a multi-tier app that spans multiple subnets, you probably need to specify your nodenames in the FQDN format.

In the first three lines of this snippet, you convert the resource ID [WindowsFeature] FailoverCluster to a Base64-encoded string. When the GetResourceState method is invoked with this encoded string, it returns either true or false based on the state of the resource on the target node.

This method uses a cache for retrieving the resource state and therefore it may not always be the current state of the resource. Here's an example to explain this:

```
Configuration AudioService
{
    Node S16-JB
    {
        Service AudioService
```

```
        {
            Name = 'AudioSrv'
            State = 'Running'
            Ensure = 'Present'

        }

    }

}
```

AudioService

Compile this configuration and enact it. This will set the Windows Audio service into a running state. Now, from a remote system, execute the GetResourceState method again, targeting the resource Id [Service]AudioService and have the computer name set to where the above configuration was enacted. See Figure 11-10.

```
PS C:\scripts> $resourceId = '[Service]AudioService'
$buf = [Text.Encoding]::Unicode.GetBytes($resourceId)
$data = [System.Convert]::ToBase64String($buf)

$computerName = 'S16-JB'

$result = Invoke-WSManAction -ResourceURI http://schemas.microsoft.com/wbem/wsman/1/wmi/root/microsoft/windows/DesiredStateC
                -action GetResourceState -ComputerName $computerName -valueset @{ConfigurationData = "$data" } `
                -Authentication None
$result.State
true
```

Figure 11-10. *GetResourceState right after an enact*

Now, stop the Windows Audio service on the node and then try GetResourceState again. It will still return true, indicating that the resource is in desired state, but it is not. This is because the GetResourceState method is using the LCM cache to retrieve the resource state instead of using Test-DscConfiguration. You can update the resource cache to include the current state of the resource by running the Test-DscConfiguration or wait for a consistency check to trigger.

This is by design and there is an open user voice item that I created. Read http://azrs.tk/dscissue for more information.

If you examine the code snippet that invokes the GetResourceState method, you will see that the –Authentication parameter is set to None. By doing so, the local WinRM client makes an anonymous request to the target node when invoking this method. The WinRM service, starting WMF 5.0, has been modified to allow a limited number of anonymous requests to a specific namespace and in this case the DesiredStateConfigurationProxy namespace.

Limitations

While cross-node synchronization looks like an attractive feature, the lack of community examples indicate that this feature is not widely used. The following are some reasons why. The WaitForX resources do not check the functional state of the resource. They only check if the resource is in the desired state or not. This was evident when you learned about the GetResourceState method. From the cluster example, WaitForAll will only wait until each node returns true for the WindowFeature resource. If the resource is buggy, it may return true even when the resource is not in the desired state and therefore may cause the node waiting on these configurations to proceed with the dependent configuration. However, in the very first example, you saw the xWaitForADDomain resource, which will indeed check if the domain is available or not. As this is a functional test, this could present a more reliable means for controlled and orchestrated configurations.

Personally, I have never had a reason to use the WaitForAny or WaitForSome resources, which is why I didn't present a full example for either. They could, however, be precisely what you need, which is why I attempted to describe them in as detailed a manner as I possibly could.

Summary

Cross-node synchronization lets you perform multi-node configurations in a cross-node dependent manner. The three resources meant for this purpose are WaitForAll, WaitForAny, and WaitForSome. The resource for a scenario depends on how many nodes should achieve the desired state. The underlying interface, GetResourceState, is implemented in the MSFT_DSCProxy class in the root/Microsoft/Windows/ DesiredStateConfigurationProxy namespace. By using cross-node synchronization it is possible to orchestrate a multi-tier application deployment.

CHAPTER 12

Debugging DSC Resources

In Chapter 7, you learned how to perform unit and integration tests of your custom DSC resources. Testing is a great way to ensure that the functionality you intend to build is indeed available and not broken. You saw in Chapter 9 how DSC debug and analytics logs can help you retrieve more information about DSC operations. However, there may be bugs that get introduced because of an environmental configuration where the resource module is being used or could just be a test miss. In this case, you need to use the available debugging techniques to root-cause the bug and fix it. DSC as a platform offers a way to debug resource modules while the enact is in progress. In this chapter, you will learn how to debug DSC resource module issues. This is going to be a quick one but I really suggest that you practice the debugging technique that you will learn with not just the simple example in this chapter but with a module of your own too. Let's get started.

Lab Requirements

To try the examples and exercises in this chapter, you will need at minimum two or more systems with Windows Server 2008 R2 or above with WMF 5.1 installed. I recommend a system with Windows Server 2016.

LCM DebugMode

All resource instance configuration enacting happens in the context of the LCM. By default, the LCM does not let you debug a resource enact process unless you configure it do so. Figure 12-1 shows the default value of the DebugMode setting in the LCM configuration.

© Ravikanth Chaganti 2018

R. Chaganti, *Pro PowerShell Desired State Configuration*, https://doi.org/10.1007/978-1-4842-3483-9_12

```
PS C:\> Get-DscLocalConfigurationManager


ActionAfterReboot                 : ContinueConfiguration
AgentId                           : 188DDA33-7F58-11E7-B424-00155D87B20A
AllowModuleOverwrite              : False
CertificateID                     :
ConfigurationDownloadManagers     : {}
ConfigurationID                   :
ConfigurationMode                 : ApplyAndMonitor
ConfigurationModeFrequencyMins    : 15
Credential                        :
DebugMode                         : {NONE}
```

Figure 12-1. *DebugMode in the LCM settings*

As shown in Figure 12-1, by default the DebugMode setting in the meta configuration is set to None. There are four possible values for this setting. This can be examined by using the GetCimClassProperty.ps1 script shown in earlier chapters.

.\GetCimClassProperty.ps1 -ClassName MSFT_DSCMetaConfiguration -Namespace root/microsoft/windows/desiredstateconfiguration |
            Select Name, CimType, AllowedValues

The allowed values for the DebugMode setting are shown in Figure 12-2 and explained in Table 12-1.

```
Name                           CimType AllowedValues
----                           ------- -------------
ActionAfterReboot               String {ContinueConfiguration, StopConfiguration}
AgentId                         String
AllowModuleOverwrite           Boolean
CertificateID                   String
ConfigurationDownloadManagers InstanceArray
ConfigurationID                 String
ConfigurationMode               String {ApplyOnly, ApplyAndMonitor, ApplyAndAutoCorrect}
ConfigurationModeFrequencyMins  UInt32
Credential                    Instance                                              |
DebugMode                  StringArray {None, ForceModuleImport, All, ResourceScriptBreakAll}
DownloadManagerCustomData InstanceArray
```

Figure 12-2. *Allowed values of DebugMode settings*

Table 12-1. *DebugMode Settings*

DebugMode Setting	Description
None	Default value and does not allow breaking into a running DSC resource script.
ForceModuleImport	Specifies that the resource module should be reloaded before enact.
ResourceScriptBreakAll	Specifies that the LCM should enable breaking into a resource script during enact.
All	Same as ForceModuleImport. In the preview releases of WMF 5.0, this was used to enable both debugging and forced module import.

On a production system, the DebugMode setting should always be the default value, which is None since production systems should always run validated code and resources only. ForceModuleImport, All, and ResourceScriptBreakAll are useful when authoring resource modules and/or debugging issues related to the configuration enact process on target nodes.

Note   Although Figure 12-2 lists ResourceScriptBreakAll as a valid allowed value for DebugMode, setting this using a meta configuration script is not allowed.

Since ResourceScriptBreakAll cannot be set using a meta configuration document, only forced module import can be configured using a meta MOF. This can be done either by setting the DebugMode value to All or ForceModuleImport.

The DebugMode can be set manually using a meta configuration document. Here is a sample meta configuration document that shows setting DebugMode to All:

```
[DSCLocalConfigurationManager()]

Configuration DebugSetting
{
    Settings
    {
        DebugMode = 'All'
    }
}
```

DebugSetting

```
Set-DscLocalConfigurationManager -Path DebugSetting
```

To set the DebugMode value to ResourceScriptBreakAll or, in other words, to configure the LCM to break into the resource scripts while enacting, you should use the Enable-DscDebug cmdlet:

```
Enable-DscDebug -BreakAll -Verbose
```

The Enable-DscDebug cmdlet does an incremental change of the DebugMode setting. So, if you have the DebugMode already set to All, it will only add ResourceScriptBrealAll.

The LCM configuration after this cmdlet execution is shown in Figure 12-3.

```
PS C:\Scripts> Get-DscLocalConfigurationManager


ActionAfterReboot                   : ContinueConfiguration
AgentId                             : 188DDA33-7F58-11E7-B424-00155D87B20A
AllowModuleOverWrite                : False
CertificateID                       :
ConfigurationDownloadManagers       : {}
ConfigurationID                     :
ConfigurationMode                   : ApplyOnly
ConfigurationModeFrequencyMins      : 15
Credential                          :
DebugMode                           : {All, ResourceScriptBreakAll}
DownloadManagerCustomData           :
```

Figure 12-3. *Meta configuration after Enable-DscDebug*

Before you get to the debugging of DSC resource modules/scripts, let's first look into the need for the ForceModuleImport and All values of the DebugMode setting.

Forcing Module Import

For performance reasons, the LCM caches the resource modules loaded during the configuration enact process. So, any enact that uses the same resource module will not have to reload the resource module from disk. This is a useful feature since the module import can be an expensive operation. However, when you are authoring DSC resource modules and testing the functionality, there is a chance that the changes you make to the resource modules may not get loaded as you would expect because the resource still in the cache is used instead of the modified version. To address this need, the DebugMode setting can be configured to force resource module import always.

Note   When using WMF 4.0, you need to restart the WMI host process where the DSC LCM provider is loaded to ensure that the LCM loads the updated resource module.

This seems like a useful feature but how do you test this behavior?

Ok! Let's start with LCM DebugMode in its default setting:

```
[DSCLocalConfigurationManager()]

Configuration DebugSetting
{
    Settings
    {
        DebugMode = 'None'
    }
}

DebugSetting

Set-DscLocalConfigurationManager -Path DebugSetting
```

Download and extract the ForceModuleImportDemo.zip from this chapter's source code to the C:\ProgramFiles\WindowsPowerShell\Modules folder as ForceModuleImportDemo.

Note   You may want to review the resource module script before you proceed to the configuration. I have deliberately created a buggy Test-TargetResource function.

Now, compile the following configuration and try an enact:

```
Configuration ForceModuleImportDemo
{
    Import-DscResource -Module ForceModuleImportDemo

    Node localhost
    {
        ForceModuleImport Demo
        {
```

```
        DummyKey = "DSC is fun!"
    }
  }
}
```

ForceModuleImportDemo

When you enact this, you will see an error, as shown in Figure 12-4.

```
PS C:\> Start-DscConfiguration -Path .\ForceModuleImportDemo -Wait -Verbose -Force
VERBOSE: Perform operation 'Invoke CimMethod' with following parameters, ''methodNa
me' = SendConfigurationApply,'className' = MSFT_DSCLocalConfigurationManager,'names
paceName' = root/Microsoft/Windows/DesiredStateConfiguration'.
VERBOSE: An LCM method call arrived from computer S16-JB with user sid S-1-5-21-689
661094-3032901192-2251061677-500.
VERBOSE: [S16-JB]: LCM:  [ Start  Set      ]
VERBOSE: [S16-JB]: LCM:  [ Start  Resource ]  [[ForceModuleImport]Demo]
VERBOSE: [S16-JB]: LCM:  [ Start  Test     ]  [[ForceModuleImport]Demo]
VERBOSE: [S16-JB]: LCM:  [ End    Test     ]  [[ForceModuleImport]Demo]  in 0.0310
seconds.
The PowerShell DSC resource C:\Program Files\WindowsPowerShell\Modules\ForceModule
ImportDemo\DscResources\ForceModuleImport returned results in a format that is
not valid. The results from running Test-TargetResource must be the boolean value
True or False.
    + CategoryInfo          : InvalidResult: (:) [], CimException
    + FullyQualifiedErrorId : TestTargetResourceInvalidResultFormat
    + PSComputerName        : localhost
```

Figure 12-4. *Test-TargetResource bug*

Now that you know what the error is, just open up ForceModuleImport.psm1 from the Module folder and update the Test-TargetResource function with the working definition:

```
function Test-TargetResource
{
    param
    (
        [Parameter(Mandatory = $true)]
        [String]
        $DummyKey
    )

    return $false
}
```

With this updated module script, try the enact again. What do you see? The same error that Test-TargetResource returned results in an invalid format?

To force the module import, let's configure DebugMode to the ForceModuleImport setting:

```
[DSCLocalConfigurationManager()]

Configuration DebugSetting
{
    Settings
    {
        DebugMode = 'ForceModuleImport'
    }
}

DebugSetting

Set-DscLocalConfigurationManager -Path DebugSetting
```

Note   If your intention is not to debug the DSC resource scripts, don't use Enable-DscDebug. It will break into the resource script and leave the LCM in debug mode.

Try an enact of the configuration again and see if the enact completes with no error messages. Once you are done with this example, don't forget to set the DebugMode back to None.

Debugging the DSC Resource Script

To demonstrate the method to debug DSC resources, you will use a buggy resource module. I have introduced one bug. You can copy BuggyResource.zip from the source code of this chapter and extract it to C:\Program Files\WindowsPowerShell\Modules folder as BuggyResource. This contains a BuggyHostsFile resource.

First, try to compile and enact the following configuration:

```
Configuration DebugDemo
{
    Import-DscResource -ModuleName BuggyResource -Name BuggyHostsFile

    BuggyHostsFile BugDebug
    {
        HostName = 'TestServer11'
        IPAddress = '10.10.10.11'
        Ensure = 'Present'
    }
}

DebugDemo
```

A result of this enact is shown in Figure 12-5.

```
PS C:\Scripts> Start-DscConfiguration -Path .\DebugDemo -Wait -Verbose -Force
VERBOSE: Perform operation 'Invoke CimMethod' with following parameters, ''methodName' = SendConfiguration
Apply,'className' = MSFT_DSCLocalConfigurationManager,'namespaceName' = root/Microsoft/Windows/DesiredStat
eConfiguration'.
VERBOSE: An LCM method call arrived from computer S16-JB with user sid S-1-5-21-689661094-3032901192-22510
61677-500.
VERBOSE: [S16-JB]: LCM:  [ Start  Set      ]
VERBOSE: [S16-JB]: LCM:  [ Start  Resource ]  [[BuggyHostsFile]BugDebug]
VERBOSE: [S16-JB]: LCM:  [ Start  Test     ]  [[BuggyHostsFile]BugDebug]
VERBOSE: [S16-JB]:                             [[BuggyHostsFile]BugDebug] Checking if the hosts file entry
exists.
VERBOSE: [S16-JB]:                             [[BuggyHostsFile]BugDebug] Did not find a hosts file entry f
or TestServer11 and 10.10.10.11.
VERBOSE: [S16-JB]: LCM:  [ End    Test     ]  [[BuggyHostsFile]BugDebug]  in 0.0160 seconds.
VERBOSE: [S16-JB]: LCM:  [ Start  Set      ]  [[BuggyHostsFile]BugDebug]
VERBOSE: [S16-JB]:                             [[BuggyHostsFile]BugDebug] Creating a hosts file entry with
TestServer11 and 10.10.10.11.
VERBOSE: [S16-JB]: LCM:  [ End    Set      ]  [[BuggyHostsFile]BugDebug]  in 0.0310 seconds.
VERBOSE: [S16-JB]: LCM:  [ End    Resource ]  [[BuggyHostsFile]BugDebug]
VERBOSE: [S16-JB]: LCM:  [ End    Set      ]
VERBOSE: [S16-JB]: LCM:  [ End    Set      ]   in  0.1250 seconds.
VERBOSE: Operation 'Invoke CimMethod' complete.
VERBOSE: Time taken for configuration job to complete is 0.166 seconds
```

***Figure 12-5.** Enact of a buggy resource*

Once this enact is complete, try the same one more time. You will see that the resource tries to add the resource again. You will see the same output as in Figure 12-5, but it should have skipped the Set method completely. So, let's debug this.

> **Note**   This example is meant to show you how to initiate a debugging session; it's not a demonstration of complex issue debugging.

As you have learned already, enabling the LCM to break into the resource script can be done using the Enable-DscDebug cmdlet. If the target node where you are seeing the resource configuration issue is a remote node, you can use the -CimSession parameter of the Enable-DscDebug cmdlet to remotely enable DSC resource script debugging on target nodes.

```
Enable-DscDebug -CimSession S16-01, S16-02 -BreakAll -Verbose
```

Using Get-DscLocalConfigurationManager against these nodes shows the new value set on DebugMode in the meta configuration.

```
Get-DscLocalConfigurationManager -CimSession S16-01, S16-02 | Select-Object
-Property DebugMode
```

Figure 12-6 shows the output of this command.

```
PS C:\> Get-DscLocalConfigurationManager -CimSession S16-01, S16-02

DebugMode
---------
{ForceModuleImport, ResourceScriptBreakAll}
{ForceModuleImport, ResourceScriptBreakAll}
```

Figure 12-6.   *DebugMode on target nodes after Enable-DscDebug*

> **Note**   For class-based resource debugging, the system where you want to enact/debug the class resource must be running WMF 5.1 or above. Class resource debugging in WMF 5.0 is not very clean and requires multiple step-ins before it hits the method.

The DSC resource script debugging leverages the PowerShell remote script debugging feature. Therefore, it is important that remote nodes have PowerShell remoting enabled for this to work. If the remote systems do not have PowerShell remoting enabled, you can enable the same using the Enable-PSRemoting cmdlet. If you are trying the DSC resource debugging on a remote node, this chapter assumes that you have PowerShell remoting enabled on the remote node and all systems are domain-joined.

Note   If you are using a remote system for working on the exercises in this section, ensure that the custom DSC resource module in `BuggyResource.zip` is extracted to the remote systems as well.

Once the debug is enabled in the LCM, try the enact of the above configuration again. You will see what is shown in Figure 12-7.

```
VERBOSE: [S16-JB]:                              [DSCEngine] Importing the module C:\Program Files\WindowsPow
erShell\Modules\BuggyResource\BuggyResource.psd1 in force mode.
VERBOSE: [S16-JB]: LCM:  [ Start  Resource ]  [[BuggyHostsFile]BugDebug]
VERBOSE: [S16-JB]: LCM:  [ Start  Test     ]  [[BuggyHostsFile]BugDebug]
VERBOSE: [S16-JB]:                              [[BuggyHostsFile]BugDebug] Importing the module BuggyResourc
e in force mode.
WARNING: [S16-JB]:                              [[BuggyHostsFile]BugDebug] Resource is waiting for PowerShel
l script debugger to attach.  Use the following commands to begin debugging this resource script:
Enter-PSSession -ComputerName S16-JB -Credential <credentials>
Enter-PSHostProcess -Id 2404 -AppDomainName DscPsPluginWkr_AppDomain
Debug-Runspace -Id 4
```

Figure 12-7. *Partial output from the enact after Debug is enabled*

You can see that the LCM suspends the enact process and provides instructions to attach the debugger to the host process where the enact is running. At this point in time, open PowerShell ISE as administrator and start executing the following commands:

Note   Opening ISE as administrator is important. If you don't do so, you will see an access denied error.

```
Enter-PSSession -ComputerName S16-JB
Enter-PSHostProcess -Id 2404 -AppDomainName DscPsPluginWkr_AppDomain
Debug-Runspace -Id 4
```

Note   The last two commands on your system will be different from what you see here. Ensure that you have the right arguments as shown in the output of the enact.

Once you complete the running of the last command, `Debug-RunSpace`, the remote resource script will open in the ISE editor, ready for you start stepping into the script.

At this point, step into the script by pressing F11 or s at the command line. Step into until the $entryExist variable is assigned a value (line 39). At this point, check if there is a match found by examining the value of $entryExist. This variable won't have any value, essentially indicating that no match is found for "$($this.IPAddress)\s+$($this.HostName)" which would translate to '10.10.10.11 TestServer11' with at least one space between the IP address and hostname. Figure 12-8 shows that $entryExist has an empty value during the debug session.

```
PowerShell 1   PowerShell 2 X

[Remote File] BuggyResource.psm1 [Read Only] X

21 ⊟{
22          [DscProperty(Key)]
23          [String]
24          $HostName
25
26          [DscProperty(Mandatory = $true)]
27          [String]
28          $IPAddress
29
30          [DscProperty()]
31          [ValidateSet('Present','Absent')]
32          [String]
33          $Ensure
34
35          [Bool] Test()
36 ⊟       {
37              Write-Verbose -Message $Script:localizedData
38              $content = Get-Content "${env:windir}\system
39              $entryExist = ($content -match "^\s*$($this.
40              if ($this.E⌐            ┐sure]::Present)
41 ⊟           {            $entryExist =
                            ‥ ‥        ‥ ‥
```

Figure 12-8. *No match found in the hosts file*

This leads us to what the Set method might be doing since that is where the hosts file entry is getting added. This is done on line 70. While adding the entry, you must inject the space between the IP address and host name. Closely examining this line tells you that the tab that you intend to inject between these values isn't really being added since there is a '`'' missing to escape the tab.

Therefore, fixing this line will resolve the Set issue. At this point, stop debugging by pressing Ctrl+C and typing exit at the command prompt.

In the `BuggyResource.psm1`, update line 69 to the following:

`$hostEntry = "`n$($this.IPAddress)`t$($this.HostName)"`

Once this update is complete, clean up the hosts file to ensure old and buggy entries are removed. Also, ensure that you disable DSC debug using the `Disable-DscDebug` command and retry the enact twice. The first time, `Set` gets called and does the hosts file update. The second, or re-enact, will now point that the entry exists and skip the Set method. This is shown in Figure 12-9.

```
PS C:\Scripts> Start-DscConfiguration -Path .\DebugDemo -Wait -Verbose -Force
VERBOSE: Perform operation 'Invoke CimMethod' with following parameters, ''methodName' = SendConfi
amespaceName' = root/Microsoft/Windows/DesiredStateConfiguration'.
VERBOSE: An LCM method call arrived from computer S16-JB with user sid S-1-5-21-689661094-30329011
VERBOSE: [S16-JB]: LCM:  [ Start  Set     ]
VERBOSE: [S16-JB]:                          [DSCEngine] Importing the module C:\Program Files\Wi
e mode.
VERBOSE: [S16-JB]: LCM:  [ Start  Resource ]  [[BuggyHostsFile]BugDebug]
VERBOSE: [S16-JB]: LCM:  [ Start  Test     ]  [[BuggyHostsFile]BugDebug]
VERBOSE: [S16-JB]:                             [[BuggyHostsFile]BugDebug] Importing the module Bugg
VERBOSE: [S16-JB]:                             [[BuggyHostsFile]BugDebug] Checking if the hosts fil
VERBOSE: [S16-JB]:                             [[BuggyHostsFile]BugDebug] Found a hosts file entry
VERBOSE: [S16-JB]: LCM:  [ End    Test     ]  [[BuggyHostsFile]BugDebug]  in 0.0470 seconds.
VERBOSE: [S16-JB]: LCM:  [ Skip   Set      ]  [[BuggyHostsFile]BugDebug]
VERBOSE: [S16-JB]: LCM:  [ End    Resource ]  [[BuggyHostsFile]BugDebug]
VERBOSE: [S16-JB]: LCM:  [ End    Set      ]
VERBOSE: [S16-JB]: LCM:  [ End    Set      ]     in  0.2500 seconds.
VERBOSE: Operation 'Invoke CimMethod' complete.
```

Figure 12-9. *The enact after the module is fixed*

This method of debugging resource modules applies to both MOF and class-based resources. What you have seen here is only the foundation of debugging DSC resources. In fact, you need to try the method that you just learned in a live debugging session to gain full experience. I encourage you to try this with a few more DSC resource modules. However, remember that you cannot ask or configure the LCM to break only for a certain DSC resource module. So, if you have a configuration resource, you will see that the debugger gets triggered every time a resource needs to get enacted. This can be avoided by using the `Invoke-DscResource` cmdlet to debug only the specific resource you are interested in. This saves a lot of time when debugging configurations that involve multiple resources.

Summary

In this chapter, you learned how to configure the LCM to force a module import and break into a DSC resource module when debugging a resource script issue. When developing DSC resource modules, you always need a near-perfect test plan for both unit and integration. You saw this implemented as a set of Pester test scripts along with a few other testing techniques in Chapter 7. However, a perfectly tested DSC resource module does not necessarily mean that there are no bugs. There may be hidden bugs that will surface only in a certain environment. This is where the debugging technique you learned in this chapter will help you.

CHAPTER 13

Security in DSC

In Chapter 5, you learned how to secure credentials or other sensitive data such as API keys in a DSC configuration document. This ensures that passwords and other sensitive strings are encrypted in the compiled configuration MOF to anyone reading it. You also saw, as a part of the configuration life cycle in Chapter 3, that once the enact completes successfully, the enacted configuration gets stored as `current.mof` in the `C:\Windows\System32\Configuration` folder. In this chapter, you will learn how DSC secures the MOF documents at rest in the local configuration store and how you can ensure that the LCM enacts only trusted configurations and uses only trusted resource modules.

Lab Requirements

To try the examples and exercises in this chapter, you will need at minimum two or more systems with Windows Server 2008 R2 or above with WMF 5.1 installed. I recommend a system with Windows Server 2016. The configuration and module signing requires a code signing certificate, so you will need a certificate authority or a self-signed certificate in order to try the examples in the signature validation section.

Configuration Encryption

Securing configuration documents is not just about encrypting the credentials and other sensitive strings in it. The configuration documents describe a blueprint of the configuration on the system where they are enacted. Therefore, we must consider the contents of the entire MOF as sensitive information. Prior to WMF 5.0, there was no way to encrypt the MOFs present in the local configuration store of a node. Even if you could encrypt it yourself, the LCM had no way to decrypt the contents for the purposes of a consistency check and the no-demand current state check using the `Get-DscConfiguration` cmdlet. Without any encryption for these configuration MOF files,

© Ravikanth Chaganti 2018

R. Chaganti, *Pro PowerShell Desired State Configuration*, https://doi.org/10.1007/978-1-4842-3483-9_13

anyone with access to the local configuration store could open it on the same node or
transfer it to another node to read the contents of the MOF and maybe enact the same
MOF elsewhere.

To address these security concerns, WMF 5.0 and above encrypt the MOFs at rest in
the local configuration store. This behavior is neither configurable nor is it something
that we can enable or disable. There are no certificates needed for this encryption since
it uses the Windows Data Protection API (DPAPI). This encryption of the MOFs in the
local configuration store can be considered security through obscurity; you will learn
more about this later in the chapter. Remember that the configuration MOF generated by
compiling a configuration document is not encrypted. It gets encrypted only when this
MOF gets published as a pending configuration or gets enacted and stored in the local
configuration store. Figure 13-1 illustrates this.

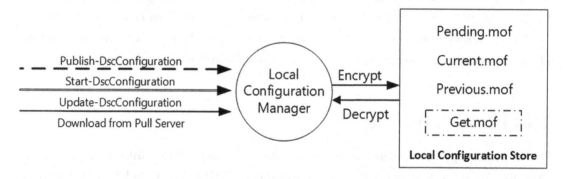

Figure 13-1. *MOF encryption in the local configuration store*

The DSC pull service available in WMF 4.0 and above does not encrypt the MOF files at
rest. This is one of the reasons why you should avoid using PSDscAllowPlainTextPassword
in the DSC configuration data to force the use of plain-text passwords. The Azure
Automation DSC service discussed in Chapter 17 encrypts MOF files at rest.

To experiment with this, compile the following configuration and publish to a target
node using the Publish-DscConfiguration cmdlet:

```
Configuration DemoWebServer
{
    Import-DscResource -ModuleName PSDesiredStateConfiguration
    -ModuleVersion 1.1

    Node S16-01
```

```
    {
        WindowsFeature DemoWebServer
        {
            Name = 'Web-Server'
            IncludeAllSubFeature = $true
            Ensure = 'Present'
        }
    }
}
```

```
DemoWebServer -OutputPath .\DemoWebServer
Publish-DscConfiguration -Path .\DemoWebServer -Verbose
```

After the configuration is published, try to read the contents of the pending.mof on the target node.

```
Get-Content -Path '\\S16-01\C$\Windows\System32\configuration\pending.mof'
```

As shown in Figure 13-2, all you will see when reading a MOF file from the target node configuration store is encrypted text. This pending.mof can only be enacted on the target node where it was received by the LCM and encrypted. You can copy this to a different or local system and try the Start-DscConfiguration cmdlet with the -UseExisting switch, like so:

```
Copy-Item -Path '\\S16-01\C$\Windows\System32\configuration\pending.mof'
-Destination C:\Windows\System32\Configuration\Pending.mof
```

```
Start-DscConfiguration -UseExisting -Force -Verbose -Wait
```

```
PS C:\scripts> Get-Content -Path '\\S16-01\C$\Windows\System32\configuration\pending.mof'
     ÐŒßÑŒz ÀOÂ-ë    5°þ7úkF¾. Zòé        f          KYÖöìàÓiá-•b$gfþ5Íþ}o
+¾Ò÷oa    €         × Þüf    ENc-_ãSÜ« ûiá‹y®Bè{+EB    µMôÍê@ˆ!§ö•å Mdàde»€>–W!ËöW>=¢¾KáÚÄz!
õ]õˆ9ë'%Y Ì À &Z#yª.y%°"_«#†UX-p[[!ƒÀ³ŽAeÉÁÇ„ù^š6ÏÍA-ëï‹k†‹‡/ÄŠ'P62þþŸï¿ˆ»Q)ÝÆ  s*²À= »àãi
ý¹"""–‡|O"b!ÏæPá,sv XìR«7Ó]†']°"Û‡NkŠ([4ü'9ÚšUo¤"j™*Ì§éF'Ñ,ä¢þ; Kˆ0šˆæ&9‹ÊÒ÷wCˆ,Ø)×¶$^åaÕ3
%èÇÇrCBÂä ÷é{ßŒ"Ž>Û
PšÚí%~éX"~%K7°%Ž1o- ,»3t‹§néZSL)·~‡Z£RÖ‹ `øæ_)°VëØT%êdþ'…älDm}>‡fºB'ö_dä-h¿=¡RÈ/Ð1dQWÿÃ%.}!
mÄþþþfrá¿Qñ«"Œ
ï‹³qì,ÿÙ1ÓÁŒ-éÝÀ]_µ¤ñäÈ-SÎç·a@™úŠ"ØéAo5…«ÝÆcàAÀRåu-õ (Ùò'š~KG¾F9-@Ðm»r¦ë@\j&Gó!y"@=…Ó‡æ9>
³vÌû~Êí)'™ ç+ð\^õ$%¯põ²oË"=Á]'-£Vç™[ë8kN}ßÛGúFèÔHK%¦Kãì´ó>þlv"6³Úã.ù-) ðWY- *4J]ÝóAlâ:#ƒ
;¶³|•   µW™÷Š9ÃVÀ:h'ê'}6+¢ë!È^¦.ÝòÂ-ãZˆÕP;1Q×Oƒµ'=*m||Ì"NÆÚ->ÀÚÙu\µ²‹óÛî%Bï„ë€ÚB
ÜÁ†ÇÂS"ÈæA¦‹ïD &ï¿\¥Ýn[45f"ØØÌÏÛK ^¤Â§… á«÷A@ÂFëÀP¾÷îþÀF" Ï¿+ð„twjþð(~
Û}mÂR%Í÷NC|Ç"¬-oaåêX1¥s¨ïæ}óc2}•pm%(ÑŒ^…ÕÐÝ¡ßŠÃî³ñ{ð µ=G™ÿµ³†§§XbH $öSÕIgÀ÷T;Û¡ˆ[9Ý^ÿ:Ç32
7í¾fž¬a,>¿Õ×ñÕpèÚXhÿZ\ËwäÞT m³+UZ9uò•T¿þ ÃM¾&‡ÿ'o®÷ßO¾Ø%«g{äÈü?
,Ž_/é?"V!M
Â-Q!q‹'Ñˆ5'0-{ã¡Œ±‡Ë¬µ!b    Ô-f³»‹pÞE6ØM>äjÜÿ·®;gT-63æ¾zI    mÂÀRr°YLåG9ˆ[ø÷‹P¿?~˜Ê,‹eôðW‹'
(é-‹3wõ%rM(¨kó _±™ÔÎþ(K+¦Îa:µsÙ$%Q$/
á€ù%Õxe™%1BP¾ˆmeCs ´z®FÅoœ>N˜Í·:˜µ§&ìq=vV    J…ã0&"´šÕ±ì\òT$ÛoÔsü0„²Ð×7|UØsh¬²~4YtÄËj¢à×ÿ[
º¦ÿwDn˜Jí8\>º'¡UÉ%×èì
0¿íæ](× á `Yƒ}6=~'!¨!wçÐ.ØÏ\ö8c;FÃcæoÅkÈ÷vr, rz7pý4Ð,«œúâ€Çþzg¬´$>Š;3Ã ‡&YÿZWÖ§Ûƒ%x"K¬¾÷ä!
ÎØ&Ì¢¢«GNÖC!B]¯ößþV¹¾ÑTŽá ú@Ä+h¬jd$
```

Figure 13-2. *Contents of the encrypted pending.mof*

Figure 13-3 shows that a local enact of an encrypted pending MOF from a different node fails because the LCM cannot decrypt it.

```
PS C:\scripts> Start-DscConfiguration -UseExisting -Force -Verbose -Wait
VERBOSE: Perform operation 'Invoke CimMethod' with following parameters, ''methodName' = ApplyConfigurat
t/Microsoft/Windows/DesiredStateConfiguration'.
VERBOSE: An LCM method call arrived from computer S16-JB with user sid S-1-5-21-2403796847-1381111412-25
VERBOSE: [S16-JB]:                          [] Starting consistency engine.
VERBOSE: [S16-JB]:            |             [] A pending configuration exists. DSC will process a set
VERBOSE: [S16-JB]:                          [] Consistency check completed.
Syntax Error. Number value is not valid: empty number string
 At line:1, char:0
 Buffer:
^?
 LCM failed to start desired state configuration manually.
    + CategoryInfo          : SyntaxError: (root/Microsoft/...gurationManager:String) [], CimException
    + FullyQualifiedErrorId : MiClientApiError_Failed
    + PSComputerName        : localhost

VERBOSE: Operation 'Invoke CimMethod' complete.
VERBOSE: Time taken for configuration job to complete is 0.102 seconds
```

Figure 13-3. *The LCM fails to decrypt*

From Figure 13-3, it may not be really obvious that the LCM failed to decrypt the MOF but the error during enact is essentially due to that. This is because the MOF was encrypted using a key on the target node that is not available on the local node for decryption.

Try the following: compile any configuration to a MOF file, rename the MOF to Pending.mof, and copy it to the local node configuration store. Do you see it encrypted? No, it won't get encrypted. This action is performed outside the LCM scope and so the LCM will not encrypt. Also, once this manually copied configuration is enacted, the current.mof in the configuration store will not be in an encrypted form as well. This is why you need to use the Publish-DscConfiguration cmdlet to publish the pending configuration or use Start-DscConfiguration with the -Path parameter to send the pending configuration, which gets encrypted and then enacted right after that.

What you have seen secures the MOF at rest in the local configuration store of a node. If a user has access to a node's configuration store to copy the encrypted MOF file, that user can also decrypt the MOF contents since the keys used to encrypt that MOF are locally available and can be accessed using the DPAPI.

So, how can you prevent the LCM from even receiving and enacting a configuration that is not trusted? Also, imagine another scenario where you have a pull server that is used to stage compiled configuration MOF files and resource modules. Let's say that this server is compromised. In such a scenario, an attacker can modify the configuration MOF files and resource modules stored on the pull server and therefore compromise all target nodes that receive either configuration MOFs and/or resource modules from this pull server.

With WMF 5.1 and above, the LCM can be configured to receive and enact only signed configuration documents. Let's see how this is done.

Signature Validation

It should be nothing new that PowerShell supports an execution policy that can be used to ensure that only signed PowerShell scripts can be executed. For example, when you set the execution policy to AllSigned, PowerShell expects that the script you are running is signed using a trusted code signing certificate with the objective of ensuring the integrity of the script content. With WMF 5.1 and above, this known method of signing scripts is extended to configuration documents and resource modules as well. In this section, you will learn the process of signing configurations and resource modules and then you will configure the LCM to perform signature validation so that the untrusted configurations are not enacted and untrusted resource modules are not used during the enact process.

Signing a Certificate

Before you can sign configuration documents or resource modules, you will need a code signing certificate. I recommend that you use a trusted certificate authority or the PKI in your organization obtain these certificates or a PKI that you set up for demo purpose or you can use self-signed certificates, as shown below:

```
$certPath = 'C:\Certificates\ProDscSignature.cer'

if (-Not (Test-Path -Path (Split-Path -Path $certPath -Parent)))
{
    $null = New-Item -Path C:\Certificates -ItemType Directory -Force
}

$cert = New-SelfSignedCertificate -Subject 'ProDscSignature' -Type
CodeSigning -CertStoreLocation Cert:\CurrentUser\My
$cert | Export-Certificate -FilePath $certPath
Import-Certificate -FilePath $certPath -CertStoreLocation Cert:\
CurrentUser\Root\
```

This code snippet helps create a self-signed code signing certificate. Once you have a code signing certificate, export the public key and save it a local folder on the authoring station where you will be signing configurations and resource modules. The last command, `Import-Certificate`, prompts you if you really want to install the certificate. You need to click Yes.

The exported public key file should be imported on the target nodes before the LCM can be configured to use that for signature validation. Here is how to do so:

```
foreach ($node in 'S16-01','S16-02')
{
    $session = New-PSSession -ComputerName $node
    $certPath = 'C:\Certificates\ProDscSignature.cer'
    $certStore = 'Cert:\LocalMachine\DSCStore'

    Invoke-Command -Session $session -ScriptBlock {
            #Create Certifcates folder
            $certFolder = 'C:\Certificates'
            if (-not (Test-Path -Path $certFolder))
            {
```

```
            $null = New-Item -Path $certFolder -ItemType Directory
        }

        #Create DSC Store
        if (-not ($using:certStore))
        {
            $null = New-Item -Path $using:certStore -ItemType Directory
        }
    }

    #Copy the public key to target node
    Copy-Item -Path $certPath -ToSession $session -Destination $certPath
    -Force

    #Import the certificate
    Invoke-Command -Session $session -ScriptBlock {
        Import-Certificate -FilePath $using:certPath -CertStoreLocation
        Cert:\LocalMachine\Root\
        Import-Certificate -FilePath $using:certPath -CertStoreLocation
        $using:certStore
    }
}
```

This code snippet assumes that you have remoting enabled on the target nodes to be able to copy the public key and invoke the Import-Certificatecmdlet. Also, note that in this example you are creating a custom certificate store called DSCStore to store the code signing certificate. A custom store is not mandatory but helps organize the certificates used with DSC into a separate store.

Once this is complete, you can move on to configuring the LCM for signature validation.

Note   Since you are using self-signed certificates, you need to import the certificate into both the trusted root and the custom store. The LCM, by default, checks the Windows trusted publisher store for the code signing certificate. If you are using the code signing certificate from a trusted publisher and not a self-signed certificate, then importing the certificate to the custom store is good enough.

The LCM Configuration for Signature Validation

You have seen several examples of performing the meta configuration already in this book. In Chapter 3, you looked at the different properties of the MSFT_ DSCMetaConfiguration class, and the SignatureValidations property of this class is represented by the MSFT_SignatureValidation CIM class in the DSC namespace. You can examine the MSFT_SignatureValidation class further to see what properties are needed.

```
.\getCimClassProperty.ps1 -ClassName MSFT_SignatureValidation -Namespace
root/Microsoft/Windows/DesiredStateConfiguration | ft
```

The output from the above command is shown in Figure 13-4.

Name	CimType	EmbeddedInstanceOf	IsReadyOnly	AllowedValues	IsKey
ResourceId	String		False		False
SourceInfo	String		False		False
SignedItemType	StringArray		False	{Configuration, Module}	False
TrustedStorePath	String		False		False

Figure 13-4. *MSFT_SignatureValidation CIM class*

The ResourceId and SourceInfo properties are internal and need not be specified as a part of the meta configuration. The TrustedStorePath property is used to specify where the code signing certificate exists and the SignedItemType specifies if the LCM should validate signatures of configurations or modules or both.

With this knowledge, here is the meta configuration document for the target nodes:

```
[DSCLocalConfigurationManager()]
Configuration LCMSignatureValidation
{
    param
    (
        [Parameter(Mandatory = $true)]
        [String]
        $CertificateStore,

        [Parameter(Mandatory = $true)]
        [String[]]
        $Nodes
    )
```

```
foreach ($node in $Nodes)
{
    Node $node
    {
        SignatureValidation LCMSignatureValidation
        {
            TrustedStorePath = $CertificateStore
            SignedItemType = 'Configuration', 'Module'
        }
    }
}
}

LCMSignatureValidation -Nodes @('S16-01','S16-02') -CertificateStore
'Cert:\LocalMachine\DSCStore'
```

You can compile and enact this meta configuration. Once the enact is complete, you can verify the LCM meta configuration using the Get-DscLocalConfigurationManager cmdlet, like so:

```
(Get-DscLocalConfigurationManager -CimSession 'S16-01','S16-02').
SignatureValidations
```

The output of this command is shown in Figure 13-5.

```
ResourceId        : [SignatureValidation]LCMSignatureValidation
SourceInfo        : ::19::13::SignatureValidation
SignedItemType    : {Configuration, Module}
TrustedStorePath  : Cert:\LocalMachine\DSCStore
PSComputerName    : S16-01

ResourceId        : [SignatureValidation]LCMSignatureValidation
SourceInfo        : ::19::13::SignatureValidation
SignedItemType    : {Configuration, Module}
TrustedStorePath  : Cert:\LocalMachine\DSCStore
PSComputerName    : S16-02
```

Figure 13-5. *Signature validation meta configuration*

413

Signature validation for a configuration is performed only during a completely new enact. It is not performed when executing commands like Test-DscConfiguration cmdlet or Get-DscConfiguration or Start-DscConfiguration with -UseExisting. You can verify this by executing any of these cmdlets on a system that is configured for signature validation and with an existing current configuration. In these scenarios, it is assumed that the MOFs in the local configuration store are already trusted. With the MOF encryption method that you just learned about, there is no way one can tamper with the MOF and enact it again.

Note   As mentioned, this method does not prevent an administrator from copying an unencrypted pending MOF into the local configuration store and enacting it. The configuration signing is used to ensure the integrity of the compiled configuration. Remember that an administrator can reconfigure the LCM to not perform signature validation at all. Overall, administrative privileges, when not used with good intentions, are evil. You will learn later in this chapter to apply the least privilege principals using Just Enough Administration (JEA).

Therefore, verifying the configuration signatures only on a new enact completely makes sense.

To verify if this signature validation is working or not, let's use the MOF you compiled at the beginning of this chapter and try to enact it again:

```
Start-DscConfiguration -Path C:\scripts\DemoWebServer -Verbose -Wait
```

This will result in an error, as shown in Figure 13-6.

```
PS C:\> Start-DscConfiguration -Path C:\scripts\DemoWebServer -Verbose -Wait
VERBOSE: Perform operation 'Invoke CimMethod' with following parameters, ''methodName' = SendConfigurationApply,'
  root/Microsoft/Windows/DesiredStateConfiguration'.
VERBOSE: An LCM method call arrived from computer S16-JB with user sid S-1-5-21-2403796847-1381111412-2575929524-
VERBOSE: [S16-01]: LCM:  [ Start  Set     ]
VERBOSE: [S16-01]: LCM:  [ End    Set     ]
Validating the signature of the configuration document failed. The signature status on the document is NotSigned.
    + CategoryInfo          : SecurityError: (root/Microsoft/...gurationManager:String) [], CimException
    + FullyQualifiedErrorId : MOFSignatureVerificationFailed
    + PSComputerName        : S16-01

VERBOSE: Operation 'Invoke CimMethod' complete.
VERBOSE: Time taken for configuration job to complete is 1.209 seconds
```

Figure 13-6. *Signature validation failure upon re-enact*

So, to be able to enact this configuration, you must sign it. This can be done by the Set-AuthenticodeSignature cmdlet. This is the same cmdlet that you use to sign your PowerShell scripts.

```
$certificate = Get-ChildItem Cert:\CurrentUser\My -CodeSigningCert
Set-AuthenticodeSignature -Certificate $certificate -FilePath C:\Scripts\
DemoWebServer\S16-01.mof -IncludeChain all -Force
```

When you execute the above commands, you should see that the signing is complete, with status shown as Valid. The signature validation won't work if the signing status is shown as UnknownError. Once the configuration is signed, you can try an enact again. It should work this time since the LCM will be able to validate the signature using the certificate in the trusted certificate store configured in the LCM settings. Figure 13-7 shows successful signature validation in action.

```
PS C:\scripts> Start-DscConfiguration -Path C:\scripts\DemoWebServer -Verbose -Wait
VERBOSE: Perform operation 'Invoke CimMethod' with following parameters, ''methodName' = SendConfiguratio
nApply,'className' = MSFT_DSCLocalConfigurationManager,'namespaceName' = root/Microsoft/Windows/DesiredSt
ateConfiguration'.
VERBOSE: An LCM method call arrived from computer S16-JB with user sid S-1-5-21-2403796847-1381111412-257
5929524-500.
VERBOSE: [S16-01]: LCM:  [ Start  Set      ]
VERBOSE: [S16-01]: LCM:  [ Start  Resource ]  [[WindowsFeature]DemoWebServer]
VERBOSE: [S16-01]: LCM:  [ Start  Test     ]  [[WindowsFeature]DemoWebServer]
VERBOSE: [S16-01]:                             [[WindowsFeature]DemoWebServer] The operation 'Get-WindowsF
eature' started: Web-Server
VERBOSE: [S16-01]:                             [[WindowsFeature]DemoWebServer] The operation 'Get-WindowsF
eature' succeeded: Web-Server
```

Figure 13-7. *Successful Signature validation*

If you are using a pull server for configuration MOF staging and distribution, ensure that the signing is complete before creating the checksum file. Configuration signing adds the signature at the end of the MOF file and this changes the checksum associated with the MOF file.

With the configuration signing and validation complete, let's look at the resource module signing.

Signing DSC Resource Modules

You already have the infrastructure in place for the code signing certificates and have the certificate already imported on a couple of target nodes. And, you have configured the LCM to perform signature validation on both configurations and modules. You can now get started with DSC resource module signing.

This is a two-step process:

- Create a module catalog file.

- Sign the module catalog file.

For this example, you will use the HostsFile resource module you built in Chapter 6.

Creating a Module Catalog File

Before packaging the custom DSC resource module and placing it on either a pull server for distribution or copying it to target nodes directly, you need to create a catalog file for the module. A catalog file contains hashes of all files at the specified path. This is done using the New-FileCatalog cmdlet.

```
$moduleFolder = 'C:\Scripts\ProDSC'
$moduleName = 'ProDSC'
New-FileCatalog -Path $moduleFolder -CatalogFilePath
"$moduleFolder\$moduleName.cat" -CatalogVersion 1.0
```

Once the catalog file is created, you need to sign it so that the LCM target node can verify the authenticity of the module that is present. Similar to the configuration signing, you need to use the Set-AuthenticodeSignature cmdlet to sign the module catalog file as well.

```
$certificate = Get-ChildItem Cert:\CurrentUser\My -CodeSigningCert
Set-AuthenticodeSignature -Certificate $certificate -IncludeChain all
-FilePath "$moduleFolder\$moduleName.cat"
```

At this point, package the module as a zip file; you learned this in Chapter 8. Next, place it on the pull server for distribution to the target nodes. Like the configuration file checksum, ensure that you have signed the catalog and packaged the module as a zip file before creating a checksum.

Note   Manual copy of the module files to the target node circumvents the signature validation by the LCM. The LCM will validate the signature only when it downloads the module and installs it before an enact.

You can compile the following configuration and sign it using the same code signing certificate that you used earlier for the other examples:

```
Configuration ProDscHosts
{
    param
    (
        [Parameter(Mandatory = $true)]
        [String]
        $HostName,

        [Parameter(Mandatory = $true)]
        [String]
        $IPAddress

    )

    Import-DscResource -ModuleName ProDsc -Name HostsFile -ModuleVersion
    1.0.0.0

    Node S16-01
    {
        HostsFile DemoHosts
        {
            HostName = $HostName
            IPAddress = $IPAddress
            Ensure = 'Present'
        }
    }
}

ProDscHosts -HostName 'testServer10' -IPAddress '10.10.10.10' -Verbose
$certificate = Get-ChildItem Cert:\CurrentUser\My -CodeSigningCert
Set-AuthenticodeSignature -Certificate $certificate -FilePath C:\Scripts\
ProDscHosts\S16-01.mof -IncludeChain all -Force
```

Once you have compiled the configuration, you can either wait for the consistency check to occur or use the Update-DscConfiguration cmdlet to download both modules and configuration from a pull server share.

Note   Similar to the configuration signature validation, module catalog signature validation is performed only when the resource module is downloaded and installed from a pull server. The subsequent enacts using the same version of the module will not trigger module signature validation.

At any point in time, if you want to ensure that the module files have not been tampered with, you can validate that using the Test-FileCatalog cmdlet. See Figure 13-8.

```
PS C:\scripts> Test-FileCatalog -Detailed -CatalogFilePath .\ProDSC\ProDSC.cat


Status        : Valid
HashAlgorithm : SHA1
CatalogItems  : {[ProDSC.psd1, CDE7D71ED5A3B4B68B5FF41AE37DFA8F4509E91A],
                [DSCResources\HostsFile\HostsFile.Schema.mof,
                C3D049CF0514EA21B08748DA6BB29C3F5E465DC4], [DSCResources\HostsFile\HostsFile.psm1,
                9F26055D8FF07103BADE0A69F3C2710AD7BCFAC4]}
PathItems     : {[ProDSC.psd1, CDE7D71ED5A3B4B68B5FF41AE37DFA8F4509E91A],
                [DSCResources\HostsFile\HostsFile.psm1, 9F26055D8FF07103BADE0A69F3C2710AD7BCFAC4],
                [DSCResources\HostsFile\HostsFile.Schema.mof, C3D049CF0514EA21B08748DA6BB29C3F5E465DC4]}
Signature     : System.Management.Automation.Signature
```

Figure 13-8. *Validation of module file catalog*

This concludes our discussion on configuration and module signing and enforcing signature validation using the LCM meta configuration. You will see how module and configuration signing can become part of the continuous integration processes in Chapters 14 and 15.

Enabling DSC Access Delegation

DSC, by default, enables only members of the local administrators group to invoke DSC related actions. This behavior can be changed to allow non-administrator users to perform DSC operations. You saw in Chapter 2 that DSC is implemented as a set of WMI providers. And you saw in Chapter 3 that most of the DSC operations are implemented in the DesiredStateConfiguration namespace in root/Microsoft/Windows. You can provide a non-administrator user access to this namespace to enable the user to execute DSC operations.

Enabling Non-Administrator User Permissions

There are a few ways to enable non-administrators to access WMI namespaces. In the first method, you can use the WMI Control configuration in the computer management console. Figure 13-9 shows this configuration option.

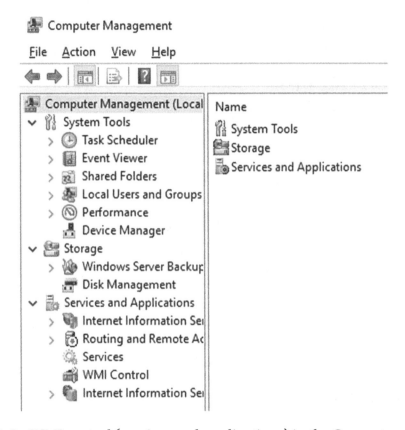

Figure 13-9. *WMI control (services and applications) in the Computer Management console*

In the MMC, right-click WMI Control and select Properties to navigate to the Security tab. Expand the root and select `Microsoft` > `Windows` > `DesiredStateConfiguration`. See `Figure` 13-10.

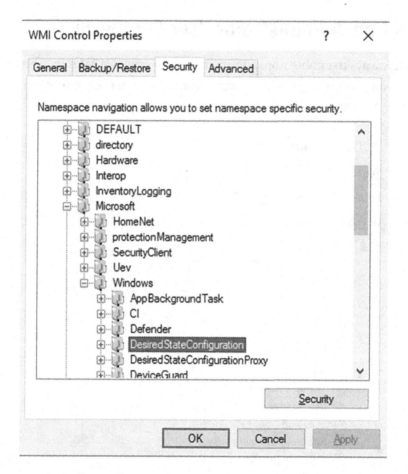

Figure 13-10. *WMI Control namespaces*

Click Security and then click Add to select the user. See Figure 13-11.

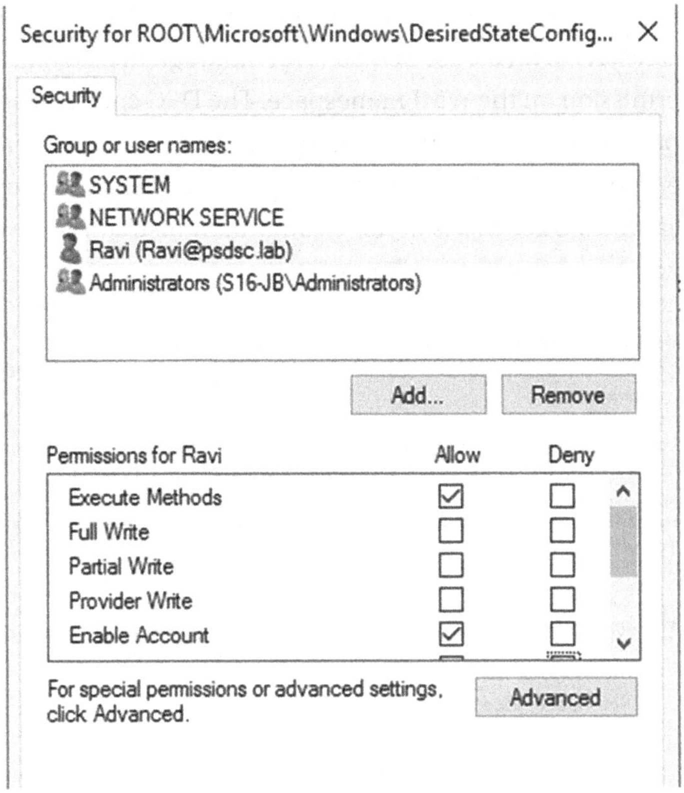

Figure 13-11. *WMI namespace permissions*

In the "Permissions for" box, select *Execute Methods, Enable Account*, and *Remote Enable* under Allow; this is also shown in Figure 13-11.

Note   Without the Remote Enable privilege, the non-administrator can locally log on to the target node and perform DSC operations. Remote Enable is must if the user needs to perform the DSC operations remotely from another node.

Once these permissions are updated, log in to any of the remote nodes as the non-administrator user and try Get-DscLocalConfigurationManager against the node where the WMI permissions are updated.

As shown in Figure 13-12, when a non-administrator user tries to perform a DSC action remotely, it results in an access denied error although the user has been granted *Remote Enable* permission on the WMI namespace. The DSC cmdlets use WinRM as the underlying transport. Therefore, it is important that the user is a member of the Remote Management Users group on the target node on which the user needs permission to perform DSC operations. Once this is done, the non-administrator user will be able to perform DSC operations remotely. See Figure 13-13.

```
PS C:\> Get-DscLocalConfigurationManager -CimSession S16-JB
Get-DscLocalConfigurationManager : S16-JB: Cannot connect to CIM server.
Access is denied.
At line:1 char:1
+ Get-DscLocalConfigurationManager -CimSession S16-JB
+ ~~~~~~~~~~~~~~~~~~~~~~~~~~~~~~~~~~~~~~~~~~~~~~~~~~~~~
    + CategoryInfo          : ResourceUnavailable: (MSFT_DSCLocalConfiguration
   Manager:String) [Get-DscLocalConfigurationManager], CimJobException
    + FullyQualifiedErrorId : CimJob_BrokenCimSession,Get-DscLocalConfiguratio
   nManager
```

Figure 13-12. *Access denied when trying remotely as a non-administrator user*

```
PS C:\> Get-DscLocalConfigurationManager -CimSession S16-JB


ActionAfterReboot              : ContinueConfiguration
AgentId                        : 5B3A9214-0D9F-11E8-9C0B-00155D161903
AllowModuleOverWrite           : False
CertificateID                  :
ConfigurationDownloadManagers  : {}
ConfigurationID                :
ConfigurationMode              : ApplyAndMonitor
```

Figure 13-13. *Non-administrator access to remote DSC operations*

Whatever configuration you have seen so far can be done using DSC as well. The WMI namespace permissions can be modified using the WMINamespaceSecurity DSC resource and the group membership can be done using the Group in-box DSC resource. Here is an example of this configuration document:

```
Configuration DSCNonAdminOperation
{
    param
    (
        [Parameter(Mandatory = $true)]
        [String]
```

```
        $User
    )

    Import-DSCResource -ModuleName WmiNamespaceSecurity -ModuleVersion 0.2.0
    Import-DSCResource -ModuleName PSDesiredStateConfiguration
    -ModuleVersion 1.1

    WMINamespaceSecurity DesiredStateConfiguration
    {
        Path = 'root/Microsoft/Windows/DesiredStateConfiguration'
        AppliesTo = 'Self'
        Principal = $User
        Permission = 'Enable', 'MethodExecute', 'RemoteAccess'
        AccessType = 'Allow'
        Ensure = 'Present'
    }

    Group RemoteManagement
    {
        GroupName = 'Remote Management Users'
        MembersToInclude = $User
        Ensure = 'Present'
    }
}

DSCNonAdminOperation -User 'psdsc\ravi'
```

Note   Ensure that you install the WMINamespaceSecurity DSC resource module (on the authoring station as well as the target node) from the PowerShell gallery before compiling and enacting this configuration.

Once you compile and enact this configuration, the node will be configured to allow non-administrator user access to the DSC operations either locally or remotely.

These configuration steps can be completed by implementing a group policy to update the WMI namespace permissions and the group membership, which is a well-known management method within enterprise IT.

The method of adding a non-administrator user to the Remote Management Users group gives the user not just DSC operations access but access to several other remote management tasks. Also, the WMI namespace permissions mean that the non-administrator user can perform any action that is available in the namespace. With the WMI namespace permissions, the non-administrators can use cmdlets such as `Invoke-DscResource` either locally or remotely (with Remote Enable permission). Using this method, a non-administrator user with bad intent can invoke the `Set` method of the `Script` resource and run any arbitrary code as SYSTEM. This can be very dangerous.

So, what if you want to give only `Get-*` cmdlet access to the non-administrator user so that they can just monitor the node and LCM configurations and not provide any WMI namespace permissions to the non-administrator user. This can be achieved using Just Enough Administration. Using JEA, you can restrict what commands a remote user can execute on the target node. This is done by registering a new session configuration with a role capability definition that is limited only to the cmdlets within the `PSDesiredStateConfiguration`.

The complete overview of JEA is outside the scope of this book and I recommend that you take a look at the documentation at `http://azrs.tk/JEA`. This will give you a very clear head-start into JEA and you will be able to create restricted session configurations.

Note   JEA requires PowerShell remoting to enable constrained management of systems remotely. Remember that enabling PowerShell remoting is not a requirement for DSC unless there is a need to debug DSC resource scripts and/or use JEA to enable delegated access to DSC operations on target nodes.

Creating a JEA Endpoint for DSC

Before you proceed, if you have already made the non-administrator domain user a member of the Remote Management Users group, undo that. Also, remove any WMI namespace permissions given to the non-administrator user.

You will learn how to use JEA to give this user only the cmdlets that this non-administrator needs and nothing more.

As mentioned, enabling JEA endpoints is a two-step process. You need to first create a role capability that defines what the user or group of users can perform on the target nodes and then create a remoting session configuration and attach the role capability. Let's get started.

DSC Role Capability

As example, you will create a role capability that restricts the non-administrator user only to the Get cmdlets in the PSDesiredStateConfiguration. The role capability must exist as a module at the $env:PSModulePath.

```
# Create the folder structure for the module
$null = New-Item -Path .\ProDSCJEA\RoleCapabilities -ItemType Directory
-Force

# Create the role capability file
$guid = (New-Guid).Guid
$roleCapability = @"
@{
    GUID = `'$guid`'
    Author = 'DSCFan'
    CompanyName = 'The Awesome DSC Inc.'
    Copyright = '(c) 2018 DSCFan. All rights reserved.'
    VisibleCmdlets = 'PSDesiredStateConfiguration\Get-*'
}
"@

$roleCapability | Out-File -FilePath .\ProDSCJEA\RoleCapabilities\
ProDscGet.psrc
```

In this code snippet, the hash table wrapped in a here string will be used as the content of the role capability file. The VisibleCmdlets key in the role capability definition constrains what the user can perform to only the Get-* cmdlets in the PSDesiredStateConfiguration module. You store this as a ProDscGet.psrc file in the RoleCapabilities folder at the module root. You can use the New-PSRoleCapabilityFile cmdlet to create this file as well. Since what you need is just the above keys in the PSRC file, I chose to do it using a here-string and hash literal.

Like every other PowerShell module, you need to create a module manifest as well:

```
#Module manifest
$manifestGuid = (New-Guid).Guid

$manifestSplat = @{
    Guid = $manifestGuid
    ModuleVersion = '1.0.0.0'
    Author = 'DSCFan'
    Company = 'The Awesome DSC Inc.'
    Description = 'Pro DSC JEA endpoint'
    Path = 'C:\Scripts\ProDscJEA\ProDscJEA.psd1'
}

New-ModuleManifest @manifestSplat
```

The JEA role capabilities are now defined. Figure 13-14 shows the folder structure you just created.

```
PS C:\scripts> tree /F /A .\ProDSCJEA
Folder PATH listing
Volume serial number is C8D6-C055
C:\SCRIPTS\PRODSCJEA
|    ProDscJEA.psd1
|
\---RoleCapabilities
            ProDscGet.psrc
```

Figure 13-14. *JEA role capabilities*

You need to copy this to a folder represented by $env:PSModulePath. I chose to copy it to the C:\Program Files\WindowsPowerShell\Modules folder.

Session Configuration

Once the role capability definition is complete, you need to create a session configuration and attach the role capability. Within the session configuration, you will also define which user or group of users will be able to connect to the target node using this session configuration.

```
#User or group for which the JEA endpoint is being created
$principal = 'psdsc\ravi'

$sessionSplat = @{
    RunAsVirtualAccount = $true
    RoleDefinitions     = @{$principal = @{RoleCapabilities = 'ProDscGet'}}
    SessionType         = 'RestrictedRemoteServer'
    Path                = 'C:\scripts\ProDscJEA.pssc'
}

New-PSSessionConfigurationFile @sessionSplat
```

In this code snippet, you set $principal to a domain user who will be performing a few DSC operations on a target node remotely. You then define a hash table containing a few more parameters needed for session configuration. The RunAsVirtualAccount when set to $true ensures that a virtual identity is used to perform the action under local administrator context and that will be available only while the session is alive. You use the RoleDefinitions to specify the role capabilities or the commands available through this session configuration to the user or group principal.

Once the session configuration file is created, you can validate the same using the Test-PSSessionConfigurationFile cmdlet. This should return True.

Session Registration

You have the session configuration created with a role capability file associated to it. You can now register the session configuration so that the non-administrator user can remotely connect to this.

```
$registrationSplat = @{
    Name  = 'ProDSCJEA'
    Path  = $sessionSplat.Path
    Force = $true
}
Register-PSSessionConfiguration @registrationSplat
```

Note   The Register-PSSessionConfiguration cmdlet restarts the WinRM service.

Once the session configuration registration is complete, it can be seen in the output of the Get-PSSessionConfiguration cmdlet. See Figure 13-15.

```
PS C:\scripts> Get-PSSessionConfiguration | Select Name, Permission

Name                                             Permission
----                                             ----------
microsoft.powershell                             NT AUTHORITY\INTERACTIVE Ac
microsoft.powershell.workflow                    BUILTIN\Administrators Acce
microsoft.powershell32                           NT AUTHORITY\INTERACTIVE Ac
microsoft.windows.servermanagerworkflows NT AUTHORITY\INTERACTIVE Ac
ProDSCJEA                                         PSDSC\Ravi AccessAllowed
```

Figure 13-15. *Session configuration*

You are all set. It is now time to hit this new session configuration and see if it really works. This can be done by running the Enter-PSSession cmdlet with the non-administrator credentials.

Once you are in the remote session, run the Get-Command cmdlet to see what capabilities are available. The output from my system is shown in Figure 13-16.

```
[S16-JB]: PS> Get-Command

CommandType    Name                             Version   Source
-----------    ----                             -------   ------
Function       Clear-Host
Function       Exit-PSSession
Function       Get-Command
Function       Get-DscConfiguration             1.1       PSDesiredStateConfiguration
Function       Get-DscConfigurationStatus       1.1       PSDesiredStateConfiguration
Function       Get-DscLocalConfigurationManager 1.1       PSDesiredStateConfiguration
Function       Get-DscResource                  1.1       PSDesiredStateConfiguration
Function       Get-FormatData
Function       Get-Help
Function       Measure-Object
Function       Out-Default
Function       Select-Object
```

Figure 13-16. *Available commands in the session*

At this point, the non-administrator can run any of the Get commands from the PSDesiredStateConfiguration module on the target node.

Using JEA, you have created a constrained endpoint on one of the target nodes and allowed a non-administrator domain user to access this and perform the DSC operations. This is so far one to one. However, you can deploy this role capability module on multiple systems and then register the session configuration that allows the non-administrator user to perform DSC operations across multiple target nodes remotely. This can be achieved using the DSC resources available to deploy JEA endpoints. I recommend that you read the article on multi-machine configuration with DSC at http://azrs.tk/jeaDSC for information on how to use resources in the JustEnoughAdministration DSC resource module.

Note   You need to download this module from the GitHub repository at http:// azrs.tk/jeaDSCresource.

Here is how you can enable DSC-delegated access using the JEA DSC resources:

```
Configuration DSCNonAdminOperation
{
    param
    (
        [Parameter(Mandatory = $true)]
        [String]
        $Principal,

        [Parameter(Mandatory = $true)]
        [String]
        $JEAModuleShare
    )

    Import-DSCResource -ModuleName PSDesiredStateConfiguration
    -ModuleVersion 1.1
    Import-DscResource -ModuleName JustEnoughAdministration
    -ModuleVersion 1.0

    Node @('S16-01','S16-02')
    {
        File RoleCapability
        {
            SourcePath = $JEAModuleShare
            DestinationPath = 'C:\Program Files\WindowsPowerShell\Modules\
                            ProDSCJEA'
            Checksum = 'SHA-256'
```

```
            Ensure = 'Present'
            Type = 'Directory'
            Recurse = $true
        }

        JeaEndpoint ProDSCJEAEndpoint
        {
            EndpointName = 'ProDscJEA'
            RoleDefinitions = "@{ `'$Principal`' = @{ RoleCapabilities =
                                'ProDscGet' } }"
            TranscriptDirectory = 'C:\ProgramData\JEAConfiguration\
                                Transcripts'
            DependsOn = '[File]RoleCapability'
        }
    }
}

DSCNonAdminOperation -Principal 'psdsc\ravi' -JEAModuleShare '\\S16-JB\
ProDSCJEA'
```

Note   Before you enact this configuration, ensure that the target nodes are either configured to download the required `JustEnoughAdministration` module from a pull server or manually copy it over to the target nodes.

When you compile and enact the above configuration, you may see an error message in the enact output that says that the WS-Management service cannot process the operation. This is because the WinRM service gets restarted during the session registration. You can safely ignore this.

```
$nodes = 'S16-01', 'S16-02'
$cred = Get-Credential 'psdsc\ravi'
$config = 'ProDscJEA'
$result = Invoke-Command -ComputerName $nodes -ScriptBlock { Get-
DscLocalConfigurationManager} -ConfigurationName $config -Credential $cred
$result | Select-Object RefreshMode, ConfigurationMode, PSComputerName
```

This should show output similar to what is shown in Figure 13-17.

```
RefreshMode ConfigurationMode PSComputerName
----------- ----------------- --------------
PUSH        ApplyAndMonitor   S16-01
PUSH        ApplyAndMonitor   S16-02
```

Figure 13-17. *LCM configuration settings from remote nodes*

Note   When using JEA endpoints for DSC operations, the non-administrator user will be constrained by the language mode and language features available in a session. For example, when using interactive remoting through the `Enter-PSSession` cmdlet, the tab completion feature won't be available. Similarly, when using the `Invoke-Command` cmdlet, the script block cannot contain language features such as the `Where({})` method or do `while`/`until` loops. As described at `http://azrs.tk/useJEA`, it is recommended to use implicit remoting with JEA endpoints.

Summary

This chapter certainly ran longer than I thought it would! After all, security is an important aspect of IaC and configuration management. In this chapter, you learned about the security features available in DSC, such as the MOF encryption at rest in the local configuration store and signature validation of configurations and resource modules. You also looked at the delegated access control to provide non-administrator users access (either local or remote) to DSC operations on target nodes. You looked at the different ways to achieve this using the WMI namespace security combined with the remote management users group membership. You looked at how JEA can be used to further limit what a non-administrator can perform remotely. Security must be a part of your configuration management or IaC thought process and what you learned in this chapter will help you implement these best practices in your organization.

PART III

DSC and the Release Pipeline

By now, you know how to author custom DSC resources and test them using Pester. You looked at different methods of publishing DSC resource modules such as the PowerShell gallery and an SMB share-based private PowerShell repository. It is important that you automate these processes to eliminate any human errors and ensure that you are continuously validating the resources that you author.

This part of the book looks at automating the DSC resource module release processes from source control to a repository. You first look at creating a release pipeline for your modules using a few community-developed modules such as PSake, Pester, and PSDeploy. You conclude this section by implementing a similar pipeline using AppVeyor and GitHub.

## CHAPTER 14

DSC and the Release Pipeline

You started your learning in Chapter 1 by looking at Infrastructure as Code and how it enables continuous integration and delivery for any DSC resource modules you author and the node configurations you prepare for compiling and enacting. However, you have not seen a practical implementation of this yet. In Chapter 6, you learned how to author your own DSC resource modules and looked at validating these resource scripts in Chapter 7. You learned how to publish the module to a private PowerShell repository hosted on an SMB share as well. It was all manual. But, with the help of a release pipeline implementation, this entire process can be automated from source control to a private repository. In this chapter, you will explore one such implementation using a few community PowerShell modules that enable a build-to-release pipeline implementation. Let's get started.

Lab Requirements

To try the examples and exercises in this chapter, you will need at minimum two or more systems with Windows Server 2008 R2 or above with WMF 5.1 installed. I recommend a system with Windows Server 2016. To build the complete release pipeline, you will use modules such as PSake, Pester, PSScriptAnalyzer, and PSDeploy. You will need these modules on the system where you want to perform the end-to-end testing and release. You will also be using Git as the source control system.

If you are new to release pipeline concepts, I strongly recommend that you read the whitepaper by Michael Greene and Steven Murawski on this subject; go to http://aka. ms/thereleasepipelinemodelpdf. Our implementation of a release pipeline is heavily influenced by this whitepaper.

© Ravikanth Chaganti 2018
R. Chaganti, *Pro PowerShell Desired State Configuration*, https://doi.org/10.1007/978-1-4842-3483-9_14

At a high level, Figure 14-1 shows the release pipeline that you will implement.

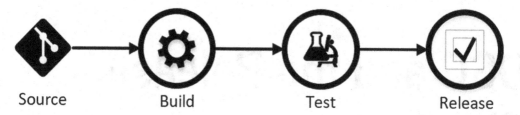

Figure 14-1. *Release pipeline stages*

In this implementation of the release pipeline for the DSC resource modules, you will be using all community-developed PowerShell modules.

- **Source**: For source control, you will use Git. You will have the module files version controlled locally and kick-start the build process from the same Git repository.

- **Build**: For this stage of the pipeline, you will use the PSake module that enables execution of individual tasks within the Test and Release stages.

- **Test**: For testing the DSC resource scripts, you will use Pester and PSScriptAnalyzer modules.

- **Release**: Finally, once the tests are complete with no errors, you will release this module to a private PowerShell repository using PSDeploy. You will also see how these modules can be published to a pull server in the infrastructure for distribution to target nodes that are pull clients.

Note   This chapter is not a deep dive into the individual modules used to build the release pipeline. Instead, this chapter provides examples of using each of these modules in a release pipeline. If you want to get familiar with the core functionality of these modules, I recommend that you read the module documentation.

Let's get started by looking at each of these stages and then you'll build the release pipeline in an incremental manner.

Source Control

As mentioned, you will use Git as the source control system for this release pipeline. If you don't already have Git installed on your system, you can download and install it from https://git-scm.com.

Once you have Git installed, create a folder called Source and a folder called ProDsc under that.

```
$null = New-Item -Path C:\Source\ProDsc -ItemType Directory -Force
```

Now, copy the ProDSC MOF-based module that you built in Chapter 6 into the ProDsc folder. Figure 14-2 shows the folder structure on my build system.

```
PS C:\Source\ProDSC> tree /F /A
Folder PATH listing
Volume serial number is 0000008A C8D6:C055
C:.
\---ProDsc
    |   ProDSC.psd1
    |
    \---DSCResources
        \---HostsFile
                HostsFile.psm1
                HostsFile.Schema.mof
```

Figure 14-2. *Folder structure inside the source folder*

Once this is done, open the PowerShell console or command prompt and navigate to the C:\Source\ProDsc folder and execute the git init command. This initializes the module folder as a git repository.

From this point onwards any changes to the files in the module folder will be version tracked and will have to be committed into the repository.

Build

To orchestrate various tasks in the release pipeline, you need a build script. This build script will be used to ensure that the required modules are present on the build system. Once you verify that the dependent modules are available, you invoke the build script that contains the tasks for the release pipeline.

```
[CmdletBinding()]
param
(
    [Parameter()]
    [string[]]
    $Task = 'default'
)

$dependentModules = @('Pester','PSScriptAnalyzer','Psake','PSDeploy')

try
{
    #Ensure all dependent modules are present
    foreach ($module in $dependentModules)
    {
        if (!(Get-Module -Name $module -ListAvailable))
        {
            Install-Module -Name $module -Force
        }
    }

    Invoke-Psake -BuildFile "$PSScriptRoot\moduleBuild.ps1" -TaskList
    $Task -Verbose
}
catch
{
    Write-Error $_
}
```

Save this script as build.ps1 at the root of the module folder.

You now need the actual build script that executes the release pipeline tasks.

```
properties {
    $resourceName       = 'HostsFile'
    $moduleScript       = "$PSScriptRoot\DSCResources\$resourceName\
                          $resourceName.psm1"
    $testFolder         = "$PSScriptRoot\Tests"
    $unitTestsFolder    = "$testFolder\Unit"
```

```
    $integrationTestsFolder = "$testFolder\Integration"
    $deployFile             = '.\deployment.yml'
}

task default -depends StyleCheck, UnitTest, IntegrationTest, DeployModule

task StyleCheck {
    $sCheck = Invoke-ScriptAnalyzer -Path $moduleScript -Severity 'Error'
    -Recurse -Verbose:$false
    if ($sCheck) {
        $sCheck
        throw 'PS Script Analyzer returned one or more errors. Release
        pipeline execution will halt.'
    }
}

task UnitTest {
    $unitTestResults = Invoke-Pester -Path $unitTestsFolder -PassThru
    if ($unitTestResults.FailedCount -gt 0) {
        $unitTestResults | Format-List
        throw 'Module Unit tests returned one or more errors. Release
        pipeline execution will halt.'
    }
}

task IntegrationTest {
    $intTestResults = Invoke-Pester -Path $integrationTestsFolder -PassThru
    if ($intTestResults.FailedCount -gt 0) {
        $intTestResults | Format-List
        throw 'Module integration tests returned one or more errors.
        Release pipeline execution will halt.'
    }
}

task DeployModule -depends StyleCheck, UnitTest, IntegrationTest {
    Invoke-PSDeployment -Path $deployFile -Force -Verbose
}
```

Save this file as `moduleBuild.ps1` at the module root.

What you see above is a PSake build script. It has multiple tasks related to the test and release stages of the pipeline. The properties block at the beginning defines the values that are needed for the subsequent tasks. This includes the path to the tests folders and the deployment YAML file that contains where the module needs to be published to if everything gets tested without errors.

The `StyleCheck` task will use `PSScriptAnalyzer` module to verify that there are no errors reported from the static code analysis.

The `UnitTest` and `IntegrationTest` tasks help you perform automated testing of the resource module. These tasks use the Pester module. You wrote the test scripts in Chapter 7 so simply copy the same test scripts to the `Tests` folder.

Finally, the `DeployModule` task will use the `PSDeploy` module to deploy the module to a private local repository. This task invokes `PSDeploy` deployment with the `deployment.yml` file, which defines that source and targets for the module deployment. You have not authored this yet.

As you can see in this build script, you have defined dependencies, and when a task fails, it throws an error message so that the pipeline halts there. This is important since you don't want the pipeline to continue to subsequent tasks if a dependent task fails.

Test

In the test stage of this release pipeline, you check for style guidelines and perform unit and integration tests. You copy the unit and integration tests for the `HostsFile`, written in Chapter 7, into a folder called `Tests` at the module root. At the end of this step, the module folder structure will look like what is shown in Figure 14-3.

```
PS C:\Source\ProDSC> tree /F /A
Folder PATH listing
Volume serial number is 000000D3 C8D6:C055
C:.
|   build.ps1
|   moduleBuild.ps1
|
\---ProDsc
    |   ProDSC.psd1
    |
    +---DSCResources
    |   \---HostsFile
    |           HostsFile.psm1
    |           HostsFile.Schema.mof
    |
    \---Tests
        +---Integration
        |       HostsFile.Config.ps1
        |       HostsFile.Integration.Tests.ps1
        |
        \---Unit
                HostsFile.Tests.ps1
```

Figure 14-3. *Module structure after adding Tests*

Since the test scripts clone the DSCResource.Tests repository from GitHub, the system where you plan to run the build process should have connectivity to the Internet. Also, you need to add a .gitignore file in the repository to ensure that the DSCResource. Tests folder does not get committed to your local repository when you use git commit.

```
@'
ProDsc/DscResource.Tests
ProDsc/DscResource.Tests/*
'@ | Out-File -Path C:\Source\ProDsc.gitignore -force
```

This command will create a .gitignore file in the local git repository.

Deploy

Once all tests are complete without any errors, you can publish the module to the internal PowerShell repository. In Chapter 6, you saw how to configure an internal PowerShell repository in a local file share and publish modules to it using the Publish-Module cmdlet.

If you don't have this private repository created, create it now using the following code snippet:

```
$localRepository = @{
    Name               = 'ProDscRepo'
    SourceLocation     = '\\S16-JB\ProDSCRepo'
    PublishLocation    = '\\S16-JB\ProDSCRepo'
    InstallationPolicy = 'Trusted'
}

Register-PSRepository @localRepository
```

For PSDeploy in the deploy task to know where the source and target for the module are, you need to define a deployment.yml file. Here is what you need to put in the deployment.yml file:

```
ProDscModuleDeployment:
  Source:
    - '.\'
  Destination:
    - 'ProDscRepo'
  DeploymentType: PSGalleryModule
```

Save this as deployment.yml at the root of the module. Figure 14-4 shows the module structure after adding this YAML file.

```
PS C:\Source\ProDSC> tree /F /A
Folder PATH listing
Volume serial number is 00000085 C8D6:C055
C:.
|   build.ps1
|   deployment.yml
|   moduleBuild.ps1
|
\---ProDsc
    |   ProDSC.psd1
    |
    +---DSCResources
    |   \---HostsFile
    |           HostsFile.psm1
    |           HostsFile.Schema.mof
    |
    \---Tests
        +---Integration
        |       HostsFile.Config.ps1
        |       HostsFile.Integration.Tests.ps1
        |
        \---Unit
                HostsFile.Tests.ps1
```

Figure 14-4. *Module structure including deployment.yml*

Executing the Build Script

Before you execute the build script, commit all changes in the git repository using the git commit command.

```
git add *
git commit -m 'Initial release of ProDsc 1.0.0.0'
```

Once the files are committed, you can check the status of the repository like so:

```
git status
```

Once you have all these artifacts in place, you can execute the build.ps1 script.

```
.\build.ps1
```

The output will be rather long when everything works. Figure 14-5 shows the partial output from the release pipeline tasks.

```
......  .
VERBOSE: Total package yield:'0' for the specified package 'ProDsc'.
VERBOSE: Performing the operation "Publish-Module" on target "Version '1.0.0.0' of module '
ProDsc'".
VERBOSE: Successfully published module 'ProDsc' to the module publish location '\\S16-JB\Pr
oDSCRepo'. Please allow few minutes for 'ProDsc' to show up in the search results.

Build Succeeded!

------------------------------------------------------------------
Build Time Report
------------------------------------------------------------------
Name            Duration
----            --------
StyleCheck      00:00:00.045
UnitTest        00:00:01.018
IntegrationTest 00:00:00.984
DeployModule    00:00:06.173
Total:          00:00:08.232
```

Figure 14-5. *Output from the build script*

As you can see from Figure 14-5, at the end of the release pipeline tasks, the ProDsc module is published to the private PowerShell repository.

This is all good but it's still a manual process. How do you automate this?

Automating the Release Pipeline with Git Hooks

Since you are using a local git repository, you can use the git hooks feature to run the build script on every commit. Git offers several hooks for different purposes. One of them is post-commit hook. Using it, you can run a shell script after a git commit is complete. You can use this as a trigger for starting an automated build process. The pre-commit hooks can be used to perform linting and style checks and disallow a commit at all.

Git Hooks

Each git repository contains a hidden folder named .git. This folder contains the git database for the repository and additional git-related artifacts. One such artifact is the hooks folder which contains several shell scripts. Figure 14-6 shows the contents of this folder.

```
PS C:\Source\ProDSC> Get-ChildItem -Path .\.git\hooks -Force


    Directory: C:\Source\ProDSC\.git\hooks


Mode                 LastWriteTime         Length Name
----                 -------------         ------ ----
-a----        2/25/2018  12:47 PM            478 applypatch-msg.sample
-a----        2/25/2018  12:47 PM            896 commit-msg.sample
-a----        2/25/2018  12:47 PM           3327 fsmonitor-watchman.sample
------        2/25/2018   6:38 PM            173 post-commit
-a----        2/25/2018   5:25 PM            316 post-commit.ps1
-a----        2/25/2018  12:47 PM            189 post-update.sample
-a----        2/25/2018  12:47 PM            424 pre-applypatch.sample
-a----        2/25/2018  12:47 PM           1642 pre-commit.sample
-a----        2/25/2018  12:47 PM           1348 pre-push.sample
-a----        2/25/2018  12:47 PM           4898 pre-rebase.sample
-a----        2/25/2018  12:47 PM            544 pre-receive.sample
-a----        2/25/2018  12:47 PM           1492 prepare-commit-msg.sample
-a----        2/25/2018  12:47 PM           3610 update.sample
```

Figure 14-6. *Contents of the .git/hooks folder*

Each shell script here is associated with a specific git action such as pre-commit, pre-push, and so on. For example, the pre-commit script (when present without the .sample extension) gets triggered before starting a commit. What you don't see in that list is a post-commit hook; using it, you can trigger an action after the commit complete. So, this is your choice for performing an automated build within your release pipeline. Unfortunately, Git does not support running a PowerShell script as a git hook. So, you will use the post-commit shell script to launch a PowerShell script that invokes the build.

Here is what I have in my post-commit shell script:

```
#!/bin/bash
message=$(git log -1 --format=%s

exec powershell.exe -NoProfile -ExecutionPolicy Bypass -File "$PWD/.git/
hooks/post-commit.ps1" -CommitMessage "\'$message\'"
```

Put the above shell script contents to a file and name it post-commit (without any extension) and copy the file to the .git\hooks folder in the ProDsc repository folder. Once this is complete, open Git bash and set the execute permissions on this file.

```
chmod +x post-commit
```

This is important for Git to be able to trigger the script post commit. Let's take a quick look at this shell script before we move forward.

In the line after #!/bin/bash, you are retrieving the last commit message and then invoking the post-commit.ps1 script with the message string as an argument. The commit message acts as a filter for you to understand when to invoke the build script. Let's look at the post-commit.ps1 script:

```
[CmdletBinding()]
param
(
    [Parameter()]
    [String]
    $CommitMessage
)

$buildScriptPath = Split-Path -Path (Split-Path -Path $PSScriptRoot
-Parent) -Parent
$buildScript = "$buildScriptPath\build.ps1"

if ($CommitMessage -and (-not ($CommitMessage -like "*Skip CI*")))
{
    . $buildScript
}
```

Save this as post-commit.ps1 in the same folder as the post-commit shell script. In this script, you check if the commit message contains anything like Skip CI to see if you need to run the build script or not. For example, if on a specific commit you want to skip the build process, you can simply add 'skip CI' to the commit message. This is why I said that the commit message is important in this case.

With the shell script and the PowerShell script in place, you can test the end-to-end automated build process. Simply make a small change to any of the resource module files and do a commit again.

```
git add *
git commit -m 'This is a minor change!'
```

After the commit is complete, you will see that the build.ps1 gets triggered, which in turn kick-starts the release pipeline.

Now, make another minor change like adding a comment to the resource script file and commit again but with the commit message containing the text *Skip CI*.

```
git add *
git commit -m 'Skip CI - This is a minor change!'
```

This will not trigger the build script, as shown in Figure 14-7.

```
PS C:\Source\ProDSC> git add *

PS C:\Source\ProDSC> git commit -m 'Skip CI - Adding comments to functions.'
[master cd80356] Skip CI - Adding comments to functions.
 Committer: Administrator@PSDSC.LAB <Administrator@PSDSC.LAB>
Your name and email address were configured automatically based
on your username and hostname. Please check that they are accurate.
You can suppress this message by setting them explicitly. Run the
following command and follow the instructions in your editor to edit
your configuration file:

    git config --global --edit

After doing this, you may fix the identity used for this commit with:

    git commit --amend --reset-author

 1 file changed, 1 insertion(+)
```

Figure 14-7. *Skipping the build process*

Deploying Modules to a Pull Server

The release pipeline that you just built deployed the module to a private PowerShell repository. You used the PSDeploy module to achieve that and the deployment definition itself was put into a file called deployment.yml. Now, what if you want to publish the module to a pull server as well? Whether it is an oData endpoint-based pull server or an SMB pull server, you need to package the module as a zip archive and then just copy it to the pull server. This can be achieved by adding a PSake task and a little bit of custom scripting. Let's dive into that.

The Script to Package a Module Folder

Let's once again take a look at the folder structure that you have within the Git repository you created earlier. See Figure 14-8.

```
PS C:\Source\ProDSC> tree /F /A
Folder PATH listing
Volume serial number is 00000085 C8D6:C055
C:.
|   build.ps1
|   deployment.yml
|   moduleBuild.ps1
|
\---ProDsc
    |   ProDSC.psd1
    |
    +---DSCResources
    |   \---HostsFile
    |           HostsFile.psm1
    |           HostsFile.Schema.mof
    |
    \---Tests
        +---Integration
        |       HostsFile.Config.ps1
        |       HostsFile.Integration.Tests.ps1
        |
        \---Unit
                HostsFile.Tests.ps1
```

Figure 14-8. *Module repository folder structure*

From Figure 14-8, it is clear that the entire DSC resource module is contained
within C:\Source\ProDsc\ProDsc. So, you can package this folder as a zip archive. But,
if you remember that discussion from Chapter 8, you need to add the version number
of the module in the zip file name. Essentially, the zip name has to be *moduleName_*
moduleVersion.zip. You can get the module version from the module manifest file.

Here is a simple script to help with this process:

```
[CmdletBinding()]
param
(
    [Parameter(Mandatory)]
    [String]
    $ModuleFolder
)

if (-not(Test-Path -Path $ModuleFolder))
{
    throw "$ModuleFolder not found"
}
```

```
$moduleName = (Get-Item -Path $ModuleFolder).BaseName

#Get the module version from manifest
$manifest = Import-PowerShellDataFile -Path "$ModuleFolder\$moduleName.psd1"
$moduleVersion = $manifest.ModuleVersion

#Package the folder
$parentPath = Split-Path -Path $ModuleFolder -Parent
$archivePath = "$parentPath\$($moduleName)_$($moduleVersion).zip"

if (Get-ChildItem -Path "$ModuleFolder\DscResource.Tests")
{
    #Copy module folder files to temp location to eliminate DSCResources.
    Tests folder
    $null = New-Item -Path "$($env:Temp)\$($moduleName)" -ItemType
    Directory -Force

    Get-ChildItem -Path .\ProDsc | % {
        Copy-Item $_.fullname "$($env:Temp)\$($moduleName)" -Recurse -Force
        -Exclude 'DSCResource.Tests'
    }
}

Compress-Archive -Path "$($env:Temp)\$($moduleName)\*" -DestinationPath
$archivePath -Force

$checksumPath = "$parentPath\$($moduleName)_$($moduleVersion).zip.checksum"
New-DscChecksum -Path $archivePath -OutPath $parentPath -Force

#Clean up temp folder
Remove-Item -Path "$($env:Temp)\$($moduleName)" -Recurse -Force

return @($archivePath, $checksumPath)
```

Save this file as packageModule.ps1 and store at the same level as the build.ps1 file. Once this is done, update moduleBuild.ps1 to add a new deployment step for publishing the packaged module to the pull server.

```
properties {
    $resourceName           = 'HostsFile'
    $moduleName             = 'ProDsc'
    $moduleFolder           = "$PSScriptRoot\$moduleName"
    $moduleScript           = "$PSScriptRoot\ProDsc\DSCResources\
                                $resourceName\$resourceName.psm1"
    $testFolder             = "$PSScriptRoot\ProDsc\Tests"
    $unitTestsFolder        = "$testFolder\Unit"
    $integrationTestsFolder = "$testFolder\Integration"
    $deployFile             = '.\deployment.yml'
    $pullServerPath         = '\\S16-JB\PullServer'
}

task default -depends StyleCheck, UnitTest, IntegrationTest,
DeployModuleToPrivateRepo, DeployModuleToPullServer

task StyleCheck {
    $sCheck = Invoke-ScriptAnalyzer -Path $moduleScript -Severity 'Error'
    -Recurse -Verbose:$false
    if ($sCheck) {
        $sCheck
        throw 'PS Script Analyzer returned one or more errors. Release
        pipeline execution will halt.'
    }
}

task UnitTest {
    $unitTestResults = Invoke-Pester -Path $unitTestsFolder -PassThru
    if ($unitTestResults.FailedCount -gt 0) {
        $unitTestResults | Format-List
        throw 'Module Unit tests returned one or more errors. Release
        pipeline execution will halt.'
    }
}
```

```
task IntegrationTest {
    $intTestResults = Invoke-Pester -Path $integrationTestsFolder -PassThru
    if ($intTestResults.FailedCount -gt 0) {
        $intTestResults | Format-List
        throw 'Module integration tests returned one or more errors.
        Release pipeline execution will halt.'
    }
}

task DeployModuleToPrivateRepo -depends StyleCheck, UnitTest,
IntegrationTest {
    Invoke-PSDeployment -Path $deployFile -Force -Verbose
}

task DeployModuleToPullServer -depends StyleCheck, UnitTest,
IntegrationTest {
    $filesToCopy = .\packageModule.ps1 -ModuleFolder $moduleFolder

    foreach ($file in $filesToCopy)
    {
        Copy-Item -Path $file -Destination $pullServerPath -Force
    }

    #Clean up local files after copy
    Remove-Item -Path $filesToCopy -Force
}
```

In this updated moduleBuild.ps1, you have added a few more properties for
the sake of identifying the module name and the path where you have published the
packaged module folder. Towards the end of moduleBuild.ps1 is a new PSake task
to package the module for pull server publish and eventually to publish them to the
pull server path. The earlier method of publishing the module to a private PowerShell
repository used the deployment.yml file and Invoke-PSDeployment from the PSDeploy
module and the pull server deployment used PSake task instead.

The `deployment.yml` method you saw earlier to publish the module to the private PowerShell repository can be used to publish modules to the official PowerShell gallery. Here is a sample `deployment.yml` that publishes to the official PowerShell gallery:

```
ProDscModuleDeploymentToGallery:
  Source:
    - '.\ProDsc'
  Destination:
    - 'PSGallery'
  DeploymentType: PSGalleryModule
  Options:
    ApiKey = 'your-Api_key'
```

Try this method!

Using what you have learned so far, can you build another pipeline that compiles the MOF files and publishes them to a pull server along with checksum files? You may want to add integration tests to ensure that the compiled configuration can be enacted.

Summary

Release pipelines help implement an automated build-and-release process for the DSC resource modules and configurations. This chapter showed one such implementation of the release pipeline that leverages a few community-developed modules. While this is great, you had to be concerned about the dependencies, and implementing git hooks made this whole thing work automagically end to end. There are products specifically meant for continuous integration and delivery/deployment, such as Jenkins, AppVeyor, and VSTS. They are the subject of the next chapter.

CHAPTER 15

DSC with AppVeyor CI

In Chapter 14, you implemented a release pipeline for DSC resource modules using open source tooling and libraries. However, as you saw towards the end, building a complete automated pipeline involves tinkering with Git hooks. Also, there was no reporting around the build success or failure, or any historical reporting for the builds. This is where more evolved tools such as AppVeyor, among many others, can help. In this chapter, you will implement a release pipeline, similar to what you saw in Chapter 14, with AppVeyor.

Lab Requirements

To try the examples and exercises in this chapter, you will need at minimum two or more systems with Windows Server 2008 R2 or above with WMF 5.1 installed. I recommend a system with Windows Server 2016. For building the complete release pipeline, you will use AppVeyor and modules such as `Pester` and `PSScriptAnalyzer` for style and unit/integration testing. You will use Git as the source control system. For the release pipeline implementation with AppVeyor, you need GitHub and AppVeyor accounts.

AppVeyor CI

AppVeyor is one of the most popular commercial CI/CD platforms. It is available in hosted and on-premises versions. Using hosted AppVeyor with open source software (OSS) projects is free. For the custom DSC resource module testing, you can host your module repository on GitHub and integrate with AppVeyor to perform automated builds on a commit. In this section, you will look at the different steps needed to implement the release pipeline with GitHub and AppVeyor.

453

© Ravikanth Chaganti 2018
R. Chaganti, *Pro PowerShell Desired State Configuration*, https://doi.org/10.1007/978-1-4842-3483-9_15

Publishing a Repository on GitHub

First and foremost, you need a GitHub repository containing your DSC resource module. You will use the ProDsc resource module you built in Chapter 6.

This chapter does not provide step-by-step instructions on setting up GitHub repositories. If you are totally new to GitHub, I recommend looking at the "Hello World" guide at `https://guides.github.com/activities/hello-world/`.

Once you have a repository, clone it locally using the `git clone` command.

```
git clone https://github.com/prodsc/ProDsc.git
```

This brings a copy of the remote repository to the local system where you can work on completing the resource module authoring. Once this local clone is ready, copy and paste the `ProDsc` module contents to the repository folder. Figure 15-1 shows the folder structure on my system.

```
PS C:\Github> tree /F /A
Folder PATH listing
Volume serial number is 0000004C C8D6:C055
C:.
\---ProDsc
    |    ProDSC.psd1
    |
    +---DSCResources
    |   \---HostsFile
    |           HostsFile.psm1
    |           HostsFile.Schema.mof
    |
    \---Tests
        +---Integration
        |       HostsFile.Config.ps1
        |       HostsFile.Integration.Tests.ps1
        |
        \---Unit
                HostsFile.Tests.ps1
```

Figure 15-1. *GitHub repository folder on a local system*

Connecting to AppVeyor

Once you have the repository, you can connect it to AppVeyor. This can be done once you log into AppVeyor using your GitHub account. To add a new project and connect your GitHub repository, take a look at `www.appveyor.com/docs/`.

For all of the public repositories that you add, AppVeyor will automatically add the webhooks to trigger a build every time you commit something to the repository. Figure 15-2 shows this from the repository I created.

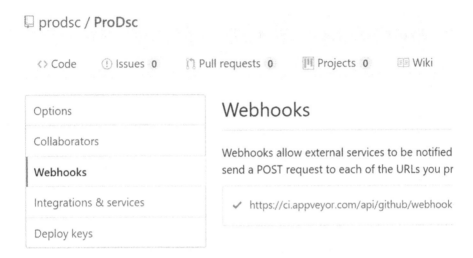

Figure 15-2. *AppVeyor webhook in the GitHub repository*

Build Configuration

Before you can commit and start a build process, you need to have the build configuration in place. A build configuration file called appveyor.yml, located at the root of the repository, defines the steps in a project build. For you, it can be used to install necessary PowerShell modules, perform unit and integration tests, and publish the module on the PowerShell gallery. This is essentially what your release pipeline did in Chapter 14.

Here is the build configuration file for the DSC resource module testing. It is same as the one generated using the Plaster template to generate the HQRM scaffold.

```
#--------------------------------#
#      environment configuration  #
#--------------------------------#
version: 1.0.{build}.0
install:
    - git clone https://github.com/PowerShell/DscResource.Tests

    - ps: |
```

```
    Import-Module -Name "$env:APPVEYOR_BUILD_FOLDER\DscResource.Tests\
    AppVeyor.psm1"
    Invoke-AppveyorInstallTask

#-------------------------------#
#      build configuration      #
#-------------------------------#

build: false


#-------------------------------#
#      test configuration       #
#-------------------------------#

test_script:
    - ps: |
        Invoke-AppveyorTestScriptTask -CodeCoverage -CodeCovIo -ExcludeTag @()

#-------------------------------#
#     deployment configuration  #
#-------------------------------#

# scripts to run before deployment
deploy_script:
  - ps: |
      Invoke-AppveyorAfterTestTask
```

Save this as appveyor.yml at the root of the repository.

In this AppVeyor build configuration, you are skipping the build task since you are testing DSC resource modules and there is no build, as such, that is needed. The test script will be invoked by the Invoke-AppveyorTestScriptTask function from the Appveyor.psm1 module contained in the DSCResources.Tests repository that gets cloned at the beginning of the AppVeyor task.

Within the command that uses Invoke-AppveyorTestScriptTask, you also specify the -CodeCoverage and -CodeCovIO switch parameters. In Chapter 7, when you ran the Pester tests, you saw 100% code coverage reported at the end of tests. The codecov.io provides similar metrics. This integration can be done in a way similar to how you integrated with AppVeyor. All you need to do is log into codecov.io with your GitHub credentials and add a project. Once this is complete, you need to add a configuration file at the root of the repository similar to appveyor.yml. Once again, the Plaster template that was used for generating the HQRM module generates the codecov.yml file too. Here it is:

```
codecov:
  notify:
    require_ci_to_pass: no

comment:
  layout: "reach, diff"
  behavior: default

coverage:
  range: 50..80
  round: down
  precision: 0

  status:
    project:
      default:
        # Set the overall project code coverage requirement to 70%
        target: 70
    patch:
      default:
        # Set the pull request requirement to not regress overall coverage
        by more than 5%
        # and let codecov.io set the goal for the code changed in the patch.
        target: auto
        threshold: 5
```

Save this file as .codecov.yml at the root of the repository. This configuration file defines the code coverage requirements for this repository.

At this point, you are all set to commit your changes to the GitHub repository to see if the AppVeyor build starts or not. This can be done using the following commands:

```
git add *
git commit -m 'Initial commit'
git push origin
```

The `git push` command will prompt for GitHub credentials.

The last command here triggers the AppVeyor task, and you can see the results at `https://ci.appveyor.com/projects`. Partial output from this is Figure 15-3.

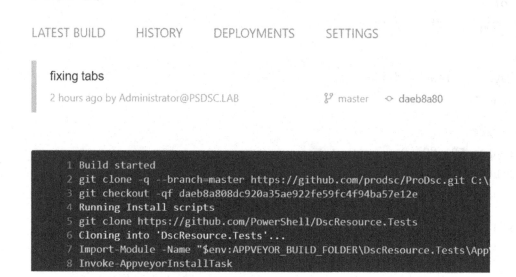

Figure 15-3. *Build status from AppVeyor*

Since you are using the same set of tests as the official PowerShell repository for DSC resources validates, you may see a few errors that you didn't see in Chapter 7 or 14. For example, the build of this resource module may fail because there are no newlines at the end of each file in the module. The error messages, if any, will be easy to understand and you must fix these issues before the build task can succeed fully.

At this point, you have the continuous integration for the tests working on AppVeyor. Every commit to the repository triggers the CI process, which in turn ensures that all unit and integration tests complete. But there may be instances where you don't want to run the CI process. For example, when you add a README to the repository, there is no need to run the tests again since you aren't checking anything specific to the README in your tests. You can tell AppVeyor to skip a specific commit by defining the same in the build configuration YAML, like so:

```
#-------------------------------#
#      environment configuration  #
#-------------------------------#
```

```
version: 1.0.{build}.0

skip_commits:
  files:
    - README.md
  message: /updated readme.*|update readme.*s|update docs.*|update
  version.*|update appveyor.*/

install:
  - git clone https://github.com/PowerShell/DscResource.Tests

  - ps: |
      Import-Module -Name "$env:APPVEYOR_BUILD_FOLDER\DscResource.Tests\
      AppVeyor.psm1"
      Invoke-AppveyorInstallTask

#-------------------------------#
#      build configuration      #
#-------------------------------#

build: false

#-------------------------------#
#      test configuration       #
#-------------------------------#

test_script:
  - ps: |
      Invoke-AppveyorTestScriptTask -CodeCoverage -CodeCovIo -ExcludeTag @
()

#-------------------------------#
#      deployment configuration #
#-------------------------------#

# scripts to run before deployment
deploy_script:
  - ps: |
      Invoke-AppveyorAfterTestTask
```

The `skip_commits` section in `appveyor.yml` is what tells AppVeyor when to ignore the commit and not run the CI.

To test this, add a `README.md` file to this project. Here is the content I have in a `README.md` file:

```
# ProDSC - HostsFile resource
This is a sample repository that is used to explain the concepts around
using AppVeyor for DSC continuous integration.
```

```
[![Build status](https://ci.appveyor.com/api/projects/
status/8snlacyyow8ate7o/branch/master?svg=true)](https://ci.appveyor.com/
project/prodsc/prodsc/branch/master)
```

```
[![codecov](https://codecov.io/gh/prodsc/ProDsc/branch/master/graph/badge.
svg)](https://codecov.io/gh/prodsc/ProDsc)
```

Save the above content as `README.md` at the root of the repository. This README contains a couple of badges that show the last build status and the code coverage through the tests in the repository. The code for these badges can be obtained from project settings in both AppVeyor and CodeCov.IO.

Once this file is added to the repository, you can commit the changes and push the commits to origin:

```
git add *
git commit -m 'Adding README.md'
git push origin
```

This should not trigger a CI build on AppVeyor. You should also see the `README.md` updated on GitHub with AppVeyor and CodeCov.IO badges. This is shown in Figure 15-4.

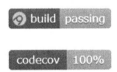

ProDSC - HostsFile resource

This is a sample repository that is used to explain the concept

Figure 15-4. Updated README.md

In Chapter 14, you created a release of the module to a local PowerShell repository and a pull server. In this chapter, you will publish a release of the module back to the GitHub repository as a zip archive after all of the tests complete successfully.

You need to update the appveyor.yml to achieve this:

```
#-------------------------------#
#     environment configuration  #
#-------------------------------#
version: 1.0.{build}.0

environment:
  auth_token:
    secure: 3lekYfC1aw4vvKr9EZ+0WrCdWrN/00te/NtKC3FUNDQeH8gjWT/i4B1FBxltbhC4

skip_commits:
  files:
    - README.md
  message: /updated readme.*|update readme.*s|update docs.*|update
  version.*|update appveyor.*/

install:
    - git clone https://github.com/PowerShell/DscResource.Tests
```

```
    - ps: |
        Import-Module -Name "$env:APPVEYOR_BUILD_FOLDER\DscResource.Tests\
        AppVeyor.psm1"
        Install-Module -Name posh-git -Force
        Invoke-AppveyorInstallTask

#-------------------------------#
#      build configuration      #
#-------------------------------#

build: false


#-------------------------------#
#      test configuration       #
#-------------------------------#

test_script:
    - ps: |
        Invoke-AppveyorTestScriptTask -CodeCoverage -CodeCovIo -ExcludeTag
@()

#-------------------------------#
#      deployment configuration #
#-------------------------------#

# scripts to run before deployment
deploy_script:
  - ps: |
      Invoke-AppveyorAfterTestTask

deploy:
  - git config --global credential.helper store
  - ps: Add-Content "$env:USERPROFILE\.git-credentials" "https://$($env:
    GitHubKey):x-oauth-basic@github.com`n"
  - git config --global user.email "Administrator@PSDSC.Lab"
  - git config --global user.name "Administrator"
  provider: GitHub
  auth_token:
    secure: 3lekYfC1aw4vvKr9EZ+OWrCdWrN/OOte/NtKC3FUNDQeH8gjWT/i4B1FBxltbhC4
```

```
artifact: /.*\.zip/
draft: false
prerelease: false
on:
  branch: master
```

In this updated build configuration, you added the GitHub access token as a secure string in the environment. This can be generated by taking the personal access token from GitHub to AppVeyor and encrypting it using the Encrypt Data option under Account settings.

You also added the deploy section in the appveyor.yml towards the end. This section ensures that the release zip created by the Invoke-AppveyorAfterTestTask is published to GitHub releases.

Once you commit this new build configuration, it triggers the build and uses the build version that is auto-incremented to generate the zip archive. This zip archive gets published to GitHub releases. See Figure 15-5.

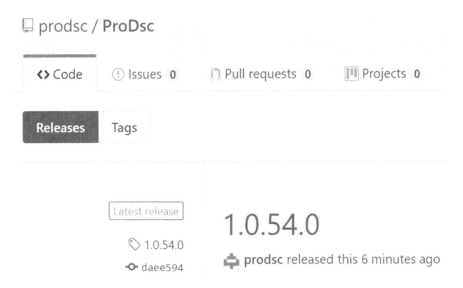

Figure 15-5. *GitHub releases*

If you plan to publish the tested module to the PowerShell gallery instead, this can be done by integrating the PSDeploy deploy task with the AppVeyor CI. PowerShell MVP Warren Frame, author of the PSDeploy module, has an excellent article about this at http://azrs.tk/psdeploy.

Summary

This chapter provided insights into how to use AppVeyor CI to perform continuous integration of your DSC resource modules in a way similar to what you saw in Chapter 14. CI/CD tooling such as AppVeyor, Jenkins, Travis CI, and VSTS provide automated and more controlled means of continuously testing and releasing PowerShell modules. While you only used AppVeyor as an example in this chapter, the concepts of CI/CD are common across most of the tooling available. It is important to adapt the CI/CD practices when developing resource modules and within IaC practices. This helps ensure that the code and configurations are continuously validated for all scenarios that the resource is designed to configure.

PART IV

DSC Platform, Cloud, and Containers

PowerShell DSC is a configuration management platform and can be used across on-premises and cloud environments alike. This final part of the book provides an overview of using DSC CIM interfaces directly in PowerShell and provides examples that can be leveraged in other programming or scripting languages.

You then look at using DSC with different public cloud providers such as Microsoft Azure, Google Cloud Platform, and Amazon Web Services. These cloud providers implement their IaaS in different ways and therefore there are different methods to use DSC with each of these providers. Chapters 17, 18, and 19 provide insights into using these different methods to configure IaaS instances using DSC.

The book concludes by taking a quick look at using DSC with Windows Server 2016 containers. Chapter 20 provides an overview of what you need to know when using DSC with Windows containers and provides examples of building DSC-configured container images.

## CHAPTER 16

DSC as a Platform

Windows PowerShell DSC is a platform rather than just a set of tools to perform configuration management. In Chapter 3, you saw how DSC is implemented as a set of WMI providers. You know that DSC uses the CIM standard data representation for node configurations and uses WS-MAN as a standard transport for sending the configurations to the target nodes. This architecture is what makes DSC a platform. The cmdlets in the PSDesiredStateConfiguration module are a way to use the interfaces provided in the DSC platform. The declarative syntax that is enabled using the Configuration command and keywords such as Node is available to make it easy to author a configuration document and compile the MOF file that the WMI providers understand. In this chapter, you will explore the platform aspect of Windows PowerShell DSC and see how to perform the DSC operations without the need for any cmdlets in the PSDesiredStateConfiguration module.

Lab Requirements

To try the examples and exercises in this chapter, you will need at minimum two or more systems with Windows Server 2008 R2 or above with WMF 5.1 installed. I recommend a system with Windows Server 2016.

The DSC Configuration Management API

You know that Windows PowerShell DSC provides an API that can be used as a part of an existing configuration management processes. It is not necessary that you use the PowerShell cmdlets provided as a part of the DSC feature to manage configurations on the target systems. In Chapter 3, you looked at the Local Configuration Manager (LCM) and you saw a list of CIM methods in the MSFT_DscLocalConfigurationManager class and how they map into the cmdlets in PSDesiredStateConfiguration module. Figure 16-1 is a recap.

© Ravikanth Chaganti 2018
R. Chaganti, *Pro PowerShell Desired State Configuration*, https://doi.org/10.1007/978-1-4842-3483-9_16

```
PS C:\> (Get-CimClass -ClassName MSFT_DscLocalConfigurationManager -Namespace root/Microsoft/Windows/DesiredStateConfiguration).CimClassMethods

Name                                ReturnType Parameters                                                                                      Qualifiers
----                                ---------- ----------                                                                                      ----------
SendConfiguration                   UInt32 {ConfigurationData, force}                                                                          {implemented, static}
SendConfigurationApply              UInt32 {ConfigurationData, force}                                                                          {implemented, static}
GetConfiguration                    UInt32 {configurationData, configurations}                                                                 {implemented, static}
TestConfiguration                   UInt32 {configurationData, InDesiredState, ResourcesInDesiredState, ResourcesNotInDesiredState} {implemented, static}
ApplyConfiguration                  UInt32 {force}                                                                                             {implemented, static}
SendMetaConfigurationApply          UInt32 {ConfigurationData, force}                                                                          {implemented, static}
GetMetaConfiguration                UInt32 {MetaConfiguration}                                                                                 {implemented, static}
RollBack                            UInt32 {configurationNumber}                                                                               {implemented, static}
PerformRequiredConfigurationChecks  UInt32 {Flags}                                                                                             {implemented, static}
StopConfiguration                   UInt32 {force}                                                                                             {implemented, static}
GetConfigurationStatus              UInt32 {All, configurationStatus}                                                                          {implemented, static}
SendConfigurationApplyAsync         UInt32 {ConfigurationData, force, jobId}                                                                   {implemented, static}
GetConfigurationResultOutput        UInt32 {jobId, resumeOutputBookmark, output}                                                               {implemented, static}
RemoveConfiguration                 UInt32 {Force, Stage}                                                                                      {implemented, static}
ResourceGet                         UInt32 {ModuleName, resourceProperty, ResourceType, configurations}                                        {implemented, static}
ResourceSet                         UInt32 {ModuleName, resourceProperty, ResourceType, RebootRequired}                                        {implemented, static}
ResourceTest                        UInt32 {ModuleName, resourceProperty, ResourceType, InDesiredState}                                        {implemented, static}
EnableDebugConfiguration            UInt32 {BreakAll}                                                                                          {implemented, static}
DisableDebugConfiguration           UInt32 {}                                                                                                  {implemented, static}
```

Figure 16-1. *CIM methods in the MSFT_DscLocalConfigurationManager class*

Table 16-1 provides a mapping between the CIM methods and the cmdlets in the PSDesiredStateConfiguration module.

Table 16-1. *Mapping Between CIM Methods and PowerShell Commands*

CIM Method	PowerShell Command
SendConfiguration	Publish-DscConfiguration
SendConfigurationApply	Start-DscConfiguration
GetConfiguration	Get-DscConfiguration
TestConfiguration	Test-DscConfiguration
ApplyConfiguration	Start-DscConfiguration with -UseExisting
SendMetaConfigurationApply	Set-DscLocalConfigurationManager
GetMetaConfiguration	Get-DscLocalConfigurationManager
RollBack	Restore-DscConfiguration
StopConfiguration	Stop-DscConfiguration
GetConfigurationStatus	Get-DscConfigurationStatus
SendMetaConfigurationApplyAsync	Start-DscConfiguration without -Wait
RemoveConfiguration	Remove-DscConfigurationDocument
ResourceGet	Invoke-DscResource with -Method Get

(*continued*)

Table 16-1. (*continued*)

CIM Method	PowerShell Command
ResourceSet	Invoke-DscResource with -Method Set
ResourceTest	Invoke-DscResource with -Method Test
EnableDebugConfiguration	Enable-DscDebug
DisableDebugConfiguration	Disable-DscDebug

In this section, you will see a few examples of how these CIM methods can be used and some tricks that you can build along. I suggest that you look at the MSDN documentation for these CIM methods before you go further. You can see this documentation at http://azrs.tk/dscapi. As you can see in the CIM method documentation, most of the methods take ConfigurationData as a parameter. When calling such CIM methods, you need to pass the contents of configuration MOF file as a byte array. So, before you look at how to call these CIM methods directly, let's look at how to convert the configuration MOF into a byte array representation.

Configuration MOF to Byte Array

Most of the CIM methods in the MSFT_DscLocalConfigurationManager take the configuration MOF contents as a byte array. Since DSC PowerShell cmdlets use CIM and CIM uses WSMAN, the way you construct this byte array depends on whether you are calling the method locally or sending the configuration data to a remote system. Depending on where the target is, you need to pad a few more bytes in the configuration data byte array. The following function explains how to do this:

```
function Get-ByteArry
{
    param
    (
        [Parameter(Mandatory = $true)]
        [string]
        $ConfigurationMof,
```

```
        [Parameter()]
        [switch]
        $Local
    )

    $configurationData = [Byte[]][System.IO.File]::ReadAllBytes
    ((Resolve-Path $ConfigurationMof))

    if (-not $local)
    {
        $totalSize = [System.BitConverter]::GetBytes($configurationData.
        Length + 4)
        $configurationData = $totalSize + $configurationData
    }

    return $configurationData
}
```

In this function, you use a -Local switch parameter to indicate if the target for the configuration is the local system. In a local system, you don't need the additional bytes in the WS-MAN payload. This function returns a byte array representation of the configuration MOF file provided as an input. In the subsequent sections, you will see how this byte array representation can be used with some of the CIM methods in the MSFT_DscLocalConfigurationManager class.

GetConfiguration

You have seen the Get-DscConfiguration cmdlet and its functionality. You know that this cmdlet returns the current state of the resource from the target systems. Remember, the current state need not be the desired state. This cmdlet calls the GetConfiguration CIM method and by default, if no configuration data byte array is provided as an input, the contents of the current.mof are used to get the current state of the resources. And this is the reason why you see an error message that says no current configuration exists when you use the Get-DscConfiguration cmdlet on a target system that never received any configuration using DSC. So, here is a trick. What if you want to find out the current state of a specific resource before you enact any configuration on to the target system?

For example, say you want to check if a specific file exists on a remote system but you don't really want to create it. Here is how to do so:

```
Configuration DemoConfig
{
    Import-DscResource -ModuleName PSDesiredStateConfiguration
    -ModuleVersion 1.1

    File FileDemo
    {
        DestinationPath = 'C:\Windows\System32\Drivers\Etc\Hosts.backup'
        Contents = ''
        Ensure = 'Present'
    }
}

$mof = DemoConfig
```

In this configuration script, you have specified the path to a hosts.backup file. And you generate the MOF file and store that file object in a variable called $mof. Now, let's see how to use the GetConfiguration CIM method to see the current state of this resource. Remember, you are not enacting it; you are simply querying for the current state of the resource.

```
$configurationData = Get-ByteArry $mof.FullName
$result = Invoke-CimMethod -ComputerName S16-Pull-01 `
                          -Namespace root/Microsoft/Windows/DesiredState
                          Configuration `
                          -ClassName MSFT_DSCLocalConfigurationManager `
                          -MethodName GetConfiguration `
                          -Arguments @{ConfigurationData = $configuration
                          Data}
```

In this example, you use the Get-ByteArray function you created at the beginning of this section. It is used to create the byte array representation of the MOF file you just generated. The $result variable is used to store the objects returned by the GetConfiguration CIM method. This method returns an array of the current state for all resources present in the MOF file. Since you have only one resource in the MOF file, $result[0] should give you the current state of the file resource. The ItemValue property of each object in this array contains the current state of the resource. This is shown in Figure 16-2.

```
PS C:\> $result[0].ItemValue


ConfigurationName     : DemoConfig
DependsOn             :
ModuleName            : PSDesiredStateConfiguration
ModuleVersion         : 1.1
PsDscRunAsCredential  :
ResourceId            : [File]FileDemo
SourceInfo            :
Attributes            :
Checksum              :
Contents              :
CreatedDate           :
Credential            :
DestinationPath       : C:\Windows\System32\Drivers\Etc\Hosts.backup
Ensure                : absent
Force                 :
MatchSource           :
ModifiedDate          :
Recurse               :
Size                  :
SourcePath            :
SubItems              :
Type                  :
PSComputerName        : S16-Pull-01
```

Figure 16-2. Result from the GetConfiguration CIM method

As you can see in Figure 16-2, the current state of the resource tells you that the Hosts.backup file does not exist at the requested path. This method can be quite useful when all you want to do it just verify the current state of a resource without enacting the configuration. This method is also a potentially better method than Test-DscConfiguration with the -ReferenceConfiguration parameter since this method provides the complete view into the schema-defined properties.

SendConfiguration

In previous chapters, you saw the Publish-DscConfiguration cmdlet publish a configuration MOF as pending.mof on the target node. The SendConfiguration CIM method is internally called by this cmdlet and this method can be used to send the configuration MOF to the target system. For this example, you will use the configuration data stored in the $configurationData variable in the previous exercise.

```
Invoke-CimMethod -ComputerName S16-Pull-01 `
                 -Namespace root/Microsoft/Windows/DesiredState
                 Configuration `
                 -ClassName MSFT_DSCLocalConfigurationManager `
                 -MethodName SendConfiguration `
                 -Arguments @{ConfigurationData = $configurationData;
                 Force = $true}
```

This example stores the byte array representation of the configuration MOF as pending.mof. You can't use this method when the target system already has a pending configuration. This can be worked around by using the Force parameter. Also, the Force parameter comes handy when you want to push configuration to a target system that is configured as a pull client. But, remember that using Force here changes the target node refresh mode to push.

ApplyConfiguration

In the preceding section, using the SendConfiguration method, you created a pending. mof file on the target system. You can use the ApplyConfiguration method to enact that configuration on the target system. This method does not have a ConfigurationData parameter and always looks for a pending.mof that can be applied. When you use the -UseExisting switch parameter with the Start-DscConfiguration cmdlet, the ApplyConfiguration CIM method gets invoked.

```
Invoke-CimMethod -ComputerName S16-Pull-01 `
                 –Namespace root/Microsoft/Windows/DesiredState
                 Configuration `
                 -ClassName MSFT_DSCLocalConfigurationManager `
                 -MethodName ApplyConfiguration
```

If you have been following the examples so far, you can run the GetConfiguration CIM method to display the current state of the resource on the target system. Remember, by applying the configuration in the preceding example, you created current.mof on the target system. Therefore, there is no need to send the configuration MOF as a byte array.

```
$result = Invoke-CimMethod -ComputerName S16-Pull-01 `
                          -Namespace root/Microsoft/Windows/DesiredState
                          Configuration `
                          -ClassName MSFT_DSCLocalConfigurationManager `
                          -MethodName GetConfiguration
```

The current state of the File resource after ApplyConfiguration is shown in Figure 16-3.

```
PS C:\> $result[0].ItemValue


ConfigurationName    : DemoConfig
DependsOn            :
ModuleName          : PSDesiredStateConfiguration
ModuleVersion       : 1.1
PsDscRunAsCredential :
ResourceId          : [File]FileDemo
SourceInfo          :
Attributes          : {archive}
Checksum            :
Contents            :
CreatedDate         : 2/16/2018 6:52:19 PM
Credential          :
DestinationPath     : C:\Windows\System32\Drivers\Etc\Hosts.backup
Ensure              : present
Force               :
MatchSource         :
ModifiedDate        : 2/16/2018 6:52:19 PM
Recurse             :
Size                : 0
SourcePath          :
SubItems            :
Type                : file
PSComputerName      : S16-Pull-01
```

Figure 16-3. *GetConfiguration result after the enact*

TestConfiguration

While the GetConfiguration method provides the current state of each resource in the configuration MOF, the TestConfiguration method tells you if the target system is in the desired state or not. This method is called by the Test-DscConfiguration cmdlet. When called with no input parameters, this method takes the current.mof and checks if each resource in that MOF is in the desired state or not. If there is no current.mof but there is a pending.mof, the pending.mof file will be used.

```
Invoke-CimMethod -ComputerName S16-Pull-01,S16-JB `
                 -Namespace root/Microsoft/Windows/DesiredState
                 Configuration `
                 -ClassName MSFT_DSCLocalConfigurationManager `
                 -MethodName TestConfiguration
```

Figure 16-4 shows this command in action.

PSComputerName	ResourcesInDesiredState	ResourcesNotInDesiredState	InDesiredState
S16-Pull-01	{[File]FileDemo}		True
S16-JB	{[HostsFile]DemoHosts}		True

Figure 16-4. *TestConfiguration output*

RollBack

Once you enact the configuration, you'll understand from our earlier discussion that the applied configuration gets stored as current.mof and any existing configuration gets stored as previous.mof. When this method is called, the previous.mof gets enacted on the target system, overwriting the current configuration. You can use the Restore-DscConfiguration cmdlet to perform the same function as the RollBack method. The Rollback method, per the MSDN documentation, has a ConfigurationNumber parameter. However, in the current implementation, this parameter is not implemented. The following example shows how this method can be invoked:

```
Invoke-CimMethod -ComputerName S16-Pull-01 `
                 -Namespace root/Microsoft/Windows/DesiredState
                 Configuration `
                 -ClassName MSFT_DSCLocalConfigurationManager `
                 -MethodName Rollback
```

Try It   With the few examples you have seen so far, try invoking other CIM methods in the MSFT_DscLocalConfigurationManager class.

Summary

This chapter is a short overview of DSC configuration management. You looked at invoking the DSC configuration management CIM methods directly using the Invoke-CimMethod cmdlet. Understanding these CIM methods and how to invoke them with the right parameters certainly helps in building custom tooling. In Chapter 9, you looked at how the DSC pull service REST endpoints can be queried using PowerShell. The same can be done in other programming languages such as Python or Ruby or Go. This enables you to build custom reports and dashboards that are not available out of the box with Windows PowerShell DSC. There are also ISV products that leverage these APIs to build an ecosystem of tools around PowerShell DSC. For example, UpGuard has DSC integration to design and compile DSC configuration MOF files, enact them remotely, and monitor the target nodes configuration status in a single console. You can read more about it at http://azrs.tk/dscupguard.

CHAPTER 17

Microsoft Azure and DSC

Microsoft Azure offers different cloud service models such as Infrastructure as a Service (IaaS), Platform as a Service (PaaS), and Software as a Service (SaaS) among many others. With the release of Microsoft Azure Stack (MAS), many of these services can now be extended into the on-premises infrastructure in a hybrid cloud deployment model as well. As a part of the IaaS offerings, the virtual machines created in the Azure cloud can be configured using PowerShell DSC in a few different ways. For the IaaS VMs on Azure, you can use the Azure VM DSC extension handler to enact configurations in the VM. Another approach that internally uses the DSC extension handler is provided by an Azure service called the Azure Automation DSC (AA DSC) service. In this chapter, you will explore how Azure IaaS virtual machines can be configured using the DSC extension handler and how the AA DSC service can be used to manage both Azure IaaS VMs and the systems on-premises.

Lab Requirements

To try the examples and exercises in this chapter, you will need at minimum one or more Azure IaaS Windows instances with Windows Server 2008 R2 or above with WMF 5.1 or above installed. I recommend Windows Server 2016 instances. If you do not have an Azure subscription, you can create one for free, and a trial subscription gives up to $200 worth of credits. Your credit card won't be charged unless you choose to enroll at the end of the trial period. This chapter does not include any instructions about creating Azure IaaS virtual machines. It is assumed that you have this expertise and this chapter builds on it to show how PowerShell DSC can be used with these IaaS VMs. You will also need the Azure PowerShell module and Azure CLI 2.0 to perform the configuration management tasks on Azure IaaS virtual machines. At the time of writing, the Azure CLI 2.0 version is 2.0.25 and the Azure RM PowerShell module version is 5.1.1. All examples have been validated only with these versions of tooling.

© Ravikanth Chaganti 2018
R. Chaganti, *Pro PowerShell Desired State Configuration*, https://doi.org/10.1007/978-1-4842-3483-9_17

The Azure IaaS virtual machines can be configured using the PowerShell DSC in more than one way:

- Setting up a pull server (what you saw in Chapter 8) in one of the IaaS virtual machines and then on-boarding the rest of the Azure VMs to this pull server in the cloud. This is no different from how you set up a DSC pull service in Chapter 8. Therefore, there is no need for any additional discussion about this method.

- Remotely push the DSC configurations to the Azure IaaS virtual machines.

- Enact a DSC configuration in an Azure VM during VM creation either using the portal or Azure CLI 2.0 or Azure PowerShell cmdlets or using Azure Resource Manager (RM) templates and the AA DSC extension handler.

- Using the AA DSC service as a pull server and on-boarding Azure IaaS and on-premises systems for DSC configurations. The AA DSC pull service addresses many limitations.

Let's explore the second, third, and fourth methods in detail.

Pushing DSC Configurations Remotely

To be able to push DSC configurations remotely, you must have the Azure VM configured with a public IP address and with inbound access to WinRM HTTP or HTTPS ports (5895/5896). By default, if you create a VM using the portal with default network settings, inbound traffic to these ports won't be enabled and therefore you need to ensure that these ports are open. You also need the firewall exceptions in the Azure VM (guest OS) to allow inbound WinRM traffic. This can be done using the commands in the NetSecurity module.

```
Set-NetFirewallRule -Name WINRM-HTTP-In-TCP-PUBLIC -RemoteAddress Any
```

One way to test if you can access port 5895, which is needed for pushing DSC configurations, is to use the Test-WSMan cmdlet. This is shown in Figure 17-1.

```
PS C:\> test-wsman -ComputerName avm-16-01.eastus2.cloudapp.azure.com


wsmid            : http://schemas.dmtf.org/wbem/wsman/identity/1/wsmanidentity.xsd
ProtocolVersion : http://schemas.dmtf.org/wbem/wsman/1/wsman.xsd
ProductVendor    : Microsoft Corporation
ProductVersion   : OS: 0.0.0 SP: 0.0 Stack: 3.0
```

Figure 17-1. *Testing if the WinRM HTTP port 5895 is accessible*

Once you have an Azure VM with an open WinRM HTTP port, you can attempt to push a DSC configuration using the Start-DscConfiguration cmdlet. Here is a simple configuration document that you will try to enact remotely:

```
Configuration WebServer
{
    param
    (
        [Parameter(Mandatory = $true)]
        [string]
        $NodeName
    )

    Import-DscResource -Module PSDesiredStateConfiguration
    -ModuleVersion 1.1
    Node $NodeName
    {
        WindowsFeature WebServer
        {
            Name = 'Web-Server'
            Ensure = 'Present'
        }
    }
}
```

You can compile this configuration. Ensure that you provide the DNS name of the Azure virtual machine as the argument to the -NodeName parameter of the configuration. See Figure 17-2.

```
WebServer -NodeName 'avm-16-01.eastus2.cloudapp.azure.com'


    Directory: C:\WebServer


Mode                LastWriteTime         Length Name
----                -------------         ------ ----
-a----         1/27/2018  12:12 PM          1920 avm-16-01.eastus2.cloudapp.azure.com.mof
```

Figure 17-2. *Compiling the configuration*

Now attempt to enact this configuration. Note that you need to supply the credentials using the -Credential parameter.

```
Start-DscConfiguration -Path .\WebServer -Credential (Get-Credential) -Wait
-Verbose
```

What happens? Did that work or do you see any error? This can be mitigated by configuring WinRM trusted hosts. See Figure 17-3.

```
Set-Item -Path WSMAN:\localhost\Client\TrustedHosts -Value *.cloudapp.
azure.com -Force
```

```
PS C:\> Start-DscConfiguration -Path .\WebServer -Credential (Get-Credential) -Wait -Verbose
cmdlet Get-Credential at command pipeline position 1
Supply values for the following parameters:
VERBOSE: Perform operation 'Invoke CimMethod' with following parameters, ''methodName' = SendConfigurationApply,'
amespaceName' = root/Microsoft/Windows/DesiredStateConfiguration'.
VERBOSE: An LCM method call arrived from computer S16-JB with user sid S-1-5-21-1824387555-1090493490-2387759169-
VERBOSE: [AVM-S16-01]: LCM:  [ Start  Set      ]
VERBOSE: [AVM-S16-01]: LCM:  [ Start  Resource ]  [[WindowsFeature]WebServer]
VERBOSE: [AVM-S16-01]: LCM:  [ Start  Test     ]  [[WindowsFeature]WebServer]
VERBOSE: [AVM-S16-01]:                             [[WindowsFeature]WebServer] The operation 'Get-WindowsFeature'
VERBOSE: [AVM-S16-01]:                             [[WindowsFeature]WebServer] The operation 'Get-WindowsFeature'
VERBOSE: [AVM-S16-01]: LCM:  [ End    Test     ]  [[WindowsFeature]WebServer]  in 1.7990 seconds.
```

Figure 17-3. *Successful enact of configuration*

Note   This method uses WinRM HTTP (port 5895) by default. To use WinRM HTTPS (port 5896), you must first configure the WinRM listener to listen on port 5896. This requires certificates. You learned about creating WinRM HTTPS listeners in Chapter 1.

While pushing configurations remotely using the Start-DscConfiguration cmdlet works, it is not the most efficient or scalable method. This method requires you to have either a virtual network connection (using either a site-to-site VPN or point-to-site VPN) or a public IP address and DNS name assigned to the virtual machine. There are, of course, better ways than this. Let's try the second method of enacting a configuration in an Azure VM.

A DSC Configuration in an Azure VM Using the VM Extension Handler

You can enact a DSC configuration in an Azure VM using the DSC extension handler. This VM extension handler can be invoked after the VM creation (or at any time during the VM life cycle) and the associated DSC configuration gets enacted inside the VM. This extension handler can be added using the portal UI or ARM templates or Azure PowerShell or CLI.

I will not show the portal way of achieving this. Instead, I will focus on using Azure PowerShell, ARM templates, and CLI 2.0 to bootstrap the DSC extension handler in an Azure VM.

Using Azure PowerShell Cmdlets

The Azure PowerShell cmdlets provide an imperative method to deploy Azure VMs. Here is the DSC configuration that you will package enact. Copy the contents and save it as webserver.ps1.

```
Configuration WebServer
{
    Import-DscResource -Module PSDesiredStateConfiguration -ModuleVersion 1.1
    Node localhost
    {
        WindowsFeature WebServer
        {
            Name = 'Web-Server'
            Ensure = 'Present'
        }
    }
}
```

The following example is quite verbose and mostly self-explanatory if you already have experience in creating Azure VMs using this method.

```
$location = 'eastus2'
$resourceGroupName = 'ProDscAzure'
$vmName = 'avm-s16-03'
$storageAccountName = 'prodscstore'
$cred = Get-Credential

# Create a resource group
$null = New-AzureRmResourceGroup -Name $resourceGroupName -Location
$location

# Create Storage Account
$null = New-AzureRmStorageAccount -ResourceGroupName $resourceGroupName `
                                   -Name $storageAccountName -Type
                                   'Standard_LRS' `
                                   -Location $location

# Create a subnet configuration
$subnetConfig = New-AzureRmVirtualNetworkSubnetConfig -Name mySubnet `
                                   -AddressPrefix 192.168.1.0/24

# Create a virtual network
$vnet = New-AzureRmVirtualNetwork -ResourceGroupName $resourceGroupName `
                -Location $location `
                -Name MYvNET `
                -AddressPrefix 192.168.0.0/16 `
                -Subnet $subnetConfig

# Create a public IP address and specify a DNS name
$pip = New-AzureRmPublicIpAddress -ResourceGroupName $resourceGroupName `
                -Location $location `
                -AllocationMethod Static `
                -IdleTimeoutInMinutes 4 `
                -Name "$vmName_pip" `
                -DomainNameLabel $vmName
```

```
# Create an inbound network security group rule for port 80
$nsgRuleWeb = New-AzureRmNetworkSecurityRuleConfig -Name
myNetworkSecurityGroupRuleWWW
                                        -Protocol Tcp `
                                        -Direction Inbound `
                                        -Priority 1001 `
                                        -SourceAddressPrefix * `
                                        -SourcePortRange * `
                                         DestinationAddressPrefix * `
                                        -DestinationPortRange 80
                                        -Access Allow

# Create a network security group
$nsg = New-AzureRmNetworkSecurityGroup -ResourceGroupName
$resourceGroupName `
                                    -Location $location `
                                    -Name myNetworkSecurityGroup `
                                    -SecurityRules $nsgRuleWeb

# Create a virtual network card and associate with public IP address and NSG
$nic = New-AzureRmNetworkInterface -Name myNic `
                                -ResourceGroupName $resourceGroupName `
                                -Location $location `
                                -SubnetId $vnet.Subnets[0].Id `
                                -PublicIpAddressId $pip.Id `
                                -NetworkSecurityGroupId $nsg.Id

# Create a virtual machine configuration
$vmConfig = New-AzureRmVMConfig -VMName $vmName -VMSize Standard_A1 |
    Set-AzureRmVMOperatingSystem -Windows -ComputerName $vmName -Credential
    $cred |
    Set-AzureRmVMSourceImage -PublisherName MicrosoftWindowsServer -Offer
    WindowsServer
    -Skus 2016-Datacenter -Version latest | Add-AzureRmVMNetworkInterface
    -Id $nic.Id
```

```
# Create the virtual machine
New-AzureRmVM -ResourceGroupName $resourceGroupName -Location $location -VM
$vmConfig

# Set Azure DSC extension
Publish-AzureRmVMDscConfiguration -ConfigurationPath .\webserver.ps1
-ResourceGroupName $resourceGroupName `
                              -StorageAccountName $storageAccountName
                              -force

Set-AzureRmVMDscExtension -ResourceGroupName $resourceGroupName -VMName
$vmName `
                              -ArchiveStorageAccountName $storageAccountName
                              -ArchiveBlobName webserver.ps1.zip `
                              -AutoUpdate -ConfigurationName 'WebServer'
                              -Version 2.72
```

Note   Make sure you change the value of $storageAccountName in the script. It needs to be unique, and someone reading this chapter might have just used the same! :)

The last two commands in this example are the most interesting in the context of this section. First, you use the Publish-AzureRmVMDscConfiguration cmdlet to package the configuration file that is locally stored and any dependent modules that it needs for an enact as a single zip archive. If your configuration requires any custom DSC resource modules, ensure that those modules are locally available on the system where you are running this cmdlet. This cmdlet also publishes this zip archive in a storage account as a blob. In the last command, you use the Set-AzureRmVMDscExtension cmdlet to enact the configuration upload to Azure Storage account.

This method of bootstrapping DSC configuration after VM creation will take a few minutes to complete. As the VM extension gets installed and the configuration is enacted, you can see the status of the deployment in the Azure Portal. See Figure 17-4.

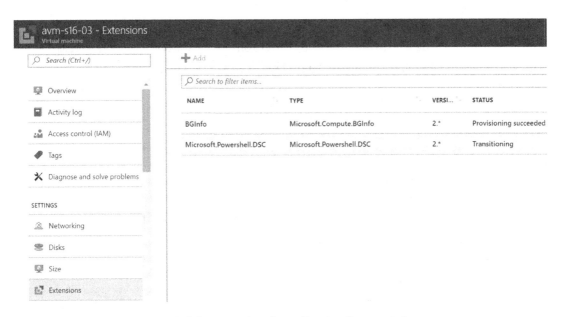

Figure 17-4. *Azure VM DSC extension handler in the portal*

Once the Azure VM creation and DSC configuration enact are complete, you can browse to the public IP or DNS name associated with the VM to check if the web server is installed or not. Remember, the above script enabled inbound access to port 80 using an NSG rule.

Using the Azure Resource Manager Template

While the Azure PowerShell module provides a way to imperatively create the VM and then enact the DSC configuration, ARM templates provide a declarative way of doing the same. My preferred choice of Azure deployments is certainly the ARM templates. The following example provides a sample ARM template:

```
{
    "$schema": "https://schema.management.azure.com/schemas/2015-01-01/
    deploymentTemplate.json#",
    "contentVersion": "1.0.0.0",
    "parameters": {
        "assetLocation": {
            "type": "string",
            "defaultValue": "https://raw.githubusercontent.com/rchaganti/
            ARMTemplates/master/",
```

485

```
            "metadata": {
                "description": "The location of resources such as templates
                and DSC modules that the script is dependent on."
            }
        },
        "vmName": {
            "type": "string",
            "defaultValue": "avm-s16-04",
            "metadata": {
                "description": "Name of the virtual machine."
            }
        },
        "adminUserName": {
            "type": "string",
            "defaultValue": "admin",
            "metadata": {
                "description": "administrator user name for the VMs."
            }
        },
        "adminPassword": {
            "type": "securestring",
            "metadata": {
                "description": "administrator user password for the VMs."
            }
        }
    },
    "variables": {
        "vNetPrefix": "172.22.176.0/20",
        "vNetName": "prodscnet",
        "vNetSubnetName": "prodscsubnet",
        "vnetSubnetPrefix": "172.22.176.",
        "vNetSubnetCIDR": "172.22.176.0/20",
        "vNetSubnetID": "[concat(resourceId('Microsoft.Network/virtual
        Networks',variables('vNetName')),'/subnets/',variables('vNetSubnet
        Name'))]"
    },
```

```json
"resources": [
    {
        "name": "prodscnsg",
        "type": "Microsoft.Network/networkSecurityGroups",
        "apiVersion": "2016-09-01",
        "location": "[resourceGroup().location]",
        "properties": {
            "securityRules": [
                {
                    "name": "allow-http-80",
                    "properties": {
                        "priority": 1001,
                        "sourceAddressPrefix": "*",
                        "protocol": "Tcp",
                        "destinationPortRange": "80",
                        "access": "Allow",
                        "direction": "Inbound",
                        "sourcePortRange": "*",
                        "destinationAddressPrefix": "*"
                    }
                }
            ]
        }
    },
    {
        "name": "[variables('vNetName')]",
        "type": "Microsoft.Network/virtualNetworks",
        "location": "[ResourceGroup().Location]",
        "apiVersion": "2015-05-01-preview",
        "dependsOn": [
            "[concat('Microsoft.Network/networkSecurityGroups/',
            'prodscnsg')]"
        ],
        "properties": {
            "addressSpace": {
                "addressPrefixes": [
```

```
                        "[variables('vNetPrefix')]"
                ]
            },
            "subnets": [
                {
                    "name": "[variables('vNetSubnetName')]",
                    "properties": {
                        "addressPrefix": "[variables('vNetSubnetCIDR')]",
                        "networkSecurityGroup": {
                            "id": "[resourceId(resourceGroup().name,
                            'Microsoft.Network/networkSecurityGroups',
                            'prodscnsg')]"
                        }
                    }
                }
            ]
        }
    },
    {
        "name": "[concat(parameters('vmName'),'-pip')]",
        "type": "Microsoft.Network/publicIpAddresses",
        "apiVersion": "2016-09-01",
        "location": "[resourceGroup().location]",
        "properties": {
            "publicIpAllocationMethod": "Dynamic",
            "dnsSettings": {
                "domainNameLabel": "[parameters('vmName')]"
            }
        }
    },
    {
        "apiVersion": "2015-05-01-preview",
        "type": "Microsoft.Network/networkInterfaces",
        "name": "[concat(parameters('vmName'), '-nif')]",
        "location": "[resourceGroup().location]",
```

```
    "dependsOn": [
        "[concat('Microsoft.Network/virtualNetworks/',
        variables('vNetName'))]",
        "[concat('Microsoft.Network/publicIpAddresses/',
        concat(parameters('vmName'),'-pip'))]"
    ],
    "properties": {
        "ipConfigurations": [
            {
                "name": "[concat(parameters('vmName'),'-
                ipconfig')]",
                "properties": {
                    "subnet": {
                        "id": "[variables('vNetSubnetID')]"
                    },
                    "publicIpAddress": {
                        "id": "[resourceId(resourceGroup().name
                        ,'Microsoft.Network/publicIpAddresses',
                        concat(parameters('vmName'),'-pip'))]"
                    }
                }
            }
        ]
    }
},
{
    "name": "[parameters('vmName')]",
    "type": "Microsoft.Compute/virtualMachines",
    "apiVersion": "2016-04-30-preview",
    "location": "[resourceGroup().location]",
    "dependsOn": [
        "[concat('Microsoft.Network/networkInterfaces/',
        concat(parameters('vmName'), '-nif'))]"
    ],
```

```
"properties": {
    "osProfile": {
        "computerName": "[parameters('vmName')]",
        "adminUsername": "[parameters('adminUsername')]",
        "adminPassword": "[parameters('adminPassword')]",
        "windowsConfiguration": {
            "provisionVmAgent": "true"
        }
    },
    "hardwareProfile": {
        "vmSize": "Standard_A1"
    },
    "storageProfile": {
        "imageReference": {
            "publisher": "MicrosoftWindowsServer",
            "offer": "WindowsServer",
            "sku": "2016-Datacenter",
            "version": "latest"
        },
        "osDisk": {
            "name": "[parameters('vmName')]",
            "createOption": "FromImage",
            "managedDisk": {
                "storageAccountType": "Standard_LRS"
            },
            "caching": "ReadWrite"
        },
        "dataDisks": []
    },
    "networkProfile": {
        "networkInterfaces": [
            {
                "id": "[resourceId('Microsoft.
                Network/networkInterfaces',
                concat(parameters('vmName'),'-nif'))]"
```

```
                    }
                ]
            }
        }
    },
    {
        "type": "Microsoft.Compute/virtualMachines/extensions",
        "name": "[concat(parameters('vmName'),'/webserver')]",
        "apiVersion": "2015-05-01-preview",
        "location": "[resourceGroup().location]",
        "dependsOn": [
            "[concat('Microsoft.Compute/virtualMachines/',
            parameters('vmName'))]"
        ],
        "properties": {
            "publisher": "Microsoft.Powershell",
            "type": "DSC",
            "typeHandlerVersion": "2.72",
            "settings": {
                "ModulesUrl": "[concat(parameters('assetLocation'),'/
                webserver.zip')]",
                "ConfigurationFunction": "webserver.ps1\\webserver"
            }
        }
    }
],
"outputs": {
    "PublicIP":{
        "type": "string",
        "value": "[reference([concat('Microsoft.Network/publicIp
        Addresses/',parameters('vmName'),'-pip')]).properties.
        ipAddress]"
    },
    "PublicDNSFQDN": {
        "type": "string",
```

```
            "value": "[reference([concat('Microsoft.Network/publicIp
            Addresses/',parameters('vmName'),'-pip')]).properties.
            dnsSettings.fqdn]"
        }
    }
}
```

This template contains the assetLocation parameter, which points to the base location where the configuration script archive is available. I took the webserver.ps1 script from the above example and packaged it into a zip archive and uploaded it to public GitHub repository. You can, however, choose to upload this to a different public location and then provide that base location (without webserver.zip) as an argument to the assetLocation parameter.

Note   If you do not prefer a pubic location, you can upload the zip archive to an Azure storage account and specify the SAS token along with the Storage account URI.

There are multiple ways to deploy this. You will use the Azure PowerShell cmdlets to deploy this. Before you can deploy this ARM template, you should have the Azure resource group created. You can do that using the New-AzureRmResourceGroup cmdlet.

```
$resourceGroupName = 'prodscazure'
$location = 'East US 2'
$null = New-AzureRmResourceGroup -Name $resourceGroupName -Location
$location
```

The ARM templates can be deployed using the New-AzureRmResourceGroupDeployment. But, before that, let's ensure that the ARM template is valid. This can be done using the Test-AzureRmResourceGroupDeployment cmdlet.

Note   This cmdlet will only tell you if the template is valid from a syntax point of view. It won't guarantee that a deployment using this template will be successful.

```
$adminPassword = Read-Host -AsSecureString
$parameters = @{
    ResourceGroupName = $resourceGroupName
    TemplateFile      = 'C:\Scripts\prodscAzureVM.json'
    AssetLocation     = 'https://raw.githubusercontent.com/rchaganti/
                        ARMTemplates/master/'
    AdminUserName     = 'Ravikanth'
    AdminPassword     = $adminPassword
}

Test-AzureRmResourceGroupDeployment @parameters -Verbose
```

If the template is valid, you will see a simple message indicating the same. This is shown in Figure 17-5.

```
PS C:\Scripts> Test-AzureRmResourceGroupDeployment @parameters -Verbose
VERBOSE: 5:20:32 PM - Template is valid.

PS C:\Scripts> |
```

***Figure 17-5.** Validating an ARM template*

You can now perform the ARM template deployment.

```
New-AzureRmResourceGroupDeployment -Name ProDSCAzureVM @parameters -Verbose
```

The verbose message stream from this cmdlet tells you the status of the deployment. This will take a few minutes and at the end, you can verify that the VM is created and the web server configuration is enacted by accessing the VM public DNS name or IP address in a browser.

The last method you will explore is the Azure CLI 2.0-based one.

Using Azure CLI 2.0

Azure CLI 2.0 is a command line tool that uses the Azure Resource Manager APIs behind the scenes. If you are command-line junkie, you will love the way Azure CLI 2.0 is written. The following example shows how to create an Azure VM and bootstrap a DSC configuration inside it using CLI 2.0:

```
# Update for your admin password
$adminUserName = 'ravikanth'
$adminPassword = Read-Host -AsSecureString

$resourceGroupName = 'ProDscAzure'
$vmName = 'avm-s16-05'

$vNetName = 'prodscvnet'
$vNetSubNet = 'prodscsubnet'

#login to Azure
az login

# Create a resource group.
az group create --name $resourceGroupName --location eastus2

# Create a vNet and subnet
az network vnet create `
    --resource-group $resourceGroupName `
    --name $vNetName `
    --address-prefix 10.0.0.0/16 `
    --subnet-name $vNetSubnet `
    --subnet-prefix 10.0.1.0/24

# Create NSG
az network nsg create `
    --resource-group $resourceGroupName `
    --name prodscnsg

# Create NSG rule to allow traffic on port 80.
az network nsg rule create `
    --resource-group $resourceGroupName `
    --nsg-name prodscnsg `
```

```
    --name http `
    --access allow `
    --protocol Tcp `
    --direction Inbound `
    --priority 100 `
    --source-address-prefix "*" `
    --source-port-range "*" `
    --destination-address-prefix "*" `
    --destination-port-range 80

# Create NSG rule to allow traffic on port 3389.
az network nsg rule create `
    --resource-group $resourceGroupName `
    --nsg-name prodscnsg `
    --name rdp `
    --access allow `
    --protocol Tcp `
    --direction Inbound `
    --priority 101 `
    --source-address-prefix "*" `
    --source-port-range "*" `
    --destination-address-prefix "*" `
    --destination-port-range 3389

# Create public IP
az network public-ip create `
    --resource-group $resourceGroupName `
    --name prodscpip `
    --dns-name $vmName `
    --allocation-method Static

# Create a NIC for the VM and attach the NSG and PIP
az network nic create `
    --resource-group $resourceGroupName `
    --name nic1 `
    --vnet-name $vNetName `
    --subnet $vNetSubnet `
```

```
    --network-security-group prodscnsg `
    --public-ip-address prodscpip

# Create a VM
az vm create `
    --resource-group $resourceGroupName `
    --name $vmName `
    --size Standard_A1 `
    --image Win2016Datacenter `
    --admin-username $adminUserName `
    --admin-password $adminPassword `
    --nics nic1

# Start DSC extension handler to use a simple bash script to update,
download scripts and install webserver
az vm extension set `
    --name DSC `
    --publisher Microsoft.Powershell `
    --version 2.72 `
    --vm-name $vmName `
    --resource-group $resourceGroupName `
    --settings "{'ModulesURL':'https://raw.githubusercontent.com/rchaganti/
    ARMTemplates/master/webserver.zip', 'configurationFunction': 'webserver.
    ps1\\webserver'}"
```

This script, although just a bunch of Azure CLI 2.0 commands, can be used to perform the same action as in the earlier two examples. You should save this as a .PS1 script (you have PowerShell variable substitution for some parameters) and then execute all the commands sequentially. Similar to the ARM template example, the path to the DSC configuration zip file is provided as an argument to the DSC extension's ModulesURL property.

All three methods you have seen so far are mostly one-to-one except the ARM template, which can be used to perform the DSC configuration on multiple VMs at the same time. Of course, you can script the Azure PowerShell cmdlets or the CLI 2.0 to perform a simultaneous configuration enact on multiple VMs. These methods are not scalable. Also, there is no centralized way to maintain configurations and resource modules, as in the case of a DSC pull service. One of the other benefits the DSC pull service offers is a way to monitor the configuration state on the target nodes. You can set up a DSC pull service instance in Azure and then on-board the Azure IaaS VM instances to that pull service. However, there are the same limitations to that approach as what you experience with the on-premises pull server.

The on-premises DSC pull server does not offer encryption at rest for the DSC configuration documents; does not offer any visualization of the node configuration status; and does not offer the ability to manage systems or VMs outside the on-premises organization unless the on-premises DSC pull service is Internet-facing.

To address some of these needs, Microsoft Azure provides a pull service in the cloud as a part of the Azure Automation service.

Azure Automation DSC

In this section, you will look at how to set up Azure Automation (standalone) and use the Azure Automation (AA) DSC pull service to on-board both on-premises and Azure IaaS virtual machines to the AA DSC pull service. Azure Automation is available as both a standalone service and as a part of the Operations Management Suite of services. This chapter will only show the deployment of a standalone AA service and use the same for all examples.

Azure Automation DSC can be used to

- Manage Azure virtual machines (both classic and v2)

- Manage physical/virtual Windows/Linux machines on-premises or in a cloud other than Azure

- Provide rich reporting capabilities for both on-premises and cloud machines

In this chapter, I will focus only on Windows VMs in the Azure cloud and on-premises. You can see on-boarding Google Compute Engine Windows VMs to the AA DSC pull service in Chapter 18 and using the AA DSC pull service with Amazon Web Services (AWS) EC2 instances in Chapter 19.

Setting Up Azure Automation

Using the Azure management portal, you just need to click a few blades to set up the Azure Automation account. However, that is no fun. You will see Azure PowerShell and Azure CLI 2.0 methods of creating an Azure Automation account.

```
$resourceGroupName = 'ProDscAzure'
$location = 'East US 2'

$null = Add-AzureRmAccount
$null = New-AzureRmResourceGroup -Name $resourceGroupName -Location
$location

$null = New-AzureRmAutomationAccount -Name 'ProDscAA' -Location 'East US 2'
-ResourceGroupName 'ProDscAzure'
```

Once the Automation account is created, you can see it in the Azure management portal or use the Get-AzureRmAutomationAccount cmdlet to retrieve the information about the newly created automation account. See Figure 17-6.

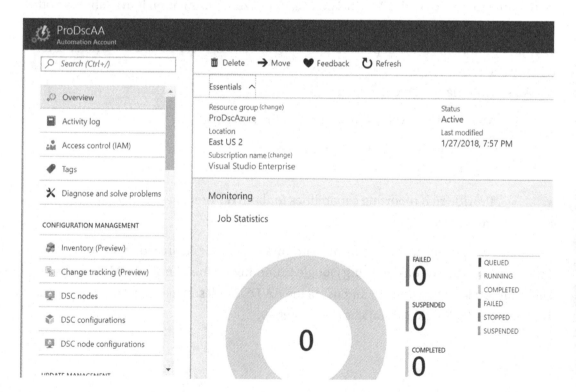

Figure 17-6. *Azure Automation account in the portal*

As you can see in Figure 17-6, the Azure Automation account contains blades that can be used manage DSC nodes, configurations, and node configurations.

- **DSC Nodes**: Used to on-board Azure VMs and see on-boarded non-Azure VMs

- **DSC Configurations**: Used to add DSC configuration scripts and compile configuration scripts

- **DSC Node Configurations**: Used to add/view compiled DSC configuration MOF files that can be assigned to nodes

Adding DSC Configurations

You can on-board either Azure VMs or non-Azure machines that are running in other clouds or on-premises without any existing node configurations in AA DSC. However, for the purpose of understanding the flow, you will first add configurations and compile them. Let's see how this can be done using Azure PowerShell cmdlets.

```
Import-AzureRmAutomationDscConfiguration -AutomationAccountName 'ProDscAA'
-ResourceGroupName $resourceGroupName -SourcePath C:\Scripts\webserver.ps1
-Published
```

The `Import-AzureRmAutomationDscConfiguration` cmdlet takes the Automation account name, resource group name, and the path to the configuration script (.ps1) as arguments. The `-Published` switch parameter specifies that the configuration script will be in published state. This published configuration can be compiled using the `Start-AzureRmAutomationDscCompilationJob` cmdlet.

```
Start-AzureRmAutomationDscCompilationJob -ConfigurationName 'webserver'
-ResourceGroupName $resourceGroupName -AutomationAccountName 'ProDscAA'
```

Once the compile job is complete, the node configuration appears in the DSC Node Configurations blade shown in Figure 17-7.

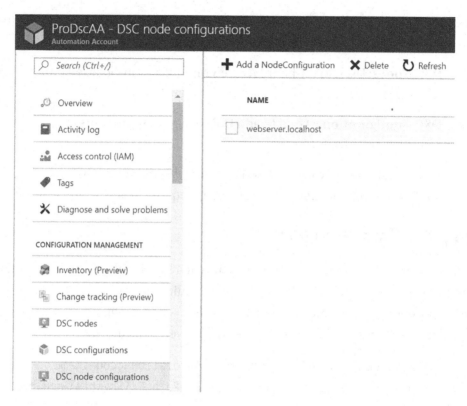

Figure 17-7. *Compiled node configuration*

Adding DSC configurations using this approach and compiling them using the DSC pull service allows you to specify separate configuration data for each compilation job.

Note   I recommend taking a look at Azure Automation in general and understanding how to use variables, credentials, and other AA assets. It is possible to use these assets when importing the DSC configuration into AA.

Try It   Your sample configuration (`webserver.ps1`) does not require any parameters or configuration data. However, this may not be a real use case. So, try publishing a configuration document that has mandatory parameters and pass the parameter arguments to the `Start-AzureRmAutomationDscCompilationJob` cmdlet. Hint: You need to use the `-Parameters` parameter of this cmdlet.

However, if the configuration is static or something that you may never reuse, you can compile the configuration locally and upload the node configuration as a MOF file directly.

Adding DSC Node Configurations

While the above process of generating node configurations (compiled) is a two-step process, you can upload compiled MOF files as node configurations directly to an automation account. This is done using the `Import-AzureRmAutomationDscNode Configuration` cmdlet.

```
Import-AzureRmAutomationDscNodeConfiguration -AutomationAccountName
'ProDscAA' -ResourceGroupName $resourceGroupName -ConfigurationName
FailoverCluster -Path C:\Scripts\FailoverCluster\localhost.mof -Force
```

Once this is uploaded, it appears as ConfigurationName.MOFFileBaseName. So, in this example, it will appear as FailoverCluster.Localhost in the DSC node configurations blade.

Since the nodename has no relevance in the AA DSC node configurations, you can specify an environment such as Dev, Test, and Prod instead of localhost to identify which environment the configuration is used in. When you add that node configuration to AA DSC, you can see those configurations as FailoverCluster.Dev, FailoverCluster.Prod, and so on. See Figure 17-8.

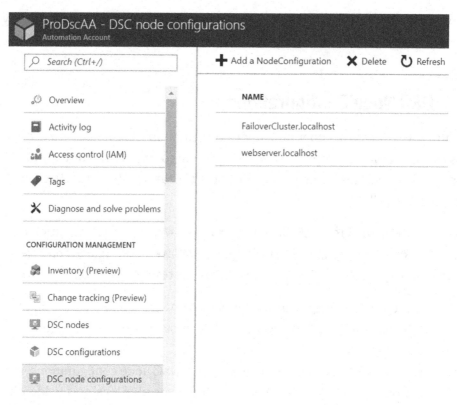

Figure 17-8. *Published node configurations*

Note   If you import a new compiled configuration that contains the same configuration name and host name in the MOF file as an existing node configuration, the existing node configuration will get overwritten.

Registering Azure and On-Premises Machines in AA DSC

Once you have the node configurations ready, you can register any Azure VM or on-premises physical and/or virtual machines to receive configuration from the AA DSC pull service. Let's first see how to register Azure VMs.

Registering Azure VMs

To register Azure IaaS VMs, you can use the `Register-AzureRmAutomationDscNode` cmdlet.

```
Register-AzureRmAutomationDscNode -AutomationAccountName 'ProDscAA'
-AzureVMName avm-s16-05 -ResourceGroupName $resourceGroupName
-NodeConfigurationName 'webserver.localhost'
```

Note   Using the `Register-AzureRmAutomationDscNode` cmdlet, it is possible to register an Azure VM without assigning any Node configuration. This will simply onboard the VM and does not associate any configuration to it.

This command installs the DSC extension handler in the VM and configures the VM to receive a configuration from the DSC pull service. At the end of this command execution, the Azure VM appears under DSC nodes in the Automation service and the state of configuration compliance can be seen there.

Note   Managing the configuration of Azure VMs with the DSC extension handler version 2.70 and above is free. The method seen above installs the latest version of the DSC extension handler in the Azure VM and therefore is free of any cost associated with AA DSC.

To retrieve the node configuration report sent to the DSC pull service, you can use the `Get-AzureRmAutomationDscNodeReport` cmdlet.

```
$Node = Get-AzureRmAutomationDscNode -ResourceGroupName $resourceGroupName
-AutomationAccountName 'ProDscAA' -Name avm-s16-05
Get-AzureRmAutomationDscNodeReport -ResourceGroupName $resourceGroupName
-AutomationAccountName 'ProDscAA' -NodeId $Node.Id
```

```
ResourceGroupName       : ProDscAzure
AutomationAccountName    : ProDscAA
StartTime               : 1/28/2018 7:29:09 AM +05:30
LastModifiedTime        : 1/28/2018 7:29:10 AM +05:30
EndTime                 : 1/28/2018 7:33:07 AM +05:30
ReportType              : Initial
Id                      : d170342d-03ce-11e8-a946-000d3a00d39c
NodeId                  : be749a9d-03ce-11e8-a946-000d3a00d39c
Status                  : Compliant
RefreshMode             : Pull
RebootRequested         : False
ReportFormatVersion     : 2.0
```

Figure 17-9. *Initial report for an Azure VM*

Figure 17-9 shows the initial report for an Azure VM. Every compliance check on the VM sends the report back to the DSC pull service. The command shown above retrieves all available reports for the node. If you are interested in seeing only the latest report, add the -Latest switch parameter to the Get-AzureRmAutomationDscNodeReport cmdlet.

Let's step back a bit and understand exactly what happened when you registered the Azure VM. You learned in Chapter 8 that the LCM needs to be configured as a pull client to be able to receive configurations from a pull server. In case of on-boarding Azure VMS to AA DSC pull service using the Register-AzureRmAutomationDscNode cmdlet, the meta is done behind the scenes. If you log into the Azure VM and run the Get-DscLocalConfigurationManager cmdlet, you will see the updated meta configuration that points to the AA DSC pull service.

If you have the necessary NSG rules and OS firewall ports enabled (you saw this earlier), you can run the Get-DscLocalConfigurationManager remotely as well. Figure 17-10 shows this.

```
$cimSession = New-CimSession -ComputerName 'avm-s16-05.eastus2.cloudapp.
azure.com' -Credential (Get-Credential)
Get-DscLocalConfigurationManager -CimSession $cimSession
```

```
ActionAfterReboot              : ContinueConfiguration
AgentId                        : BE749A9D-03CE-11E8-A946-000D3A00D39C
AllowModuleOverWrite           : False
CertificateID                  : BE0252687825E3FFA0521D4205031B9684A093FF
ConfigurationDownloadManagers  : {[ConfigurationRepositoryWeb]AzureAutomationDSC}
ConfigurationID                :
ConfigurationMode              : ApplyAndMonitor
ConfigurationModeFrequencyMins : 15
Credential                     :
DebugMode                      : {NONE}
DownloadManagerCustomData      :
DownloadManagerName            :
LCMCompatibleVersions          : {1.0, 2.0}
LCMState                       : Idle
LCMStateDetail                 :
LCMVersion                     : 2.0
StatusRetentionTimeInDays      : 10
SignatureValidationPolicy      : NONE
SignatureValidations           : {}
MaximumDownloadSizeMB          : 500
PartialConfigurations          :
RebootNodeIfNeeded             : False
RefreshFrequencyMins           : 30
RefreshMode                    : Pull
ReportManagers                 : {[ReportServerWeb]AzureAutomationDSC}
ResourceModuleManagers         : {[ResourceRepositoryWeb]AzureAutomationDSC}
PSComputerName                 : avm-s16-05.eastus2.cloudapp.azure.com
PSComputerName                 : avm-s16-05.eastus2.cloudapp.azure.com
```

Figure 17-10. *LCM meta configuration from the Azure VM*

You can access individual properties in the meta configuration to see how the node is configured. For example, Figure 17-11 shows the ConfigurationDownloadManagers setting in the meta configuration.

```
ResourceId               : [ConfigurationRepositoryWeb]AzureAutomationDSC
SourceInfo               : C:\Packages\Plugins\Microsoft.Powershell.DSC\2.74.0.0\DSCWork\Registra
                           tionMetaConfigV2.0\RegistrationMetaConfigV2.ps1::69::9::ConfigurationR
                           epositoryWeb
AllowUnsecureConnection  :
CertificateID            :
ConfigurationNames       : {webserver.localhost}
RegistrationKey          :
ServerURL                : https://eus2-agentservice-prod-1.azure-automation.net/accounts/6d0a754
                           3-89a1-4fb7-b078-152f0f314e7e
PSComputerName           : avm-s16-05.eastus2.cloudapp.azure.com
```

Figure 17-11. *Configuration Download Manager configuration in Azure VM*

As you can see in Figure 17-11, the ServerURL property is set to the Azure Automation DSC endpoint.

Try It   Similar to the above, can you try retrieving the report server and resource module manager settings?

Registering On-Premises Machines

What you have seen so far with registering Azure VMs is fairly straightforward. The AA DSC service takes care of registering the target nodes behind the scenes and you don't need to worry about details such as the pull service URL, registration keys, and other related settings. You saw in Chapter 8 that this information is necessary for on-boarding a target node as a pull client. However, in the case of AA DSC, you are neither creating any registration keys nor aware of the pull service endpoint URL. So, how do you retrieve this information necessary for on-boarding non-Azure machines?

Note   The process shown in this section can be used not just with on-premises physical or virtual machines but also machines running in a cloud other than Azure.

On-boarding non-Azure machines to AA DSC incurs cost. Refer to the pricing for using AA DSC with on-premises or non-Azure cloud machines.

Generating a Meta Configuration

To configure the LCM as a pull client, what you really need is a meta configuration document that can be used with the Set-DscLocalConfigurationManager cmdlet. Within the Azure PowerShell cmdlets module for Azure Automation, this can be done using the Get-AzureRmAutomationDscOnboardingMetaconfig cmdlet.

```
Get-AzureRmAutomationDscOnboardingMetaconfig -ResourceGroupName
$resourceGroupName -AutomationAccountName 'ProDscAA' -ComputerName S16-01,
S16-02 -OutputFolder C:\Scripts -Verbose
```

This cmdlet downloads the `meta.mof` files for the nodes S16-01 and S16-02 to a local path. You can open the MOF files in your favorite text editor to see the registration keys and endpoint URLs.

Note   While this method of downloading a meta MOF is easy, it requires you to manually edit the compiled MOF in case of any customizations. I recommend manually creating a meta configuration script and compiling it into a MOF. This is shown later in this section.

These machines are the no-premises virtual machines that I have in my DSC lab and I can perform the meta configuration using the `Set-DscLocalConfigurationManager` cmdlet. Once the configuration is complete, you can verify that these nodes are on-boarded to the AA DSC pull service by using the `Get-AzureRmAutomationDscNode` cmdlet. This is shown in Figure 17-12.

```
Get-AzureRmAutomationDscNode -ResourceGroupName $resourceGroupName
-AutomationAccountName 'ProDSCAA' | Select-Object Name,
NodeConfigurationName, Status
```

```
Name        NodeConfigurationName Status
----        --------------------- ------
avm-s16-05  webserver.localhost   Compliant
S16-01                            Compliant
S16-02                            Compliant|
```

Figure 17-12. Node in Azure Automation DSC

As you can see in Figure 17-12, there are no configurations associated with the newly on-boarded nodes. You can assign a node configuration by using the `Set-AzureRmAutomationDscNode` cmdlet.

```
$Node1 = Get-AzureRmAutomationDscNode -ResourceGroupName $resourceGroupName
-AutomationAccountName 'ProDscAA' -Name 'S16-01'
Set-AzureRmAutomationDscNode -AutomationAccountName 'ProDscAA'
-NodeConfigurationName 'FailoverCluster.Localhost' -ResourceGroupName
$resourceGroupName -Id $Node1.Id
```

```
$Node2 = Get-AzureRmAutomationDscNode -ResourceGroupName $resourceGroupName
-AutomationAccountName 'ProDscAA' -Name 'S16-02'
```

```
Set-AzureRmAutomationDscNode -AutomationAccountName 'ProDscAA'
-NodeConfigurationName 'FailoverCluster.Localhost' -ResourceGroupName
$resourceGroupName -Id $Node2.Id
```

Once the nodes are assigned a node configuration, running Get-AzureRmAutomationDscNode again tells you that there is pending configuration on these nodes. This is shown in Figure 17-13.

```
Name         NodeConfigurationName       Status
----         ---------------------       ------
avm-s16-05 webserver.localhost           Compliant
   S16-01    FailoverCluster.Localhost   Pending
   S16-02    FailoverCluster.Localhost   Pending
```

Figure 17-13. *Pending node configurations in AA DSC*

As the consistency check gets triggered on the on-premises VMs, the new configuration assigned to the node gets enacted. Once the enact is complete, you can check the node status using the Get-AzureRmAutomationDscNode cmdlet again. This is shown in Figure 17-14.

```
Name         NodeConfigurationName       Status
----         ---------------------       ------
avm-s16-05 webserver.localhost           Compliant
   S16-01    FailoverCluster.Localhost   Compliant
   S16-02    FailoverCluster.Localhost   Compliant
```

Figure 17-14. *All nodes in compliant state in AA DSC*

As noted, you can use the AA DSC for just reporting purposes. However, if you look at the DSC meta configuration that was downloaded using the Get-AzureRmAutomati onDscOnboardingMetaconfig cmdlet, it will have settings for configuration download managers, resource module mangers, and report servers. If you want to configure the target node only for reporting to the AA DSC pull service, you need the registration key and the endpoint URL. These values can be retrieved in the Azure Management portal. This can be done by navigating to the Keys blade of the Azure Automation account in the management portal, as shown in Figure 17-15.

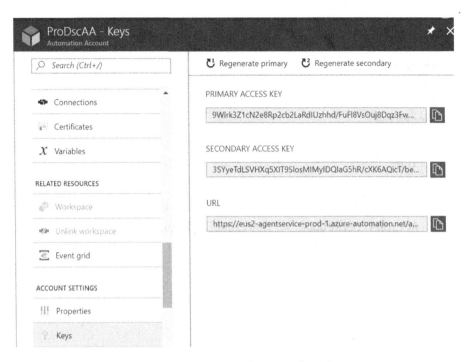

Figure 17-15. *Azure Automation Account keys and endpoint URL*

This can also be done using the Get-AzureRmAutomationRegistrationInfo cmdlet.

```
$registrationInfo = Get-AzureRmAutomationRegistrationInfo
-ResourceGroupName $resourceGroupName -AutomationAccountName 'ProDSCAA'
```

With this information handy, you can create a meta configuration document that on-boards the target node only for reporting in AA DSC. The following is an example:

```
[DscLocalConfigurationManager()]
Configuration AADscMetaConfiguration
{
    param
    (
        [Parameter(Mandatory = $true)]
        [String]
        $RegistrationKey,

        [Parameter(Mandatory = $true)]
        [String]
        $EndPointURL,
```

```
        [Parameter()]
        [String]
        $NodeName
    )

    Node $NodeName
    {
        Settings
        {
            ConfigurationMode = 'ApplyAndMonitor'
            ActionAfterReboot = 'ContinueConfiguration'
        }

        ReportServerWeb AADSCReport
        {
            ServerURL = $EndPointURL
            RegistrationKey = $RegistrationKey
        }
    }
}

$registrationInfo = Get-AzureRmAutomationRegistrationInfo
-ResourceGroupName $resourceGroupName -AutomationAccountName 'ProDSCAA'
AADscMetaConfiguration -NodeName 'S12R2-01' -RegistrationKey
$registrationInfo.PrimaryKey -EndPointURL $registrationInfo.Endpoint
-Verbose
```

Once this meta configuration compiled and the enact is complete, the target node can be seen in the Azure Portal as a DSC node without any configuration associated with it. This is shown in Figure 17-16.

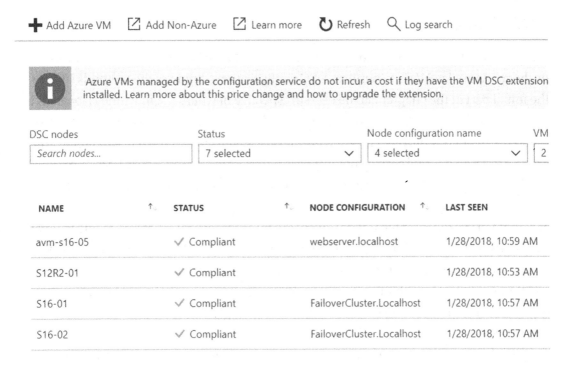

Figure 17-16. *Azure automation DSC nodes*

This brings us to the end of this session. One aspect that you did not see is how to upload custom DSC resource modules to the AA DSC pull service.

Adding DSC Resource Modules to the AA DSC

This can be done directly from the PowerShell gallery by clicking the **Deploy To Azure Automation button** on the module page or you can use the New-AzureRmAutomationModule cmdlet.

```
New-AzureRmAutomationModule -ContentLinkUri 'https://raw.githubusercontent.
com/rchaganti/ARMTemplates/master/NetworkingDsc.zip' -Name NetworkingDsc
-ResourceGroupName $resourceGroupName -AutomationAccountName 'ProDscAA'
-Verbose
```

Once this module import is complete, it can be seen in the Modules blade of the Azure Automation service in management portal.

Summary

This chapter provided details about using DSC with Azure IaaS VMs and different ways to on-board Azure IaaS VMs to perform DSC configurations. Some of the methods seen in the initial part of the chapter can be used irrespective of where the machine is located (in a cloud or on-premises). You saw an overview of what the Azure Automation DSC service is and the benefits it provides over the on-premises pull server shown in Chapter 8. You can use the AA DSC pull service not just with Azure VMs but non-Azure VMs or physical machines running either on-premises and/or in a cloud other than Azure. This service, when integrated with Operations Management Suite (OMS) solutions, provides the capability to see rich graphical reporting of the node configuration status. While you have not seen any in-depth content on integrating the standalone AA DSC service with OMS, let me tell you that it is not rocket science. I recommend that you look at this integration and understand the capabilities it can provide. In the next two chapters, you will see how the AA DSC service can be used with VMs running in Google Cloud Platform and Amazon Web Services.

Ben Gelens, my good friend and the technical reviewer of this book, published an excellent video series on the Azure Automation DSC. You can watch it on Channel 9 at `http://azrs.tk/CH9Dsc`. If you are looking for more details on this AA DSC service, I strongly recommend taking a look at his video series.

CHAPTER 18

DSC and Google Cloud Platform

Google Cloud Platform (GCP) is yet another but very important player in the Infrastructure as a Service (IaaS) public cloud space. As a part of Google Compute Engine (GCE), GCP offers a wide range of IaaS VM instances and operating systems. Windows Server 2008 R2, Windows Server 2012 R2, Windows Server 2016, and Windows Server 2016 version 1709 are a part these GCE offerings. In this chapter, you will learn how to use DSC to configure the GCE Windows instances.

Lab Requirements

To try the examples and exercises in this chapter, you will need at minimum one or more GCE IaaS Windows instances with Windows Server 2008 R2 or above with WMF 5.1 or above installed. I recommend Windows Server 2016 instances. If you do not have a GCP subscription, you can create one for free and a trial subscription includes up to $300 worth of credits. Your credit card won't be charged unless you choose to enroll at the end of the trial period. This chapter does not provide any in-depth overview of GCP or GCE VM instances. You will also need the Google Cloud SDK for the gcloud CLI and PowerShell cmdlets. You will also need an active Azure subscription for on-boarding a GCE instance to the AA DSC pull service.

Before using the gcloud CLI or GoogleCloud PowerShell module, you must ensure that you authenticate with Google Cloud. Upon installing the Google Cloud SDK, you get a configuration option to log into GCP. You must complete this and create a project.

```
gcloud init
```

© Ravikanth Chaganti 2018

R. Chaganti, *Pro PowerShell Desired State Configuration*, https://doi.org/10.1007/978-1-4842-3483-9_18

This command will initialize the authentication process and walk you through the on-boarding steps. You must set the default region and zone in the project settings.

```
gcloud config set compute/region asia-east1
gcloud config set compute/zone asia-east1-a
```

You can override these settings using the -Region and -Zone parameters when available.

For the GCP project that you created during the initialization, you should enable the relevant APIs. At minimum, you should enable the Google Compute Engine, Cloud Storage, and Cloud Storage JSON APIs. To do this, navigate to the project in the Google cloud console and go to API & Services.

For the GCP project, you should also have a billing account associated. Your card won't be charged.

Using DSC with GCE Windows Instances

The GCE Windows instances can be configured using PowerShell DSC in more than one way.

- Setting up a pull server (what you saw in Chapter 8) in one of the IaaS virtual machines and then on-boarding the rest of the GCE Windows instances to this pull server in the cloud. This is no different than how you set up a DSC pull service in Chapter 8. Therefore, there is no need for any additional discussion about this method.

- Another method is to remotely push the DSC configurations to the GCE Windows instances.

- Enact the DSC configuration in a GCE Windows instance during the start up of the instance.

- You can use the AA DSC service as a pull server and on-board GCE Windows instances so that the GCE instance configurations can be managed and monitored from AA DSC.

Let's explore the last three methods in the above list.

Pushing DSC Configurations Remotely

To be able to push DSC configurations remotely, you must have the GCE Windows instance configured with a public IP address and with inbound access to WinRM HTTP or HTTPS ports (5895/5896).

To allow WinRM HTTP or HTTPS traffic into a GCE Windows instance, you must first create the firewall rules at the VPC network level. The following code snippet will add both WinRM HTTP and HTTP firewall rules for the 'default' network:

```
$projectID      = 'prodsc-gce-01'
$allowedHTTP    = New-GceFirewallProtocol "tcp" -Port 5985
$winrmhttpTag   = 'winrmhttp'

$winrmhttpsTag  = 'winrmhttps'
$allowedHTTPS   = New-GceFirewallProtocol "tcp" -Port 5986

#Create the HTTP firewall rule
Add-GceFirewall -Name 'allow-winrm-http' `
                -AllowedProtocol $allowedHTTP `
                -Project $projectID `
                -Network "default" `
                -SourceRange '0.0.0.0/0' `
                -TargetTag $winrmhttpTag

#Create the HTTPS firewall rule
Add-GceFirewall -Name 'allow-winrm-https' `
                -AllowedProtocol $allowedHTTPS `
                -Project $projectID `
                -Network "default" `
                -SourceRange '0.0.0.0/0' `
                -TargetTag $winrmhttpsTag
```

Note   Ensure you update the value of $projectID.

Once this is complete, you will be able to see the new firewall rule in VPC Network ➤ Firewall Rules, as shown in Figure 18-1 or in the Get-GceFirewall cmdlet output.

Firewall rules   ➕ CREATE FIREWALL RULE   ↻ REFRESH   🗑 DELETE

Firewall rules control incoming or outgoing traffic to an instance. By default, incoming traffic from outside your network is blocked. Learn more

Note: App Engine firewalls are managed here.

Ingress   Egress

Name	Targets	Source filters	Protocols / ports
☐ allow-winrm-http	winrmhttp	IP ranges: 0.0.0.0/0	tcp:5985
☐ allow-winrm-https	winrmhttps	IP ranges: 0.0.0.0/0	tcp:5986

Figure 18-1. *WinRM HTTP rule in VPC Network*

For Windows instances within GCE, a WinRM HTTPS listener gets created with a self-signed certificate and the WinRM HTTPS firewall rules in the OS are enabled. Therefore, if you plan to use only the WinRM HTTPS listener to connect and push configurations remotely, no further configuration is required. However, if you plan to use the WinRM HTTP (not recommended) for pushing DSC configurations, you will need to enable the firewall rule in the OS.

Before you create the GCE Windows instance and enable the WinRM HTTP firewall rule in the OS, save the following command to a PowerShell script named `firewallconfig.ps1` and upload it to a public location that can be accessed from Google Compute instance:

```
Set-NetFirewallRule -Name WINRM-HTTP-In-TCP-PUBLIC -RemoteAddress Any
```

I chose to upload this as a public gist on GitHub. This script will be used as a startup script to configure the WinRM HTTP firewall rule in the OS.

With the script uploaded a public location, you can create a new Windows instance and attach the above script as a startup script and add the firewall tags -- `$winrmhttpTag` and `$winrmhttpsTag`. This ensures that the GCE instance is allowed both inbound WinRM HTTP and HTTPS traffic.

You can create a GCE Windows instance using the following snippet:

```
$disk = Get-GceImage -Project 'windows-cloud' -Family 'windows-2016'
$config = New-GceInstanceConfig 'prodscgce1' `
    -MachineType 'n1-standard-1' `
    -BootDiskImage $disk `
```

```
-Metadata @{ "windows-startup-script-url" = "https://gist.
githubusercontent.com/rchaganti/e635e5f90847780763fd61b6f6198863/raw/98
3e42f7205efb309969b6f759515decd7b8e147/firewallconfig.ps1" } `
-Tag $winrmhttpTag, $winrmhttpsTag

$gceInstance = $config | Add-GceInstance -Project $projectID
```

Note   Since you are adding `firewallconfig.ps1` as a startup script, it will run after every reboot.

It is possible to use a Google Cloud Storage bucket for the startup script. It requires you to specify the GCS bucket URL with the access token.

This creates the instance but the default Windows user password won't be available until you reset it. There is no PowerShell cmdlet to do this. Instead, you use the gcloud CLI. Run the following command and follow the on-screen instructions. At the end of the action, you will see the public IP address and the username and password to use:

```
gcloud compute reset-windows-password prodscgce1
```

Note the username/password and proceed to the next section. This command shows the public IP address of the GCE instance as well.

Note   You may have to wait for a few minutes before trying to reset the password. Don't forget to replace the instance name `prodscgce1` with name of the instance you chose to deploy.

Pushing a Configuration Over WinRM HTTPS

Since the firewall rules at both the VPC level and the OS level are in place, you can start by creating a CIM session to the GCE instance.

```
$cimSessionOptions = New-CimSessionOption -SkipCACheck -SkipCNCheck -UseSsl
-Verbose
$cimsession = New-CimSession -ComputerName 35.229.193.26 -Credential
(Get-Credential) -SessionOption $cimSessionOptions
```

Note   When specifying credentials, ensure that you prefix the GCE instance host name with the user name.

This creates a CIM session. Since the WinRM HTTPS listener gets created using a self-signed certificate, you can work around any certificate checks by using the -SkipCACheck and -SkipCNCheck parameters with the New-CimSessionOption cmdlet and use this CIM session option object with the New-CimSession cmdlet.

At this point, if you run the Get-DscConfiguration cmdlet, you should see a message saying that there is no existing current configuration. This is shown in Figure 18-2.

```
PS C:\scripts\GCE> Get-DscConfiguration -CimSession $cimsession
Get-DscConfiguration : Current configuration does not exist. Execute Start-DscConfiguration command with -Path
parameter to specify a configuration file and create a current configuration first.
At line:1 char:1
+ Get-DscConfiguration -CimSession $cimsession
+ ~~~~~~~~~~~~~~~~~~~~~~~~~~~~~~~~~~~~~~~~~~~~~~
    + CategoryInfo          : NotSpecified: (MSFT_DSCLocalConfigurationManager:root/Microsoft/...gurationManager)
    [Get-DscConfiguration], CimException
    + FullyQualifiedErrorId : MI RESULT 1,Get-DscConfiguration
    + PSComputerName        : 35.229.193.26
```

Figure 18-2. *Get-DscConfiguration error*

Let's now compile and enact the following configuration using the CIM session that you created for the WinRM HTTPS endpoint:

```
Configuration GCEDemo
{
    param
    (
        [Parameter(Mandatory = $true)]
        [String]
        $NodeName
    )

    Import-DscResource -ModuleName PSDesiredStateConfiguration
    -ModuleVersion 1.1

    Node $NodeName
    {
        WindowsFeature WebServer
```

```
    {
        Name = 'Web-Server'
        Ensure = 'Present'
    }
  }
}

GCEDemo -NodeName '35.229.193.26' -OutputPath C:\Scripts\GCE\GCEDemo


Start-DscConfiguration -CimSession $cimsession -Wait -Verbose -Path .\
GCEDemo
```

When you enact this, the GCE instance receives the configuration MOF and the web server feature gets configured.

Pushing a Configuration Over WinRM HTTP

With the WinRM HTTP endpoint, pushing a DSC configuration using Start-DscConfiguration is just about providing the credentials. For this example, you set the Ensure property in the above configuration to Absent.

Note   Before trying this example, set the TrustedHosts value at wsman:\localhost\Client to either '*' or the IP address of the GCE instance.

```
Configuration GCEDemo
{
    param
    (
        [Parameter(Mandatory = $true)]
        [String]
        $NodeName

    )

    Import-DscResource -ModuleName PSDesiredStateConfiguration
    -ModuleVersion 1.1
```

```
    Node $NodeName
    {
        WindowsFeature WebServer
        {
            Name = 'Web-Server'
            Ensure = 'Absent'
        }
    }
}

GCEDemo -NodeName '35.229.193.26' -OutputPath C:\Scripts\GCE\GCEDemo

Start-DscConfiguration -Wait -Verbose -Path .\GCEDemo -Credential
(Get-Credential)
```

This is it really.

Enact During a GCE Instance Startup

You saw how to use the startup scripts in the previous example. Let's use the same mechanism to directly enact a DSC configuration. Here is the configuration document that you will enact as a startup script:

```
Configuration GCEDemo
{
    Import-DscResource -ModuleName PSDesiredStateConfiguration
    -ModuleVersion 1.1

    Node 'localhost'
    {
        WindowsFeature WebServer
        {
            Name = 'Web-Server'
            Ensure = 'Present'
        }
    }
}
```

```
GCEDemo -OutputPath "$env:Temp\GCEDemo"
Start-DscConfiguration -Wait -Verbose -Path "$env:Temp\GCEDemo"
```

Save this as startupConfig.ps1 and upload it to a public location accessible from your GCE instance. Once again, I chose to do this as a gist on GitHub.

```
$projectID = 'prodsc-gcp-01'
$disk = Get-GceImage -Project 'windows-cloud' -Family 'windows-2016'
$config = New-GceInstanceConfig 'prodscgce2' `
    -MachineType 'n1-standard-1' `
    -BootDiskImage $disk `
    -Metadata @{ "windows-startup-script-url" = "https://gist.
    githubusercontent.com/rchaganti/feaf23ade96269925c6ddf97ee757f28/raw/55
    99e91f15cf76d9c1bb6ad3aaa036fe67f89928/startupConfig.ps1" } `
    -Tag $winrmhttpsTag

$gceInstance = $config | Add-GceInstance -Project $projectID
```

This command will create a new GCE instance and attach the winrmhttps network tag for enabling inbound WinRM HTTPS traffic to the instance. At the end of the instance creation, startupConfig.ps1 gets executed and completes the web server feature install. The output from this can be seen in the serial port 1 (console) log in the Google Cloud console. Figure 18-3 shows this.

Note   This may take a while since the OS activation has to complete.

```
2018/02/27 15:28:30 windows-startup-script-url:    Directory: C:\Windows\TEMP\GCEDemo
2018/02/27 15:28:30 windows-startup-script-url:
2018/02/27 15:28:30 windows-startup-script-url:
2018/02/27 15:28:30 windows-startup-script-url: Mode              LastWriteTime         Length Name
2018/02/27 15:28:30 windows-startup-script-url: ----              -------------         ------ ----
2018/02/27 15:28:30 windows-startup-script-url: -a----       2/27/2018   3:28 PM          1996 localhost.mof
2018/02/27 15:28:31 windows-startup-script-url: VERBOSE: Perform operation 'Invoke CimMethod' with following parameters,
2018/02/27 15:28:31 windows-startup-script-url: ''methodName' = SendConfigurationApply,'className' =
2018/02/27 15:28:31 windows-startup-script-url: MSFT_DSCLocalConfigurationManager,'namespaceName' =
2018/02/27 15:28:31 windows-startup-script-url: root/Microsoft/Windows/DesiredStateConfiguration'.
2018/02/27 15:28:32 windows-startup-script-url: VERBOSE: An LCM method call arrived from computer PRODSCGCE2 with user sid
2018/02/27 15:28:32 windows-startup-script-url: S-1-5-18.
2018/02/27 15:28:32 windows-startup-script-url: VERBOSE: [PRODSCGCE2]: LCM:  [ Start  Set      ]
2018/02/27 15:28:39 windows-startup-script-url: VERBOSE: [PRODSCGCE2]: LCM:  [ Start  Resource ] [[WindowsFeature]WebServer]
2018/02/27 15:28:40 windows-startup-script-url: VERBOSE: [PRODSCGCE2]: LCM:  [ Start  Test     ] [[WindowsFeature]WebServer]
2018/02/27 15:28:41 windows-startup-script-url: VERBOSE: [PRODSCGCE2]:                            [[WindowsFeature]WebServer]
2018/02/27 15:28:41 windows-startup-script-url: The operation 'Get-WindowsFeature' started: Web-Server
2018/02/27 15:28:42 windows-startup-script-url: VERBOSE: [PRODSCGCE2]:                            [[WindowsFeature]WebServer]
2018/02/27 15:28:42 windows-startup-script-url: The operation 'Get-WindowsFeature' succeeded: Web-Server
2018/02/27 15:28:42 windows-startup-script-url: VERBOSE: [PRODSCGCE2]: LCM:  [ End    Test     ] [[WindowsFeature]WebServer]
```

Figure 18-3. *Serial console log showing the startupConfig.ps1 enact*

Since you enabled inbound WinRM HTTPS traffic, you should be able to retrieve the current configuration on the GCE instance.

```
$cimSessionOptions = New-CimSessionOption -SkipCACheck -SkipCNCheck -UseSsl
-Verbose
$cimsession = New-CimSession -ComputerName 35.194.248.7 -Credential
(Get-Credential) -SessionOption $cimSessionOptions

Get-DscConfiguration -CimSession $cimsession
```

Note   You will have to reset and retrieve the GCE instance credentials using the gcloud CLI, as you saw earlier.

The current configuration of the GCE instance is shown in Figure 18-4.

```
ConfigurationName     : GCEDemo
DependsOn             :
ModuleName           : PSDesiredStateConfiguration
ModuleVersion        : 1.1
PsDscRunAsCredential :
ResourceId           : [WindowsFeature]WebServer
SourceInfo           :
Credential           :
DisplayName          : Web Server (IIS)
Ensure               : Present
IncludeAllSubFeature : False
LogPath              :
Name                 : Web-Server
Source               :
PSComputerName       : 35.194.248.7
CimClassName         : MSFT_RoleResource
```

Figure 18-4. *Current configuration on the GCE instance*

If your configuration requires custom DSC resource modules, you should add the
Install-Module cmdlet or other means of downloading and installing the modules on
the GCE instance to the startup script.

Since you have the configuration document as a startup script, the script gets run
every time the instance reboots. You can remove the startup script from the metadata
using the following code snippet:

```
$projectID = 'prodsc-gcp-01'
$gceInstance = Get-GceInstance -Name prodscgce2 -Project $projectID
Set-GceInstance -Object $gceInstance -RemoveMetadata 'windows-startup-
script-url'
```

On-Boarding a GCE Instance to AA DSC Pull Service

The final method to explore here is to on-board the GCE instances to the AA DSC pull
service. This can be done using the startup script as well.

Note   On-boarding a GCE instance to the AA DSC pull service is not free. There
is a per-node cost associated with this service. See the Azure Automation pricing
information in your region.

You can follow the instructions in the "Setting Up Azure Automation" section
in Chapter 17 to create a new Azure Automation account. Once you have an Azure
Automation account, you can publish the node configuration to AA DSC.

You will use one of the earlier configuration scripts you created. Save the following configuration script as webserver.ps1:

```
Configuration WebServer
{
    Import-DscResource -ModuleName PSDesiredStateConfiguration
    -ModuleVersion 1.1

    Node 'localhost'
    {
        WindowsFeature WebServer
        {
            Name = 'Web-Server'
            Ensure = 'Present'
        }
    }
}
```

Once the script is saved locally, run the Import-AzureRmAutomationDscConfiguration cmdlet to publish this script as a node configuration:

```
Import-AzureRmAutomationDscConfiguration -AutomationAccountName 'ProDscAA'
-ResourceGroupName $resourceGroupName -SourcePath C:\Scripts\GCE\webserver.
ps1 -Published
```

This published configuration can be compiled using the Start-AzureRmAutomation DscCompilationJob cmdlet as shown below:

```
Start-AzureRmAutomationDscCompilationJob -ConfigurationName 'webserver'
-ResourceGroupName $resourceGroupName -AutomationAccountName 'ProDscAA'
```

Now that you have a compiled configuration in the AA DSC service, you can on-board the GCE instance using a startup script. Before you can do that, you need the AA DSC pull service endpoint URL and the registration key. You can gather these details using the Get-AzureRmAutomationRegistrationInfo cmdlet:

```
$registrationInfo = Get-AzureRmAutomationRegistrationInfo
-ResourceGroupName $resourceGroupName -AutomationAccountName 'ProDSCAA'
```

The Endpoint and PrimaryKey properties of $registrationInfo will be used in the meta configuration document. Here is the meta configuration document. You will use it as the startup script. Therefore, save this locally as GceMetaConfig.ps1.

```
[DscLocalConfigurationManager()]
Configuration GCEDscMetaConfig
{
    param
    (
        [Parameter(Mandatory = $true)]
        [String]
        $RegistrationUrl,

        [Parameter(Mandatory = $True)]
        [String]
        $RegistrationKey,

        [Parameter(Mandatory = $true)]
        [String[]]
        $ConfigurationNames
    )

    Node localhost
    {

        Settings
        {
            RefreshMode = 'Pull'
        }

        ConfigurationRepositoryWeb AzureAutomationDSC
        {
            ServerUrl = $RegistrationUrl
            RegistrationKey = $RegistrationKey
            ConfigurationNames = $ConfigurationNames
        }
```

```
        ResourceRepositoryWeb AzureAutomationDSC
        {
            ServerUrl = $RegistrationUrl
            RegistrationKey = $RegistrationKey
        }

        ReportServerWeb AzureAutomationDSC
        {
            ServerUrl = $RegistrationUrl
            RegistrationKey = $RegistrationKey
        }
    }
}

$Params = @{
    RegistrationUrl     = 'Endpoint-URL-Here'
    RegistrationKey     = 'Registration-Key-Here'
    ConfigurationNames = 'webserver.localhost'
    OutputPath          = "$env:TEMP\MetaConfig"
}

GCEDscMetaConfig @Params

Set-DscLocalConfigurationManager -Path "$env:TEMP\MetaConfig" -Verbose
```

Note   In this script, replace the values of `RegistrationURL` and `RegistrationKey` to match your Azure Automation account details.

Since this startup script contains sensitive information such as the endpoint URL and registration key, you don't want to upload this to a public location. Instead, put it in a Google storage bucket and assign the appropriate permissions to the compute default service account so that you can use this script in the GCS bucket to perform the node meta configuration.

Configuring Service Account Permissions

For the demo purpose here, you can grant the default compute service account in the project storage object admin permissions so that the GCE instance can download the script from a storage bucket and execute it. This can be done using the cmdlets in the Google Cloud PowerShell module.

```
#Grant service account storage viewer role
$projectID = 'prodsc-gcp-01'
$project = (Get-GcpProject -Name $projectID).Where({$_.LifecycleState -eq
'ACTIVE'})
$defaultSvcAccount = "$($project.ProjectNumber)-compute@developer.
gserviceaccount.com"
$null = Add-GcIamPolicyBinding -Project $projectID -ServiceAccount
$defaultSvcAccount -Role roles/storage.objectAdmin
$svcAccount = New-GceServiceAccountConfig -Email $defaultSvcAccount
```

Once these permissions are in place, you can create the instance.

Creating a GCS Bucket and Uploading the Meta Configuration Script

The next step is to create the GCS bucket for uploading the meta configuration script and assigning the right permissions.

```
#Create a GCS bucket
$bucketName = 'prodscscripts'
$objectName = 'gcemetaconfig.ps1'
New-GcsBucket -Name $bucketName -Project $projectID -DefaultBucketAcl
ProjectPrivate -DefaultObjectAcl BucketOwnerFullControl
$startupScript = New-GcsObject -Bucket $bucketName -ObjectName $objectName
-File C:\scripts\GCE\GCeMetaConfig.ps1 -Force
```

This will create the GCS bucket and upload the meta configuration document at C:\Scripts\GCE to the GCS bucket as gcemetaconfig.ps1.

Creating a GCE Instance and Enacting the Meta Configuration

As in the previous sections, you will use the Google Cloud PowerShell cmdlets to create an instance that uses a script located in the GCS bucket as the startup script.

```
$config = New-GceInstanceConfig 'prodscgce3' `
    -MachineType 'n1-standard-1' `
    -BootDiskImage $disk `
    -Metadata @{ "windows-startup-script-url" =
    "gs://$bucketName/$objectName" } `
    -Tag $winrmhttpsTag `
    -ServiceAccount $svcAccount -Verbose

$gceInstance = $config | Add-GceInstance -Project $projectID
```

In this code snippet, you use the default compute service account to which you have given the storage object administrator permission and use gs://prodscscripts/gcemetaconfig.ps1 as the Windows startup script URL. This method can be used with node configurations that contain sensitive strings as well.

Once the GCE instance is created, the meta configuration in gcemetaconfig.ps1 gets enacted. This is shown in Figure 18-5.

```
2018/03/01 02:57:37 windows-startup-script-url: Mode              LastWriteTime        Length Name
2018/03/01 02:57:38 windows-startup-script-url: ----              -------------        ------ ----
2018/03/01 02:57:38 windows-startup-script-url: -a----    3/1/2018    2:57 AM            4564 localhost.meta.mof
2018/03/01 02:57:38 windows-startup-script-url: VERBOSE: Performing the operation "Start-DscConfiguration:
2018/03/01 02:57:38 windows-startup-script-url: SendMetaConfigurationApply" on target "MSFT_DSCLocalConfigurationManager".
2018/03/01 02:57:38 windows-startup-script-url: VERBOSE: Perform operation 'Invoke CimMethod' with following parameters,
2018/03/01 02:57:38 windows-startup-script-url: ''methodName' = SendMetaConfigurationApply,'className' =
2018/03/01 02:57:38 windows-startup-script-url: MSFT_DSCLocalConfigurationManager,'namespaceName' =
2018/03/01 02:57:38 windows-startup-script-url: root/Microsoft/Windows/DesiredStateConfiguration'.
2018/03/01 02:57:40 windows-startup-script-url: VERBOSE: An LCM method call arrived from computer PRODSCGCE4 with user sid
2018/03/01 02:57:40 windows-startup-script-url: S-1-5-18.
2018/03/01 02:57:40 windows-startup-script-url: VERBOSE: [PRODSCGCE4]: LCM:  [ Start  Set      ]
2018/03/01 02:57:43 windows-startup-script-url: VERBOSE: [PRODSCGCE4]: LCM:  [ Start  Resource ] [MSFT_DSCMetaConfiguration]
2018/03/01 02:57:43 windows-startup-script-url: VERBOSE: [PRODSCGCE4]: LCM:  [ Start  Set      ] [MSFT_DSCMetaConfiguration]
2018/03/01 02:57:44 windows-startup-script-url: VERBOSE: [PRODSCGCE4]: LCM:  [ End    Set      ] [MSFT_DSCMetaConfiguration]
2018/03/01 02:57:44 windows-startup-script-url: in 0.1450 seconds.
2018/03/01 02:57:45 windows-startup-script-url: VERBOSE: [PRODSCGCE4]: LCM:  [ End    Resource ] [MSFT_DSCMetaConfiguration]
2018/03/01 02:57:49 windows-startup-script-url: VERBOSE: [PRODSCGCE4]:                            [] Registration of the Dsc
2018/03/01 02:57:49 windows-startup-script-url: Agent with the server
2018/03/01 02:57:49 windows-startup-script-url: https://eus2-agentservice-prod-1.azure-automation.net/accounts/7471b7ce-95d2-47
```

Figure 18-5. Partial output from GCE instance serial console logs

Figure 18-6 shows that the GCE instance is registered as the AA DSC pull service.

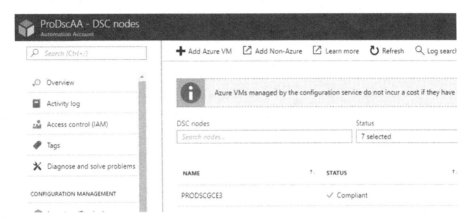

Figure 18-6. *GCE instance in the AA DSC pull service*

Note   Once again, the startup script will execute every time the instance reboots. Therefore, once the initial run is successful, you can remove the startup script using the -RemoveMetadata parameter of the Set-GceInstance cmdlet.

The instance eventually pulls the webserver.localhost configuration and enacts it. The node configuration status can be seen on the Azure Portal or can be verified using the Azure Automation PowerShell cmdlets.

Summary

In this chapter, you learned how to create and configure GCE instances. For the most part, you used the Google Cloud PowerShell cmdlets but you also saw a few examples of using the gcloud CLI too. This chapter is not an in-depth guide to GCE or Google Cloud; you only looked at three different methods for using DSC with GCE instances. Google Cloud supports deployment of GCE instances using Google Cloud deployment manager templates written in Python or Jinja2; this is outside the scope of this chapter and this book. What you learned in this chapter with regards to using the startup scripts will still be applicable in templates as well.

CHAPTER 19

Amazon Web Services and DSC

In the two pervious chapters, you learned how to use PowerShell Desired State Configuration with Windows instances running on Azure and Google Cloud services. You learned how the Azure Automation DSC service can help with both cloud and on-premises instances of Windows systems. In this chapter, you will learn how to use DSC with AWS Elastic Compute 2 (EC2) instances.

Lab Requirements

To try the examples and exercises in this chapter, you will need at minimum two or more EC2 Windows instances with Windows Server 2008 R2 or above with WMF 5.1 or above installed. I recommend Windows Server 2016 instances. If you do not have an AWS account, you can create one for free and subscribe to the free tier. Your credit card won't be charged as long as you stay within the free tier limits. The examples and exercises in this chapter do not need anything more than what is available in the AWS free tier. This chapter does not include any instructions for creating EC2 instances. If you are completely new to AWS, I recommend first looking at the AWS EC2 documentation to understand how to provision EC2 virtual machines. You will also need the AWSPowerShell module to deploy the CloudFormation (CFN) templates and invoke EC2 Systems Manager Run commands.

There are multiple methods through which you can use DSC in the AWS cloud. You can deploy the pull server infrastructure within AWS EC2 and on-board all other EC2 instances to this pull server infrastructure. This is no different from how you do it on-premises. Whatever you learned in Chapter 8 should be sufficient to set up a pull server infrastructure in AWS. You can simply push a configuration to an EC2 instance with an

© Ravikanth Chaganti 2018
R. Chaganti, *Pro PowerShell Desired State Configuration*, https://doi.org/10.1007/978-1-4842-3483-9_19

assumption that you have public IP attached to the instance and you have the necessary security groups and firewall rules enabled. You will see this as the first method in this chapter.

You can also on-board AWS EC2 instances Azure Automation DSC (AA DSC) like the on-premises virtual machines or physical servers. You will see an example of this and what other tooling is available to perform this.

You can also use the CloudFormation templates to provision an EC2 instance and bootstrap it with the necessary configuration. You will see this as well in this chapter.

You can also use EC2 Systems Manager capabilities such as the Run command to push a configuration into an EC2 Windows instance. I will discuss this in detail in this chapter.

Let's start!

Push a Configuration to an EC2 Instance

To be able to remotely push configurations to an EC2 instance, you must have the following prerequisites configured.

- The EC2 instance should be configured to allow inbound WinRM HTTP or HTTPS traffic. This can be done by adding new security group rules on the EC2 instance. See Figure 19-1

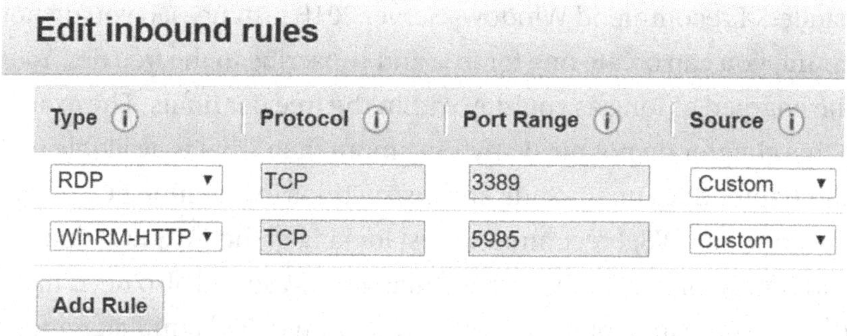

Edit inbound rules

Type (i)	Protocol (i)	Port Range (i)	Source (i)
RDP ▾	TCP	3389	Custom ▾
WinRM-HTTP ▾	TCP	5985	Custom ▾

Add Rule

Figure 19-1. EC2 instance security groups

- There should be a firewall rule to allow remote WSMAN traffic. This can be achieved by running the following command in the EC2 instance guest OS:

```
Set-NetFirewallRule -Name WINRM-HTTP-In-TCP-PUBLIC -RemoteAddress Any
```

If these prerequisites are already met, you can compile and enact a configuration remotely using the Start-DscConfiguration cmdlet. Here is the sample configuration that you will enact on an EC2 instance:

Note   Using a WinRM HTTPS endpoint is the most recommended method for pushing DSC configurations remotely. However, this requires setting up an HTTPS listener with certificates. This is not in the scope of this chapter.

```
$ec2Name = 'ec2-18-218-88-255.us-east-2.compute.amazonaws.com'

Configuration WebServer
{
    param
    (
        [Parameter(Mandatory = $true)]
        [String]
        $NodeName
    )

    Node $NodeName
    {
        WindowsFeature WebServer
        {
            Name = 'Web-Server'
            Ensure = 'Present'
        }
    }
}

WebServer -NodeName $ec2Name
```

This configuration can be compiled and enacted using:

```
Start-DscConfiguration -Path .\WebServer -Credential (Get-Credential) -Wait
-Verbose
```

It is important that you pass the credentials to authenticate to the EC2 instance to start the enact. You may have to configure the `TrustedHosts` property of the WinRM client to ensure that you can successfully enact the configuration remotely. This can be done by using the `Set-Item` cmdlet on the WSMAN:\Localhost\Client\TrustedHosts property and set it to either a specific EC2 instance DNS name or * (less secure).

Note   The password needed to authenticate with the EC2 instance can be retrieved using the key-pair created during the instance creation.

On-Board EC2 Instances to AA DSC

In Chapter 17, you looked at the AA DSC service in depth. You used it to on-board both VMs running in the Azure cloud and an on-premises data center infrastructure. It is possible to on-board EC2 Windows instances on Amazon Web Services to Azure Automation DSC. These EC2 instances can be treated like on-premises systems and can simply perform the meta configuration changes to on-board them to AA DSC. Let's look at an example of this meta configuration:

Note   Keep in mind that AA DSC service is not free for non-Azure machines. Refer to the pricing information before you decide to use AA DSC for configuration management of AWS EC2 instances.

```
[DscLocalConfigurationManager()]
Configuration AWSEC2MetaConfig
{
    param
    (
        [Parameter(Mandatory = $true)]
        [String]
        $RegistrationUrl,

        [Parameter(Mandatory = $true)]
        [String]
        $RegistrationKey,
```

```
    [Parameter(Mandatory = $true)]
    [String[]]
    $ConfigurationNames,

    [Parameter(Mandatory = $true)]
    [String[]]
    $NodeName
)

Node $NodeName
{
    Settings
    {
        RefreshMode = 'PULL'
    }

    ConfigurationRepositoryWeb AADSCConfigWeb
    {
        ServerUrl = $RegistrationUrl
        RegistrationKey = $RegistrationKey
        ConfigurationNames = $ConfigurationNames
    }
}
}
```

This meta configuration document has three parameters to provide the AA DSC registration URL, registration keys, and the configuration names that will be pulled from the AA DSC service. From Chapter 17, you already know how to gather the registration URL and key from the AA DSC service. To use the Set-DscLocalConfigurationManager cmdlet remotely to push the meta configuration, the same prerequisites as in the previous section must be met.

Once these prerequisites are met, you can compile and remotely enact the meta configuration using the Set-DscLocalConfigurationManager cmdlet. See Figure 19-2.

```
AWSEC2MetaConfig -RegistrationUrl 'https://cid-agentservice-prod-1.azure-
automation.net/accounts/78373be3-84aa-432b-8be6-5dcbeae5eff2' `
                -RegistrationKey 'keEiP98x6pNKaGwi1pJITEgzNgcneDQZwBxR+J5I
                jKZqPf6t19KGgVRI2beAvVPFtypVQNEbOmKJtRq9pSX+2w==' `
```

```
            -ConfigurationNames 'WebServer.localhost' `
            -NodeName 'ec2-13-59-154-158.us-east-2.compute.amazonaws.com'
Set-DscLocalConfigurationManager -Path .\AWSEC2MetaConfig -Verbose
-Credential (Get-Credential) -Force
```

Note   The configuration names specified as an argument to the
-ConfgurationNames parameter should exist as compiled configurations in AA DSC.

```
PS C:\Scripts> Set-DscLocalConfigurationManager -Path .\AWSEC2MetaConfig -Verbose -Credential (Get-Credential) -Force
cmdlet Get-Credential at command pipeline position 1
Supply values for the following parameters:
VERBOSE: Performing the operation "Start-DscConfiguration: SendMetaConfigurationApply" on target "MSFT_DSCLocalConfigu
VERBOSE: Perform operation 'Invoke CimMethod' with following parameters, ''methodName' = SendMetaConfigurationApply,'c
r,'namespaceName' = root/Microsoft/Windows/DesiredStateConfiguration'.
VERBOSE: An LCM method call arrived from computer S16-JB with user sid S-1-5-21-248859308-185110412-2079184118-500.
VERBOSE: [EC2AMAZ-H8VBNDA]: LCM:  [ Start  Set      ]
VERBOSE: [EC2AMAZ-H8VBNDA]: LCM:  [ Start  Resource ]  [MSFT_DSCMetaConfiguration]
VERBOSE: [EC2AMAZ-H8VBNDA]: LCM:  [ Start  Set      ]  [MSFT_DSCMetaConfiguration]
VERBOSE: [EC2AMAZ-H8VBNDA]: LCM:  [ End    Set      ]  [MSFT_DSCMetaConfiguration]  in 0.0160 seconds.
VERBOSE: [EC2AMAZ-H8VBNDA]: LCM:  [ End    Resource ]  [MSFT_DSCMetaConfiguration]
VERBOSE: [EC2AMAZ-H8VBNDA]:                           [] Registration of the Dsc Agent with the server https://cid-ag
nts/78373be3-84aa-432b-8be6-5dcbeae5eff2 was successful.
VERBOSE: [EC2AMAZ-H8VBNDA]: LCM:  [ End    Set      ]
VERBOSE: [EC2AMAZ-H8VBNDA]: LCM:  [ End    Set      ]   in  2.2030 seconds.
VERBOSE: Operation 'Invoke CimMethod' complete.
VERBOSE: Set-DscLocalConfigurationManager finished in 3.969 seconds.
```

Figure 19-2. *Meta configuration enact*

Once this meta configuration is complete, you can see the node listed in the AA DSC
service. See Figure 19-3.

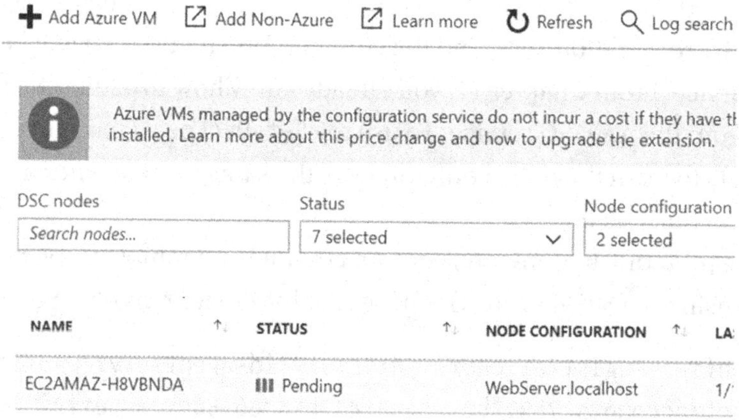

Figure 19-3. *The on-boarded AWS EC2 node*

This node will eventually complete the pending configuration, and the state of the configuration can be seen in the Azure portal. The PowerShell team at Microsoft started developing a module to help on-board EC2 instances to the AA DSC pull service. It is available in the PowerShell gallery as `AwsDscToolkit` and it is open sourced on GitHub (`https://github.com/PowerShell/AwsDscToolkit`). There is no significant development on this module. As an exercise, you can try this module to on-board EC2 instances to the AA DSC pull service. This module uses the EC2 Systems Manager Run commands. You will learn about EC2 Run commands towards the end of this chapter.

DSC Configuration Using CloudFormation

AWS CloudFormation provides a template-based method to describe and provision AWS resources. These templates can be in a JSON or YAML format. The following code snippet provides the basic syntax of an AWS CloudFormation JSON template:

```
{
    "AWSTemplateFormatVersion": "version date",
    "Description": "JSON string",
    "Metadata": {
        templatemetadata
    },
    "Parameters": {
        setofparameters
    },
    "Mappings": {
        setofmappings
    },
    "Conditions": {
        setofconditions
    },
    "Resources": {
        setofresources
    },
```

```
    "Outputs": {
        setofoutputs
    }
}
```

Within the CFN templates, you can use the `cfn-init` script to enact the DSC configuration. But, before that, you need to package the configuration scripts in a ZIP file and ensure that it is available at a location that can be accessed using CloudFormation for deploying the stack. Here is the basic configuration for the Web-Server Windows feature:

```
Configuration WebServerDemo
{
    WindowsFeature WebServer
    {
        Name = 'Web-Server'
        IncludeAllSubFeature = $true
        Ensure = 'Present'
    }
}

if (-not (test-path C:\Temp))
{
    $null = New-Item -Path C:\temp -ItemType Directory
}

WebServerDemo -OutputPath C:\Temp\WebServerDemo

Start-DscConfiguration -Path C:\Temp\WebServerDemo -Force -Wait -Verbose
```

This configuration document is used for setting the web server after an EC2 instance is created. You also need a tear-down script to remove the configuration when the stack is deleted. For the tear-down action, you simply set `Ensure` to `Absent` in the configuration script:

```
Configuration WebServerDemoTearDown
{
    WindowsFeature WebServer
```

```
    {
        Name = 'Web-Server'
        IncludeAllSubFeature = $true
        Ensure = 'Absent'
    }
}
```

```
WebServerDemo -OutputPath C:\Temp
Start-DscConfiguration -Path C:\Temp\WebServerDemoTearDown -Force -Wait
-Verbose
```

Finally, you also need a script to set up the firewall rules to allow inbound WinRM HTTP ports:

```
Set-NetFirewallRule -Name WINRM-HTTP-In-TCP-PUBLIC -RemoteAddress Any
```

Save these scripts as .PS1 files and package them into a zip archive and upload it to an Internet location that is accessible to the CloudFormation deployment engine. I chose to upload this to a public GitHub repository. Since this is not a book on CloudFormation templates, let's jump directly to the template that deploys the EC2 instance and enacts a DSC configuration. I will discuss a few components within this template.

```
{
  "AWSTemplateFormatVersion": "2010-09-09",
  "Description": "A template to deploy a web server using DSC bootstrap
  from a Github repository.",
  "Parameters": {
    "BootstrapperScript": {
      "Description": "The URL to a ZIP file containing the PowerShell
      script package to bootstrap EC2 instance in this CloudFormation
      template.",
      "Type": "String",
      "Default": "https://github.com/rchaganti/cfnDSC/raw/master/
      WebServerDSCBootstrap.zip"
    },
    "KeyPairName": {
      "Description": "The EC2 key pair used to launch web instance",
      "Type": "AWS::EC2::KeyPair::KeyName",
```

```json
        "Default": "DSCInstance"
      },
      "WebserverImageId": {
        "Description": "The EC2 AmiId to use for web",
        "Type": "String",
        "Default": "ami-89cce7ec"
      },
      "WebserverInstanceType": {
        "Description": "The EC2 instance type to use for web",
        "Type": "String",
        "Default": "t2.micro"
      }
    },
    "Resources": {
      "WebSecurityGroup": {
        "Type": "AWS::EC2::SecurityGroup",
        "Properties": {
          "GroupDescription": "Allow inbound HTTP, RDP, and WinRM HTTP",
          "SecurityGroupIngress": [
            {
              "IpProtocol": "tcp",
              "FromPort": "80",
              "ToPort": "80",
              "CidrIp": "0.0.0.0/0"
            },
            {
              "IpProtocol": "tcp",
              "FromPort": "3389",
              "ToPort": "3389",
              "CidrIp": "0.0.0.0/0"
            },
            {
              "IpProtocol": "tcp",
              "FromPort": "5985",
              "ToPort": "5985",
              "CidrIp": "0.0.0.0/0"
```

```json
        }
      ]
    }
  },
  "DSCWebServer": {
    "Type": "AWS::EC2::Instance",
    "Metadata": {
      "AWS::CloudFormation::Init": {
        "config": {
          "sources": {
            "c:\\cfn\\Zephyr\\Scripts": {
              "Ref": "BootstrapperScript"
            }
          },
          "files": {
            "c:\\cfn\\cfn-hup.conf": {
              "content": {
                "Fn::Join": [
                  "",
                  [
                    "[main]\n",
                    "stack=",
                    {
                      "Ref": "AWS::StackId"
                    },
                    "\n",
                    "region=",
                    {
                      "Ref": "AWS::Region"
                    },
                    "\n"
                  ]
                ]
              }
            },
```

```
"c:\\cfn\\hooks.d\\cfn-auto-reloader.conf": {
  "content": {
    "Fn::Join": [
      "",
      [
        "[cfn-auto-reloader-hook]\n",
        "triggers=post.update\n",

        "path=Resources.DSCWebServer.Metadata.
        AWS::CloudFormation::Init\n",
        "action=cfn-init.exe -v -s ",
        {
          "Ref": "AWS::StackId"
        },
        " -r DSCWebServer",
        " --region ",
        {
          "Ref": "AWS::Region"
        },
        "\n"
      ]
    ]
  }
},
"c:\\cfn\\hooks.d\\cfn-teardown.conf": {
  "content": {
    "Fn::Join": [
      "",
      [
        "[cfn-teardown-hook]\n",
        "triggers=post.remove\n",

        "path=Resources.DSCWebServer.Metadata.
        AWS::CloudFormation::Init\n",
        "action=powershell.exe -Command C:\\cfn\\Zephyr\\
        Scripts\\Teardown.ps1\n"
      ]
```

```
            ]
          }
        }
      },
      "commands": {
        "00-set-execution-policy": {
          "command": "powershell.exe -Command Set-ExecutionPolicy
          Unrestricted -Force",
          "waitAfterCompletion": "0"
        },
        "01-set-firewall-rule": {
          "command": "powershell.exe -Command C:\\cfn\\Zephyr\\
          Scripts\\ConfigureFirewall.ps1",
          "waitAfterCompletion": "0"
        },
        "02-configure-webserver": {
          "command": "powershell.exe -Command C:\\cfn\\Zephyr\\
          Scripts\\WebServerDSCBootstrap.ps1",
          "waitAfterCompletion": "0"
        }
      },
      "services": {
        "windows": {
          "cfn-hup": {
            "enabled": "true",
            "ensureRunning": "true",
            "files": [
              "c:\\cfn\\cfn-hup.conf",
              "c:\\cfn\\hooks.d\\cfn-auto-reloader.conf"
            ]
          }
        }
      }
    }
  }
},
```

```json
"Properties": {
  "ImageId": {
    "Ref": "WebserverImageId"
  },
  "InstanceType": {
    "Ref": "WebserverInstanceType"
  },
  "SecurityGroups": [
    {
      "Ref": "WebSecurityGroup"
    }
  ],
  "KeyName": {
    "Ref": "KeyPairName"
  },
  "UserData": {
    "Fn::Base64": {
      "Fn::Join": [
        "",
        [
          "<script>\n",
          "cfn-init.exe -v -s ",
          {
            "Ref": "AWS::StackId"
          },
          " -r DSCWebServer",
          " --region ",
          {
            "Ref": "AWS::Region"
          },
          "\n",
          "</script>"
        ]
      ]
    }
  }
```

```
        }
      }
    }
  }
}
```

In this template are four parameters with default values already set.

- BootStrapperScript takes the argument to the location where the configuration zip archive is available.

- KeyPairName is the key pair that will be used to encrypt and decrypt login information. This needs to be pre-provisioned in the region where you want to deploy the EC2 instance.

- WebServerImageId is the AMI image identifier within the region where you plan to deploy the CFN template.

- WebserverInstanceType is the instance type of an AWS instance that needs to be deployed.

Within this template is a resource named DSCWebServer. Within this resource's metadata is the CloudFormation configuration that defines what commands need to be run at the of EC2 instance creation. Within this are the scripts for configuring the firewall and compiling and enacting the web server configuration. Save this template as a JSON file.

To deploy this CFN template, you use the commands in the AWSPowerShell module.

Note   If you do not have the AWS PowerShell module, you can use Install-Module -Name AWSPowerShell to install it from the PowerShell gallery.

The AWS credentials such as Access Key and Secret Key can be retrieved from the AWS console by going to Users in the navigation pane.

```
#Set AWS Credentials
Set-AWSCredential -AccessKey 'accessKey' -SecretKey 'secretKey'

#Set Default AWS region
Set-DefaultAwsRegion -Region us-east-2
```

```
#Validate a CFN template
$templateBody = Get-Content -Path .\cfnTemplate.json -raw
Test-CFNTemplate -TemplateBody $templateBody

#Deploy a CFN template
$parameters = @(
    @{
        ParameterKey = "KeyPairName"
        ParameterValue = "DSCInstance"
    },
    @{
        ParameterKey = "WebserverInstanceType"
        ParameterValue = "t2.micro"
    },
    @{
        ParameterKey = "BootstrapperScript"
        ParameterValue = "https://github.com/rchaganti/cfnDSC/raw/master/
        WebServerDSCBootstrap.zip"
    },
    @{
        ParameterKey = "WebserverImageId"
        ParameterValue = "ami-89cce7ec"
    }
)

New-CfnStack -StackName DscCfnStack -TemplateBody $templateBody -Parameter
$parameters -Verbose
```

Note   The AMI identifier may be different between different AWS regions. Verify
that the AMI identifier is for the region you are deploying.

In this snippet, the first command sets the AWS credentials to access the AWS
resources and deploy the CFN template. The $parameters variable specifies the
arguments needed for the template parameters. You will have to update these
parameters as needed before trying out this example. When the New-CFNStack cmdlet is
executed, a new stack deployment gets initiated and completes in a few minutes.

Once the deployment is complete, you can use the `Get-DscConfiguration` cmdlet to check if the node configuration completed successfully or not. The CFN command execution might take a few minutes before you see the enacted configuration in the `Get-DscConfiguration` output, shown in Figure 19-4.

```
$ec2Name = 'amazonInstanceDnsName'

$cimSessionOption = New-CimSessionOption -Protocol Wsman
$cimSession = New-CimSession -SessionOption $cimSessionOption -ComputerName
$ec2Name -Port 5985 -Credential (Get-Credential)

Get-DscConfiguration -CimSession $cimSession
```

Note   In this code snippet, replace the value of $ec2Name with the public DNS name of the EC2 instance you created.

```
Get-DscConfiguration -CimSession $cimSession
cmdlet Get-Credential at command pipeline position 1
Supply values for the following parameters:


ConfigurationName     : WebServerDemo
DependsOn             :
ModuleName            : PsDesiredStateConfiguration
ModuleVersion         : 1.1
PsDscRunAsCredential  :
ResourceId            : [WindowsFeature]WebServer
SourceInfo            :
Credential            :
DisplayName           : Web Server (IIS)
Ensure                : Present
IncludeAllSubFeature  : True
LogPath               :
Name                  : Web-Server
Source                :
PSComputerName        : ec2-13-59-44-163.us-east-2.compute.amazonaws.com
CimClassName          : MSFT_RoleResource
```

Figure 19-4.   Output from Get-DscConfiguration

In this code snippet, the creation of a CIM session is mandatory since you need to authenticate to the EC2 instance, and when using the –CimSession parameter with the Start-DscConfiguration cmdlet, there is no option to pass the credentials.

Using the EC2 Systems Manager Run Command

One more way to enact DSC configurations is to use the EC2 Systems Manager Run command. The EC2 Systems Manager provides interfaces to view the operational data from across different AWS services and provides methods to automate operational tasks. The Systems Manager service allows management of services running in the AWS cloud as well as systems running on-premises. The Systems Manager supports secure execution of remote tasks using the Run command interfaces. The Run command uses artifacts called documents to execute the remote tasks, and there are many predefined public documents already present in AWS. In this section, you will use the AWS-RunPowerShellScript document. You can gather more information about this document using the Get-SSMDocumentDescription cmdlet in the AWSPowerShell module.

Note   A list of available SSM documents can be seen by running the Get-SSMDocumentList cmdlet.

```
PS C:\Scripts> Get-SSMDocumentDescription -Name AWS-RunPowerShellScript


CreatedDate       : 8/31/2017 8:52:31 PM
DefaultVersion    : 1
Description       : Run a PowerShell script or specify the paths to scripts to run.
DocumentFormat    : JSON
DocumentType      : Command
DocumentVersion   : 1
Hash              : 2142e42a19e0955cc09e43600bf2e633df1917b69d2be9693737dfd62e0fdf61
HashType          : Sha256
LatestVersion     : 1
Name              : AWS-RunPowerShellScript
Owner             : Amazon
Parameters        : {commands, workingDirectory, executionTimeout}
PlatformTypes     : {Windows, Linux}
SchemaVersion     : 1.2
Sha1              :
Status            : Active
Tags              : {}
TargetType        :
```

***Figure 19-5.** AWS-RunPowerShellScript document description*

As seen in Figure 19-5, there are three parameters available in this document and commands is the only required parameter. The Send-SSMCommand cmdlet is used to invoke a remote task.

> **Note**   Before running an SSM command, ensure that the EC2 has an associated IAM role.

Let's look at an example:

```
$commandBlock = @'
$scripts = 'https://github.com/rchaganti/cfnDSC/raw/master/
WebServerDSCBootstrap.zip'

if (-not (Test-Path -Path C:\Temp))
{
    $null = New-Item -Path C:\Temp -ItemType Directory -Force -Verbose
}

#Download the scripts archive
$archivePath = 'C:\temp\WebServerDSCBootstrap.zip'
Invoke-WebRequest -Uri $scripts -OutFile $archivePath -Verbose

#Expand the achive
Add-Type -assembly "system.io.compression.filesystem"
[io.compression.zipfile]::ExtractToDirectory($archivePath, 'C:\Temp')

Set-Location -Path C:\Temp
.\ConfigureFirewall.ps1
.\WebServerDSCBootstrap.ps1

Start-DscConfiguration -Path C:\Temp\WebServerDemo -wait -Verbose
'@

$instanceID = 'i-0cd0a54070119de93'

$configCommand = Send-SSMCommand -instanceId $instanceID `
                                 -DocumentName AWS-RunPowerShellScript `
                                 -Comment 'DSC configuration onboarding
                                 using SSM Command' `
                                 -Parameter @{'commands'=@($commandBlock)}
                                 -Verbose
```

Note 'The instance ID of the EC2 instance can be retrieved using the
`Get-EC2Instance` cmdlet.

This code snippet is a script block that you run on the EC2 instance using the SSM command. This command takes a few minutes to complete and the status can be monitored using the `Get-SSMCommand` cmdlet. See Figure 19-6.

```
PS C:\Scripts> Get-SSMCommand -instanceId $instanceID

CommandId            : 1c3477e3-d0a0-442d-9601-9e357b536347
Comment              : DSC configuration onboarding using SSM Command
CompletedCount       : 0
DocumentName         : AWS-RunPowerShellScript
ErrorCount           : 0
ExpiresAfter         : 1/13/2018 5:14:52 PM
InstanceIds          : {i-0cd0a54070119de93}
MaxConcurrency       : 50
MaxErrors            : 0
NotificationConfig   : Amazon.SimpleSystemsManagement.Model.NotificationConfig
OutputS3BucketName   :
OutputS3KeyPrefix    :
OutputS3Region       :
Parameters           : {[commands, Amazon.Runtime.Internal.Util.AlwaysSendList`1[System.String]]}
RequestedDateTime    : 1/13/2018 3:14:52 PM
ServiceRole          :
Status               : InProgress
StatusDetails        : InProgress
TargetCount          : 1
Targets              : {}
```

Figure 19-6. *SSM command progress*

Since you are using the same scripts as in the CFN template, once this SSM command is complete, you should be able to use the `Get-DscConfiguration` command remotely to gather the current configuration status from the EC2 instance. You saw how to do this in the earlier section.

Summary

In this chapter, you learned how to push a configuration to an EC2 instance remotely, on-board EC2 instances to the Azure Automation DSC service, use CloudFormation templates to bootstrap DSC configurations, and use the EC2 Systems Manager Run command to execute PowerShell scripts that contain DSC configurations as remote tasks. Depending on what level of security group and OS firewall rules can be changed, you have a choice of different methods here. I personally prefer the CloudFormation templates because they allow us to define the entire infrastructure needed along with EC2 instances in a single version-controlled document that is idempotent and reusable. The EC2 Systems Manager Parameter store can be used to supply parameters to the DSC configuration documents or any scripts in general whether you are using the Run command or CFN templates. I will leave this to you as an exercise to try a few CFN templates that use values from the parameter store. Mind you, the parameter store only supports three type values. So, there is not much choice there.

CHAPTER 20

DSC with Containers

Containers have existed for a while in the Linux world; now with Windows 10 and Windows Server 2016 containers have entered the Microsoft Windows world too. Containers accelerate application development, testing, and deployment and are useful in the dynamic data center and cloud environments where DevOps practices are implemented. You can get an application from a development environment to production in a completely automated way by building the container images in the development stage and then shipping the same image through validation and finally to production. The configuration needed for the application to work can be packaged into the image itself. In this chapter, you will explore how to use DSC with Windows containers using Server Core.

Lab Requirements

To try the examples and exercises in this chapter, you will need at minimum two or more systems with Windows Server 2016 or above or Windows 10 Fall Creators Update (FCU) and above. Container images require that the container host is running the most recent Windows updates. Therefore, ensure that you have a system with the most recent Windows updates installed.

Getting Started with Windows Containers

Starting in Windows Server 2016, containers are a built-in OS feature. This feature can be installed using the `Install-WindowsFeature` cmdlet. However, the next step, which requires you to install the Microsoft Docker Provider, installs this feature for you automatically.

```
Install-Module -Name DockerMsftProvider -Repository PSGallery -Force
Install-Package -Name docker -ProviderName DockerMsftProvider
```

© Ravikanth Chaganti 2018
R. Chaganti, *Pro PowerShell Desired State Configuration*, https://doi.org/10.1007/978-1-4842-3483-9_20

Restart the system after the Docker package has been installed. At this point, this system acts as the container host on which container images can be deployed.

After the restart, verify that the docker service is running by executing the following command and you should see that the service is in the running state, as shown in Figure 20-1.

```
Get-Service -name Docker
```

```
PS C:\> Get-Service -name Docker

Status    Name                DisplayName
------    ----                -----------
Running   Docker              Docker
```

Figure 20-1. *Docker service on the container host*

Running the following command shows the version of the docker server and client on the container host. This is shown in Figure 20-2.

```
docker version
```

```
PS C:\> docker version
Client:
 Version:      17.06.2-ee-6
 API version:  1.30
 Go version:   go1.8.3
 Git commit:   e75fdb8
 Built:        Mon Nov 27 22:46:09 2017
 OS/Arch:      windows/amd64

Server:
 Version:      17.06.2-ee-6
 API version:  1.30 (minimum version 1.24)
 Go version:   go1.8.3
 Git commit:   e75fdb8
 Built:        Mon Nov 27 22:55:16 2017
 OS/Arch:      windows/amd64
 Experimental: false
```

Figure 20-2. *Docker client and server versions*

At this point, you are ready to download and run container images. By default, there won't be container images on the host. This can be verified by running the docker images command.

Pulling Container Images

The docker pull command can be used to download the supported Windows Container images. Since I am using Windows Server 2016 as the container host, I can pull both Server Core and Nano Server container images from the docker hub registry.

```
docker pull microsoft/windowsservercore
```

The above command downloads the Windows Server Core container image from the Docker hub; it will take a while to download the 10GB image. The result of this is shown in Figure 20-3.

```
PS C:\> docker pull microsoft/windowsservercore
Using default tag: latest
latest: Pulling from microsoft/windowsservercore
3889bb8d808b: Pulling fs layer
cfb27c9ba25f: Pulling fs layer
cfb27c9ba25f: Verifying Checksum
cfb27c9ba25f: Download complete
3889bb8d808b: Verifying Checksum
3889bb8d808b: Download complete
3889bb8d808b: Pull complete
cfb27c9ba25f: Pull complete
Digest: sha256:554b69722f31381f10a2f3ddd81e4cb50beba7af8561e9014a9e431a52c8f825
Status: Downloaded newer image for microsoft/windowsservercore:latest
```

Figure 20-3. *Pulling a Windows Server Core image*

Once the image is pulled, you can use it to start a container from this image. You will start the container to run in the background. However, given the Docker container execution model, the container will be stopped if there is no synchronous process inside the container. You can work around this by using a simple PowerShell sleep command.

```
docker container run -d --name winservercore microsoft/windowsservercore
powershell.exe -command {while(1) {sleep 1000}}
```

This starts the container named winservercore. This is shown in Figure 20-4.

```
PS C:\> docker ps
CONTAINER ID        IMAGE                              COMMAND              CREATED
      STATUS              PORTS               NAMES
0910255bdf96        microsoft/windowsservercore        "powershell.exe -e..."   2 minutes ago
      Up 2 minutes                            winservercore
```

Figure 20-4. *Running Windows Server Core Container*

Before you proceed, let's gather some container configuration settings. This can be done using the docker inspect command.

```
$containerID = (docker ps -aqf "name=winservercore")
$container = (docker inspect $containerID) | ConvertFrom-Json
```

The docker inspect command takes the Container ID as the argument. You already know this from the output in Figure 20-4. This command gives you a JSON string. Using the ConvertFrom-Json cmdlet you convert it to a PS object.

Figure 20-5 shows the host name retrieved as a part of the $container.Config object.

```
PS C:\> $container.Config


Hostname      : 0910255bdf96
Domainname    :
User          :
AttachStdin   : False
AttachStdout  : False
AttachStderr  : False
Tty           : False
OpenStdin     : False
StdinOnce     : False
Env           :
Cmd           : {powershell.exe, -encodedCommand,
                IAB3AGgAaQBsAGUAKAAxACkAIAB7ACAAcwBsAGUAZQBwACAAMQAwADAAMAAgAHAA,
                -inputFormat...}
Image         : microsoft/windowsservercore
Volumes       :
WorkingDir    :
Entrypoint    :
OnBuild       :
Labels        :
```

Figure 20-5. *Container host name and other configuration*

Note   By default, the host name of the container will be the same as the container ID. But make it a practice to always retrieve it using docker inspect. This will be helpful when you have configurations that change the host name.

At this point, you know that your container is running and you know the host name. You can try the Test-WsMan cmdlet to ensure that the WinRM service is running. The result of this is shown in Figure 20-6.

```
Test-WSMan -ComputerName $container.Config.Hostname
```

```
PS C:\> Test-WSMan -ComputerName $container.Config.Hostname


wsmid            : http://schemas.dmtf.org/wbem/wsman/identity/1/wsmanidentity.xsd
ProtocolVersion : http://schemas.dmtf.org/wbem/wsman/1/wsman.xsd
ProductVendor   : Microsoft Corporation
ProductVersion  : OS: 0.0.0 SP: 0.0 Stack: 3.0
```

Figure 20-6. *Test-WsMan output*

DSC Configurations in a Container

To be able to push configurations into a container, you need to use the Start-
DscConfiguration. However, the container you created just now is neither domain-
joined nor do you have the administrator user credentials for the container login. For
example, compile the following configuration and try an enact:

```
$containerID = (docker ps -aqf "name=winservercore")
$container = (docker inspect $containerID) | ConvertFrom-Json
$hostName = $container.Config.Hostname

Configuration ContainerDemo
{
    param
    (
        [Parameter(Mandatory = $true)]
        [String]
        $NodeName
    )

    Import-DscResource -ModuleName PSDesiredStateConfiguration
    -ModuleVersion 1.1

    Node $NodeName
    {
        WindowsFeature NET-Framework-45-Core
        {
            Name = 'NET-Framework-45-Core'
            Ensure = 'Present'
        }
    }
}
```

```
ContainerDemo -OutputPath C:\scripts\ContainerDemo -NodeName $hostName
Start-DscConfiguration -Path C:\scripts\ContainerDemo -Wait -Verbose
```

The result of this attempt is shown in Figure 20-7.

```
VERBOSE: Perform operation 'Invoke CimMethod' with following parameters, ''methodName' = Se
ndConfigurationApply,'className' = MSFT_DSCLocalConfigurationManager,'namespaceName' = root
/Microsoft/Windows/DesiredStateConfiguration'.
WinRM cannot process the request. The following error occurred while using Kerberos
authentication: Cannot find the computer 0910255bdf96. Verify that the computer exists on
the network and that the name provided is spelled correctly.
    + CategoryInfo          : NotSpecified: (root/Microsoft/...gurationManager:String) []
    , CimException
    + FullyQualifiedErrorId : HRESULT 0x80070035
    + PSComputerName        : 0910255bdf96

VERBOSE: Operation 'Invoke CimMethod' complete.
VERBOSE: Time taken for configuration job to complete is 0.086 seconds
```

Figure 20-7. *Error in enact*

In fact, you will see a similar error when you try any of the DSC commands against the container's host name as the -CimSession argument. In the earlier chapters, for a normal VM or bare-metal system, you saw that this can be worked around by creating the CIM session with credentials. However, in this case of containers, you do not have the administrator credentials handy. So, what are your options here? There are many but let's look at the following two options:

- Copy the configuration script into the container and invoke it inside the container.

- Automate the above method using dockerfiles.

Let's explore these methods.

Copy the Configuration and Enact

In this method, you will copy the compiled configuration document into the container and execute that script remotely from the container host. Here is the configuration document you will compile and copy into the container:

```
Configuration ContainerCopyDemo
{
    param
    (
```

```
    [Parameter(Mandatory = $true)]
    [String]
    $NodeName
)

Import-DscResource -ModuleName PSDesiredStateConfiguration
-ModuleVersion 1.1

Node $NodeName
{
    WindowsFeature NET-Framework-45-Core
    {
        Name = 'NET-Framework-45-Core'
        Ensure = 'Present'
    }
}
}
```

```
ContainerCopyDemo -NodeName 'localhost' -outputPath C:\scripts\
ContainerCopyDemo
```

Once you have the compiled MOF, you can copy it into the container using a couple of methods. The first method uses the docker cp command.

```
docker cp C:\scripts\ContainerCopyDemo\localhost.mof winservercore:/
windows/temp/localhost.mof
```

Note   This command will not work if you are using containers in Hyper-V isolation mode.

The other method is to use a PowerShell remoting session to copy the file.

```
$containerID = (docker ps -aqf "name=winservercore")
$container = (docker inspect $containerID) | ConvertFrom-Json

$containerSession = New-PSSession -ContainerId $container.Id
-RunAsAdministrator
```

```
Copy-Item -Path C:\scripts\ContainerCopyDemo\localhost.mof -ToSession
$containerSession -Destination C:\Windows\Temp -Force
```

You can verify if this copied or not using the following command. See the results in Figure 20-8.

```
Invoke-Command -ContainerId $container.Id -ScriptBlock { Get-ChildItem
-Path C:\Windows\Temp } -RunAsAdministrator
```

```
    Directory: C:\Windows\Temp


Mode                LastWriteTime       Length Name                PSComputerName
----                -------------       ------ ----                --------------
-a----       2/24/2018     8:40 PM        1962 localhost.mof       0910255bdf96b74459c8
                                                                   69053a8c6254f89b0b1b
                                                                   6bd3c57deadce597e367
                                                                   f96f
-a----       2/12/2018     9:46 PM        1276 MpCmdRun.log        0910255bdf96b74459c8
                                                                   69053a8c6254f89b0b1b
                                                                   6bd3c57deadce597e367
                                                                   f96f
-a----       2/24/2018     7:56 PM         102 silconfig.log       0910255bdf96b74459c8
                                                                   69053a8c6254f89b0b1b
                                                                   6bd3c57deadce597e367
                                                                   f96f
```

Figure 20-8. *Compiled MOF in the container*

The -RunAsAdministrator switch parameter is important since C:\Windows\Temp can only be accessed by members of the local administrators group. Once you verify this, you can start an enact docker exec:

```
docker container exec winservercore powershell -command { Strat-
DscConfiguration -Path C:\Windows\Temp -Wait -Verbose }
```

Note   You need to input the name of the container you used to create the container.

Or the enact can be started using Invoke-Command:

```
Invoke-Command -ContainerId $container.Id -ScriptBlock { Start-
DscConfiguration -Path C:\Windows\Temp -Verbose -Wait } -RunAsAdministrator
```

The result of this enact is shown in Figure 20-9.

```
VERBOSE: Perform operation 'Invoke CimMethod' with following parameters, ''methodName' = Se
ndConfigurationApply,'className' = MSFT_DSCLocalConfigurationManager,'namespaceName' = root
/Microsoft/Windows/DesiredStateConfiguration'.
VERBOSE: An LCM method call arrived from computer 1A5827C9A9DF with user sid S-1-5-93-2-1.
VERBOSE: [1A5827C9A9DF]: LCM:  [ Start  Set       ]
VERBOSE: [1A5827C9A9DF]: LCM:  [ Start  Resource ] [[WindowsFeature]NET-Framework-45-Core]
VERBOSE: [1A5827C9A9DF]: LCM:  [ Start  Test     ] [[WindowsFeature]NET-Framework-45-Core]
VERBOSE: [1A5827C9A9DF]:                            [[WindowsFeature]NET-Framework-45-Core]
 The operation 'Get-WindowsFeature' started: NET-Framework-45-Core
VERBOSE: [1A5827C9A9DF]:                            [[WindowsFeature]NET-Framework-45-Core]
 The operation 'Get-WindowsFeature' succeeded: NET-Framework-45-Core
VERBOSE: [1A5827C9A9DF]: LCM:  [ End    Test     ] [[WindowsFeature]NET-Framework-45-Core]
   in 1.4450 seconds.
VERBOSE: [1A5827C9A9DF]: LCM:  [ Skip   Set      ] [[WindowsFeature]NET-Framework-45-Core]
VERBOSE: [1A5827C9A9DF]: LCM:  [ End    Resource ] [[WindowsFeature]NET-Framework-45-Core]
VERBOSE: [1A5827C9A9DF]: LCM:  [ End    Set      ]
VERBOSE: [1A5827C9A9DF]: LCM:  [ End    Set      ]    in  7.1200 seconds.
VERBOSE: Operation 'Invoke CimMethod' complete.
VERBOSE: Time taken for configuration job to complete is 7.662 seconds
```

Figure 20-9. *Enact in the container*

You can now save this container as an image and run it or create new docker containers from it at a later point. This is done using docker commit. However, unlike Linux containers, Windows containers cannot be committed to an image unless they are stopped. So, here are the commands you need to execute in a sequence:

Note   To avoid consistency checks within the docker container, you can use the Remove-DscConfigurationDocument cmdlet with -Stage Current as the parameter with docker exec, as seen earlier.

```
docker stop $container.Id
docker commit $container.Id myimages/servercoredsc
```

Using a Dockerfile

The above process is rather manual and involves several steps. However, when building or configuring an infrastructure using release pipelines, it is important to have a rather automated process. This is where docker build with dockerfiles will be helpful.

Docker can build images automatically from instructions in a file called a dockerfile. Think of a dockerfile as an orchestration template that has a bunch of commands that need to be executed to accomplish a task. Here is the dockerfile for the image and the configuration you created earlier:

```
if (-not (Test-Path -Path C:\scripts\dockerbuild))
{
    $null = New-Item -Path C:\scripts\dockerbuild -ItemType Directory
-force
}

@'
FROM microsoft/windowsservercore
ADD containerdsc.ps1 /windows/temp/containerdsc.ps1
RUN powershell.exe -executionpolicy bypass c:\windows\temp\containerdsc.ps1
'@ | Out-File C:\scripts\dockerbuild\Dockerfile -Encoding utf8 -Force
```

Once the dockerfile is ready, save the following configuration script as containerdsc.ps1 in the C:\scripts\dockerbuild folder:

```
Configuration ContainerCopyDemo
{
    param
    (
        [Parameter(Mandatory = $true)]
        [String]
        $NodeName
    )

    Import-DscResource -ModuleName PSDesiredStateConfiguration
-ModuleVersion 1.1

    Node $NodeName
    {
        WindowsFeature NET-Framework-45-Core
        {
```

```
        Name = 'NET-Framework-45-Core'
        Ensure = 'Present'
    }
  }
}

ContainerCopyDemo -NodeName 'localhost' -outputPath C:\Windows\Temp
Start-DscConfiguration -Path C:\Windows\Temp -Wait -Verbose -Force
```

Open a command prompt or PowerShell console and navigate to C:\scripts\
dockerbuild and execute the following command:

```
docker build.
```

This will create a docker image from the dockerfile and save it locally. Here is the
output from that process on my system:

```
PS C:\scripts\dockerbuild> docker build.
Sending build context to Docker daemon   6.144kB

Step 1/3: FROM microsoft/windowsservercore
 ---> 1a599239a62c
Step 2/3: ADD containerdsc.ps1 /windows/temp/containerdsc.ps1
 ---> 036f64eb0f12
Removing intermediate container 0b8e40f872d9
Step 3/3: RUN powershell.exe -executionpolicy bypass c:\windows\temp\
containerdsc.ps1
 ---> Running in b2c0090ddf47

    Directory: C:\Windows\Temp

Mode              LastWriteTime         Length Name
----              -------------         ------ ----
-a----      2/24/2018  10:54 PM           2074 localhost.mof
VERBOSE: Perform operation 'Invoke CimMethod' with following parameters,
''methodName' = SendConfigurationApply,'className' =
MSFT_DSCLocalConfigurationManager,'namespaceName' =
root/Microsoft/Windows/DesiredStateConfiguration'.
VERBOSE: An LCM method call arrived from computer B2C0090DDF47 with user sid
S-1-5-93-2-1.
```

```
VERBOSE: [B2C0090DDF47]: LCM:  [ Start  Set       ]
VERBOSE: [B2C0090DDF47]: LCM:  [ Start  Resource  ]
[[WindowsFeature]NET-Framework-45-Core]
VERBOSE: [B2C0090DDF47]: LCM:  [ Start  Test      ]
[[WindowsFeature]NET-Framework-45-Core]
VERBOSE: [B2C0090DDF47]:
[[WindowsFeature]NET-Framework-45-Core] The operation 'Get-WindowsFeature'
started: NET-Framework-45-Core
VERBOSE: [B2C0090DDF47]:
[[WindowsFeature]NET-Framework-45-Core] The operation 'Get-WindowsFeature'
succeeded: NET-Framework-45-Core
VERBOSE: [B2C0090DDF47]: LCM:  [ End    Test      ]
[[WindowsFeature]NET-Framework-45-Core]  in 2.1920 seconds.
VERBOSE: [B2C0090DDF47]: LCM:  [ Skip   Set       ]
[[WindowsFeature]NET-Framework-45-Core]
VERBOSE: [B2C0090DDF47]: LCM:  [ End    Resource  ]
[[WindowsFeature]NET-Framework-45-Core]
VERBOSE: [B2C0090DDF47]: LCM:  [ End    Set       ]
VERBOSE: [B2C0090DDF47]: LCM:  [ End    Set       ]    in  8.6760 seconds.
VERBOSE: Operation 'Invoke CimMethod' complete.
VERBOSE: Time taken for configuration job to complete is 9.849 seconds

 ---> 58a66aa850d5
Removing intermediate container b2c0090ddf47
Successfully built 58a66aa850d5
```

Once the image is created, it can be seen in the docker images command output. The image ID for this new docker image is shown at the bottom of the above output as well. You can now create a new docker container from this image and ensure that the configuration was enacted by using the Get-DscConfiguration command.

```
docker container run -it 58a66aa850d5 powershell -command {start-sleep 60;
Get-dscConfiguration}

ConfigurationName   : ContainerCopyDemo
DependsOn           :
ModuleName          : PSDesiredStateConfiguration
ModuleVersion       : 1.1
```

```
PsDscRunAsCredential :
ResourceId           : [WindowsFeature]NET-Framework-45-Core
SourceInfo           :
Credential           :
DisplayName          : .NET Framework 4.6
Ensure               : Present
IncludeAllSubFeature : False
LogPath              :
Name                 : NET-Framework-45-Core
Source               :
PSComputerName       :
CimClassName         : MSFT_RoleResource
```

In this command, the start-sleep is required since the LCM starts a consistency check as soon as the containers starts, and without the sleep, you will see an error that the Get-DscConfiguration cannot be performed.

This method of using a dockerfile can be very useful in a release pipeline or a deployment pipeline. As mentioned, there are other ways to get DSC configurations into Windows docker containers. But the methods you saw in this section, especially the dockerfile method, are widely used.

Summary

This brings you to the end of the chapter on how to manage configurations inside containers using DSC. You learned how to use docker client and PowerShell remoting together to enact configuration inside Windows Server core containers and looked at how a dockerfile can be used to simplify that process. Using a dockerfile can be very helpful in a release and/or deployment pipeline.

This chapter completes this book as well. What a journey it has been! You started with the very basics of IaC, learned about DSC basics and advanced concepts, looked at how DSC can be used in a release pipeline, and used that knowledge to build your own pipeline using PowerShell modules and AppVeyor. You also looked at how to use DSC with multiple public cloud providers and containers. I learned a lot while writing this book and I hope you found it useful as well. Thank you for reading!

Index

© Ravikanth Chaganti 2018
R. Chaganti, *Pro PowerShell Desired State Configuration*, https://doi.org/10.1007/978-1-4842-3483-9

Get the eBook for only $5!

Why limit yourself?

With most of our titles available in both PDF and ePUB format, you can access your content wherever and however you wish—on your PC, phone, tablet, or reader.

Since you've purchased this print book, we are happy to offer you the eBook for just $5.

To learn more, go to http://www.apress.com/companion or contact support@apress.com.

Apress®

All Apress eBooks are subject to copyright. All rights are reserved by the Publisher, whether the whole or part of the material is concerned, specifically the rights of translation, reprinting, reuse of illustrations, recitation, broadcasting, reproduction on microfilms or in any other physical way, and transmission or information storage and retrieval, electronic adaptation, computer software, or by similar or dissimilar methodology now known or hereafter developed. Exempted from this legal reservation are brief excerpts in connection with reviews or scholarly analysis or material supplied specifically for the purpose of being entered and executed on a computer system, for exclusive use by the purchaser of the work. Duplication of this publication or parts thereof is permitted only under the provisions of the Copyright Law of the Publisher's location, in its current version, and permission for use must always be obtained from Springer. Permissions for use may be obtained through RightsLink at the Copyright Clearance Center. Violations are liable to prosecution under the respective Copyright Law.

Printed in the United States
By Bookmasters